FOREIGN AID IN A CHANGING WORLD

ISSUES IN THIRD WORLD POLITICS

Series Editor: Vicky Randall, Department of Government,
University of Essex.

Current titles:
Peter Burnell: Foreign aid in a changing world
Heather Deegan: The Middle East and problems of democracy
Jeff Haynes: Religion in Third World politics
Robert Pinkney: Democracy in the Third World
Georgina Waylen: Gender in Third World politics

FOREIGN AID IN A CHANGING WORLD

Peter Burnell

OPEN UNIVERSITY PRESS
Buckingham • Philadelphia

Open University Press
Celtic Court
22 Ballmoor
Buckingham
MK18 1XW

and
1900 Frost Road, Suite 101
Bristol, PA 19007, USA

First Published 1997

A catalogue record of this book is available from the British Library

ISBN   0 335 19524 5 (pb)   0 335 19525 3 (hb)

Library of Congress Cataloging-in-Publication Data
Burnell, Peter J.
    Foreign aid in a changing world / Peter Burnell.
        p.   cm.—(Issues in Third World politics series)
    Includes bibliographical references and index.
    ISBN 0–335–19525–3 (hc).—ISBN 0–335–19524–5 (pbk.)
    1. Economic assistance.   2. Technical assistance.   3. Economic development—International cooperation.   I. Title.   II. Series: Issues in Third World politics.
HC60.B884   1997
338.91—dc21   97–9043
                                                                  CIP

Typeset by Graphicraft Typesetters Ltd, Hong Kong
Printed in Great Britain by St Edmundsbury Press, Bury St Edmunds, Suffolk

Contents

Series editor's introduction

When I was invited to edit this series, I thought long and hard about what it should be called. I ended up going back to the well-worn phrase 'Third World' but recognizing that this very term raises problems that both this Introduction and the books in the series would need to address. Its advantage is that to most people it signals something fairly clear cut and recognizable. The expression 'Third World' has come to connote the regions and individual countries of Africa, Asia, the Caribbean, Latin America and the Middle East. It is the politics, in the broadest sense, of this part of the world, and of its relationship with the rest of the world, that constitutes the subject matter of this series.

Yet the notion of a single 'Third World' has always been problematic. When it became clear that the nations so designated were not going to follow a third, 'non-aligned', economic and political route between the capitalist West and the communist world, it was argued that they none the less shared a common predicament. Directly or indirectly they suffered the after-effects of colonization and they came late and on disadvantageous terms into the competitive world economy. Even then there was tremendous variety – in culture, experience of colonial rule, forms and levels of economic activity – between and within Third World regions.

Over time this internal differentiation seems to have grown. On the one hand we have the oil-rich states and the Newly Industrializing Countries (NICs), on the other the World Bank has identified a 'Fourth World' of lower income countries like Bangladesh or Tanzania, distinguished from the lower-middle income countries like Mexico and Malaysia. Then from the later 1980s we have witnessed the disintegration of most of the 'Second World' of state socialist societies – where does that leave the First and the Third?

These developments certainly threaten the coherence of the concept of a Third World. They must make us wonder whether the concept is any longer plausible or useful in categorizing what are by now well over 100 countries, containing three-quarters of the world's population. Recently writers both on the Right and on the Left have suggested that the notion of a Third World functions primarily as a myth: for the former it is a projection of the guilt of First World liberals while for the latter it evokes for the West a reassuring image of its own opposite, all that it has succeeded in not becoming.

The arguments are not all one way, however. When Nigel Harris writes about the 'end of the Third World' and its dissolution into one world economic system, he is referring to objective economic trends which still have a long way to go and which are by no means automatically accompanied by a decline in Western economic nationalism or cultural chauvinism. Third World countries do still at least some of the time recognize their common status *vis-à-vis* the developed world and the need to stick together, as was apparent at the Rio Earth Summit in June 1992. The fact that some Third World nations may have 'made it' into the developed world, does not negate the existence of the Third World they have left behind. It does, however, undermine the more deterministic arguments of dependency theorists, who have maintained that it is impossible to break out of economic dependence and underdevelopment. The dissolution of the Second World, it could be argued, leaves the confrontation and contrast between First and Third World starker than ever (this might of course indicate the use of a different nomenclature, such as North and South). On the other hand the countries of the old Second World will not be transformed overnight into members of the First and there is a case for retaining a Second World category to refer to countries only recently emerged from a prolonged period of communist rule.

But my purpose here is not to insist on the continuing usefulness of the notion of a Third World so much as to signal the question as part of the agenda I hope that authors in this series will address. It seems to me that there *are* respects in which most of the countries conventionally included in the Third World do continue to share a common predicament and about which it is up to a point legitimate to generalize. But unless we also explore the differences between them, our powers of political explanation will be limited and it may be that it is these differences which now hold answers to the most important and interesting questions we want to ask.

Turning to the present volume, the topic of foreign aid incidentally provides an excellent illustration of the problems associated with an unrevised concept of a 'Third World'. Here, for instance, we encounter former Third World countries acting as donors, and countries of the former 'Second World' Soviet bloc clamouring for aid. Peter Burnell's impressive survey differs from some other titles in this series, in that rather than providing an initial exploration of a hitherto neglected dimension of Third World politics, he offers an invaluable and critical analysis of the extensive existing literature on this important question. In so doing, he asks the questions we would want to raise ourselves – 'Does aid do good?', '*can* aid do good?' – although his meticulous examination provides no easy, or especially comforting, answers.

Vicky Randall

Acknowledgements

The encouragement given by Open University Press is gratefully acknowledged. So too is the constructive advice given by series editor Vicky Randall and Michael Edwards, who deserves special mention for reading a manuscript that would add little to his existing knowledge. I am also indebted to the many students who have followed my courses in this subject area. All mistakes and errors of judgement in the book are my responsibility alone.

List of abbreviations

ACP	Africa, Caribbean, Pacific countries (associated with EU)
AIDS	Acquired immune deficiency syndrome
APEC	Asia Pacific Economic Cooperation
ATP	Aid and Trade Provision
CAP	Common Agricultural Policy (EU)
CEEC	Central and East European Country
CFCs	Chlorofluorocarbons
CMEA	Council for Mutual Economic Assistance
DAC	Development Assistance Committee (OECD)
EBRD	European Bank for Reconstruction and Development
EDF	European Development Fund (EU)
ERP	European Recovery Programme
ESAF	Enhanced Structural Adjustment Facility (IMF)
EU	European Union
FAO	Food and Agriculture Organisation (United Nations)
G7	Group of Seven 'most industrialised nations'
GATT	General Agreement on Tariffs and Trade
GDP	Gross Domestic Product
GDR	German Democratic Republic (East Germany)
GEF	Global Environment Facility
GNP	Gross National Product
HIV	Human immune deficiency
IBRD	International Bank for Reconstruction and Development
ICRC	International Committee of the Red Cross
IDA	International Development Association
IFAD	International Fund for Agricultural Development
IFC	International Finance Corporation
ILO	International Labour Organisation
IMF	International Monetary Fund

LDC	Less developed country
LIC	Low income country
LLDC	Least developed country
MFA	Multi-Fibre Arrangement
NAFTA	North American Free Trade Agreement
NATO	North Atlantic Treaty Organisation
NGO	Non-governmental organisation
NIEO	New International Economic Order
NIS	Newly Independent State (of the former Soviet Union)
NNGO	Northern non-governmental organisation
OAU	Organisation of African Unity
ODA	Overseas Development Administration (British government)
oda	official development assistance
OECD	Organisation for Economic Cooperation and Development
OPEC	Organisation of Petroleum Exporting Countries
PLO	Palestine Liberation Organisation
PVO	Private and Voluntary Organisation
SAL	Structural Adjustment Loan
SAP	Structural Adjustment Programme
SILIC	Severely indebted low income country
SNGO	Southern non-governmental organisation
UN	United Nations
UNCTAD	United Nations Conference on Trade and Development
UNDP	United Nations Development Programme
UNEP	United Nations Environment Programme
UNESCO	United Nations Educational, Scientific and Cultural Organisation
UNHCR	United Nations High Commissioner for Refugees
UNICEF	United Nations Children's Fund
UNIDO	United Nations Industrial Development Organisation
USAID	United States Agency for International Development
WDM	World Development Movement
WFP	World Food Programme
WHO	World Health Organisation
WID	Women-in-development
WTO	World Trade Organisation

1 Introduction

Some people call it foreign aid, others prefer international assistance, and still others development cooperation, even partnership. These labels are normative statements, but whatever the designation, the subject is 'huge, complex and fragmented' (Tomasevski 1993: 52). Many actors of different kinds are involved in aid. Aid goes to a variety of destinations: states, proto-states and would-be states, even countries with whom the provider does not have normal diplomatic ties, for instance North Korea's receipt of rice aid from South Korea and Japan. Aid goes to central governments and to their opponents, for example in the 1970s the World Council of Churches Programme to Combat Racism sent material assistance to liberation movements in Southern Africa. Aid increasingly goes to non-governmental organisations, many of them reputedly non-political, to community groups and to international organisations. The sources of aid are many, and include states lacking universal recognition like Israel and Taiwan, would-be governments (the Palestine Liberation Organisation funded 'solidarity projects' in Guinea and Guinea-Bissau), 'autonomous' organisations financed from the public purse such as the United States National Endowment for Democracy, charities like Oxfam and private individuals acting on their own. Intergovernmental and multilateral bodies raise funds both on a regular basis and through special appeals. Some approach only governments, for example the International Development Association, established in 1960 as the soft loan window of the World Bank; others also make appeals to the public at large, for instance the United Nations Children's Fund (UNICEF).

Aid has been much picked on and picked over by academics, journalists and aid practitioners alike. There are many who damn it, some with faint praise and others without even that; few laud it to the skies. Everyone seems to have a view. Yet notwithstanding the criticisms, a recurrent theme of the last half century has been that there is simply not enough aid, and there needs to be more.

2 Foreign aid in a changing world

From the start an important issue has to be how we understand the meaning of 'aid'. On the one hand, there seems to be a great deal of it, and its portfolio multifarious, if we believe the newspaper accounts. Thus, in life-threatening emergencies there is humanitarian aid of the sort associated with several United Nations agencies and private disaster relief. Also, transfers of lethal equipment between governments in the North and the South have regularly taken place under special financial arrangements called military assistance and military support. Then there is 'regional aid', especially the structural fund payments by the European Union and its predecessor the European Community (EU) to.depressed regions in the EU and cohesion funds for the poorest member countries. Together these account for a third of the annual EU budget in excess of £70 billion (billion = one thousand million). The tax incentives and cash grants member states offer to attract inward corporate investment are also often referred to as aid. 'Aid' crops up in conjunction with loans made by the International Monetary Fund (IMF), International Bank for Reconstruction and Development (World Bank) and regional development banks, although much of their financing is at interest rates barely more favourable than commercial or near-to-market terms. Reports of the more than $40 billion in international financial support which the United States (US) government mobilised for Mexico in response to the financial crisis which broke in December 1994 characteristically called it an aid package. Yet the main components, which included a loan from the US Exchange Stabilisation Fund for currency support and IMF standby credit, were fundamentally different from grants to development projects. Different again is the import of Lavigne's (1995: 235) claim that trade arrangements granting Central and Eastern Europe improved access to Western markets are indisputably a form of aid.

In 1960 the General Assembly of the United Nations (UN) adopted a 1 per cent target of Gross National Product (GNP) for net flows of external financial resources from developed to developing countries. In the many subsequent claims that have been made about how extensively the rich world aids the poor world, direct corporate investment and private portfolio capital flows have often been included. At the other extreme, there are always critics who calculate net aid after deducting any dividend remittances and profit repatriation to their home base by private foreign investors as well as the costs of servicing international debt. In 1970 the UN General Assembly decided to adopt a proposal of the Commission on International Development (1969) or Pearson Commission that there be a separate target for official development assistance (oda), set at 0.7 per cent of donors' GNP.

The total oda sums are modest by comparison with the more encompassing interpretations of aid. What is sometimes called real aid could actually be very small, although even here, notions differ. Stokke (1996: 56) called real aid resource transfers aimed at creating long-term, sustainable development. The Independent Group on British Aid, which was formed in 1982 when Britain's oda looked like becoming increasingly commercialised, defined it as aid that has an immediate and positive effect on the welfare and productive capacity of poor people, especially the poorest, in the Third World. On that score much so-called aid could well be 'sham aid' (Watkins 1995a: 200). Indeed, if aid is supposed to do good in the recipient countries then various commentators argue that much of what is called aid does not pass the test. For example, Barratt Brown (1995: 346), writing from a left-wing perspective, believes most aid to Africa has been useless if not harmful; from the right, Bauer (*The Times*, 5 February 1980) goes so far as to claim aid does harm rather than good. Griffin (1986: 44) concluded that since aid 'is doing little to promote growth in the Third World and less to alleviate poverty . . . the time may have come to abandon the enterprise, to set ourselves the goal, not of increasing foreign aid, but of reducing it . . .' Aid is nothing if not controversial. But before explaining the reasons why, we must first address the question, what exactly is aid?

Defining aid

How do we go about defining aid, when common usage fails to provide a clear and consistent lead? One answer is to start with the force that prompts aid giving. Foreign aid can be construed as inter societal transfers of resources that are intended by all the relevant parties, especially the provider, to serve first and foremost the recipients' needs, interests or wants. In Malek's (1991: 1) words, 'By its very definition the sole motive behind aid is altruism'; and Zinkin (1978: 272): 'Aid is charity. If it is not charity, it is not aid. It may be enlightened self-interest; mutual defence; a boost for the export trade; a sop to a troublesome ally; it cannot be aid'. These are demanding stipulations. If we were to accept them there would probably be little of aid to study. Much human behaviour is characterised by mixed motives. There is no a priori reason to suppose that transfers cannot assist the recipients just because they are offered on grounds that include self-interest. Equally, the best of intentions can produce action that is so misguided or badly executed that it wreaks havoc on intended beneficiaries. Aid defined in this way could turn out to be aid that does not aid, though it may still profit the donor as an unintended by-product.

An alternative approach is to focus on effects. Perhaps aid should be understood in terms of transfers that actually benefit the recipient, notwithstanding self-interested reasons for giving. However, this facility is not exclusive to aid. Normal commercial or market-based transactions are entered into on the expectation of mutual gain, even if the results sometimes disappoint. A miscalculation by one party to a market relationship which commits it to incurring costs without sharing in the gains could be construed as very charitable, by the beneficiaries. If aid's reference point comprises only good effects, then transfers advanced in a spirit of great generosity would not qualify if the consequences prove negative. But that can happen due to circumstances outside the control of aid providers and beyond any reasonable foresight. It might even stem from avoidable failings for which the recipient is wholly responsible.

Further questions are raised about the nature of the effects or benefits that should be intended, or which might follow from aid. What matters most: needs, wants or interests, and which kinds are eligible? Are social values on a par with economic purposes? Should security objectives be given equal weight? Aid recipients supply the most authentic view of what they want, but could the providers have a superior insight into their interests and needs? The parties to aid negotiations do not always see eye to eye. Even when they do, there can be other actors who should have been (or who feel they should have been) included in the discussions, and who will be affected by the outcome. Who or what should be the target beneficiary – whole countries, or societies and groups defined more narrowly?

Aid defined

Foreign aid is the subject of a large social science literature. The lion's share in the last few decades particularly in Europe has been contributed by development economists, who provide an important constituent of the aid policy community. In contrast the 1960s flush of writings by political scientists and foreign policy analysts in the United States reflected US aid's more overt concern for strategic and political considerations, in a context of superpower confrontation. Nevertheless, over the years an institutional definition of aid has come to be accepted for the most part as being the cleanest way out of the definitional *impasse*. The label official development assistance (oda) has been given by the Development Assistance Committee (DAC) of the Organisation for Economic Cooperation and Development (OECD). The DAC dates from the early 1960s (originally under the name Development Assistance Group), and was established for the purposes of increasing aid and improving its terms and forms, and to encourage burden sharing and cooperation among donors. The DAC membership comprises 21 of the member states of the OECD in North America, Western Europe, Australasia and Japan, plus the European Commission; on South Korea's accession in 1996 the OECD numbered 29 states.

The DAC defines oda as resources transferred on concessional financial terms with the promotion of the economic development and welfare of developing countries as the main declared objective. This embraces humanitarian assistance and emergency relief, which have a longer history than development project aid. For instance, the US sent relief to the Soviet Union (USSR) in the early 1920s. Humanitarian and development assistance overlap anyway. The shortcomings of development assistance can contribute to disaster-proneness; and in many instances the provision of disaster relief should merge into rehabilitation, recovery and reconstruction aid, which in turn provide a basis for development efforts. People whose lives are constantly threatened by poverty-related diseases are said to face a silent emergency day in and day out, quite apart from sudden natural catastrophes or the onset of a man-made disorder like war. Ideally, oda will offer a remedy.

In addition to the flows included in oda calculations, there are private or voluntary flows of a concessionary nature sourced by non-governmental organisations (NGOs) having humanitarian and developmental objectives. The entitlement to be included in the overall construct of aid is self-evident. Indeed, there is a body of opinion that NGOs come closest to providing real aid; and in the North their perceived contribution to overseas emergencies is legendary.

Following the demise of the Second World at the end of the 1980s, especially the collapse of the USSR, the DAC supplemented the idea of oda with what it calls official aid. While sharing the defining features of oda, this differs in being made available to a separate 'Part II List of Aid Recipients'. They are thirteen of the more advanced countries of the former Soviet bloc including seven former Soviet republics, or 'countries in transition'. Other countries and territories that attain a significant level of development are being added, for instance Kuwait, Brunei and Singapore. Concessionality lies at the heart of both oda and official aid. Concessionality derives from the financial terms. An unconditional cash grant is wholly concessional. For loans, the concessionality or grant element is a function of the interest rate, the period of grace before repayment of principal must begin (on average around eight years for loans from DAC members) and the number of years within which full repayment must be made (the date of maturity). Since 1972 the DAC has stipulated that there must be a grant element of at least 25 per cent if a loan is to qualify as assistance. The grant equivalent of a loan is a function of the face value multiplied by the grant element.

Alongside oda, official aid and NGO equivalents there are official resource flows intended to finance development but where a concessional element is absent or is insufficient to fulfil the stated requirements. Where oda loans are cancelled, only the interest forgiven is counted as new oda. There are refinements which blur the grants/loans classification and extend aid's compass, and marginal changes have occurred such as the inclusion of debt cancellation in instances where the loans were not originally reported as oda. Now, the upkeep of developing country refugees in DAC countries may be counted as oda, although for the first year only. According to Watkins (1995b) this accounted for 11 per cent of Canada's oda in 1995. The transfer of items like this from other budget headings in government expenditure to oda has been called a form of budget pollution (Box 1994: 51). Nevertheless, the basic understanding of oda has been applied more or less consistently over the years in which the DAC has collected and published data – an exercise that provides an important part of the definition's appeal. Of course, the borderlines can look somewhat arbitrary. Thus, even non-concessional finance like government export credits will be highly prized when other sources are unavailable. On a similar basis, Ryrie counts as aid official lending at market rates by a non-profit distributing body like the International Finance Corporation (IFC) – an affiliate of the World Bank and the 'leading private-sector aid agency in the world' (Ryrie 1995: xiv). The recipients of IFC loans and equity investment are companies with no more than 50 per cent public ownership, and the purpose is economic development. Also, any lender's relaxation of its usual terms and conditions, or an unusual windfall offer of finance that is extraordinarily helpful, might seem concessional even when not qualifying as oda. An example is the IMF's innovative financial package for Mexico in 1986, which offered compensatory funding in the event of a fall in the price of Mexico's oil exports or a reduction in its GDP growth below an agreed threshold. The unexpected offer of a substantial fixed rate subsidised loan by the United Arab Emirates to Pakistan in 1996, a time when Pakistan had badly depleted its foreign reserves and faced looming external debt repayment liabilities, might be considered another example.

As defined and recorded, oda notably came to exclude the price subsidies which strongly marked trade between the USSR, European members of the Council for Mutual Economic Assistance (CMEA) and a few favoured countries like Cuba. These were estimated to be worth more than $4.5 billion annually to Cuba in the late 1980s. The Soviets' provision of convertible currency backed Cuba's trade arrangements with Western countries and underpinned its creditworthiness with international commercial banks. That led Dominguez (1978: 154) to maintain that in 'a very fundamental sense, then, the credits Cuba has received from capitalist countries should also be considered a form of Soviet aid to Cuba'. Measuring the worth of Soviet project loans is also complicated where repayments took the form of merchandise supplied to the USSR possibly at below world prices (and then sometimes resold by the USSR on world markets, at the expense of the producer countries' market share and unit price earnings). Needless to say, Soviet and CMEA claims about the size of their aid programmes were always understated by DAC estimates of their oda. Other departures from the DAC definition include new forms of assistance pioneered by the Islamic Development Bank (OECD 1995: 108), whose proscription on usury has steered it towards making interest-free loans ever since it was established in 1973.

Development, the military and the political

The developmental objective built into oda and official aid is potentially misleading, for two reasons. First, aid received for development can have the effect of promoting other purposes including military ones, because of the fungibility of financial and economic resources (that is to say, by expanding the recipient's resources oda may effectively underwrite expenditures other than those intended by and agreed with the donor). The oda is then a substitute for domestic resources that would have been allocated to development. Additionally, a recipient government may practise straightforward transfers between budget heads, with or without the knowledge or tacit approval of donors. Also, the employment of civic soldiers on dual-purpose tasks such as road building can obscure the dividing line between military and developmental activities, particularly where the armed forces constitute a large part of the governing administration. In principle development might benefit from military assistance that is a substitute for domestic spending that would have taken place on the armed forces. In practice, heightened levels of consumption like luxury imports have often been the form in which the benefits are realised. Military assistance could secure a country's chances of developing in peace, and has been used to guard development projects and their workers from saboteurs. In contrast, humanitarian supplies intended for civilians in war-torn lands are sometimes appropriated by combatants and occasionally converted into funds for the purchase of arms.

Second, official donors usually have a number of aims, objectives and goals of aid. Different donors will have different combinations and their own order of priorities, which may change over time. Development could be served by the promotion of some intermediary condition such as political stability. Development might be both an objective in its own right and a means to advance some further ends, such as the recipient's (and the donor's) national security. Ball (1988: 237–94) described how the US and USSR provided economic assistance to enable countries to maintain artificially high levels of military spending. The developmental and non-developmental objectives will be valued for their presumed contribution to donor interests, construed in commercial, economic, political, strategic or some other terms. Donor and recipient interests might or might not largely coincide.

All aid can be given a financial value, but money transfers and financial credits are not the only forms of aid. Forms of aid matter not least because different forms send different signals: 'The symbolic effects of military aid and disaster relief are quite different even though the actual economic impact may be the same' Baldwin (1985: 305). There is aid-in-kind, as embodied in material assistance. Commodities, particularly food, are a long-established form attracting media prominence in emergencies, although much greater amounts have been shipped as programme food aid to governments on a regular basis, providing balance of payments and budgetary support. From being half of all oda initially (and over a third of US oda in 1970), food aid has declined to under 10 per cent. Technical assistance and technical cooperation (treated here as being closely related) are a major constituent of all aid, worth up to $15 billion annually. The purpose includes augmenting and developing human resources and institutions through improved levels of skill, knowledge and productive aptitudes. Another growth area has been general programme aid, which provides financial support to the balance of payments and/or public sector budget of a country, in contrast to earmarking aid for specific projects or programmes of works like dams and agricultural improvement schemes. Retrospective terms adjustment to debts previously incurred also qualifies as oda, if the terms are sufficiently generous, as in debt cancellation. Debt relief and programme aid have comprised around a quarter of all oda in recent years.

Military aid takes various forms too, including the transfer of items of equipment not normally available for purchase in world markets. Military assistance differs from exercises in military cooperation between the armed forces of friendly countries, and has included military education and training programmes as well as arms transfers. Although there are far less reliable data than for oda, the largest programmes have been mounted by the US and the USSR. The US established a Military Assistance Programme for grant financing of equipment purchases in 1949. By 1971 total US military exports had a grant component of two thirds. Then came a significant hardening of terms and a growth in military sales credits. By 1980 concessional and non-concessional credits together were financing a third of arms transfers. At the same time the US Economic Support Fund, while not funding military purchases directly, became a significant instrument for helping selected countries cope with the costs of militarisation. It advanced grants and loans for balance of payments support and infrastructure development, under the rubric of oda. The cancellation of several billion dollars' worth of military sales debts owed by Egypt in the wake of the 1991 Gulf war is another example of US military aid.

The intentions that lie behind the giving of oda including aid that proves to be developmentally effective can resemble the strategic objectives of military assistance. Hence Ball deploys the concept of security assistance, which comprises military assistance and security-related economic aid. Ball (1988: 293) concluded from a comparative study of US security assistance to around 95 Third World countries (Soviet security assistance went to around 40 countries) that receipt of such assistance has the potential to assist development. But much will depend on recipient government policy – something that is true of oda generally. Security will not be enhanced if it encourages the adoption of a more aggressive foreign policy or causes other states to be hostile (Ball 1988: 294). Anyway, most countries have received too little such assistance for it to make a major economic contribution. Of course the forgiveness of military debts could benefit development and can actually have that as its aim, especially since the Cold War now that major donors' security concerns have moved on from former preoccupations, as has the nature of many recipient states.

Military and related assistance was a significant component of world aid. Indeed, alms-racing in the service of arms-racing was a familiar feature of East–West rivalry in many parts of the developing world. The aid-assisted export of weaponry by the superpowers and their principal allies was employed directly in the cause of securing client states and regional spheres of influence. By expanding the production runs it increases the economic viability of the research, development and procurement expenditures that are incurred on behalf of the armed forces at home. During President Reagan's second term of office in the US direct spending on military aid rose to over a third of the entire aid programme. Almost two thirds of aid outlays including the Economic Support Fund were attributable to military and security purposes. Only around 15 per cent of all US aid expenditure was administered by the Agency for International Development (USAID). In the developing countries in the late 1980s military expenditure was estimated to be more than three times the value of DAC oda receipts. At an average figure of 5 per cent of Gross Domestic Product (GDP) it compared favourably with public spending on health and education, exceeding their combined totals in nearly a fifth of countries, in some by factors of two or three.

Today, governments like those of the US, France and Britain continue to encourage their arms exports but on a largely commercial basis. Declining military expenditure at home enhances the importance of securing overseas orders. The customers still include developing countries as well as richer countries like Saudi Arabia and Taiwan. In the case of Bosnia's Muslims fighting against Serb forces in 1994–5, inward shipments of arms from Iran and Saudi Arabia were presumably supplied gratis. They probably enjoyed the approval of a US administration which, for diplomatic reasons, could not be seen to assist directly at that time. Aid and arms entanglements persisted even as the Cold War finally drew to a close. Britain's offer of financial support to Malaysia's Pergau dam and Malaysia's agreement to purchase Tornado fighter aircraft proceeded in parallel during the second half of the 1980s. The two were connected, implicitly if not explicitly. Newspaper accounts (*Observer*, 13 November 1994) suggest there may be other occasions where British diplomacy has taken oda decisions in the light of anticipated defence equipment sales, in Indonesia and Nigeria.

Nevertheless, Russia is unable to continue the USSR's role as provider of military assistance (by 1994 its arms exports accounted for just 6 per cent of the global market); and the reduction of tension in some previously conflict-ridden regions such as Central America, Southern Africa and Ethiopia point to a decline in military aid absolutely and proportional to all aid. Formally, the position taken now by some DAC donors, especially Germany and Japan, the IMF and the World Bank, indicates that the military spending of governments seeking financial support will be reviewed when the size of new aid pledges comes under consideration. But the difficulties of knowing whether a government is inclining towards an unacceptable 'military burden' should not be ignored, especially if its security requirements touch on the donors' own strategic interests (Ball 1992). This recent development in oda does not yet seem to warrant the term military conditionality, and is being applied mostly to some weak, very aid-dependent countries. Even so, since 1987 the value of international arms deliveries to the Third World has fallen. Arms imports into Africa fell from around $8 billion in 1981 to less than one billion ten years later (current prices). Severe financial and economic difficulties are partly responsible. Defence spending fell for the world as a whole from 4.8 per cent of GDP in 1985 to 2.4 per cent in 1995. The Middle East (where Israel and Egypt will probably continue to receive large US military assistance packages) and South-East Asia are notable exceptions, fuelling an international arms trade still worth around $30 billion annually (compared with $78.6 billion in 1987).

If military assistance is ebbing, recent years have witnessed a growing interest in aid for certain kinds of political reform, especially so-called democracy assistance and good governance, and 'political aid' specifically. Typical examples of political aid are help given to the strengthening of advocacy and lobby groups and other civic associations, and political parties. As Robinson (1995: 75) says, the overall objectives of such aid are often vague and ill-defined. The forms include training courses, equipment grants, travel grants to conferences and even cash transfers. Germany's *Stiftungen* (political foundations linked to the country's principal parties) have been active in this field since the 1950s (Pinto-Duschinsky 1991), furthering good relations between Germany and political figures, some of whom go on to high public office. The US has provided substantial political aid over the years, in Europe and Latin America especially, and in 1992 Britain followed suit with its Westminster Foundation for Democracy (budget of £2.5 million of public money for 1995–6). The present interest of DAC donors in supporting political pluralism and democratic consolidation in Central and Eastern Europe, Southern Africa and elsewhere is a distinctive feature of the 1990s (explored in Chapter 10), although even in the mid-1980s South Africa's African National Congress was reputedly receiving each year up to $24 million in kind from the USSR and $20 million in cash from Scandinavian sources. Foreign support to liberation movements, freedom fighters, 'rebel forces' and the like are more ancient features of the high politics of inter-state and sub-state relations, and can still be found in several parts of the world, Afghanistan for example. The total magnitude of such support and its overall impact on history cannot even be guessed. It lies beyond the conventional study of aid.

Never mind the quantity, think about the quality

World oda stood at not much more than $59 billion net disbursements in 1995. Behind this figure lies an uneven pattern of growth. In real terms, oda experienced average growth of 3 per cent per annum in 1950–65 followed by a period of stability. 1970–80 saw average annual increases of 5 per cent, owing largely to the emergence of aid from some Organisation of Petroleum Exporting Countries (OPEC) members after 1972 and increased funding of multilateral institutions. A real terms annual decline in world aid of 2.5 per cent in the first half of the 1980s, when OPEC aid fell back, produced a fairly static picture for the decade despite a real terms increase in DAC oda of 31 per cent for 1981–2 to 1991–2. The disappearance of Soviet aid at the end of the 1980s has not been compensated elsewhere. Few DAC members are currently increasing their aid in real terms. 1993 saw both a real and nominal terms fall in collective net disbursements and, following a nominal recovery in 1994, oda fell by around 9 per cent in real terms in 1995.

In the quarter century up to 1994 oda remained in the range 0.30–0.36 per cent of average DAC members' GNP. There has been no sustained progress towards the UN target of 0.7 per cent. Indeed, some countries, most notably the US, have moved in the opposite direction, and in that sense the US's oda performance is now the least impressive (0.10 per cent of GNP in 1995, compared with 3.2 per cent of GNP in 1949). The DAC performance overall has been drifting down to around 0.27 per cent (1995), having fallen in recent years in more than half the donors including some formerly strong performers like Canada and Sweden. An aid high of 0.53 was recorded in 1962–3, when the US together with small French and British programmes accounted for 80 per cent of Western aid.

DAC records of aid flows, based on donor submissions and related to the DAC's definition of oda, exaggerate the amounts received because of the costs of administering the budgets. The conversion of totals into dollar values exposes national comparisons to fluctuations in currency exchange rates, and the available data for some donors, especially non-DAC countries, and for NGOs is usually incomplete and can be unreliable. Promises of aid sometimes remain just promises; and donors' multi-year payments to some multilateral organisations tend to be lumpy, giving distorted annual pictures of their aid giving. Moreover, aid disbursements often lag behind commitments, for a variety of reasons. These can include problems with the kind of aid that has been pledged and its unsuitability, difficulties in donor–recipient relations, bureaucratic obstacles and lengthy procedures as exhibited by the EU's European Development Fund (EDF) for instance. A donor government might be unable to secure legislative authorisation, or finds itself short of funds; recipient countries that descend into civil disorder lead development agencies to suspend their operations. Conversely, an initial aid loan may come to understate the actual disbursement if it becomes 'non-performing', perhaps because the borrower cannot meet the repayment terms or declares a moratorium, or reneges for political reasons.

Donors and recipients will each have their own understanding of what is most valuable about oda and an aid relationship. All parties might agree that the primary importance lies in aid's potential contribution to economic development, yet the economic value placed on the sums will diverge depending on the wealth and poverty of donor and recipient. Aid partners perceive the worth of a given transfer differently because their opportunity costs, capital productivity, time horizons and discount rates all differ. The valuation placed on non-pecuniary aid and technical assistance especially is a case in point: parties in need of the second are almost bound to be unfamiliar with its full potential. Donors and recipients may make different assessments of the known outcomes and effects of assistance, absolutely and relative to stated objectives, where their objectives diverge. The *actual* cost to creditors of debt forgiveness to defaulters, in terms of probable interest and repayments receipts that are foregone, could be considerably less than the face value; the debtor enjoys much greater benefit if it thereby becomes more attractive to new capital inflows, commercial, private or public.

Furthermore, quantity is not everything. The quality of aid and so its chances of being effective in achieving its ends are no less important. The determination of what should count as a measure of effectiveness will be a function of where the assessors stand, their functional responsibilities and the purposes they ascribe to aid. On the donor side, the diplomatic corps will think in terms of foreign policy objectives and the maintenance of good intergovernmental relations; trade and industry ministries are attuned to aid's performance in promoting international market share for exports and securing employment prospects at home; private donors to voluntary relief organisations may seek reassurance in the number of lives saved from unnecessary death; others may look for some contribution to international understanding and peace. Financial auditors everywhere place emphasis on value-for-money, irrespective of how the purpose is defined.

Development workers are, unsurprisingly, interested in aid's contribution to development; and there is now a broadly based interest in establishing the extent of aid's developmental effectiveness, more so than before when strategic and political considerations were uppermost for some major donors. A clutch of criteria has evolved for assessing the quality of a donor's overall approach to oda, although such an assessment cannot be divorced from qualities pertaining to discrete projects or programmes, and which should include a commitment to rigorous appraisal, monitoring and evaluation procedures. The criteria do not guarantee good results. They relate not so much to undisputed features of oda's record of achievement, as to the means and modalities which are presumed to enhance the chances of high achievement. Some criteria are more generally agreed upon than others. Their status varies over time, and not all are endorsed by every aid recipient. Donors individually tend to advance first and foremost the criteria which show their own performance in the most favourable light. The following are leading candidates.

First, the more an aid programme is targeted on countries that are among the poorest, the higher its quality. A measure of arbitrariness exists in how poor countries are delineated. The category of low income countries (LICs) as determined by the World Bank (in 1996, possessing annual average per capita incomes of $725 or less in 1994) has been given closer (if equally debatable) specification in respect of least developed countries (LLDCs), by the UN Economic and Social Commission in 1971. LLDCs have low average incomes and also the additional handicaps of weak social development and low economic diversification. China, India and Pakistan are notable exclusions. Donors differ in targeting the more than 60 LICs or the smaller number of LLDCs. For example, in 1993 two thirds of Portugal's oda went to LLDCs (chiefly Mozambique in the form of debt rescheduling) but for Spain the figure was 11 per cent, because trade and investment partners in Latin America were more highly favoured. The World Bank (*World Development Report 1990*: 127–8) could identify only 8 per cent of the US aid programme as development assistance devoted to LICs, in 1986. According to DAC data LLDCs and around 100 middle income countries (possessing average per capita incomes in the range $726–8955 in 1994) each account for approximately a quarter of all oda. The Independent Commission on Population and Quality of Life (1996: 11) calculated that countries with average real incomes below $2000 a year received aid of only $8.23 per person in 1991, whereas those in the $4–5000 range received twelve times as much.

Second, as a general rule a higher grant element is associated with greater oda quality. Grants are often considered superior to loans. For many donors the grant share and grant element now approach 100 per cent of their aid. Japan's oda is an exception – the grant share is less than half and the grant element only three quarters. Loans have been a significant feature. However in Japan, where the idea of self-help is central to development cooperation, the justification for loans is that they impose discipline on the recipient to use the resources wisely. Writers like Ryrie (1995: 114) worry that grants induce dependence on charity. Some voluntary aid agencies operate revolving credit schemes in community development programmes, which they say are more likely than gifts to generate a sense of achievement and self-worth among successful participants, with greater possibilities for self-reliance. Knorr (1973: 172) said prospective recipients not unusually rejected gifts, and preferred the explicit spelling out of reciprocal obligations such as repayment terms, to allay suspicion of the real motives of grant offerers.

The grants versus loans issue should not overshadow the traditional reluctance of donors to fund local and recurrent costs of development expenditure – a stance justified in terms of encouraging recipients to make a corresponding commitment (i.e. to become 'stakeholders'), as well as the desirability for donors of setting a finite limit to their involvement. However, while the restriction means that donors are more able to recoup their aid outflows through exports, the consequence has been an import- and, often, capital-intensive bias to oda for its recipients, which could obstruct the development of their own resources. One legacy has been projects that fall idle after completion due to a host government's inability to service their needs – school buildings without teachers or books, hospitals bereft of medicines and staff – although more attention is being paid these days to introducing local cost-recovery schemes. Aid that finances recurrent local expenditures can offer high social rates of return. Accordingly, the flexibility of an aid programme may be counted a third important dimension of oda quality. Aid that can be adjusted easily to the particular needs of recipients is superior to aid whose content and form is made inappropriate by the imposition of donors' self-interested requirements – an example being food aid allocations that are dictated by donor needs to dispose of agricultural surpluses in ways that are commercially non-damaging and politically acceptable at home.

By extension, flexibility means that good aid is not procurement tied. In other words, it does not have to take the form of goods or services from the donor country and is fully and freely available for essentially worldwide procurement. Donors vary considerably. Aid from the Arab OPEC countries is customarily untied, and well over half of aid from Japan, the US and Sweden is wholly untied. For Britain and Italy the norms are less than two fifths, and Belgium's oda has been under one fifth untied. The full extent of informal tying is not reflected by the DAC's average figure for untied aid of around 38 per cent. Economists agree procurement tying reduces oda's value: Jepma (1996: 251) conservatively estimates it probably reduces aid's real value relative to its nominal value by between 10 and 15 per cent. Aid recipients are prevented from taking advantage of international competition when placing orders and might have to accept inappropriate merchandise. Tying biases aid towards a high import content. Producers in the aid recipient as well as other LDCs may be denied equal chances to compete. Commodity aid is similarly defective. The cash value of some food aid to recipients has been estimated at one third of the reported value because of administration, transport and distribution costs. Tying has been defended by saying it enables donor governments to justify the aid to taxpayers, by establishing a clear link with economic benefit at home. Hence, with less tying there would be less support for aid, and so the budget would be smaller. However, this argument is not borne out by cross-national comparisons among donors, although it might carry some weight in a few countries.

Fourth, good aid is channelled through multilateral institutions, such as the World Bank group and United Nations agencies. True multilaterals include recipient as well as donor countries as full members. In contrast to bilateral aid, which bears the impress of donor interests, multilaterals are constitutionally obliged to pursue developmental or humanitarian ends. They do not get involved in military assistance. They devote around three quarters of their disbursements to LICs, including around 40 per cent to LLDCs in sub-Saharan Africa. The International Development Association (IDA) lends to countries with average per capita incomes of up to $865 (in 1996 79 countries were eligible), and usually to much poorer countries. Stokke (1996: 91) maintains that around 43 per cent of IDA investment lending is for poverty alleviation.

There has long been a mark of idealism associated with multilateralism, said to symbolise a commitment to aid as a shared international responsibility. The reality is critically examined in Chapter 9. Suffice to say here that the presumption in favour, widely held in the 1970s, has given way to a more questioning attitude which harbours doubts about the effectiveness and efficiency of several such organisations. Furthermore, some of the advances in their approach, like improved awareness of gender and participatory issues, have actually come about as a result of promptings from certain bilateral agencies, for example in Canada, Britain and Scandinavia. Having grown rapidly to a third of all DAC oda, multilateral aid inclusive of EU oda reached a plateau and then declined to the current level of around 30 per cent, partly due to donor attachment to commercial objectives that are best promoted bilaterally, and growing hostility in the US

Congress especially. The UN agencies, where developing countries have equal rights of representation, have been subjected to far less criticism from the developing world than from the principal funders. Developing countries probably experience a greater sense of shared ownership of a body like the United Nations Development Programme (UNDP), which provides grants, than of the Bretton Woods institutions (IMF and World Bank) where power is perceived to lie with the major subscribers (voting rights on the board of executive directors being proportional to capital subscription). Third World governments have usually been most vocal in criticising the IMF and the World Bank since the early 1980s, for their insistence on making lending highly conditional, although the Bank has also come under increasing fire in the US especially and also Europe, first for poor environmental practice and then over managerial shortcomings (highlighted by an internal Bank report – the Wapenhans report – in 1992). The tardiness of UN development bodies to undertake rigorous self-evaluation and slowness to conform to the pro-market, anti-state orientation that became prominent in the World Bank and among bilateral agencies in the 1980s, further mirrors differences of character among the multilaterals, and has occasioned some impatience in the West.

From this point on, criteria for assessing the quality of a donor's overall approach to oda become even more judgemental. Chris Patten cited one example when speaking to the House of Commons (17 March 1989) as Britain's Overseas Development Minister: 'All attempts to use the nongovernmental organisations more and to put more through the volunteer organisations help to enhance the quality of our total aid programme'. The NGOS are credited with doing some things better than government, like targeting the people who most need help. They are presumed to be generally more cost-effective than official aid agencies. Because most NGOs are small they can think small; and legend maintains small is beautiful. Hence, the greater the proportion of a country's aid effort that is channelled through NGOs, the better are the chances that it will be 'real aid', delivering sound developmental and welfare objectives. NGOs have become central to the distribution of humanitarian assistance in emergencies. For instance, around three quarters of Britain's food aid is administered by NGOs.

These presumptions too warrant careful examination (see Chapter 9). The seemingly exponential growth of NGOs' aid activities bears out the claim that they 'have done well out of the poor' (Edwards and Hulme 1996b: 18). But there may be a size of aid programme above which the employment of NGOs becomes self-defeating – an NGO begins to lose some of the distinguishing characteristics by virtue of which it lays claim to comparative advantage. An alternative would be to control for the size of NGOs and distribute oda through an ever-increasing number. But this engenders a different set of problems such as poor coordination, which has long been considered a weak point in the international aid effort. In any case, the relationships that obtain between official and non-official aid sectors could be even more relevant to the quality of the total aid effort than is the volume of resources channelled through the NGOs. Moreover, the record of NGOs and their allies includes campaigning for increased government aid efforts. They do not by and large aspire to replace government agency, but to be a complementary force instead.

For many years the attaching of political strings to aid was considered symptomatic of a donor's lack of interest in the developmental outcomes. Indeed, political, strategic and diplomatic goals have been responsible for much aid being given to countries that are not among the poorest. The same point applies to commercially motivated aid. Aid-seeking governments that do not attach a high priority to development can feel more comfortable with aid advanced solely on acceptable political grounds. If aid's developmental effectiveness is a function of the extent to which development really is the primary object, then it is tempting to draw the inference that good aid is non-political.

However, such a reading would fit best the Cold War years and must be amended, although not jettisoned completely, in the light of the modern politics of aid (see Chapter 10). That some countries need political reform before sustainable development is feasible has become a cardinal belief since the late 1980s, and is ubiquitous among DAC donors. The giving of aid to corrupt and oppressive regimes was once commonplace, but is now called into question more than ever before. Good governance is believed to be a significant determinant of the developmental returns to oda. On these grounds political conditionalities are being attached to oda, and aid is being given for purposes of political reform. Many US aid officials for instance now believe countries cannot be helped to develop economically unless explicit attention is paid to their political development (Carothers 1995: 69). Tomasevski (1993: 174–5) maintains that if aid is to have an economically sustainable developmental effect it must first be subjected to a human rights impact assessment, so adding further political content to the idea of quality oda.

The checklist for a high quality aid programme could be extended further by an assortment of additional criteria. One candidate is environmental sustainability. Aid must promote environmentally sustainable development, a widely used formulation being development that meets the needs of the present without compromising the ability of future generations to meet their own needs. Another criterion asks, what does the aid effort do for women? That special attention should be paid to women's rights, entitlements and needs is widely endorsed in the DAC and not just because women comprise a majority of the world's poor, although a shortage of gender-based data and statistical analysis remains a problem. But, just as voices have been raised in the developing world against 'green imperialism', so there is concern in some quarters that women-in-development and other gender-related initiatives can become vehicles for cultural imperialism. Where significant local opposition is aroused, on these or other grounds, the chances are that aid's effectiveness could be reduced.

Finally, some consideration must be given to the relationships between aid quantity and quality. Instinct suggests that as the former increases so the latter will decrease unless aid agencies commit adequate manpower resources to preparing and administering the flows – a commitment that has often seemed absent in aid agencies with large budgets. A separate thesis maintains that as the quality of official aid is improved, so the tax-paying public will become more supportive and demand an increase in the resources committed to aid (Mosley 1985). However, survey evidence from several donor countries indicates that public perceptions of aid can be very inaccurate. Even if support grows, competition for public spending in other policy areas and resistance from the finance ministry may prove over-whelming. In fact, there has been growing concern in recent years that aid's poor reputation as an instrument of development could be damaging the case for oda.

Aid in perspective

Aid is only one of many different kinds of relationship between countries and is not the most important one at that. The fact that oda flows have not accounted for more than 1.5 per cent of the combined GNP of developing countries is one statement of its significance. Of course, volume is only a partial counter, for development experts have described oda's principal role in several different ways. For example it is a catalyst that mobilises resource flows from other quarters (the same point is also made about the IMF's non-concessionary loans, whose seal of approval can unlock both conces-sionary and private commercial flows); it helps remove bottlenecks in an economy; it is a device for transferring skills in policy analysis and eco-nomic management, so raising the profile of developmental considerations in public policy formation. Aid is neither a necessary nor a sufficient con-dition for development or economic growth. Even the DAC acknowledges that oda is less important than 'healthy access' to international markets, cap-ital, and technology, and that all of the external factors play only a second-ary role to the efforts of the people in the developing countries (OECD 1994: 9). Figures consistently bear out a positive correlation between eco-nomic growth rates in the developing world and integration into world markets for goods, services, capital and labour.

In 1995 total net resource flows from OECD countries into developing countries reached a new high around $240 billion. Aid and other financial resources are not direct substitutes for one another, but history shows that inward corporate investment, foreign commercial bank loans and port-folio investment as well as trade credits have all been more volatile, indi-vidually and collectively. Largely because of movements in one or more of these, oda's proportional contribution to the net flow of financial resources from DAC countries to developing countries and multilateral organisations has fluctuated markedly over the period since 1945. Official development finance, of which oda is the major component, increased from under a third of total net receipts of developing countries in 1980 to a half in 1989, before falling back in the 1990s. Private flows now regularly account for over two thirds of all capital inflows to developing countries. Moreover, economists claim the demands posed by such flows provide a valuable agency of restraint on host government temptations to pursue distortionary economic policy regimes – regimes that would be designed less to maximise the nation's economic well-being than to privilege the rent-seeking of politically influential minority interests.

Nevertheless, for LLDCs oda consistently accounts for the largest share of resource inflows. Private flows to the developing world, equity investment especially, were buoyant in the first half of the 1990s and quadrupled on an annual average basis in money terms between 1980–5 and 1992–3 alone. But a few countries in East Asia, most notably China and to a lesser extent Latin America, have benefited most. Just eight countries representing 30 per cent of developing country GDP accounted for two thirds of overall foreign direct investment flows to developing countries in 1990–3; around one third went to China alone, exceeding $35 in 1995. In contrast, sub-Saharan Africa receives less than 5 per cent of direct investment. Of the 20 countries who between them received 80 per cent of all private financial flows in 1989–93, only three were LICs: China, India and Indonesia.

Whatever benefits developing countries might derive from oda, the significance of the economic contribution cannot be assessed in isolation from the full gamut of their transactions, in trade, commerce and finance. To illustrate, by the end of the 1980s developing countries were paying up to $70 billion more each year in interest and principal repayments on their foreign borrowings than they were receiving in new aid disbursements. Debt service payments continue to increase, to $194 billion in 1995. Over the years there have been widely differing estimates of the losses Northern trade protectionism has inflicted on developing countries' export earnings, ranging from twice to ten times their annual oda inflows. In the 1980s non-tariff barriers against developing country exports actually increased (Spero 1990: 222–30). The conclusion of the Uruguay round of world trade negotiations under the General Agreement on Tariffs and Trade (GATT) in 1994 made considerable progress in reducing tariff and non-tariff barriers in the industrialised world, and is projected to generate additional export earnings for developing countries of more than $65 billion annually by the year 2002. Again, the chief gainers will be the more developed countries of Asia and Latin America. In contrast, some estimates reckon the least developed countries mainly in Africa could lose up to $2.6 billion annually, largely by having to pay more for imported foodstuffs (due to the required cuts in subsidies on Northern food exports), and reduced export revenues caused by erosion of preferential tariff status. A collapse in commodity export prices in the 1980s meant that 45 least developed states in the Africa, Caribbean, Pacific (ACP) group of countries associated with the EU lost income of $100 billion – twice the aid received from all sources (Goutier 1996: 4).

Hence Stokke's (1996: 62) remark that a yet further role for aid in the years ahead might be to repair the damage the evolving trade regime could inflict on poor country losers. Even so, the protectionist measures which sub-Saharan African countries insist on retaining for themselves are reckoned to be costing them as much as $11 billion each year (equivalent to the region's entire oda receipts in 1991), because indirectly they harm the region's export competitiveness.

That rich world initiatives such as in trade (especially the arms trade) and the treatment of foreign debt are sometimes contrary to aid's developmental objectives is so widely acknowledged that a coded language has arisen to characterise the phenomenon: in the 1970s there was talk of the desirability of a more 'integrated development policy' and an 'integrated economic policy' towards the developing world, and now the need is said to be for greater 'policy consistency', 'policy coherence' and 'complementarity'. The degree of success with which the OECD countries manage their own domestic economies also clearly has major import for LDCs; thus Toye (1993) instanced the significance for developing countries of the global level of real interest rates. In addition there are particular factors of special relevance to certain countries. For example, Stokke (1996: 55) reports claims about the economic costs to Southern Africa of apartheid South Africa's regional destabilisation and warfare as high as $46.9 billion (for 1980–8) and $100 billion (1990–4); Barratt Brown's (1995: 111) more conservative estimate of $10 billion losses (1980–5) also exceeds all oda receipts. For the sub-Saharan African countries who belong to the franc zone the 50 per cent devaluation of the CFA (Communauté Financière Africaine) franc relative to the French franc in January 1994 was highly significant, as was France's former unwillingness to countenance such a step. For post-communist states in Central and Eastern Europe, accession to the EU and World Trade Organisation should provide far greater and more lasting economic benefit than all the aid they are likely to receive in the meantime.

In sum, there is a belief that for all its weaknesses and limitations oda 'remains one of the most important mechanisms for relieving poverty and its destructive effects' (Watkins 1995a: 174). Nevertheless, there is growing evidence in support of Gilpin's (1987: 313) advice against overestimating oda's significance to the world economy, especially in the current era of increasing globalisation. He was also right to draw attention to aid's subordinate status to the foreign policy objectives of donor states.

Aid as a political relationship

There have been many attempts to define politics. One of the most enduring sees power as its essence. Power too has been defined in different ways. The various members of the family of concepts of which power is an umbrella term can be usefully distinguished, for instance physical force, influence and manipulation. The possession of power resources, wealth for example, denotes a potential to exercise power, which could remain idle or be used inefficiently. Attempts to influence and persuade can be unsuccessful, even counter-productive. The exercise of power and its achievements can be measured in relation to a number of variables, such as range, scope, the extent and significance of the changes that are caused and the amount of resistance that is overcome. Central is a measure of distance between the initial positions of the different parties to the relationship.

The political nature of the aid relationship too can be conceptualised in different ways. Indeed, the aid literature is thoroughly confusing in its unsystematised employment of such terms as leverage, pressure, coercion, conditionality and dialogue. This partly reflects unavoidable semantic difficulties. But also, there are not one but several different kinds of aid relationship to be found in reality. Moreover, the parties to a particular relationship may not share identical views of the nature of that relationship, and outside observers could have their own understandings, different again. Thus for instance Gordon (1992: 25) identifies three models of interpretation, which he associates with donors, left-wing critics and development economists: aid as a gift, aid as an instrument of domination, and aid as a form of purchase. The fact that the conduct of aid relationships is a process, perhaps proceeding by way of several distinct stages, adds further complexities, and the relations may be dynamic over time. Donors undertake a commitment after first making an offer; prior to that, there will be an indication that an offer might be made. This could arise in the context of a set of expectations that have been generated within an established aid relation. The maintenance of a commitment and, conversely, threats to consider suspending aid deliveries, the withholding of aid, abandoning a relationship and excluding a possible recipient from further consideration, are all opportunities to attempt to exercise power. Aid recipients too take initiatives. For instance, on occasions a particular relationship has been terminated contrary to the donor's wishes.

Aid negotiations are invariably preceded by, or embellished with, conditions, usually formal, and sometimes tacit understandings that apply to the commitment and disbursement of aid. The conditions usually originate with donor suggestions, but take final shape following discussions with recipients. They vary from terms to which recipients can freely assent without any sense of having made a major concession, to matters where agreement is given only with great reluctance. Some conditions, like aid itself, may prove to be fungible. Aid seekers might exploit competition and divisions among donors to advantage, and take opportunities to win a relaxation of agreed conditions or a renegotiation of terms that once seemed settled. On the other side, performance monitoring and aid tranching (staged disbursement conditional on satisfactory performance) should enhance the donor's chances of securing compliance. The outcomes of aid negotiations and of attempts to enforce conditionalities will depend in part on the balance of power resources and the skills of the parties, and on how determined they are to reach agreement and maintain aid relations.

Traditionally, conditions have related to the financial terms and administrative arrangements for aid, and to the specifics of projects or programmes for which the resources are earmarked – the intention being to make aid expenditures conform to accounting requirements and fit for the purpose. There have also been exchange conditions or reverse transfers – often referred to as strings – such as a donor's use of a military base on recipient territory, commercial opportunities and political allegiance. These are the quid pro quos, sought in anticipation of some benefit to the donor. An unusual example from 1995 involves acceptance of the return of 40,000 Vietnamese guest workers formerly based in the German Democratic Republic (GDR), by Vietnam, in exchange for German oda worth £40 million. Japan's oda to Tanzania, which acknowledged Tanzanian 'understanding' of Japan's need to trade with apartheid South Africa (Tanzania being the 'bellweather of African public opinion and the moral voice in the region's politics') furnishes another example, from the 1980s (Ampiah 1996: 123).

In addition to exchange conditions there are what have come to be known since the early 1980s as conditionalities. These are the changes at the systemic levels of economy and polity, including institutions as well as policies, that are insisted on by donors and conceived to be of benefit to the recipient. The principal expressions are fiscal stabilisation and macroeconomic liberalisation which became prominent in the 1980s – also called first generation conditionalities (Stokke 1995: 7) – and in the 1990s the 'good governance' and other reforms involving democratisation and human rights, or second generation conditionalities.

The analytical distinction between a voluntary arrangement based on exchange conditions, which as Baldwin (1985: 294) pointed out resembles trade, and conditionality bargains of the kind common in the last 15 years seems clear. However, the practical significance may not be equally great everywhere. In all cases the donor's intention is to influence recipient behaviour. Aid seekers could be reluctant to give ground whatever the proposed requirements. Certain exchange conditions can be no less sensitive politically than are conditionalities. The latter might entail least deviation from actual (rather than revealed) intentions of an aid seeker. Where the substance of the conditionalities is inescapable but bound to be unpopular, the opportunity an aid recipient has to externalise responsibility can provide a welcome shield. Conditions are like conditionalities in that they invite aid seekers to calculate the balance of net gains, in terms of their own interests. The aid can be so highly prized as to make a distinction between the two look relatively unimportant. In either case the general nature of the required concessions could be less important than opportunities to participate in refining the details and shape the final agreement.

Moreover, even conditionalities that are formulated primarily to benefit the recipient will not be immaterial to donor interests. The smooth functioning of the global economy and a stable world order are vital public goods for the international community. The belief that economic and political circumstances in developing countries will have a significant bearing on these informs much aid giving. What is more, aid lenders have a stake in facilitating the chances of debt service and repayment, which an effective use of aid and first generation conditionalities especially are supposed to advance. Donors who believe their aid giving equates to making a sacrifice have an interest in seeing recipients develop to the point where aid is no longer necessary. That objective too is supposed to lie behind many of the conditionalities. Thus, the principal difference between exchange conditions and conditionality could turn less on any distinction between self-regarding and other-regarding conduct on the part of donors, and more on the expected form of the returns. Are they specific and anticipated in the near future, or instead are they indirect, diffuse and longer-term?

Anyway, aid conditionality has become an increasingly dominant feature of much international aid. Views differ on the political interpretation that should be placed on such conditionality (see Stokke 1995: 11–13). One perspective sees an offer of conditional aid by X to Y as a bribe or induce-ment, even a purchase (of policy influence, for example) which increases the recipient's range of choice. A more usual characterisation is in terms of power, or coercive influence, where it involves a threat of sanctions in the event of non-compliance by Y with X's wishes. Conditional aid goes well beyond mere persuasion (where X is not intentionally implicated in the structure of alternatives facing Y). It seems more than attempted influence, where X's best efforts may possibly be ignored with impunity; even so, Y might be influenced to respond quite contrarily to the way X had intended. Even successful influence might not involve the subordination of Y's wishes to X's intentions.

Conditional aid is two-faced in that it can be construed as a 'carrot' – sometimes called positive linkage – and it is also prospectively a 'stick' – negative linkage. By implication, if the requisite conditions are not agreed to or are not met, the aid will not be advanced or an offer could be with-drawn. Conditional aid creates a sanction which donors may threaten to apply. Non-compliance invokes at least the possibility, and perhaps the certainty, of a cost, in the form of aid denial. Where this formula effects a change of behaviour by Y contrary to Y's wishes then it exhibits a funda-mental attribute of power. Thus many analysts consider conditional aid to be a form of pressure at the very least; and in some circumstances it has been identified with coercion.

These circumstances include, first, where an offer of aid can reasonably be regarded as an entitlement, and the addition of conditionalities is illegit-imate for that reason. The history of an oda relationship may give rise to a reasonable expectation that aid will continue to be offered on the usual terms, such as minimal or no conditionality. It could also be construed as repayment by the donor of a moral debt. Second, Y might judge that its refusal to accept a conditional aid offer would entail *very severe* penalties. Y's financial and economic situation might be dire. Aid termination could lead to an unbearable loss of access to virtually all trade credit. If the option to do without aid is not realistic, then the donor's imposition of conditions on aid becomes an imposition of conditions on the recipient. Arguably a third circumstance is where the magnitude of an aid offer is so great as to be irresistible. However, it should be noted that in many situations an exertion of donor pressure and attempts to coerce are not bound to secure the desired response. That the threat of sanctions has proven inadequate will become evident when the sanctions are actually invoked. Then, conditional aid's power potential will be redeemed if, and when, the punitive steps finally secure compliance. Put differently, power over aid flows does not necessarily denote power over aid seekers and recipients. Furthermore, none of these powers is synonymous with power over final outcomes and events.

Limits to aid power

Aid seekers can feel strongly pressurised as a result of the asymmetry typical of donor–recipient relationships, even when there is no aid conditionality or intention to coerce. Equally, the direction indicated by an external aid pressure placed on Y could actually coincide with Y's wishes, where Y's behaviour has been restrained by the force of contrary pressures pointing in other directions. This is a not unusual situation facing governments. In any case, dependence on one or just a few sources of aid will have different implications from a dependence on aid as such; and a narrow concentration of aid sources may not itself betoken a reliance on aid. Moreover, many recipients are not highly aid dependent when measured by such yardsticks as the ratio of aid to GNP. At times, even apparent weakness can be a bargaining point, as when the social chaos and political instability that might ensue from the denial of assistance to a country could spread to states where donors have major oda commitments, or highly profitable economic involvements or strategic interests. Fears that the government of politically isolated North Korea might react to the contraction of the country's economy (by up to 25 per cent since 1989) and to growing food insecurity (both the 1995 and 1996 harvests were badly affected by flooding) by becoming more belligerent towards South Korea have prompted the US to make food aid available under the UN's World Food Programme. There is also a fear that political implosion in the North might seriously affect South Korea. A desire to avoid political embarrassment at home can impel DAC governments to respond positively to disasters in seemingly helpless countries where the foreign policy inclination is to abstain, once media attention and NGO campaigning focus public sympathies, as happened during the 1984–5 Ethiopian famine.

Moreover, a donor can come to value the benefits it derives from aid so highly as to make the relationship closer to reciprocal dependency, or interdependence. At the extreme, a reverse dependence of donor on recipient emerges: the perceived cost that would be incurred by the donor (including writing off the sunk costs of past aid) exceeds the cost the recipient would acknowledge from a disruption of relations. Conteh-Morgan (1990:

225) said the US commitment to South Korea 'reached a point of no return such that the commitment itself acts as a leverage over the donor to the advantage of the recipient'. Situations of inverted conditions may be rare, but as a general rule Baldwin (1985: 308) maintained that the greater a donor's interest in making the recipient dependent, the more dependent the *donor* becomes. Donors having the fewest joint interests with recipients and who are most indifferent to the aid relation are the ones who can most credibly threaten to exploit the full power potential of recipient dependency.

The political balance within aid relationships does not remain static: changes in the external environment and the effects of aid itself can relatively advantage either side. An example of effective measures to reduce aid dependence is India's drive to become self-sufficient in grain. That followed reliance on concessionary and commercial imports from the US and US attempts to influence macro-economic policy in the mid-1960s (the 'short-tether' policy). The ability of much smaller donor countries to coerce much larger developing countries is strictly limited. Also, there are many examples of donors seeming not to enforce their apparent power advantage. This can be due to an unwillingness to jeopardise the wider set of diplomatic, commercial and other relationships and the priority given to other interests. Thus, although acute food insecurity would seem to render a country highly vulnerable to external pressure, food aid never quite fulfilled its promise as the 'weapon' of US foreign policy denoted by Agriculture Secretary Earl Butz, in 1974. In that respect (and notwithstanding the occasional deployment of food power against certain regimes since 1974), food aid shared a broadly similar fate to the Middle East's oil weapon (which in 1973–4 threatened oil sanctions against Israel's international supporters), and against which US food aid was projected to be a countervailing power. The reasons include increased competition for Third World markets from other surplus producers. The US share of food aid has declined from 90 per cent in 1965 to not much over half. Only in 1986 did the EU formally detach its humanitarian food aid programme from the persistent tendency of the Common Agricultural Policy (CAP) to generate surpluses, and by 1991 the members accounted for almost a third of world food aid expenditure. And while US strategic interests have also been a limiting factor, so has been the political influence of US agricultural interests who suffer when their government embargoes commercial or food aid exports to significant customers. The objective of cultivating markets for US commercial sales was laid down early on, in the Agricultural Trade Development and Assistance Act (1954), the starting point for what came to be known as PL480 food aid. Now, food aid tends to be bound up more with the economic and political conditionalities attached to programme loans than with more traditional donor exercises in self-serving *realpolitik*. And Uvin (1992) demonstrates that a multilateral 'food aid regime' has evolved since the 1970s, which embodies binding commitments to supply specified amounts and exhibits greater concern for world food security than the general political

and economic self-interests of the donors – interests that were never effectively promoted by food aid.

The ability of the superpowers to enjoy power over other countries has
been due to much more than aid. The limits to aid's potential as a political tool is borne out by the many occasions on which major bilateral
donors have resorted to more dramatic (usually more costly) policy instruments – such as the imposition of trade sanctions and economic embargoes,
even military intervention – which have sometimes been judged potentially
more effective even *vis-à-vis* small, very poor states. Other instruments
include quiet diplomacy, restrictions on visas and bans on arms sales. At
times, all such measures have proven incapable of achieving the sought-for
effects, and aid is no exception. The absence of a significant connection
between aid-recipient voting behaviour in the United Nations and bilateral
aid flows, especially from the US, is a particularly well-documented illustration (Wittkopf 1973; Gonzalez 1984; Kegley and Hook 1991). Similarly,
Geldenhuys (1990: 429) notes that major recipients of Israeli aid in Africa
were consistently less helpful to Israel in UN votes than were some minor
recipients; and, after reviewing the statistical evidence for both the US and
USSR, Mosley (1987: 38) determined that countries 'which use aid as a
means of buying political support get very little for their money'.

Of course, UN voting is only one of many possible ways in which
recipients might signify compliance with a donor's wishes. It may never
have been a policy objective for most donors. Even so, it is undeniably
significant that the Reagan administration's strategy of refusing aid to countries routinely opposing US positions in the UN was so unsuccessful that
it was abandoned soon after being introduced in 1986. Indeed, states for
whom US aid represented a relatively large proportion of their GNP (El
Salvador for example) were no more likely to defer to the US than were
states for whom US aid was proportionately less important (Kegley and
Hook 1991: 307). The moral seems to be that donors seeking influence must
take cognisance of the national interests, values and perceptions espoused
by aid-seeking governments; they might also have to compete with politically influential local groups and social forces whose sectional interests are
at odds with the donors' intentions.

Thus, aid, its conditions and conditionalities provide no certainty of
control over events. On occasions donors have been embroiled in the
manoeuvrings between opposing political forces and conflicting personalities inside recipient states. Thus, as a donor Cuba became 'entangled but
ineffective in its clients' internal politics': Domínguez (1984: 679) cited this
as evidence that aid's political performance conforms to a 'power wasting'
hypothesis. While some major donors have stoked the flames of regional
conflict in parts of the Third World, development cooperation has also
implicated donors unwittingly in some regional tensions and even out-
breaks of warfare. Valued bilateral relations have been endangered. For
many years Soviet military aid to India was viewed by China as provoca-
tion, to the advantage of neither. Disreputable behaviour such as human

rights abuse or the maladministration of aid in a recipient country tarnishes the reputation of donors who are closely associated with the government, even though they may be unable to improve matters. In consequence they could lose diplomatic ground when the domestic political situation changes dramatically, as recently happened to France in Rwanda. Situations where donors have wished to stem their losses and extricate themselves are matched by the cases of failure to win even friendship and local applause.

Again, the US is a good test case, not just because of its size as a donor but because of its exceptional use of aid in pursuit of power political ends (McKinlay and Little 1977 and 1979). According to Eldridge (1969) the US in India gained disproportionately less prestige than the USSR despite having a much larger aid programme; Burns (1985: 172) demonstrates that considerable US aid to Egypt made an adversary of President Nasser whose government was 'psychologically and politically unprepared to make the sorts of concessions that the American government expected in return for its aid'. Aid does not guarantee the stability of a firm ally, not just where unfavourable local circumstances develop their own internal dynamic, but also where other international circumstances prove adverse. Damaging movements in the terms of trade or world interest rates are examples. In places the very aid relationship has undermined a government whose client status eroded its authority and increased its vulnerability to attack by the likes of nationalists and ideological opponents. Zimmerman (1993) presents a familiar argument that US aid has ill served overseas development because it has been the handmaiden of US short-term political and security objectives. The unhelpful results share responsibility for the social unrest and political instability that eventually brought down the governments and produced hostile successor regimes like those in Ethiopia and Iran, after the fall of the Emperor Haile Selassie (1974) and the Shah (1979) respectively, or created power vacuums and political decay of no obvious lasting benefit to the US, as in Liberia and Zaire. But the US is not a unique source of examples; Gérard Prunier, writing about France's unpopularity among the peoples of some francophone countries in Africa, says: 'The chickens are really coming home to roost. We have been behaving like slobs, and finally we have to pay the bill' (*Financial Times*, 14 November 1996). When seen against this kind of background, the measurement of aid's political effectiveness has to be highly contingent on the time horizon donors adopt when undertaking such 'political investment' (May, Schumacher and Malek 1989: 15–16).

In summary, the political value of aid to donors will vary from case to case, but overall judgement is that aid's worth as an instrument of leverage can easily be overestimated. What makes this particularly likely is that donors individually and collectively pursue multiple objectives which sometimes compete. When they place a high value on securing certain exchange conditions, the chances are that involuntary compliance with conditionalities will be more difficult to achieve. Indeed, some close observers of the way in which economic conditionalities have been incorporated into aid agreements and then disregarded characterise the whole less in terms either of trade or politics than as being more like a game, a 'fantasy' even (Collier 1991: 350). Finally, full compliance with donor-specified conditionalities will not necessarily guarantee the donor objectives, including developmental ones, for at least three reasons. For one thing, the situation of the aided country could have been misdiagnosed, and the prescription contained in the conditionalities could rest on a mistaken understanding of the means–ends relationships. For another, compensating manoeuvres may be effected in recipient countries in areas where they retain freedom of action. Further, shocks, which can just as well originate in the international environment as in the internal affairs of countries, have demonstrated the capability to overwhelm even the results of sound analysis and good advice by donors and faithful recipient compliance. Berg (1991: 87–8) concluded that a great deal of 1980s economic conditionality was inappropriate, largely ineffective and often counter-productive. In time, similar judgements might have to be reached about the 1990s sequel of politically conditioned aid. But while this places aid in political perspective, it does not mean aid is without influence or only rarely has political effects.

2

Who would manage an aid agency?

As chief executive of an aid agency, how would *you* decide who should be offered oda? In global terms, aid is a scarce resource relative to demand. Aid agencies must apply a rationing principle or set of principles to countries seeking aid. An approach that has much to commend it bases the determinants on an understanding of recipient-oriented qualifications, such as need, desert and merit. This chapter surveys the criteria.

Allocative criteria

Demography

Demographic size in the developing world ranges from the largest country of all – China, population approaching 1.2 billion and receiving $3.23 billion of oda in 1994, more than any other country – to micro-states and territories of under one million people. Small states face particular obstacles to development. They cannot source the full range of developmentally necessary skills, and have to turn to imports (which require foreign exchange) to satisfy their material desires and, perhaps, basic needs. The economics of scale make it impracticable to have a very diversified economy and fully competitive internal markets. Some small islands and land-locked countries are vulnerable to dependency on larger neighbours; a number are physically remote, at the margin of the global economy. Most LLDCs are relatively small (a major exception is Bangladesh), but in terms of aid received per capita and share of bilateral aid many small developing countries have been favourably treated relative to their average incomes. Partly this is a relic of empire – Britain and France especially collected small island colonies, overseas territories and dependencies in Oceania and the Caribbean. To illustrate, at one point in the mid-1980s the Falkland Islanders were easily the largest beneficiaries of British oda on an annual per capita basis, at £5350 each. Administration costs should place some sort of floor to the minimum size of aid programmes anyway. Small countries can be convenient places to pioneer new ideas in development, minimising the casualties and written-off costs in the event of failure.

Nevertheless, neither small size nor an absence of obvious physical resources are insuperable barriers to economic progress. In fact, generally speaking the growth performance of countries has been inversely related to dependence on natural resource exports. And the greatest extent of need is in the largest poor countries. Hence McKinlay and Little's (1978: 323) claim that covariance of aid and population size 'is compatible with a primitive or basic conception of humanitarianism', and Lipton's (1986: 5) comment, when noting that more than one third of allocable aid went to countries containing a mere 2.7 per cent of the population of the developing world, that aid allocation is 'little short of a scandal'. The sheer number of very poor people in, say, India and Bangladesh commands attention, and in terms of total aid flows these two, China, Pakistan and some other sizeable countries consistently head the recipients' league. The EU employs a mathematical formula based on population for aid allocations to its privileged group of associated ACP states, under the Lomé Convention.

With regard to aid projects, large countries would seem to offer most scope for replicating successful initiatives, spreading out the benefits and grossing up the scale. The costs of harmful aid interventions might be dissipated more easily in a large landscape, and the risks of inducing an unhealthily high level of aid dependence are reduced. Big societies offer greater possibilities of making an absolutely large impact on the world's population growth, regardless of whether improved prospects for development rest on a decline in the birth rate, or, alternatively, rising living standards are the single most effective way to a diminution of family size. However, we must not assume the populous nature of a country necessarily makes its development problems more intractable and so more demanding of help; inter-communal divisions such as those grounded on religion, race or ethnicity have impeded development even in some relatively small states like Sri Lanka. On the other hand, countries with populations of less than one million are more commonly liberal democratic than larger countries.

Economics

There are sound economic arguments for selecting countries where the marginal productivity of assistance promises to be greatest. The idea of *triage* introduced in First World War field hospitals recommended medical orderlies prioritise those casualties who were most likely to recover. The weakest are allowed to perish. Similarly, a concentration of oda on the developing countries that appear most dynamic should help them graduate from the ranks of the developing world sooner. The result would reduce the countries seeking aid and expand the number able to provide aid, possibly increasing world aid supply. Japan, a significant recipient of US aid in 1949–61, and for a time the second largest borrower after India from the World Bank (borrower status lapsed in 1966), lends support to this approach, for Japan is now the world's biggest donor. South Korea and Taiwan are further examples. By 1980 Taiwan, recipient of US aid, mainly grants, worth more than $1.5 billion between 1951 and 1965 (when it graduated from concessional transfers), was providing technical missions to over 50 countries. There are expectations that other Asian 'tigers' too should become more significant contributors to the Asian Development Fund for instance. The positive economic effect of directing a critical mass of oda at potential growth pole countries could be a large multiple of the initial stimulus, because of the benefits to trade, investment or labour flows and remittances within the region and beyond. South Korean manufacturers are now locating in India for example; a possible prospective case is South Africa, which has been much touted as a future engine of growth for black Africa. An additional if incalculable benefit is the inspiration that successful role models can provide to other countries and the boost to morale by showing there is no fixed division of nations into rich and poor.

Even with a strategy of backing winners, differences between present and prospective future marginal product impose further choices. But countries with only a small absorptive capacity for aid will be displaced, as might those who show no early promise of transcending low income status. Thus, on the basis of their absorptive capacity some European post-communist societies become eligible for aid even though prior to 1990 almost all of them enjoyed higher per capita incomes and more advanced social conditions than most developing countries. However, their capacity to make use of resource inflows in a manner comparable to the earlier experience of the European Recovery Programme or Marshall aid (1948–51) in Western Europe should not be exaggerated (see Chapter 11).

The difficulties of identifying priority countries by reference to the prospective economic returns to aid should not be underestimated. Forecasters often disagree. Their estimates can fluctuate widely at short notice, due to changing economic circumstances and political events. For a time some Westerners called India a 'basket case', implying aid should not be wasted on the country. Now, India is a major industrial country registering significant technological accomplishments. Moreover, there are ethical reservations about preferring countries by virtue of their already enjoying a relatively privileged economic disposition. Other countries would be threatened with double jeopardy – denied assistance by virtue of having weak resource endowments and infrastructures. Global inequalities in wealth distribution would be compounded, in the short run at least. The economies that are performing badly, not those that are (or should be) performing well, are most in need of help. An emphasis on economic growth is, perhaps, more redolent of investment banking than the criterion that came to be identified in the 1970s as one of oda's main objectives, the satisfaction of basic material needs.

The well-known thesis that the benefits of economic growth will ultimately trickle down and raise living standards throughout society occasions much dispute even among economists. But few social scientists deny
the long-run importance of economic vitality. The higher the poverty line
is set (i.e. the greater the proportion of the population judged to be poor),
then the more tautological is the argument that growth is essential to poverty alleviation; yet in many LLDCs, even optimistic estimates of feasible
growth will not be sufficient to reduce mass poverty dramatically. Of
course, the appropriateness of different ways of tackling poverty is related
to how poverty is defined. For example, the destitute are served by welfare
transfers targeting immediate redistribution, but in all but the short run
more generalised forms of economic assistance, and appropriate adjustments to macro and meso level economic policy and institutional environments, could be more efficacious for many poor. Nevertheless, a desirable
component of any strategy for aid and development is widely agreed to
be an increase in the productive capacity of the poor to meet their own
needs; and in the 1990s increased attention is being paid to the desirability
of making aid a more focused instrument for reducing poverty. In its *World
Development Report 1990* (iii, 133, 136) the World Bank said loan allocations
must be linked more closely to the commitment countries show to development programmes geared to poverty reduction. This acknowledges that
insufficient weight had been given to such a consideration in previous years.

Poverty and suffering

A concentration of oda on the poorest countries has already been flagged
up in connection with the qualitative dimension of aid programmes. These
countries can be denoted by average incomes per head, and relevant data
are readily available even if their accuracy is uneven. The growing practice
of comparing countries on the basis of purchasing power parity has also
impacted on the rank ordering of countries, and in some cases automatically makes the international poverty gap look less dramatic. The world's
poor are concentrated in around 65 LICs. More than 300 million people are
reckoned to live in absolute poverty in sub-Saharan Africa alone, and at
least another 350 million are in South Asia. A further 150 million live in
East Asia and 100 million in each of North Africa/Middle East and Latin
America. Clearly, poverty alone cannot provide a sufficiently discriminating criterion for allocating the resources of just one aid agency, although
this is not such a problem for organisations like UNICEF and Save the
Children, who start by trying to stem the estimated 13 million child
mortalities caused each year by diseases of poverty including malnutrition.
Development experts agree that targeting the poorest people, rather than
simply the poorest countries, is a desirable refinement to our understanding
of high aid quality. Countries with the most extensive poverty headcount
do not necessarily harbour the deepest poverty or most severe poverty
(inequality among the poor). Poverty is multifaceted and multidimensional.

The measurement of absolute poverty and the identification of the very poorest people – the ultra-poor – can be problematic, and the methodology that is chosen will determine the perceived extent of the problem. The particular significance we attach to relative poverty introduces further complications. In some surroundings poverty is seasonal and will fluctuate from year to year, such as with the success of the harvest. Apart from income levels, other indicators vie as proxies to capture the essence of poverty, such as calorie and nutritional intake, proportion of income spent on food, consumption expenditure, anthropometric and medical indicators. The picture has been amplified since 1990 by the publication by the UNDP of indicators for human development, comprising real GDP per capita, life expectancy, adult literacy and mean years of schooling. Some indicators have improved over the years: average life expectancy in the developing world has increased from 56 years in 1970 to 65 years in 1993. But averages do little justice to the chronically (non-transitory) poor or destitute, who are dependent on transfers from others and often hide in the shadows, or are deliberately kept out of sight. The population of ethnic minorities who suffer negative discrimination and low caste groups, the elderly, sick and infirm, many women and slaves can all come within this category. In countries undergoing severe economic dislocation a further distinction is between the poor and the new poor. The latter suffer greater problems of adjustment and could have fewer coping strategies, and as a result may be more inclined to take political action.

Poverty assessments of countries are complex and difficult to make. Experience has taught that providing oda in forms that will effect a sustained improvement in the living conditions of the very poorest, and bring about a permanent reduction in extreme poverty, is not easy, especially for the poor in geographically remote areas. Oda has made only a very limited measurable contribution here. One explanation applicable to some major donors lies in the reasons why they provide aid; UNICEF estimates have suggested that less than 10 per cent of all bilateral aid tends to be directly targeted to meeting the basic needs of the poorest. The haste by aid agencies to spend their budgets within the financial year and an aversion to funding local and recurrent costs have also been unhelpful. However, the fact that even NGOs often fail to reach the poorest indicates that the problems are severe. Usually, progress will greatly depend on the attitudes shown by the socio-economic and political elites in the developing countries. That many governments have not displayed a sustained and overriding commitment to poverty reduction is trite but true. Thus, one proposal (see Watkins 1995a, for example) is that aid allocations should prioritise poor countries whose governments strongly want to address poverty, and should be so constructed as to encourage governments to move in this direction (in other words, a third generation of aid conditionality).

Nevertheless, in some situations it is not possible to target the poor without paying a significant price in terms of buying off the non-poor, whose cooperation or acquiescence could prove indispensable. Alternatively, by involving the non-poor a progressive element of cross-subsidisation might be possible. Avoidance techniques concentrate on delivering assistance in forms that do not interest the non-poor, for instance 'inferior goods', or in indivisible units that are difficult to usurp, and public goods benefiting everyone. Carefully administered food-for-work projects offer one way of reaching some of the deserving poor, especially if the wage or food value are set below market levels. But generally speaking attempts to make food aid combine humanitarian and developmental objectives have proven to be problematic. The same is true of aid that is intended to benefit the poor at some cost to the non-poor. Chambers' (1983: 163) argument remains valid, that ignoring the power and interests of local elites possibly accounts more than any other factor for project aid's failure to benefit the poor.

Currently fashionable definitions of poverty focus on a lack of entitlements or the means to claim due entitlements, following pioneering analysis by Amartya Sen (1981). Poverty described by low income or consumption expenditure can be distinguished from insecurity or vulnerability to shocks – a condition of being without assets such as land and other forms of 'insurance'. Institutionalised disadvantage is more serious than merely temporary vulnerability, and the destitute have neither income nor assets. Generally speaking poverty as such need not preclude happiness but in these situations a reasonable assumption is that misery will be an almost inevitable accompaniment. In practice the victims of catastrophes such as drought (hunger is responsible for just over half of all deaths caused by 'natural disasters') make signal claims on donors. Much of the suffering here is rooted in poverty, which makes for high vulnerability to disaster agents. Thus, countries that are particularly prone to disasters and are unable to withstand their effects are strong candidates for development assistance, not just humanitarian relief. Of course, neither form will suffice in circumstances where only constructive political intervention, possibly outside military involvement, can secure a viable peace. In many cases disaster proneness seems to be largely self-inflicted, most notably in what have come to be known as complex emergencies. The difficulties of transition from relief through rehabilitation to development assistance in 'post-conflict' recovery situations, where state structures remain weak, fragile, and unable to take responsibility and effect decisions, have become increasingly salient in recent years (see Macrae, Zwi and Forsyth 1995).

War and civil war make even relief interventions difficult to execute and politically fraught. Even military-led humanitarian interventions have been prone to shortcomings; and in some conflict situations humanitarian aid has been held responsible for prolonging the violence. Aid that deflects efforts from conflict resolution may actually increase the loss of life. In these sorts of situations aid agencies tend to be criticised if they intervene and criticised if they hold back. The Biafran war (1967–70) furnished an early example. More recently in Bosnia, the United Nations High Commissioner for Refugees (UNHCR) found itself caught between appearing to be an accomplice to Serb-inspired 'ethnic cleansing', by helping people at risk to flee danger, and encouraging people to remain in 'safe areas' that were to be insecure. Generally speaking, the responsiveness of the international community to disasters has been highly variable – selective, even arbitrary in relation to need, because of reasons of domestic and international politics (see Burnell 1991b: Chapter 7). For instance Kent (1987: 79–81) drew attention to the significance of donor politics to disaster relief, citing US Secretary of State Henry Kissinger's admission that relief is a major instrument of US foreign policy. Refugee migrations have been an increasingly prominent accompaniment of 'man-made disasters' and complex emergencies – there are at present probably more than 23 million refugees and even more internally displaced persons (who have to flee their homes but remain inside national borders), half of them in Africa. Decisions about who qualifies for refugee status provide further evidence of the influence of extraneous considerations (the 1951 UN Convention relating to the Status of Refugees offers special protection whereby signatories are legally obliged not to return refugees to persecution or danger). For instance, on the one side the British authorities disputed the US government's (and UNHCR's) view that Vietnamese 'boat people' reaching Hong Kong in the second half of the 1980s were refugees; on the other side, the US insisted that Haitians fleeing their island's brutal dictatorship were just economic migrants, unentitled to asylum in the US. The UN definition of a refugee is itself a Cold War product, geared to the needs of people fleeing communism in Europe. It is not well suited to the very different circumstances that have given rise to mass displacements of people within as well as beyond the borders of Third World and other states.

Special relationships

Good reasons direct aid agencies to focus on countries with whom there is a special relationship, perhaps the consequence of a former colonial bond, commonalities of culture or official language. A good working relationship based on mutual understanding, not sentiment alone, is desirable. Success may be enhanced by choosing partners who are regarded as equals in some sense – partners with the ability and confidence to make their own contributions to the design and implementation of oda transfers. Most DAC states contain pools of development professionals with more detailed knowledge of some developing countries than others; and a solid record of trade and diplomatic ties could also be helpful. So, even NGOs in the wealthier Commonwealth countries especially Britain have chosen to develop links primarily with poorer Commonwealth members, despite broadly duplicating the official choice of bilateral aid relationships. While another country's proximity might make it important to a donor's national security, that will not necessarily convey superior insights into the country's needs.

Most donors have acquired distinctive patterns of aid relationships, and a new aid agency could justifiably look for countries that have been persistently ignored or fallen out of favour for no defensible reason. Thus while Egypt and Kenya fare consistently well in the international aid lottery, some countries like Nicaragua and Cambodia (the latter diplomatically isolated by the West for most of the 1980s) have seen their fortunes fluctuate wildly, for reasons that owe a lot to international politics. Apartheid South Africa was embargoed; the collapse of the USSR means Cuba's aid inflows have collapsed. In the last decade new and initially uncrowded territory has become available for aid because of the proliferation of states, some of them in Europe having the advantage of being without an aid dependency culture and not weighed down by its debilitating effects. Stories of aid misuse and rampant corruption now circulating out of Cambodia and other countries currently on the aid frontier remind us that a sudden aid inrush can be corrosive and wasteful. The advice to donors is to exercise restraint. To some degree the Eritrean authorities, appreciating the merits of self-reliance, have imposed a self-denying ordinance *vis-à-vis* aid.

Past performance and indebtedness

Donors should assess the performance of aid projects and programmes in terms of achievement of objectives, overall impact, cost-effectiveness, and general development results (Carlsson, Kohlin and Ekbom 1994: 9). The levels of attainment among these dimensions may not be well correlated. Indeed, Riddell *et al.* (1995) found that NGOs' development impact consistently fell short of their attainment of their objectives. Countries that make the best use of oda may not be the same as the developing economies that are performing most impressively, or have the brightest prospects for economic take-off. Furthermore, past economic performance provides no guarantee of future results. Calculations for both will be sensitive to the variables selected for purpose of measurement – savings, physical investment, human capital formation, exports (or import substitution, in the industrialisation models formerly favoured in Latin America and the USSR), and so on – and the extent of time over which a performance review is judged appropriate.

Who is responsible for past performance, especially an ineffectual application of aid? The fact that legal mechanisms may not exist whereby donor countries can be made internationally accountable for their aid interventions does not mean they should be free of all blame. It would be irrational to penalise potential aid candidates today for having been unlucky in their 'choice' of donors in the past, or for the adverse impact on aid's results of external factors over which they had no control. Such considerations as these are important to how we approach the issue of sovereign indebtedness – something the world began to notice when the Mexican debt crisis broke in 1982. Since then, arguments for debt forgiveness and debt write-offs have been vigorously presented by Third World pressure groups in the North and political leaders in the South, partly on the grounds that institutions controlled in the North encouraged irresponsible levels of borrowing and so should help resolve the ensuing financial difficulties. A variety of measures such as rescheduling, refinancing, partial and complete debt cancellation have been arranged. To illustrate, multilateral restructurings of official and/or commercial bank debt were concluded with 68 governments between 1980 and 1994, and in 11 countries the debt was restructured ten or more times. Yet developing country debt has continued to grow, to over $1945 billion.

Debt relief is considered a form of aid if the terms and conditions are sufficiently generous. In the 1990s it has become an increasingly prominent feature – in 1992 for instance, debt forgiveness exceeded 14 per cent of oda. The potential benefit is obvious where governments have to take fiscal and economic policy measures that depress living standards and frustrate growth simply in order to service existing loans and qualify for further credit. However, the origins of the present indebtedness are not identical for all countries, and are liable to various interpretations. The mix of factors makes it difficult to apportion responsibility exactly or to be wholly confident that similar financial problems could not recur (and, indeed, might be made more likely to recur if debt relief is handled clumsily now). Mexico's peso crisis in December 1994 is illustrative. Even now several countries such as Brazil, Chile, Colombia and the Philippines are running large current account deficits on their trade which could prove unserviceable before long.

Aid's contribution to debt formation is ambiguous. On the one hand it is clear that some oda loans have not generated the means to honour the interest and repayment schedules. On the other hand, a shortfall of concessional support helps explain why governments came to make excessive borrowings at commercial rates. The enthusiasm with which commercial banks in the 1970s made loans in order to recycle petro-dollars (total sums estimated around $300 billion) emanated from two steep increases in the world traded price of oil (1973–4 and 1978–9), which might never happen again. The same cannot be said of the other elements, like OECD governments' rashness in guaranteeing trade credit deals; the contraction of world export markets and depreciation of Third World currencies following the adoption of deflationary measures in the West, which led also to higher interest rates; the economically unproductive uses to which loans were put, and a commitment to unsound economic policies; and finally the trigger – a dramatic reduction of private financial flows (notably in commercial bank lending), which destroyed the cycle in which debtors had come to rely on new borrowing in order to service their existing debt.

In principle, the restoration of a country's creditworthiness in the eyes of private international capital is a legitimate developmental objective of oda. In practice, the use of publicly funded concessionary money to enable debtors to clear their arrears with private banks has been more difficult to justify. Of course, NGOs especially have tried hard to address some of the adverse social consequences of financial crisis. Furthermore, positive political developments in a number of indebted countries in recent years blur the issue.

Regimes that contracted excessive foreign debts tended to be unrepresentative of the interests and wishes of the majority of their people. They did not consult widely. Many were not democratically elected. Most were not publicly accountable. The lenders knew this at the time. Since then, many such regimes have been discredited and replaced. Some of the successors now fully profess agreement with the donors' neo-liberal nostrums and are effecting economic and political reforms. Take Zambia, whose per capita debt is one of the highest in the world. The one-party state which contracted external debt of over $6 billion (equivalent to 170 per cent of GDP) was replaced by competitive party politics. A new government took office in 1991, imbued with a degree of economic realism alien to its predecessor.

Throwing good new money where old monies have been squandered and have created insupportable debt *can* make sense in a changed environment, and once other reasonable means to solving debt problems have been fully explored, like debt–equity and debt–environment swaps. The argument that debt cancellation and fresh oda can only exacerbate these countries' difficulties is illogical. And the relevance of old debts is even more questionable when *both* parties have undergone dramatic change. A case in point is Ethiopia's $3.2 billion debt to the former USSR, much of it credit for arms purchases that were advanced to promote Soviet strategic objectives in the region, and were used in Ethiopia's internal war. Now, the reformed Ethiopian government is unwilling to honour the debt. In a nice parallel, Jacques Attali, the first president of the European Bank for Reconstruction and Development (EBRD), reportedly told his hosts in Moscow that Russia's new democracy should not have to repay its own external debts incurred under the previous Soviet dictatorship (Zhukov 1995: 327).

The debt burden takes different forms and dimensions in different places. The countries that draw most attention can vary depending on what is believed to be the most crucial indicator: the volume of the debt stock or its ratio to GNP (or to GDP); the ratio of annual debt service (interest payments plus amortisation) to GNP (GDP) or to export earnings, or to government income and expenditure overall; and instead of the overall size of a country's debt (or debt servicing) the figures that could be calculated on an average per capita basis (and perhaps with some comparison to average incomes). The largest debts are in Latin America (Brazil's debt exceeds $125 billion), where the leading economies have experienced substantial private capital inflows in the 1990s and wealthy citizens have even begun to repatriate savings previously lodged abroad. The main outstanding obligations are to commercial banks, the IMF and the World Bank. By February 1997 sixteen countries (only two of them in Africa) had participated in 'Brady plan' arrangements to convert non-performing commercial bank loans into bonds, under IMF auspices. This provides temporary relief. Other major debtors include Turkey and fast-growing economies in East Asia, notably South Korea and Thailand. These countries are not in greatest need of concessionary support. India's position is debatable. While not getting into financial difficulties in the 1980s, borrowings since then mean interest payments now account for a large slice of government receipts (47 per cent in 1994), and the total debt of around $100 billion is among the largest.

The poorest debt-distressed countries who have virtually no access to private resources flows would seem to merit greatest consideration. There are around 40 severely indebted low income countries (SILICs), mainly in sub-Saharan Africa. The debt volumes are smaller partly because the countries are poor and have traditionally had to rely largely on concessionary transfers. The debts have typically amounted to less than $10 billion. However, the ratio of debt stock to GNP is virtually treble that for all developing countries – the average for sub-Saharan Africa being 82 per cent in 1994 (compared with 30 per cent in 1980), with countries like Tanzania and Mozambique exceeding 100 per cent. A comparable South American example is Guyana, where per capita debt of $2650 (1995) exceeded that of Brazil and equated to 420 per cent of GDP. Most SILICs are not judged creditworthy by commercial moneylenders. They hold few attractions to foreign corporate investors, apart from in mining, especially while they remain highly indebted. They are extremely unlikely simply to grow out of their present difficulties. Because of this the World Bank launched a Special Programme of Assistance for SILICs in sub-Saharan Africa in 1987 and, as will be seen below, now supports a more ambitious approach.

Bilateral official debt accounts for approximately two thirds of all long-term public debt stock of the SILICs, approaching $200 billion. Unlike the Bretton Woods institutions, bilateral donors are free to write off debt. The major bilateral creditors (the so-called Paris club) agreed modest general terms for reducing official bilateral debt and debt service for SILICs in Toronto (1988); they considered further proposals in Trinidad (1990) and agreed to enhanced Toronto terms in 1991. In 1994 agreement was reached on Naples terms for relief of up to 67 per cent of eligible bilateral debt, all offers to be conditional on commitments to financial stabilisation and economic adjustment. However, the SILICs' need to service multilateral debt now amounts to approximately half their required debt payments (one fifth in 1980). Uganda, among the first to benefit from Naples terms debt cancellation (worth $71 million in 1995) owes three quarters of its external debt to the multilaterals. With total debt in excess of $3.4 billion Uganda's external repayments in 1996 amounted to ten times the budget for primary health care and seven times that for primary education. Debt service corresponds to a quarter of the export value of goods and services. For many countries like Uganda much of the value of new aid is effectively being recycled back to 'preferred creditors', especially the World Bank and the IMF (since 1987 the IMF has received $4 billion more in repayments from all SILICs than it has provided in new loans). Watkins (1995a; 1995b) calls this the theatre of the absurd. Meanwhile, an accumulation of arrears means African debt continues to increase.

By 1996 the World Bank was airing proposals for a multilateral debt facility, a trust fund that would buy up debt stock and so clear principal and service payments on loans owed to bodies like the IMF, International Development Association (IDA) and African Development Bank, on behalf of governments displaying sensible economic management. There was initial resistance from the IMF and some government donors, who alleged funds would be diverted away from new aid (IDA replenishment for example) and from prudent but needy countries. There is also a fear for the World Bank's credit rating which, if affected adversely, would increase the cost of future fund-raising from capital markets. Some critics continue to argue that weak political commitment to sound economic policies and implementation failures still pose greater difficulties in many indebted countries, and that neither fresh oda nor debt relief will be sufficient there, let alone in countries wracked by civil strife. Debt forgiveness, seen by some analysts to be a necessary condition for many SILICs to have any chance of economic recovery, is charged with signalling to governments that they can escape penalty for financial and economic mismanagement.

Following months of dispute over how to share the costs, agreement was finally reached among the main creditor bodies on steps to reduce 'unsustainable debt burdens' (i.e. where the debt ratio to annual value of exports is 200–250 per cent or higher, and ratio of debt service costs to export earnings exceeds 20–25 per cent), in October 1996. The decision to proceed will be made on a country by country basis, conditional on acceptable economic policy performance over a period of three to six years. Around twenty SILICs might qualify in full. Paris club members will write off up to 80 per cent of bilateral debt, as part of the arrangements agreed with the World Bank and the IMF. The IMF will take part notwithstanding German opposition to the selling of around $2 billion of its $40 billion gold reserves, so putting its Enhanced Structural Adjustment Facility on a more permanent footing. Following an initial Bank contribution of $500 million, estimates of the eventual value of the trust fund range up to $7.7 billion. There will be no formal writing off of multilateral debt. And the chances are that serious debt problems will remain for a number of countries, inside and outside these new arrangements, not least because around a quarter of all developing country foreign debt is owed to countries that fall outside (Russia and Arab institutions are owed up to $300 billion).

Planning for the future

Ideally, oda's long-range purpose should be to work itself out of a job, but in the meantime lesser horizons will also preoccupy bodies that have a vested interest in maintaining oda. Aid agencies must attend to their own survival, if only so as to be able to continue pursuing their developmental, humanitarian and other formal objectives directly and through influencing others. There need be no cynicism about this, but it can be taken to indicate targeting countries where aid's beneficial effects will be most visible. That could mean fairly small countries, where it is possible to make a 'splash'. Also, essential local cooperation might be anticipated where few other donors are heavily involved. The power of television to influence public awareness and shape opinions at home is another important factor, which could favour allocations to areas that are easily accessible to television journalists and stay in the public eye. This helps explain why the international community has responded more readily in some emergencies than others that were comparable in terms of humanitarian need. Thus, in the aftermath of the Gulf war (1991) NGOs with a strong interest in Africa complained that funding for work there was suffering because media attention focused on the plight of the Kurds in northern Iraq. Victoria Brittan (*The Guardian*, 26 April 1991) noted: 'For every Kurd wretched on the mountains of northern Iraq there are nine Africans threatened with hunger and starvation. But the ratio of media interest has been far more than nine times over in favour of the Kurds'.

In general, disasters and relief operations command more attention from the mass public than less dramatic development work. International assistance is a competitive business especially for NGOs. Involvement in fashionable activities in countries that are in the spotlight can advance an aid agency's standing among its peers, help staff recruitment and not least improve its chances of attracting funding – including monies from multilateral bodies like the UNHCR which employ NGOs on a contractual basis for operational work. The media also influences public perceptions of success and views about what constitutes an acceptable rate of failure. There is a bias against publicising failure among aid agencies including NGOs, despite the OECD's (1985: 253) wise counsel that any organisation claiming 'to have no failures on its books would be either lying or admitting that it had evaded the hard jobs'.

Allocative decisions on aid are not made in a vacuum. Such considerations as internal bureaucratic constraints, procedural requirements, inter-organisational politics and the domestic political environment may have to be taken into account by agencies as they plan their progress, so as to further their legitimate aims. Government bodies for overseas development rarely enjoy great autonomy. In bilateral aid agreements made by oil-rich Gulf states the heads of the ruling family have frequently been decisive, and in DAC countries the people's elected representatives have regular opportunities to review and comment upon the official aid programme. Public attitude surveys in Britain and the US reveal that society invariably overestimates the magnitude of aid, and is also prone to distractions which, if translated faithfully into policy, could diminish aid's constancy and further undermine its performance. Furthermore few NGOs are membership organisations with highly participatory structures. For the most part, voluntary donations betoken a limited interest in what aid agencies do. The very act of giving usually indicates a preference against taking a more active involvement. Put differently, charities, even examples run on amateurish lines, fulfil the function of professional conscience of the nation. For these reasons it is debatable whether governments and NGOs should pay special heed to the ultimate paymasters when deliberating aid allocations, unless suitable steps are taken first to ensure society has an adequate grasp of the issues. In fact there is a consensus that much remains to be achieved in the field of 'development education'. Total DAC public expenditure on this has typically been less than $50 million annually, and in only a few countries like Canada, the Netherlands and Norway has there been strong government support. Anyway, Olsen's (1996: 342) findings in several countries indicate that mass public opinion has never had much direct influence on foreign aid policy. He detected a passive acceptance of government decisions.

There is a larger problematic here: to whom *should* aid agencies be chiefly responsible? For, *if* aid is analogous to a market (a proposition that is anathema to some idealisations of development cooperation that are voiced from the NGO community), then who is 'purchasing' what? One answer maintains it is the donors who can be likened to consumers, of satisfaction from giving aid, or of pleasure from believing the results will be good (Morton 1996: 57). Alternatively, they may be buying influence over the recipients. Yet neither taxpayers nor charitable givers have direct experience of much of what the aid agencies supply, whether projects, programmes, processes or technical advice. But if the ultimate paymasters cannot make informed comparisons between alternative products in this market, then neither can oda's recipients. They cannot be likened to buyers in a free market either. Many have few means to influence the supply, even when profoundly dissatisfied with the 'product'. There are conundrums facing aid agencies in knowing what is the right balance to strike between the statutory legal and financial accounting requirements at home, professional obligations to achieve their mandated developmental and humanitarian objectives, and an appropriate responsiveness to the expressed wishes of overseas partners and the people who are supposed to be the ultimate beneficiaries – the 'shareholders' (Edwards and Hulme 1995: 221) in development. The conundrum is particularly complex for NGOs especially in respect of funds received from government. Their partners are often intermediary NGOs in the South and they may not deal directly with grass-roots bodies, who in turn work most closely with the people that NGO support is supposed to help. Indeed, Edwards and Hulme (1995) conclude the problem is so difficult that it may never be solved, and at best can only be managed.

Let the market decide?

According to DAC sources (OECD 1970: 27) donors should not 'look at recipients through field glasses as at horses at a race track and then place their bets in the form of aid allocations'. Countries that need aid are the authentic interpreters of what they want. America's European allies were involved at an early stage in the designs for Marshall aid, and jointly submitted their lists of requirements in advance of the allocative decisions. Official donors maintain that they invite their overseas partners to specify what they would like aid for, and Japan in particular has always said a 'request first' basis governs its bilateral funding relations (often, the requests appear to have been formulated after advice received from Japanese businessmen seeking oda-funded contracts). A long-standing demand in the developing world is that voting arrangements in multilateral institutions grant equal rights to funders and funded, rich and poor countries, North and South.

However, it is a fanciful notion that aid seekers should determine among themselves the allocation of available oda. For one thing, they comprise a clear majority of all countries, which underlines the need for some further criteria that would identify the most eligible claimants. In a free-for-all, advantage might well accrue to countries that are already well equipped to present a cogent case and who are most skilled at building supportive coalitions. Weak and underresourced countries, who could formulate sound aid bids only with the help of foreign assistance, would be disadvantaged. The European parties to Marshall aid reached agreement on reconstruction plans, but not without some cost in the form of provoking divisions in their ranks. The fractious nature of the Non-Aligned Movement and its decline over the last 20 years do not inspire confidence that a global forum of today's many and very diverse aid seekers would be a harmonious and efficient mechanism for arriving at a fair and fruitful distribution of aid.

Many or few?

Some donors provide aid to well over 100 countries. That maximises the variety of experiences their aid agencies can accumulate, increases the scope for cross-fertilisation of ideas, and reduces exposure to localised shocks. Backing many horses is less of a gamble than trying to pick only the winner. However, portfolios that are spread widely and thinly increase the organisational and administrative costs. Aid agencies are no different from other bureaucracies in attracting criticism when they appear to spend excessively on themselves. But they can also be open to criticism when the interests of administrative convenience seem to dominate the choice of operational behaviour. Donors that form many aid partnerships increase the chances of different aid agencies having overlapping domains and duplicating one another's efforts. Those symptoms too have been the subject of much criticism, and the potential scope for cost-sharing and exchange of information about successful formulae has often gone unrealised. Against this background, a focused approach to selecting countries commends itself. It facilitates the development of a close familiarity with the individual circumstances, especially when recipients share some family resemblance that permits the donor to cultivate excellence in a specialised field. In the 1990s several donors have decided to increase the concentration of their oda on priority countries, if only because of tightening constraints on their budgets.

Conclusions

One of the most important questions any organisation that dispenses resources must address is, who shall benefit? In theory aid agencies have
learned that thorough familiarisation with potential partners is advisable
before making commitments to transfer aid, and that decisions once taken
can be difficult to reverse – like 'turning an oil tanker around' (Ryrie 1986:
9). Judith Hart's (1973: 183) experience on becoming Minister responsible
for Britain's overseas development cooperation is worth quoting, for on
canvassing her officials over the criteria they had been using to determine
aid allocations she 'received almost as many answers as there were people
present'. The issue of how many criteria can be comfortably factored into
the equation could be as pertinent as deciding the optimum number of aid
partners. The appropriate model to adopt for the decision-making process
is also a fit subject for consideration. What role should be afforded to aid
seekers, and how far can aid agencies' own organisational goals be given
legitimate representation?

In any case, the DAC's preoccupation in the early years with devising
general allocative principles for aid has not been sustained. Experience has
taught the enduring importance of political, commercial and other non-
developmental influences, leading Mosley (1987: 60) to conclude that the
'only thing which country allocations are *not* determined by, broadly speaking, is "effectiveness" in the sense of the ability of aid flows to achieve high
rates of return or influence the rate of economic growth'. Other analysts
too have noted that, historically speaking, the pattern of aid distribution
bears little relation to evidence about oda's actual or projected results.
However, times are changing. The enthusiasm for setting global targets for
aid pledges has waned. The once high ambitions to close world income and
poverty gaps have also given way. Today's preoccupations are more sober,
and include both the detailed assessment of aid needs of countries and the
fashioning of robust criteria for testing oda's developmental effectiveness.
The talk in DAC circles is of output measures and value-for-money, rather
than just a familiar plea for more resources. Not all the reasons may be
viewed as the right reasons. There are fears that the world is witnessing a
weakening of the political motivation for providing aid since the end of the
Cold War, and there is intensifying competition between the different claims
within aid budgets and for the resources that could become lost to oda.

Some simple lessons emerge from simulating the aid chief executive's
dilemma over allocative principles. First, there is no sense in identifying
target countries without having clear ideas about aid's developmental
purpose(s) and the reasons why it should be advanced. These issues are
addressed in the following chapters, but it is appropriate to say here that
there are few certainties, and much disagreement, about oda's objectives
and the best ways to go about achieving them. A DAC report (OECD
1980: 53) was once so bold as to say 'A priori one knows nothing, really,
about what aid in general is supposed to do, does, or how it does it'. What

weight should be accorded to humanitarian purposes relative to the more developmental ones? What, indeed, is development? What order of priority should be accorded to development's various facets – economic, social, environmental and so on – which may not sit easily together? These are big questions. And just as developing country circumstances change over time, sometimes rapidly and in unforseeable ways, so has our understanding of why they might need oda and what aid can achieve.

Second, allocative decisions must be informed by knowledge of both the quantity and the sorts of resource available, including organisational capacity, professional capabilities and technical expertise. Occasionally, aid agencies are drawn into activities for which they are ill-adapted. All are unsure of the resources they can command in the future, and such uncertainty prejudices their choice of undertakings.

Third, while many of the criteria enumerated in this chapter may combine well, some are mutually exclusive. Hard choices have to be made, but once made, they should be subjected to re-examination from time to time in the light of changes in the world around and the lessons of experience. In development generally and oda specifically few, if any, quick fix solutions prove satisfactory. On the one side, the continuity in aid relations which enables mutual trust and understanding to form has much to commend it. On the other side, aid agencies have sometimes been vulnerable to accusations of developing too cosy a relationship with their established partners, of just going through the motions because there is a budget to be spent.

Fourth, decisions about allocative criteria among countries differing widely in their socio-economic profiles and levels of development will be influenced by value judgements. Science alone cannot tell us how to balance social needs against economic performance, or past performance against future potential. After how long is it reasonable to expect aid's impact to be measurable? What should be the threshold in terms of developmental achievements and the period over which they are sustained before it becomes reasonable to drop a country from the class of eligible oda candidates? Should aid be advanced as a reward for self-help, or should it be conceived as a stimulus to do better? Questions like these have only subjective answers. The answers will be coloured by circumstantial forces. For example, Kinoshita (1993: 120–1) hazards that the economic history of Japan could be driving its people to believe that only needy societies which are making earnest self-help efforts should be granted assistance (while not going so far as to say people who do not work should not eat). The need for aid cannot be determined purely objectively. This does not only mean that precise measurement is impossible. Political judgement is required (OECD 1992: 99). That need not be a matter for regret.

At a minimum political decisions can offer a tie-breaker between competing developmental criteria (or bundles of criteria) and the conflicting oda allocations they suggest. Political decisions could supply consistent organising principles for aid allocation. Moreover, political compatibility facilitates donor–recipient cooperation. A clear sense of political purpose can provide direction where confusion would otherwise reign. It may be needed to correct the distorting influence of an aid agency's informal objectives and bureaucratic goals. Anyway, oda that is not consciously directed at political ends may still have significant political effects, which could make oda's development objectives harder, or easier, to achieve: it is best to recognise this from the start. And the modern politics of aid highlights the importance of governance, whose significance for aid allocation now seems self-evident. Seers' (1972) proposal could be finally coming of age: financial assistance of the sort which offers immediate political gains to the recipient (the 'announcement effect') should be reserved for good governments. He argued that if oda other than humanitarian relief must go to governments who are not developmentally committed, then it should take the form of technical assistance that produces returns only in the longer term. In practice, there seems to be little evidence that the aid conditionalities either of the 1980s or the early 1990s have impacted very strongly on the geographical pattern of aid allocations, aside from one or two striking exceptions (Hewitt and Killick 1996: 153). These two analysts advise that the way in which conditionality has been applied so far is best thought of as a means of quality control, rather than a rationing device. Another finding is that some official donors including Japan, the Netherlands, France and the EU claim that rationing their available oda is less problematic than ensuring it is well spent.

Nevertheless, there are many countries who seek and rather fewer who provide aid. There is no global parity of supply and demand. The degree to which donors recognise they must locate worthy partners or clients and worthwhile objects of aid does not compare with the demand-intensity for oda supplies. Not all aid agencies are equal in terms of demonstrating good qualifications to supply oda. Hence, it would be rational of aid seekers as well as donors to reflect on appropriate criteria for forging relationships, and to identify their partners with equal care. You can try this exercise for yourself. But it might look somewhat academic. For while virtually all donors now claim to base their prescriptions for development around more or less free market economics (and politics), in the aid business it is the suppliers who for the most part determine the pattern of allocation. They also decide the total of oda, and they initiate the aid agendas too. In short, structural power lies with the donor community. Certainly, donors are faced with few genuinely straightforward choices, but there is a clear contrast with societies who truly need assistance and for whom the opportunities to exercise choice are more rare, perhaps an unaffordable luxury. When the view from the South is that the international political inequalities introduced by money are 'indestructible' (see comment in Sogge 1996: 140), the most challenging question is not who would manage an aid agency but who would prefer to be on the other side?

3

The case for giving: morality, justice and entitlement

'Needed: a case for giving', declared *The Economist* (7–13 May 1994). Why should people in relatively prosperous countries provide aid to foreigners? This chapter introduces answers structured along ethical lines and reviews arguments claiming that some countries are entitled to receive aid by virtue of their unfavourable treatment by others.

There is an important distinction between the reasons why people should give aid and what motivates governments to mount aid programmes. Popular demand has not been a necessary condition and is not a sufficient condition for governments to have aid budgets, especially in the presence of resource limitations and competing demands. But democratic logic suggests that if moral conviction moves society to call for an official aid programme, then its government should comply, unless there is an even stronger moral counter-argument. A more radical position maintains that the ethical principles which command an international redistribution of resources are strong enough to override even the opposition of a majority of voters. Indeed, some political theorists have argued that a major function of the state should be to advance the cause of moral education, rather than to obey society's wishes in every respect. A more practical issue than how closely a government should follow the electorate's express desires is whether the people's wishes are clear. Political debate especially around election time usually marginalises development cooperation issues. Particular interests such as commercial or business lobbies and the attentive public who take part in Third World pressure groups will try to influence public policy towards development cooperation but will not be representative of society as a whole.

The Commission on International Development (1969: 8) or Pearson Commission said the simplest answer to the question of why rich countries should help others is 'the moral one: that it is only right for those who have to share with those who have not'. The presumption that there is, or must be, a strong moral case for aid giving might explain why that case has been explored in the literature much less frequently than the intensive, but no more conclusive, investigation of the economic grounds. The relative neglect is significant, given: the prominence attained by arguments appealing to self-interest in the wake of the Brandt Commission report *North–South: A Programme for Survival* (Independent Commission on International Development Issues 1980); the subsequent popularisation of a root-and-branch critique of aid from the political right; and mantra-type chants that donors exhibit symptoms of aid fatigue. Riddell (1987: Chapters 2–7 especially) provided an invaluable service in dusting off a collection of moral arguments and examining their worth; readers seeking a more thorough analysis are directed to his exegesis.

Moral arguments

Moral arguments propose that a stated course of action or inaction *should* be followed even if contrary to the wants and perceived interests of the actor. For innumerable people around the world, religion and morality are inextricably intertwined, and their religious faith informs them they should endeavour to help fellow human beings less fortunate than themselves. This becomes a matter of doing what pleases God, or alternatively what God commands, usually without distinction between the needy of the same faith and other faiths or no religious conviction at all. The force of this type of reasoning is certainly not confined to Christianity, which has featured prominently in many secular as well as church-based voluntary aid agencies in the West. Religion remains a powerful social force in the United States and some continental European countries as well as in many developing areas. Needless to say, for many people religion is not an essential part of the case for giving.

Second, a venerable idea is that all human beings possess in equal measure certain natural rights, logically prior to any additional rights ascribed by public law, social custom and convention. Human rights are a special sort of moral right that specify the minimum conditions of a tolerable life. The corollary is an equivalent set of duties. Some analysts infer from the most basic right of all – the right to life – a right to the means to life, or at a minimum the right to subsistence. Vincent (1986: 13) argued the right to subsistence should be allotted at least coequal status with the right to security – both are essential if the right to life is to mean anything at all. He added that (1986: 144) 'it may even be the case that subsistence rights should be a higher priority for international society than rights to security'. The Universal Declaration of Human Rights (Article 25), adopted by United Nations General Assembly in 1948, states everyone has the right to a standard of living adequate for the health and well-being of himself and his family. The essence was later enshrined by the Assembly in the International Covenant on Economic, Social and Cultural Rights (1966). The UN Charter enjoins members to employ international machinery for the promotion of the economic and social advancement of all peoples. Thus, human beings who lack the means to life have a claim on the surplus resources of people who possess more than they need.

Third, there is the language of need and the obligation of humanity to relieve suffering and distress. In the 1970s there was considerable discussion of the thesis that the principal object of development is increasing satisfaction of basic needs. This found its way into the mission statements of many development agencies. An awareness of unfulfilled need can evoke a variety of responses all of which indicate that help should be given, for example sympathy and a sense of injustice, possibly informed by sentiment or what is sometimes called conscience, or moral sense. For Singer (1977: 24) not only is it wrong to take advantage of distress but 'if it is in our power to prevent something bad from happening, without thereby sacrificing anything of comparable moral importance, we ought, morally, to do it'. For others, the issue is more one of equal respect for persons. This is said to give rise to an obligation to pay equal consideration to each other's interests. The fact that other people might be equally well placed to assist someone in need is morally irrelevant. Some voluntary aid agencies argue that shared humanity, the brotherhood of man (sisterhood of women) entails an obligation to go further than relieve material deprivation, to give support to those who are weak and oppressed, for these conditions are thought to be intimately bound up with poverty. For example, Frank Judd (1991) maintained as director of Oxfam that solidarity is the modern meaning of charity and requires more than just aid giving: steps must be taken to change the structures that are responsible for the unsatisfied need, which can mean taking political action.

Fourth, in utilitarianism the eighteenth-century thinker Jeremy Bentham helped develop a philosophy capable of generating a case for redistribution separate from natural rights, which he regarded as an anarchical fallacy and rhetorical nonsense. The premiss is a distinctive view of human beings: 'Nature has placed us under the governance of two sovereign masters, *pain* and *pleasure*. It is for them alone to point out what we ought to do, as well as to determine what we shall do' (Bentham 1948 edn: 125). The greatest happiness, or, alternatively the greatest happiness of the greatest number, comprises the ultimate good. Whatever procures this utilitarian end is morally desirable. Many economists agree with Bentham that there is diminishing marginal utility to increasing amounts of pleasurable sources, including material wealth. The pain caused by redistributing units away from people who have a lot can be outweighed by the pleasure accruing to recipients who formerly had very little. Indeed, where such transfers are effected out of benevolence, not compulsion, the contributors' own utility will also increase. Some donors might feel good about what they have done, or delight in the improved circumstances of aid's recipients.

A utilitarian calculus was applied to aid by Russett (1978). He estimated that the marginal utility in terms of life expectancy of an incremental dollar at the lower end of the world income scale is at least 75 times greater than at the top end. Sengupta (1993: 460–1) argued that even if no more than 10 per cent of the rich world's total income generates negligible utility at home, and if only 10 per cent of that sum was earmarked for oda rather than spent on domestic social purposes, then aid worth $170 billion would be justifiable. He also believed poverty alleviation and social justice have traditionally been the most enduring and often the most important motivations of development cooperation (1993: 454), a factual claim he shares with Lumsdaine (1993).

Fifth, a case for aid can be developed from John Rawls's *A Theory of Justice* (1973), one of this century's most notable works of political philosophy. Although Rawls was not primarily interested in inter-societal relations, his contractual case for justice is apposite. His principle requires that all primary social goods – rights, liberties, power, opportunities, income and wealth – should be distributed equally unless an unequal distribution would be to the advantage of *everyone* including (especially) the least well off. Rawls claims his 'difference principle' is rational for self-interested individuals: they would endorse it if asked to judge from behind a 'veil of ignorance' about their own personal situation. This makes the principle morally obligatory. Rawls's theory does not necessarily produce a justification for absolute equality. However, it could be argued that if global economic inequalities are to be vindicated then they must optimise the economic well-being of those in the poorest rank. Since the present highly unequal distribution of primary social goods cannot be shown to be of benefit to the least advantaged, some global redistribution would seem to be necessary. Barry (1973: 129) adds that arguments which are said to lead the participants in Rawls's original position to insist on maximising the wealth of the worst off within any given community 'would even more strongly lead to an insistence that what this minimum is should not depend capriciously upon the good luck of being born into a rich society or ill luck of being born into a poor one'.

Some problems with the moral arguments

Folklore maintains the road to hell is 'paved with good intentions', which happens to be the sub-title Porter, Allen and Thompson (1991) adopted for *Development in Practice*. The moral arguments for aid encounter a number of objections alluding to dubious logic and weak empirical foundations.

First, arguments relating to needs and rights are not sufficient to warrant aid giving in the absence of evidence confirming aid's potential to achieve the objectives outlined. Remediable shortcomings are not morally devastating, but if there is doubt about aid's potential to be effective because serious weaknesses in the design and delivery of aid transfers are inevitable, or because of unavoidable limitations on the recipient side, then the obligation to provide aid must be questionable. The same is true if aid necessarily frustrates other, eminently practical and possibly more effective ways of achieving the desired objects. There would seem to be an almost irrefutable moral case *against* providing aid if Yeoman (1986: 25–6), an experienced aid worker, is right in saying: 'The only reliable rule, one that should be printed on the T-shirt of every aid worker, is that almost everything one does will be wrong'. The notion that some Third World societies are killed with kindness as a result of their contact with the West is not uncommon, even if at variance with the charge that colonialist, imperialist and other Western interventions have been purely selfish and knowingly malign. Yeoman's belief that access to modern technologies such as in medicine and hygiene has brought about the destruction of local ecologies, and contributed to unsustainably high population growth rates, is but one example. More aid would simply compound the damage even further. Hardin's (1992: 184) observation of Norwegian aid agency staff who 'seemed to feel obligated to scrutinize and publicize their naiveté' provides little moral comfort in these circumstances.

Second, the idea that there are such things as natural or even human rights is not accepted by everyone, and supporters disagree over the substance. Some consider the most that can be derived from a right to life is a right to an equal opportunity to acquire the means to life. A contrary position gives precedence to an imputed absolute right to property legally acquired, and to the liberty of the producer. The material needs of the underprivileged are considered to be subordinate. Other commentators disallow claims on the abundance of wealthy countries by any poor peoples who disregard or wilfully make ineffectual use of their own economic potential, while conceding that a right to the material means to life has a more compelling moral force where resource endowments are indubitably mean. Even so, the impressive achievements of Singapore, now universally acknowledged to have one of the most competitive economies of all, tells us that a lack of obvious physical resources is no absolute bar to prosperity. A World Bank exercise which measured countries' riches in terms of their stock of assets, in 1995, found human resources accounted for two thirds of wealth on average, and 81 per cent in Japan! The inference is that neither natural nor manufactured physical capital are binding preconditions for sustainable development, if society shows resourcefulness and invests wisely in human potential.

Third, there is no agreement on how extensive is the obligation to provide aid based on the claims that invoke needs and rights, and even individual statements like Singer's seem open to different interpretations (Opeskin 1996). What is the threshold of abundance that triggers an obligation to provide aid? To what condition should rich societies reduce themselves in order to discharge their moral obligation fully? Is the requirement more extensive than simply to alleviate suffering? Morton (1996: 248) for instance invites us to consider whether it is really moral to keep people alive (by relief aid for example) in ways that do not solve their long-term problems; and Sir Shridath Ramphal, a former Commonwealth Secretary-General (1975–90), has argued the ethical impulse must be directed at the promotion of good, or development, not just human survival. Development is a far more open-ended commitment than, say, combatting world hunger with famine relief. But development is the superior means to eradicate hunger in the long run. *If* there is an obligation to help establish the *developmental* conditions in which undernourishment and malnourishment need never arise, does that obligation run to effecting the socio-political conditions which may be as essential as the economic ones? Even a minimal requirement to attend to basic needs encounters some unsettled questions (see Streeten 1984), the first being who should determine the relevant needs. The freedom to define one's own needs is, perhaps, the most basic need of all.

Fourth, the rectitude of aid cannot be determined without measuring the impact on the donors' well-being and on their proclivities for wealth creation. In theory, everyone's living standards could suffer if the taxes that finance aid have a severely depressive effect; and the relocation of resources away from productive uses in rich countries towards less productive uses in recipient countries could have lasting adverse consequences. A thorough application of utilitarianism would take these considerations into account. It would indicate that resources be redistributed up to the point where marginal benefit equates to marginal cost. In practice, calculations of this sort will be dogged by imperfect information. Academic exercises to identify the welfare functions of individuals and show how much wealth can be redistributed at little or no cost often lack conviction. And where a legitimate part of the overall calculus comprises the pleasure derived from beneficence, then should donors be expected to take all reasonable steps to establish that aid really will augment recipient welfare, and to know by how much?

Utilitarianism is widely faulted for resting on too simplistic an understanding of human nature. Aid inflows might contribute pleasure to a needy society and yet have harmful side-effects, for example a decline in self-respect or sense of dignity, even an erosion of prized spirituality, quite apart from placing the recipient in thrall to the donor. These matters do not comfortably fall within the utilitarian calculus and could go unrecognised as independent values. They cannot be objectively quantified and compared against one another, let alone against pleasure and pain. There is some evidence, however, that aid dependence can bring psychological damage and in some instances has carried racist overtones. Anyway, Bentham's inclination was to place weight on securing the expectations of the propertied (and modern psychological research confirms that people evaluate losses as larger changes in their welfare than equal-size gains). Notwithstanding diminishing marginal utility, his verdict would constrain involuntary redistribution, in the name of the greatest happiness or social utility.

Finally, Rawls's theory has been subjected to a great deal of comment, much of it highly critical according to Lessnoff (1986: 140). Here is not the place to review that literature. But once the device of the veil of ignorance is jettisoned, and thought processes are predicted against the background of actual socio-economic and cultural surroundings, Rawls's conclusions are likely to be disputed. That his argument would ignore the actual effects of transfers on donor communities is judged a weakness. Another challenge is that human beings are believed to attach considerable value to eminence and would be unpersuaded of the virtues of a distributive arrangement which infringes its scope, even if that arrangement abolished absolute deprivation – a condition into which they might possibly fall. Put simply, not everyone is risk averse. A deduction from this is that arrangements which maximise not the lowest level but the average level of welfare could gain greater approval. In any case, the application of Rawls's theory to foreign aid is said to be invalid because his premiss of a mutually advantageous cooperative venture, even if realistic for societies, cannot be endorsed at the global level (Opeskin 1996: 30).

1066 and all that came later

While the reflections of writers like Rawls are of great interest to philosophers, arguments in more mundane circles resound more to the themes of guilt, atonement and entitlement, in other words corrective justice. One such argument emphasises the entitlement of Third World countries to redress for injuries done to them in the past (Tucker 1975; Cooper 1979: 252–6). Another stresses the requirement of rich countries to compensate for wrongs they commit in the course of current interactions and for how present-day relationships are managed and organised. The two versions are not mutually exclusive and are often advanced together. Aid transfers which tax the less well off in some rich countries and benefit the better off in some poor countries might seem capable of justification, on both counts.

Over the last five centuries more than 130 countries and territories belonging to today's developing world are generally recognised to have experienced some form of colonial rule, by one or more of a dozen foreign powers. Almost all such powers have belonged to the richer North (an exception is South Africa's sway over the territory of Namibia, 1915–90). The length of exposure has varied considerably. The dates of constitutional independence range from the sixteenth century for Spanish and Portuguese colonies in South America, through the 1960s and the great scramble out of Africa particularly by Britain and France, to a dwindling number of more recent examples. Decolonisation is still incomplete, but the colonial era has often been said to leave behind a special obligation. For instance, Douglas Hurd speaking as Britain's Secretary of State for Foreign and Commonwealth Affairs has said that in regard to Africa Britain has particular responsibilities by virtue of history.

For some peoples in the developing world the years following constitutional independence have been no more kind than was the colonial experience. This is not only because malign external influences persisted, as in the form of proxy wars that were fought by surrogates of much greater powers, but also due to domestic misrule and economic mismanagement. This does not dismiss the case for reparations in situations of proven harm done by colonial intervention, especially where the unfavourable post-colonial developments can themselves be traced to the legacy of the colonial impact. The social, economic and cultural impact of externally imposed relationships and their specific forms can last indefinitely. Nor is the entitlement case affected by any finding that the countries which accumulated the most colonies did themselves a disservice in the process, such as by becoming too accustomed to living off the fruits and subsequently proving unable to adjust easily to the loss of empire. There can be extra moral ingredients too. Thus the 1991 summit meeting of the Organisation of African Unity (OAU) witnessed Nigeria's President Babangida call from the chair for international aid to Africa, specifically as restitution for the slave trade which blighted African peoples, mainly in the seventeeth and eighteenth centuries. In Britain the Africa Reparations Movement campaigns on a similar basis.

These arguments raise as many questions as they provide answers. The historical argument needs considerable refinement if it is to offer guidance about which of all past relationships of foreign aggression, invasion, occupation and control now merit some kind of recompense. Does the historical case obsolesce with the passage of time, and if so, how quickly? Should France pay reparations to Britain because of the Norman conquest in 1066? Should Russia recompense Central and Eastern European countries for the Soviet state's imposition of puppet regimes? The US and Britain too were implicated, by virtue of participation along with the USSR in the 1945 Yalta conference, and for instance Carothers (1996: 116–17) found Romanians now regard current Western aid to them as a payback of debt incurred by this earlier betrayal.

The composition of societies and the territorial map of states have been subject to so many changes down the years that a rigorous attempt to determine who should be paid what and from whom, and in respect of which misdemeanours, would be an extremely daunting task. The nature of the items on the charge sheet must be clarified first. They do not all sit easily together even with respect to the colonisation of the Third World, viz. foreign domination and a failure to prepare societies adequately for self-government (in many cases pressures from those societies accelerated the decolonisation process). In some cases like Belize colonial withdrawal was contrary to local wishes; and a majority of Bermudans who voted in a referendum in 1995 declined independence.

Colonial rule took different forms in different places; for instance France attempted to facilitate a form of political representation for francophone Africa in Paris. Today's largest donors were not the chief colonial powers. Some very poor societies escaped colonial imposition, and others were subjugated by neighbours whose descendants belong to the Third World today. In many parts of the Third World the sovereign entities and their territorial boundaries are themselves a product of the colonial impact. The implications for aid entitlement are ambivalent. Jackson's (1990) view is that most countries which acquired independence after 1950 are only quasi-states. Their continued existence owes a good deal to international recognition expressed partly in the form of foreign aid. They lack secure internal foundations and the empirical substance associated with modern statehood. Is aid an obligation here, or could it be an insult that compounds the original mischief, especially in those cases where the chances of successful state-building look slim regardless of how much aid is received? What bearing does the OAU's express commitment to observing the inherited borders have on the suggestion that European countries should give aid in recognition of the arbitrariness of the borderlines they left on the map?

Moral demands for recompense may be grounded on the subjection of the ancestors to violence. But that too needs close specification, if the strength of the claim is to be assessed and appropriate recompense agreed. The degree of inhumanity shown, the amount of brutality visited on people, and the level of humiliation borne may all be relevant, but are not synonymous. Should the power that has been exercised not so much by physical force but mystique and reputational effect also be included in the reckoning? Apart from foreign occupation of land, which has occasioned a number of formal reparations agreements, the strongest moral consensus usually coalesces around atoning for systematic aggression against a people defined in terms of such features as race, creed or colour, and the intent (or the actual consequence) of driving them from their land, perhaps even pushing them close to the brink of extinction: in short, actions tantamount to genocide. In recent decades West Germany's development cooperation with Israel is an example of a special aid relation, which emerged from the Nazis' treatment of the Jews. A formal reparations agreement existed between 1953 and 1970, and Israel has consistently been a major recipient of German bilateral oda, for instance being third largest recipient both in 1970–1 and 20 years later.

The demographic consequences of genocidal-type behaviour and similar violence are one thing, the psychological harm done to the generations who follow or the destruction of their culture could be other grounds for arranging forgiveness through aid. The idea of recompense for the requisitioning of sexual services by the Japanese Imperial Army from up to 200,000 'comfort women' during World War II, especially in Korea, is causing considerable contention in the Far East at the present time. More commonly experienced grounds include having been subjected to foreign economic domination and exploitation, or what Lenin understood by economic imperialism. In many cases the economic, political and other phenomena are closely interwoven, but this only sharpens the case for establishing the necessary and sufficient conditions for aid to be invoked in the name of corrective justice.

Clearly, effects comparable to some of the aforementioned can arise even in the absence of invasion from outside. There may be local cooperation. African chiefs were willing sellers of African slaves (to meet a demand that was as great from the Arab world as from anywhere else). Should this have any bearing on how we judge the actions of the buyers? What is the most relevant yardstick for judging historical events – the moral conventions that prevailed at the time? In times of moral diversity and flux, which conventions should be applied? Lamentable features of the past exploits of some of today's wealthiest countries have modern equivalents inside the Third World (where parallels can also be found in the pre-colonial days). Examples include the internal colonialism which discriminates against, perhaps even seeks to eliminate, specific ethnic or racial groups, the systematic subjection of women, and slavery and related forms of servitude – more prevalent now than ever, according to the Anti-Slavery Society. Instances are not confined to the South. So-called ethnic cleansing in former Yugoslavia can be likened to tribal massacres in Burundi and Rwanda, scene of up to one million deaths in 1994. It may be possible to trace a chain of causal responsibility to outside powers, who in a former era forced different communities to cohabit against their will or exaggerated differences in order to divide and rule. But what is the relevance to the way in which we apportion moral blame for events that are happening now? At the very least, we must doubt the credentials of governments who behave in similar ways to those for which they would call for redress from others. In such circumstances the entitlement case for aid should make provision to ensure the benefits are directed to the good of the people. That could mean aid conditionalities, or donor countries exercising potentially coercive intervention now in the cause of atoning for such intervention in the past!

There can be no compensation for the victims of abuse who are no longer alive. It is their descendants who seek reparations as an entitlement. Are the claims transferable between generations, when the sins that underlie the claims cannot be hereditable? On the one side, there are historians who argue the days of empire made a permanent contribution to the power and wealth of the countries who maintained colonies, explaining how their standard of living has come to be so high. In that case, perhaps aid should be given out of gratitude rather than guilt. On the other side are historians who present a very different story. They maintain the annexation of territories by expenditures of money and lives transferred economic, spiritual and other benefits of enduring value, or as the authors of *1066 and All That* say about England: 'The Norman Conquest was a Good Thing, as from this time onwards England stopped being conquered and thus was able to become top nation' (Sellar and Yeatman 1961: 25). Many African economies were in much better shape at independence than they are today; Ryrie (1995: 20) for one maintains that in an economic sense there is very little for the former colonial powers to feel guilty about. Hong Kong illustrates how economically benign colonial rule can be, enjoying average incomes comparable to Canada and the Netherlands.

Whatever happened in the past, for the most part the counterfactual cannot be known. Perspectives change over time; history books are constantly being rewritten. Generally speaking, then, the entitlement case for

aid based on such interpretations will be difficult to operationalise satisfactorily, aside from specific exceptions where relevant parties agree there is
a legitimate claim and settle the terms. Opeskin (1996) concludes that where
the determination of reparations is arbitrary, there can be no obligation to
make a transfer as a matter of justice, for justice cannot be arbitrary. Perhaps all reparations are arbitrary, for aid may not offer a complete solution
even where the parties agree on a sum. For instance aid could not repair the
psychological damage Frantz Fanon highlighted in *Les Damnés de la Terre*
(1961), which argued that only violent action by former colonial subjects
could provide the necessary catharsis. Financial reparations cannot cancel
out gross acts of inhumanity. Indeed, the completion of a restitution programme might be self-defeating if the former aggressors believe they have
secured absolution and proceed to forget the lessons.

Among the prime demands of the Africa Reparations Movement are an
official apology from Britain and the return of cultural treasures and religious artefacts to their original lands. Far more problematic is the proposal
to establish a link to foreign debt cancellation of African states. For the pattern of debts does not correspond to the impact of the slave trade. Former
colonies elsewhere have also accumulated burdensome debts, in similar circumstances and in similar ways since gaining independence. There are other
considerations to be borne in mind too, such as the state of community
relations in countries that are multi-ethnic because of their imperial past. In
the West, aid giving has sometimes been said to strengthen racial stereotypes
among white people and confirm patronising attitudes towards black and
brown peoples. Universal acknowledgement of the justifications for reparations might prejudice the attitudes of ethnic minorities towards fellow white
citizens. One suggestion is that reparations take the form of a determined
effort to educate people everywhere about the positive contribution the
peoples of Africa and other developing areas have made and continue to
make to world history.

In sum, many different arguments have been advanced for reparations,
and in total they exhibit a confusion of aims, ranging from compensating
for the disruptive effects of international capital on indigenous pre-capitalist
societies, to changing white Northern attitudes and overcoming a lack of
self-belief among black peoples. The impact of the case for correcting historical injustice is diluted by the richness of the debate – a conclusion that
could stand for aid more generally.

Present-day inequities

The relationships between North and South since formal decolonisation
have been characterised as neo-colonial and as a form of economic imperialism. The Third World is said to suffer economic exploitation from outside. The gains from international commerce, trade, and private financial
flows are weighted in favour of the more developed world, as are the fruits
of a growing world economy. There is unequal exchange. Third World

countries do not receive fair returns for their produce and labour, particularly the commodity suppliers who face highly oligopsonistic international market situations. Barratt Brown (1995: 44) for instance reckons that in the 1980s African countries generally retained only 25 per cent of the final value of their agricultural exports, and the growers typically received less than 5 per cent. It is said that as consumers, Third World countries are required to pay inflated prices for imported merchandise; and they are prey to usurious practices in international money transactions. All things considered, poor countries are denied their just deserts, and in some accounts this results in more poverty. Slote goes so far as to say that the victims of poverty are being deprived of their right not to be killed. He says: 'One has a duty not to profit from the crimes of others (at the expense of those who have been harmed) and one has a duty not to receive stolen goods...' (Slote 1977: 145). Furthermore, 'it seems ridiculous to suppose that we have a right to omit helping the poorer nations because that would interfere with our way of life, if that way of life involves commissive business wrongdoings to many of those very nations' (1977: 144). The persistence of inequity is ascribed to how the global economy is structured. The major OECD countries enjoy superior bargaining power and shape international regimes (i.e. governing arrangements or frameworks of norms, principles, rules and decision-making procedures, both explicit and implicit) to suit their own advantage. Some analysts even believe the unequal distribution of bargaining resources introduces an element of coercion into seemingly free commercial exchange.

The arguments for aid based on an obligation to remedy present-day global inequities and redress imbalances in the distribution of gains from global economic participation are far-reaching. Some developing countries could be both entitled to receive aid and required to make aid transfers, for they also take advantage of weaker countries in their commercial dealings. Even so, the thrust of the argument has usually been considered more attractive to Third World governments than aid rationalisations couched in terms of the rights and needs of their citizens as individuals. Those rationalisations deny to recipient governments unrestricted freedom over the deployment of aid receipts. The moral imperative on donors would extend to attaching whatever conditions are needful to realising the end, and could even include bypassing Third World governments. In contrast, arguments that advance the collective due of the nation reinforce the paramountcy of the state, and make aid-seeking governments central to the arrangements.

Nevertheless, the case for aid deduced from present-day inequities seems hardly more conclusive than that based on historical wrongs, for several reasons. The proposition that international economic relations are uniformly unfair to all developing countries, and excessively generous throughout the North, is false. It should not be confused with the claim that secular trends in the international terms of trade move against major commodity exporters, whose numbers include the US, Canada, Norway and Russia. The idea that corporate investment from the advanced capitalist countries brings about decapitalisation (and denationalisation) in the developing world, as profits and payments are remitted northwards, must be tested against fuller assessments that take account of any positive externalities, the contributions to local employment, incomes and taxes. Anyway, how relevant are notions of fairness to market-based relations, even scenarios where the parties clearly do not have equal market power or are not equally desperate to strike a deal, and differ widely in their estimates of the gains to be enjoyed from doing business?

One view, germinal in Marxian thought, is that far from being exploited to excess because of their economically dependent status, Third World countries have not been exploited enough. For as their contact with the international capitalist system grows, so their production structures will be changed more comprehensively. Formerly agrarian societies will become industrialised (Warren 1980). Marxists believe that, in the right circumstances, an industrial proletariat is a revolutionary force for socialist transformation, which is good. That the West might owe compensation for having been instrumental in such an outcome looks decidedly odd. Of course, many neo-Marxists dispute that international capital plays a positive role in the Third World, and argue that it retards the prospects of true development. This is a large and complex area of debate, which cannot be entered into here. Indeed, to do so would be superfluous. For if the neo-Marxists are correct, then the most aid could offer would be a second-best resort, not a solution. A superior response would be to tackle the problem at source, by dismantling the power of international capital.

Indeed, a range of critics of the present 'liberal' international order conclude that what the Third World needs is not aid conventionally understood, but justice. By this they mean a reformulation of the international monetary and trade regimes, and of the processes by which those regimes are determined, in directions that will be more favourable to developing countries. Such has been an objective of the United Nations Conference on Trade and Development (UNCTAD) for many years, especially in its 1970s campaign for a New International Economic Order (NIEO). A recent illustration involves the collection of genetic materials by Northern-based multinational companies, who modify the material and patent the results without offering royalty payments to the countries of origin. This has been called bio-piracy. A UNDP report (Rural Advancement Foundation 1994) says it costs the developing world as much as $5.4 billion annually (the annual cost to industrialised countries of developing country piracy mainly of chemical and pharmaceutical patents is estimated at around $2.7 billion).

UNCTAD failed to achieve substantial progress, at a time when circumstances were more propitious than now, although ideas resembling a NIEO still live on. The West associated NIEO-type proposals with authoritative interventions in the operations of the global economy. Yet as a general rule, the economic neo-liberalism which has gained the ascendancy maintains that aggregate welfare is reduced by the regulation and control of economic markets. From this perspective, a more efficient approach to world poverty is further marketisation of the international economy and of financial systems too. A withering away of the IMF and World Bank has even been ruminated (Ryrie 1995). Needless to say, matters look different from the South, where several viewpoints exist. Aid that provides a manipulable resource is attractive to governments that receive it, especially now the pressure to liberalise their economies and dispose of public enterprises challenges some of the other main sources of their political power and material accumulation. But aid can never offer a perfect substitute for more advantageous trading arrangements, if only because of the discretionary power held by donors. This was explained by Senegal's Mazide Ndiaye (in Barratt Brown 1995: 339): 'We do not want charity because it demeans. With the money earned from trade you can buy what you want. You cannot demand what you need from people who are helping you'. So, a more promising way than aid to advance the welfare of people outside the government circles of patronage could well be increased participation in the world economy, especially if the terms of international exchange improve ('fair trade') and producers obtain a rewarding share of the benefits that accrue to their country.

Aid as immorality

'Lifeboat ethics' indicate that famine relief and, possibly, more generalised relief of need are immoral. Prosperous societies should do nothing that would cause the ecology of the planet and their own well-being to be threatened by the press of human numbers. The outcome would be disastrous for all. In Hardin's view (1977: 11–12) the fundamental error of the sharing ethic is that it leads to the tragedy of the commons: mutual ruin is inevitable. Far better, then, that feelings of conscience and pity towards less fortunate peoples be held in check. For well-off peoples to keep what they have does not only serve their own immediate interest. It is an obligation to their descendants, and a rational strategy for the survival of the species. A variant of this argument allows exceptions for countries suffering some purely temporary misfortune, and whose prospects are otherwise healthy. Forms of international aid specifically directed at bringing down population growth rates in hungry countries might also be justifiable.

This thesis is resonant of the spectre long associated with Rev. Thomas Malthus's *An Essay on the Principle of Population* (1798), that population grows in geometrical fashion and outstrips the arithmetic progression of resources. Today, around 800 million people including 200 children are reckoned to be chronically undernourished, and no less than 88 countries (half in Africa) are described as low income food deficit countries. World wheat stocks declined to an exceptional low in 1995–6, and a growing shortfall of rain-fed rice production in Asia is widely predicted. Global food production will have to increase by 75 per cent to match expected population growth in the next 30 years; and predicted increases in China's commercial imports of grain from three million tonnes in 1990 to possibly 40 million tonnes annually ten years later could cause world prices to skyrocket. Nevertheless, 'lifeboat ethics' are very controversial. They clash with the moral principle of 'equity now', which places equal rights of the living (or their right to equal shares of life's necessities) ahead of claims imputed to future generations, and ahead of the presumed needs of the species (Watson 1977: 115–23). The doomsday scenario of humankind pressing against the limits of the world's natural resources and progressively exhausting the available stocks is in any case an anachronism. It was a product of the early 1970s, when world oil reserves and a sudden dip in US grain stocks produced anxiety. Since then, Third World governments have become more sympathetic to population planning. Worldwide, over half of all couples are reckoned to practise family planning – a proven means of reducing population growth rates, demonstrated in large developing countries like China. Global population growth peaked in 1965–70, at around 2.1 per cent per annum. Now, the average is around 1.7 per cent. Fertility rates in LICs have declined, from 5.6 births per woman in the early 1970s to 3.3 now. World population predictions tend to contain a significant margin of error, but many demographers believe the total will decline after around 2050, having reached possibly 10–12 billion. Moreover, we must not forget that some densely populated countries have achieved affluence. Perhaps the two conditions are causally related. The more people, the greater the scope for economic specialisation or division of labour and the greater the potential economic value embodied in human capital.

Also, the amount of raw materials needed for a given unit of economic output has been dropping throughout the twentieth century, for most non-agricultural commodities. This is due to the introduction of increasingly efficient production methods and changes in consumption demand patterns towards less material-intensive forms. Mankind's proven talent for problem-solving suggests a virtually limitless capacity for technological ingenuity, tapping hitherto underutilised materials, discovering new deposits and developing unfamiliar sources of substitute energy for instance. Average world cereals yields almost doubled between 1960 and 1990, and the developing world achieved a 94 per cent increase in wheat yields between 1970 and 1994. The world grain harvest almost tripled between 1950 and 1990. Biotechnology and improvements in smallholder farming both offer considerable further potential.

The principal problem with meeting basic needs, especially guaranteeing food security to hungry communities, does not lie with the limits to productive capacity, or even with environmental constraints. The crucial variable is the highly uneven distribution of access to resources, and the skewed pattern of *effective* demand (or Sen's 'entitlements') within societies and between countries. An illustration is that while the average daily calorie intake of Africans is 6 per cent below requirements, Europeans and North Americans enjoy a third higher than needed. A child born in the advanced industrial countries will consume 40 times the natural resources of a child in the Third World, before reaching adulthood. The consumption of commercial energy per person in the industrial market economies is reckoned to be more than 80 times that of people in sub-Saharan Africa, and the divergence is widening. In some aspects high levels of consumption damage health. They erode basic self-sufficiency, for example by diverting cereal production to animal feedgrain. Hence Adamson (1975: 12) dismissed Hardin's thesis thus: 'Far from being a "lifeboat" situation, it is more a case of the rich world sinking the poor world's ship and forcing its population into the water for the sake of stocking up a luxury liner for a round-the-world-cruise'. However, these analogies have been overtaken anyway by the increase of world interdependence, globalisation, transnationalisation and growing permeability of state borders. Perhaps not for much longer will the more privileged nations be able to exist in splendid isolation from the problems that beset their less fortunate neighbours (see Chapter 4).

Conclusion

Most arguments for aid based on morality, justice and entitlement presuppose the existence of an international moral community that not everyone accepts. Johnson (1970: 17) for example says that in 'relations among sovereign nations, morality is an emotion without a cutting edge'. Arguments whose force might be acknowledged with respect to fellow citizens and members of the same national community do not travel so well in a world of nations and nation states. Recently, nationalism has gained new vitality in some regions, especially areas formerly dominated by communism. Statehood has expanded dramatically, to 185 members of the United Nations in 1995. Although most human beings do not choose their country, they often feel an overriding commitment to their kith and kin. Perhaps many expect the developing countries to accept full responsibility for their own well-being, especially if they are not themselves intentionally implicated in those countries' problems. The only obligations nations and their members have towards other countries are said to comprise what is sanctioned by positive international law. Hence, there is no moral obligation of wealthy countries to offer aid. Similarly, poor countries are not morally obliged to accept aid when it is offered (although the idea of a positive legal obligation on the part of governments to accept international humanitarian aid in emergencies is attracting discussion. See for example Griffiths et al. 1995: 45–6). In the late nineteenth century Social Darwinists argued nations, like individuals, must compete; the fittest will thrive, and the devil should be allowed to take the hindmost. At the very least, national interests must take precedence over whatever moral obligations are thought to exist at the international level if, as often seems likely, the two come into conflict.

There is a certain resilience about beliefs like these. That much is evident in the plea made by J. Brian Atwood, Administrative Head of USAID (cited in the *Financial Times*, 18 January 1995): 'Morality is not simply something for domestic consumption alone . . . It is remarkable that some who advocate a return to traditional standards in America can simultaneously argue for moral indifference in international conduct'. There is a concern that a society which retracts moral principles from its international conduct is ultimately in danger of doing likewise in its internal affairs. Of course, many individuals around the world are convinced there *is* an obligation to help fellow human beings who are less fortunate. This helps explain voluntary aid donations. Even if the absence of a true international community means there is no obligation of distributive justice at the global level, certain minimum obligations of simple humanity may still be thought to exist, such as to ensure subsistence (Opeskin 1996). Nevertheless, the critics' retort is that aid is morally permissible but not required. There is a saying that charity begins at home. And if charitable concerns and their potential beneficiaries in the affluent countries continue to grow as rapidly as they have done in recent years, then perhaps home is where most charitable endeavours will remain. For example in the US around 13 per cent of the population lives below the poverty line, and attitude surveys disclose domestic poverty is a major reason for US public indifference to funding foreign aid.

Perhaps the most critical weakness of moral and related arguments for foreign aid is that they fail the test of universal acceptance. The nineteenth-century philosopher Pierre-Joseph Proudhon observed (in *What is Property?* 1840) that to perform an act of benevolence towards one's neighbour is called in Hebrew, to do justice; in Greek to take compassion or pity; in Latin to perform an act of love or charity; in French to give alms. He argued we can trace the degradation of benevolence through these various expressions: the first signifies duty, the second only sympathy, the third simply affection (a matter of choice, not obligation), and the fourth caprice. Nowadays however, there is an entire discourse that lies outside caprice, namely arguments for aid grounded on mutual advantage and enlightened self-interest. Those arguments have gained in prominence over the last 20 years. The label development cooperation has become more resonant than development aid not simply because it seems less patronising and so more acceptable to recipients, but because it is thought to reflect more accurately the expectation of mutual gain.

The case for giving: mutual advantage and enlightened self-interest

The case for aid grounded in mutual advantage and enlightened self-interest falls here in two parts, each one anchored in a landmark report: *North–South: A Programme for Survival*, or Brandt Commission report, by the Independent Commission on International Development Issues (1980), and *Our Common Future*, or Brundtland report, by the UN-appointed World Commission on Environment and Development (1987).

Brandt's many recommendations for reforming the international economic order included increasing oda channelled through multilateral institutions. Funding would be by a sliding scale of levies on states according to their ability to pay. Revenues could be collected automatically such as by taxes on the international arms trade or trade more generally. A new World Development Fund would meet the unsatisfied oda needs of developing countries. The report argued that there are strong moral reasons for enacting its proposals, but one of its most notable features was an emphasis on the positive mutual interest of the South and North. Among donor countries an enlightened understanding would recognise that national self-interest can be pursued effectively only through taking account of mutual advantage.

Brandt came at the end of a period in which the interdependence of the West and OPEC countries made a striking impression. The report was prepared against a background of international economic recession. Large increases in traded oil prices stirred a sequence of developments that shattered comfortable illusions: no longer could the OECD mixed economies be confident in their ability to combine sustained growth, low inflation and full employment. Brandt detected growing tension in North–South relations, due to the existence of a divided world in which living standards differed sharply and large parts of the South were poor. Against this backdrop greater resource transfers could be constructive in two main ways. First, by generating effective demand for goods and services economic activity would be stimulated in DAC countries. Their access to vital raw materials would be safeguarded. Second, threats to world peace would be reduced. The benefits of economic progress, secured by increased and more rewarding integration into the global economy brought about partly by aid, would reduce the social origins of Third World discontent. The LDCs' new interest in maintaining order would bring stability to the international scene. An alternative scenario of civil unrest and power vacuums growing in Third World theatres of geo-strategic significance would be far less preferable, because of the risk that such conditions would bring the great powers into direct confrontation. Aid that effectively boosts Third World development would serve the donors' security interests more effectively than the customary bilateral aid offers that embody exchange conditions like diplomatic allegiance and rights of access to a military base.

Brandt criticised

Among DAC countries the Brandt report aroused an exceptional and sustained level of public interest, but the analysis was heavily criticised (see for example Seers 1980; Strange 1981), not least because it downplayed the counter-arguments even though it did not completely ignore them.

On the economic side, the prospective economic returns from aid including export markets gained and jobs secured have always figured in donor calculations. They continue to feature prominently in attempts to mobilise support for aid budgets. For example, in seeking to dissuade Congress from reducing US payments to the IDA President Clinto said: 'IDA recipients of yesterday – countries like South Korea, Indonesia, Turkey, China, Chile – are today among America's most important trading partners. Those who are reminded of this perhaps will be tempted to change their position' (cited in the *Financial Times*, 12 October 1995). May, Schumacher and Malek (1989: 230) calculated the total of oda-related jobs in Germany to be 110,000 (or around 0.5 per cent of total employment) and in Britain, 75,000 (0.3 per cent of employment), in 1984. Today, over 24 million workers are unemployed in the Group of Seven (G7) industrialised countries, having doubled in number since 1979, and unemployment in the EU averages around 10 per cent. The developing world is responsible for around a quarter of G7 exports and any increase in that market would be welcome. This economic argument for increasing oda continues to be made, long after Brandt (see Angelopoulos and Fagen 1994).

However, not all donors are guaranteed equal promise of mutual economic benefit. The gains would go disproportionately to the main trading nations. That is why Britain's Overseas Development Administration believes that the multilateral untying of aid would be to Britain's advantage. Some donor countries are relatively uncompetitive, and others could discover the economic multiplier of aid-induced exports brings unwelcome inflationary pressures. There are risks even for the US – Patterson (1993: 184) noted a satisfactory share of aid-generated business could be elusive if the US chose to mount a Marshall aid-type programme for Russia, because of the superior competitiveness of German and Japanese manufacturers (a consideration not present at the time of Marshall aid which was tied to US procurement). The least trade-competitive donors could face a real income loss, unredeemed by high procurement tying, which is something that can cause switching – the substitution of aid orders for orders that would have been placed anyway. The displacement of commercial exports to third countries is another possibility.

A concern in the past has been that Third World economic growth will increase competition for non-substitutable, non-renewable resources, so raising input costs in the OECD economies. Now, in a world economy where according to the International Labour Organisation (ILO) nearly a third of the workforce is un/underemployed, a clear message is that the economic success of emerging economies could impose other significant adjustment costs on the OECD countries – putting pressure on wage levels in low-skilled labour-manufacturing especially, and increasing unemployment in the absence of appropriate responses such as retraining and technical upgrading of the workforce. The prospect has been called an example of reverse leverage. Of course, even where DAC export industries flourish as a result of aid not all citizens will be net beneficiaries, after their tax contributions to the aid budget are taken into account. Anyway, there are more direct ways than oda of using public money to stir economic activity and implement social goals at home. In Britain for example, the Child Poverty Action Group reckons one quarter of the population are touched by poverty, in bad housing for instance. In such an environment politicians campaigning for election have more immediate ways of trying to win votes than by presenting the general economic case for resource transfers to the Third World.

There are LLDCs and SILICs that offer little economic return to the rich world in exchange for oda. Their markets are small and they do not control the supply of highly sought-after commodities. For example, while sub-Saharan Africa accounts for 9 per cent of world population it contributes around 2 per cent of global GDP and 1 per cent of trade. The kinds of aid needed here may well not correspond closely to the sort of expenditures that would most readily rejuvenate the depressed parts of Northern economies. Indeed, commercially motivated aid is not bound to be developmentally very effective anywhere, and it can even be harmful. The most dynamic economies in East Asia and Latin America offer considerably more opportunities for mutually beneficial economic exchange. In Brandt's day the Middle East could be included too, and soon some Central and Eastern European countries will be useful additions as well. Even in politically strategic terms some very poor countries have become more peripheral to major donors, especially since the end of the Cold War.

Aid and stability

The effectiveness of resource transfers in reducing poverty and/or socio-economic inequality inside developing countries, lessening social discontent and generating political stability there is all contingent on the policies and conduct of their governments. Brandt's reluctance to dwell on this aspect was a major weakness. The omission befitted the disinterest of some donors in poverty amelioration at the time. But in today's changed circumstances far less tolerance is extended to the hypocrisy of Southern elites who pursue socially regressive measures at home while calling for greater fairness and more equal treatment of Third World countries in the international economy.

In any case, the connections between economic growth and development, and between social improvement and political effects are highly variable and difficult to predict, especially in transitional phases and before long-run patterns emerge clearly. Poverty and stability can coexist. Governmental instability and social unrest tend to obstruct smooth development, but aid that hastens economic change can disrupt social systems and undermine civil order. Dramatic shifts in politics and foreign policy can follow. The rate and the pattern of growth are both significant. On the first, a more rapid or more uneven pace of growth disturb existing socio-cultural norms, bonds and conventions and increase the chances that expectations will be disappointed at some point. On the second, increased relative and absolute poverty can both issue from economic dynamism, in the absence of appropriate distributive mechanisms. On all counts, the consequences can include greater political instability. The correspondence between the perceived distribution of gains and losses from growth and any pre-existing social cleavages may critically influence the social peace, and so can the interpretations that different groups place on the correlations they recognise.

Many examples exist of good bilateral relations persisting between countries notwithstanding widely different economic attainments, and which owe little or nothing to aid ties. Even so, the familiar propositions which purport that international stability is positively connected in the *long run* with an equitable global distribution of wealth, or with the absence of great inequality, or with the absence of mass poverty, all look plausible, even though they have very different properties. However, the path along which the eventual outcome is reached may not be straightforward. There are too many intervening variables that can influence the passage of events, and these can have a bearing on the case for aid. Take for example the $2.3 billion which an international consultative group pledged to the Palestinian Authority in West Bank and Gaza for a five-year period, in 1994. The offer could prove worthless if enough Arabs and Jews oppose an Israeli–Palestinian compromise, or if Israeli forces do not withdraw definitively from the Occupied Territories, and continue to impede Palestinian workers' freedom of movement. Aid can help the prospects for peace in the region. But it must bring early tangible improvements in the living conditions of Palestinians. Yet donor concerns about funding 'welfarism' and the potential for aid misuse and corruption in a politically fraught environment, where administrative and managerial structures are weak, have delayed aid disbursements. This, at a critical time, when the momentum of the Middle East peace process could have benefited most from external help. Now, the disbursements have slowed to little more than $200 million annually. Of course Israel has been an extraordinary beneficiary of aid over the years. Yet political divisions in Israel between secular and religious Jews and between 'doves' and 'hawks' have become more acute, to the point where doubts have been expressed about its future as a unified state.

Clearly, societies and their sub-groups come into conflict with one another for reasons that are not reducible to economic considerations. Racial intolerance, religious bigotry and territorial disputes all play a part. Aid has not prevented such weakly integrated countries as Rwanda, Burundi, Sudan and Sri Lanka falling prey to long-running bloody conflict, just as it has not brought harmony between Taiwan and China, whose uneasy coexistence poses a major potential threat to regional security in East Asia and beyond. Some of the areas that are geopolitically significant to DAC country security interests may be of relatively modest commercial interest, and some others are not obvious candidates for aid – for example Saudi Arabia, where internal dissidence manifested itself in the terrorist bombing of US targets, in 1995 and 1996.

There are several aspects to stability and instability, including not only the pace of changes but their duration, extent, frequency and direction, as well as the manner of change. There are different levels, such as systemic international stability, stable relations between the official structures of countries that are allies or friends, stable leadership of a country and the continuity of a specific type of political regime. Broad-brush claims about aid's contribution to stability have lacked precision and often do not question whether the promotion of one or another application might be dysfunctional for others. For instance, a stable nationalist regime can be a threat to regional and international security, just as prosperity could furnish a dictatorship with the wherewithal to mount external aggression. Wealthy but weak states like Kuwait can tempt predatory invasion. In theory oda could exacerbate North–South friction which owes more to global income disparities than to absolute poverty, if the logic of economic mutuality is applied. Because when donor as well as recipient economies benefit, there are three possibilities: the gap between rich and poor countries shrinks, grows larger, or remains about the same.

Krasner's (1985) explanation of North–South conflict in terms of deep asymmetries of power, which leave Third World governments exposed to external economic shocks, raises further difficulties. Writing from a realist perspective, he argued the defining characteristic of Third World politics is not poverty but the vulnerability of its leaders. That means their inability to exercise economic control in a market-oriented global environment. Aid that helps reduce mass poverty would not of itself improve international relations. For what Third World governments seek is more relational power and meta-power – opportunities to determine international economic regimes in a direction that satisfies their own domestic requirements of political security. There is no solution in mutual economic gains which perpetuate a global economic order that produces power inequalities. In Krasner's view the solution would have to take the form of substituting a more authoritative international regime for the neo-liberal status quo, increasing the prerogatives of Third World states. However, as has already been noted that prospect has become more, not less remote since Brandt's time, owing to the progress of economic liberalisation and globalisation. Globalisation in particular means that traditional barriers between states are being transcended by rapidly expanding transnational forces in investment and trade, most notably international corporations pursuing market advantage regardless of place.

There is currently much debate about what globalisation actually means for the future of states. For the present, an inference deducible from Krasner's analysis is that even countries in the South which attain good levels of socioeconomic development could be hostile to the North, if denied tickets to the top tables. China and India – the world's third and sixth largest economies in terms of GNP measured on a purchasing power parity basis – are not invited to meetings of the G7. Neither are Mexico or Brazil, and yet Canada remains a member. This disposition looks more and more questionable as the world undergoes a secular redistribution of economic weight between nations. The G7 countries now account for under half of global economic production and the US's share is down by a third since 1945. After allowing for leads and lags, the long historical view indicates the international political displacement of large states tends to track their economic progress and relative economic size. This relationship may persist even if the collective power of states declines *vis-à-vis* other institutions embedded in the global economy and economic forces. For example, the strong claims of Japan and Germany to permanent seats on the UN Security Council will continue to draw primarily on their economic and financial strength. China is now using its heightened importance in international trade and investment to bargain for political autonomy *vis-à-vis* the US, Japan and Europe, and to promote its goal of reincorporating Taiwan. Other countries too demand growing respect as they register impressive industrial and technological achievements and, as in Iraq, accumulate a critical mass of aggressive military capability. All this is highly significant from a realist perspective.

Realists in international relations theory maintain that an erosion of the relative power enjoyed by the major states is detrimental to their security. Hegemony – the power to shape international order – is believed to be the most reliable means to avert external threats to national security. Affordability is enhanced where the reputational effect of eminence or, even better, deference to a power's ideological leadership, make costly displays like the visible deployment of military force unnecessary. *Pax Britannica* and

Pax Americana were comforting especially to the two named powers. But so were the certainties that were provided by nuclear stalemate between the two superpowers during the Cold War. By comparison moves towards multi-polarity in the world and the diffusion of power among states are unsettling (and a haemorrhage of power to non-state actors may be considered even more threatening). A possible moral for the great powers (and hence not for all donors) is to try to retain economic primacy for as long as possible so as to protect their enduring security requirements, notwithstanding the commercial stake they may have in seeing other countries prosper. Of course, this line of argument does not deny that aid policy could still contribute to their strategic interests. But the particular forms and the aid relationships that it indicates may well not coincide with what Brandt envisaged, when describing oda as a powerful tool for fighting world poverty.

Gone but not forgotten

The Brandt report was published at the end of an era. In many OECD countries a reliance on Keynesian responses to economic problems and the idea of heavy economic involvement by the state were about to be jettisoned, in preference for more neo-liberal economic agendas. Counter-inflationary measures were put in place; and the interventionist, demand-stimulating bent of Brandt stood little chance of being enacted at the international level. Thus, although several DAC states increased their aid programmes in the years that followed, Sengupta (1993: 455) is correct to say the paradigm of mutual interest remained an unrealised potential, and did not become a driving force behind the donors' aid policies.

Moreover, with hindsight we might now judge as being unduly alarmist Brandt's warning that the 1980s could witness even greater catastrophes than the 1930s. Admittedly, the ratio between the richest and poorest fifths of the world's population has continued to increase, from 30:1 to 60:1 over the last 30 years. But the possibility of violent East–West confrontation has receded, and conflict levels have been much reduced in such places as Central America and Southern Africa. Indeed, the accuracy of the realists' paradigm of international anarchy and an emphasis on states' *realpolitik* are being questioned more than ever before. New thinking detects the emergence of international order governed increasingly by collective action and subordinated to non-unitary non-state actors, including the global corporations. Where the lust for power used to divide, we are now told that more materialistic aspirations and the profit motive are bringing people together, at least in the wealthier or 'core' areas of the globe. The elevation of wealth to a primary goal is said to promote compromise and negotiation, over belligerence. Some former concerns of national security begin to look increasingly archaic.

However, security as an issue has not gone away. Far from it; for the widening and deepening of interdependence has brought enhanced attention to themes that are redolent of Brandt. Two major points stand out, and they are intrinsically connected.

The new instability

First, the geography of risk to international security has been reformulated in ways that go beyond the old East–West states' rivalry, no longer considered a major threat. Even if realist theory cannot make good sense of what is happening in the 'core', the same is not necessarily true of the 'periphery' (Goldgeier and McFaul 1992). The periphery comprises substantial parts of the Third and former Second Worlds. The last ten years has seen a growth of intra-state and sub-regional violence in areas not far from OECD countries. This has brought converts to the belief that all countries have an interest in securing the orderly evolution of a viable global system, together with its regional constituents. For most countries hegemony never was a feasible option anyway, and Nye's (1992: 94) comment on the US, today's only universally acknowledged superpower, is a telling one: 'in a world of transnational interdependence, international disorder can hurt, influence or disturb the majority of people living in the United States'. Theatres of either actual or possible instability include North Africa and Eastern Mediterranean, the Balkans and parts of Eastern Europe (all being of interest to Western European countries); the South China Sea and the Korean peninsula concern Japan; and Russia cannot be indifferent to the Caucasus and Central Asia. Typical of current thinking is Yunling's (1995: 92) claim that the most dangerous of current conflicts are those between the new minipowers, often involving ethnic, religious and nationalist antagonism.

The corrosive force of nationalism in particular has drawn attention, especially in places where the restraints formerly imposed by communist rule have disappeared. In more than a third of all countries there are ethnic sub-groups harbouring dreams of political self-determination. The idea that states must be at peace with themselves if they are to be at peace with their neighbours (Barnett 1995: 80) is now considered self-evident. Jan Pronk, long-time holder of ministerial responsibility for Dutch development cooperation, has likened recent intra-state conflicts to peat fires, because of their potential to spread (Box 1994: 56). Some of the 'hot spots' could yet rekindle antagonism between Russia and the West. While it is no more true now than in the 1980s that these sorts of problems are bound to be dispatched by economic and social improvement, especially where conflict is oriented around non-negotiable principles, development could provide an essential part of a solution. At the very least development may be a facilitator, or provide an enabling role. In the 1990s many proponents of oda seem much impressed by this way of thinking. Falk's (1995: 214) view reflects many of the pronouncements made in DAC circles: 'since security is increasingly associated with avoiding weak state crises there is present a strong nonaltruistic motivation to overcome acute poverty'.

The security 'laundry list'

Recognising new regions where the principal threats to international stability are thought most likely to originate, and dwelling on the systemic consequences of sub-state violence, identify one major point about today's security agenda. A second major point, closely connected, is the reconceptualisation of what security means, and a reappraisal of the forms threats can take. But before describing these it is worth noting that the dangers of nuclear proliferation have not gone away completely. There are up to a dozen countries preparing to join the nuclear club. India, Pakistan and Israel have reached 'threshold' status. No exercise of aid power by international donors has seemed capable of persuading India to endorse a comprehensive nuclear test ban treaty, in the absence of multilateral nuclear disarmament. In 1990 the US suspended all aid to Pakistan, which had received $7 billion in the previous decade, in order to bring pressure to bear to halt its nuclear weapons programme, but was not obviously successful. However, North Korea was persuaded to abandon its graphite reactor programme (judged capable of delivering weapons-grade plutonium) in exchange for a $4 billion construction programme of light water reactors for civilian purposes, to be funded mainly by South Korea together with the US, EU and Japan. The possibility remains that weapons of mass destruction including biological and chemical warfare could fall into hands that lack adequate political and technical control mechanisms. Currently up to ten states possess biological weapons and at least thirteen Southern states are believed to possess, or have the capacity to produce, chemical weapons.

However, it is a commonplace that the traditional state-centric concept of national security rooted in protection from organised violence, most notably military aggression, no longer has a monopoly on our understanding of security. There has developed an 'additive "laundry list" approach' (del Rosso 1995: 190) which considerably broadens 'security' in ways far more congruent with the dictionary definitions – freedom from risk or danger, freedom from doubt, anxiety and fear. Prominence is now being given to several different kinds of threats judged dangerous in and of themselves, and threatening not simply states and their territorial control. They can be related to one another in various ways; and topical discussions surmise that all have some connection with poverty or misery and state failure.

One example is the unsolicited movement of people across national frontiers, something that is caused in the places of origin by an absence of 'economic security' or by lack of 'human security' understood more broadly. The US regulates inflows of job-seekers from Mexico and the Caribbean only with difficulty; and the time could come when Japan faces similar problems *vis-à-vis* China or the Philippines, say. Development that improves employment prospects and social conditions should alleviate the problem at source. As a tool of migration management oda may prove more effective than heavier policing of border controls. For this reason Belgium, host to a sizeable community of Moroccans, funds a significant programme of agricultural improvement in Morocco, and hopes to encourage reverse migration.

Refugees and asylum-seekers are another large category. For years the total number of refugees has been rising, from lows of 2.5 million in 1970 and 4.6 million in 1978. Of course most refugees travel no further than neighbouring countries in the developing world, and international aid assists with the repatriation and resettlement – operations that have become feasible in, for example, Southern Africa, Ethiopia and Cambodia in recent years. But around 250,000 refugees from former Yugoslavia sought refuge in Germany; and in Yugoslavia alone at least four million people became dependent on humanitarian assistance. All in all, refugee work accounted for $2.5 billion of DAC oda in 1994.

Another security issue that taxes the North is the growth of organised crime, in particular international drugs-trafficking and money laundering. Action abroad may be more politically convenient than taking effective measures to reduce directly the demand for drugs at home. Poor states are seen to be weak links in the chain of effective response. Practical assistance has been provided to governments in Asia and Andean countries, particularly Bolivia and Colombia, to obtain and subvent their cooperation in applying legal controls, and to finance alternative crop production by peasant farmers (global organised crime is reckoned to have reached $1000 billion in 1996, half of it involving the US and over two thirds of it drug-related, according to a report in the *Financial Times*, 14 February 1997). Another high profile issue is international terrorism – called by President Clinton at a G7 meeting in 1996 the security challenge of the twenty-first century. Terrorist bombings in France in 1995 and 1996 show how political violence within one developing country (Algeria) can spill over into others where there is a diaspora. One danger is that such events will ignite latent racist and xenophobic tendencies, harming community relations. The purpose conventional oda might serve in this context is not so clear, and it has no bearing on the terrorism whose origins lie closer to home, whether in Ulster, Oklahoma City or the Tokyo subways. In fact when the G7 governments and Russia agreed on 25 measures to counteract international terrorism, in July 1996, aid was barely considered. Nevertheless, the spread of Islamic fundamentalism in developing areas has been portrayed as a security threat in a number of Western countries. Though not a sole cause, widespread poverty is seen to provide a very receptive environment.

Other problems that are being presented through the security lense include the spread of AIDS and HIV. The World Health Organisation (WHO) estimates up to 23 million adults worldwide were infected by HIV as of 1996 and that by the end of the decade about two million each year will die from HIV-related illness. Of the totals, around two thirds and three quarters respectively will be in sub-Saharan Africa. Apart from anything else this is bad news for human capital formation and, just as with migration flows within the South, the effects can make poverty worse and societies more unstable. The WHO has identified 30 new infectious diseases in the last 20 years. Global climate change will alter the pattern of infectious (particularly airborne) diseases, which presently claim over 17 million human lives annually, with consequences for the North. Urbanisation (well over half the world's population will be urban by 2015) and mass international travel also increase the possibilities for epidemic diseases to spread. Even so, the practical responses to such issues of common concern must be constructed carefully, if there is to be mutual benefit. The point is illustrated by fierce controversies concerning AIDS. There has been some criticism that the resources devoted to curative medicine in the West would be better spent on preventive measures that tackle the underlying socioeconomic causes in poor countries; also, channelling oda to such initiatives as 'safe sex' campaigns is depriving health programmes concerned with higher incidence risks, like malaria and tuberculosis (TB). Worldwide, TB is on the increase and is responsible for more deaths now (three million annually) than ever, most notably in Asia.

By way of summary, many of today's security themes stand comparison with the analytical structure offered by Brandt, even if the reasons why they have become so conspicuous were not foreseen in 1980 or, perhaps like the fall of communism, could not have been predicted then. Ayoob's (1995: 74) verdict is apposite when he says the components of the international system are so closely intertwined today that 'one cannot realistically contemplate a Hobbesian periphery and a Lockean core existing side by side without the former exporting some of its instabilities and insecurities to the latter'. But the interdependencies are complex and are far from identical across the globe. The best way for aid to make a constructive contribution is not identical on every issue, and on some its role is less than obvious. Much hangs on where the balances are struck between security assessments in the immediate, short, medium and longer terms. In certain matters aid's potential purchase could work fast and directly through governments, while in others it will be more indirect, through alleviating human misery and promoting economic progress. The security laundry will not respond uniformly to the same wash programme, or just one brand of international aid. In any case, faith in a neat causal sequence that runs from concessionary transfers to economic development, to social stability, to political stability, and finally to international security and peace has long been dispelled. Some present-day thinking holds that political reform must come at the start of the process. In the 'new world disorder' of the 'post post-Cold War' age there is no well-worked out theory that explains how aid can address all of the problems. But if this is a weakness it is not confined to aid. The nature, scale and pace of recent changes in world systems are challenging international relations theorising in its entirety. The challenge to humankind is even more profound in matters environmental.

Interest redefined: survival of the planet

Nowhere has the prognosis of a 'world risk society' registered more force-fully than in regard to the global environment. In 1987 the World Com-mission on Environment and Development foresaw a growing ecological crisis, in *Our Common Future* (World Commission on Environment and Development 1987). The crisis was presented as a source of political instab-ility in the Third World and a threat to security worldwide. Timberlake and Thomas (1990: 211) provide a graphic illustration:

> For the first time ever, what happens in the South poses a serious threat to Northern nations. If China rapidly increases its production and use of CFCs (chlorofluorocarbons), Britons get more skin cancer and American children breathe more smog. If the developing nations follow the lead of the North, and develop wasteful and dirty energy and industry systems, then the US Midwest dries out, and the seas around Britain rise.

In the USSR, Mikhail Gorbachev too picked up the significance of global environmental interdependence and made the inevitable inference that glo-bal cooperation is desirable, in his 1986 political report to the Communist Party. Here is an issue area that both transcended the East–West divide and seems to bestow leverage potential on actors in the South *vis-à-vis* the North. Also, it features in notions of intergenerational equity and rights-based discourse, namely the entitlement of future humanity to inherit a planet capable of sustaining well-being.

The significance of the growing environmental awareness has not been lost on the aid agencies. In the 1980s they sought to capitalise on what looked like a promising new avenue for resource mobilisation from governments and voluntary donors alike. The calling of a Conference on Environment and Development ('earth summit') by the UN General Assembly in 1992 seemed auspicious. It was attended by the largest-ever assembly of govern-ment delegations (more than 170) and heads of state (118), and was flanked by numerous NGOs. The summit displayed general agreement that con-siderable extra financial resources were needed to tackle global environ-mental problems. Estimates of the likely cost of the 'Agenda 21' action plan of more than 100 programmes range from $125–600 billion annually. Japan led the way in making a five-year oda promise of over $7 billion (equivalent to possibly not much more than $500 million in terms of new funding), for the environmental field.

The effects of environmental degradation in the South can reach the North by many routes – by damaging the global environment; by harming economies which in turn produces social and political consequences that could threaten international security; by giving rise to large migrations of environmental refugees – whose numbers are expected to grow. However, much dispute surrounds the apportioning of responsibility for environ-mental damage and the exact nature and magnitude of the environmental problems. The steps that must be taken and the best forms of action are also contested. One reason is that scientific knowledge is incomplete and prone to disagreements; another is conflicts of interests. Nevertheless, oda seems to offer both preventative and remedial possibilities; and the EU, for instance, by 1995 was claiming that environmental activities accounted for more than one tenth of its development cooperation budget.

How aid can help

Good environmental practice and economic efficiency are not necessarily incompatible. They can be complementary. However, in the presence of discordance it is understandable that countries like China will insist that near-term economic gains must take precedence. Because of this, 'what is absolutely crucial is that cooperation or participation by the South in any global environmental scheme has to be *incentive-compatible* and this necessitates side payments' (Murshed 1993: 39). Indeed, the World Bank in its *World Development Report 1992* (1992: 24 and 153) suggested not only that poor countries might reasonably expect to be recompensed, but that they may view this as being equivalent to rich world payments for imports, rather than as aid. The Bank argued that these payments should be additional to existing oda. In this way new transfers could provide both an incentive and a means for developing countries to avoid repeating the sort of ecological damage already committed by more industrialised countries, without retarding their chances of sustainable development. This point applies especially to methods of production where the cheapest technologies are relatively harmful. Some developing countries have invested heavily in acquiring such technologies and the means to produce them. Help now could tilt the economic balance in favour of technological renewal, and support the transfer of environmentally appropriate machinery, licences, and blueprints.

The 1990 London conference amendment to the Montreal Protocol on Substances that Deplete the Ozone Layer (1987) is illustrative. It provided for financial help to developing countries to defray the costs of introducing substitutes for CFCs, and undertook to ensure better technologies are made available under fair and favourable conditions. These concessions persuaded China, India and Indonesia to become signatories. By 1997 the accumulated portfolio was 59 projects valued at over $500 million. The Global Environment Facility (GEF) is the principal international mechanism for making grants to projects promising significant global environmental benefits but inadequate economic returns to developing countries (the base line was defined as countries with annual per capita incomes below $4001). The GEF, established under the World Bank, UNDP and UN Environment Programme (UNEP), started work in 1991 with an initial focus on global warming, ozone depletion, international waters and biological diversity. Agenda 21 confirmed its position and by 1995 it had been pledged over $2 billion – monies that most donors were minded to debit from their oda budgets. By 1997 approval had been given to projects totalling $214 million, to be administered by the World Bank.

Some DAC oda is directed to research and development intended to meet environmental challenges, like biodiversity conservation. To the same end international transfers maintain examples of certain natural habitats. Assistance can also be made available for the building of indigenous capacities to monitor environmental performance, enforce environmental standards and manage scarce resources sensitively, as well as to raise public awareness through education and training. Help can be offered for remedial projects – reforestation schemes are popular with some donors.

On a more general level, oda that addresses the underlying causes of poverty and helps reduce poverty, either directly or indirectly through raising economic performance, can benefit the environment. This is because poor or vulnerable people often have no choice but to behave in ways that are ecologically sub-optimal. According to Chambers (1988: 3):

> [T]here is mounting evidence that when poor people have secure rights and adequate stocks of assets to deal with contingencies, they tend to take a long view, holding on tenaciously to land, protecting and saving trees and seeking to provide for their children . . . Secure tenure and rights to resources and adequate livelihoods are prerequisites for good husbandry and sustainable management . . . Enabling poor people to gain secure and sustainable livelihoods in resource-poor and forest areas is, thus, the surest protection for the environment.

For example, by granting effective recognition to the land rights of local peoples a country could help arrest slash-and-burn agriculture, which is a significant contributor to deforestation. Community empowerment is said to lead to more environmentally sound decision-taking in economic affairs. Aid programmes can be designed to serve this purpose too, again directly or indirectly through improving living standards. Special interests motivated solely by particular economic gain will then find it more difficult to hijack decisions about resource usage. Indeed, it 'could be argued that the distribution of power and influence within society lies at the heart of most environment and development challenges' (World Commission on Environment and Development 1987: 38).

Also, debt relief is urged as being highly appropriate to countries whose international financial obligations are held responsible for their taking an environmentally unsound approach to resource exploitation. Russia's oil exports furnish an example. Of course this would not touch financially untroubled developing countries like Malaysia, whose large-scale logging activities have been much criticised in the West. Nevertheless, aid incentives can be devised that will entice public and private sector organisations routinely to incorporate environmental considerations into a wide range of policy processes. Technical advice is being given on the removal of policy distortions that encourage wasteful energy consumption, in Central and Eastern European countries for example. Green conditionality attached to oda disbursements that are not themselves earmarked for environmental purposes form another possibility that is being explored by some donors. But compliance can be problematic; and externally-driven environmentalism, especially via conditionality, creates resentment when it is thought to encroach on national sovereignty. The exercise can be counter-productive where green conditionality comes to be regarded as green imperialism – a view taken by the Brazilian military towards vociferous international concern over the Amazonian rainforest in the 1980s.

Aid's limitations as an environmental force

Aid can promote mutual environmental benefit in the North and South, but books with titles like *Exploited Earth: Britain's Aid and the Environment* (Hayter 1989) indicate that the aid industry too should clean up its act. Many developing countries bear environmental scars from aid-assisted projects and commercial activities. The existence of environmentally unsound oda has been blamed on the influence of donor commercial interests, aid agencies' haste to spend budgets, ignorance and a development ethos that excessively favours modernisation and industrialisation. Other reasons that are often cited include the absence of meaningful consultation with local communities and lack of political interest by recipient authorities.

So, the proposition that rich countries should aid poor countries for the sake of the environment is acceptable only if aid-assisted activities are themselves submitted to rigorous environmental impact assessment, before being given approval. Stringent environmental conditions may have to accompany certain project loans, and on completion there should be an environmental audit. Such procedures are becoming more widely accepted among donors, some of whom now formally incorporate 'sustainable development' in their stated objectives. In 1987 the World Bank established a central environment department and environmental units in its regional offices. It has generally become more cautious about funding large projects like hydro-electric dam schemes that involve substantial involuntary displacements of people, although in 1996 the Bank acknowledged its environmental assessment procedures still inadequately influence lending and need improvement. Outside opinions differ over how significant are the changes and whether the damage that has already been done can ever be rectified. Looking to the future, donors may anticipate good commercial opportunities from the greening of developing countries, and some oda will fund appropriate transfers for that reason. For example, Japan is tapping China's market for technologies that reduce industrial atmospheric pollution, and it has a clear environmental interest in doing so.

Second, some environmental problems important to the developing world impact less severely than others on the global environment. Being peripheral to the rich world's range of greatest concern, they may receive inadequate attention from environmental aid. Slum housing and water supplies are examples. Over 1.3 billion people including 690 million rural people in Asia are reckoned to lack access to clean water, and two billion lack adequate sanitation. The most decisive initiative of the main industrialised nations so far has been in respect of the ozone layer. That is no coincidence. Rich countries have their own environmental agendas, many of them amenity-related rather than centreing on poor societies' needs for sustainable liveli-hoods. A skewed pattern of aid allocations emerges from these agendas; and there will be no boost given to the oda prospects of Third World countries who pose no obvious threat to the global environment for the foreseeable future. Some countries are better placed than others to make credible threats to free ride on attempts by OECD states to curb global environmental pollution, unless given aid. There is an uneven distribution of environmental goods, which also feeds differential capacities to exercise eco-blackmail as a strategy to gain aid. The same point applies to the phe-nomenon of environmental refugees. The GEF, then, was shaped by a desire of G7 governments to vest control with institutions they would dominate (notably the World Bank), rather than accede to proposals for a new UN 'Green Fund' from the Group of 77 developing countries (Gibbon 1993: 50–2). The major donors have retained voting predominance in the GEF. Its early choice of projects has been criticised (Miller 1995: 140) for reflecting their preferences too strongly. It does not offer the long-term financing which many conservation activities require.

Third, if the main objective is to tackle *homo sapiens'* harmful impact on the natural environment as it affects humankind, then major donors should prioritise efforts much closer to home. Aid must not cause attention to be deflected from changes that can only be effected in the North. Take for instance global warming. There is likely to be an average global temper-ature increase of up to 1.5 degrees celsius over the next 50 years. That is ominous for small low-lying islands and countries with extensive river deltas like Bangladesh, for the global sea level could rise by as much as 35 centimetres. At the outset of the 1990s the US accounted for 24 per cent of global energy-related CO_2 emissions, followed by Russia and China (11 per cent each) and India (2.85 per cent). Obviously oda cannot reverse this western origin of global warming (indeed, commercially inspired aid projects to countries like India have included the construction of many coal-fired power stations. Worldwide, such stations account for over 70 per cent of CO_2 emissions). The World Bank estimated the economic cost in relation to GDP of stabilising greenhouse gas emissions could be almost twice as high in developing countries as the world average (*World Development Report 1992*: 160). Yet OECD countries' expenditure on more friendly renewable energy research actually fell by 40 per cent between 1982 and 1993.

Asia presently accounts for only around 20 per cent of CO_2 emis-sions. Nevertheless, China and India are estimated to treble their emissions in the next 20 years, creating a larger absolute increase than from all OECD countries combined. In OECD countries the industrial, economic and lifestyle changes needed to reduce current emission levels rapidly are politically demanding. This makes the option of concessionary transfers to developing countries for the purpose of retarding their growth of CO_2 output look relatively attractive (just as it is *economically* attractive to countries like Norway, whose baseline emissions are so modest that reductions would involve high marginal cost). A comparable point can be made about international trade. The domestic consequences of adding in the environmental costs of production to the price tags of Northern imports from the Third World are likewise politically challenging, and consumers as well as producers seem bound to resist.

However, the environmental impact made by the affluent societies cannot be excluded from consideration, even if Third World poverty and the hot pursuit of industrial growth in emerging economies are both environmentally harmful as well. The North has developed international commercial and financial structures that propel Third World countries into environmentally unsustainable production and trade (practices that may not even be in their long-term economic interest). Wasteful Northern consumption of tropical hardwoods is a prime example. In this and other ways the industrialised world has already used much of the planet's 'ecological capital' (World Commission on Environment and Development 1987: 51). Eventually, the demand side of the equation will have to be addressed. But environmentally induced changes to consumption and production patterns in the North could cause serious economic shocks to many countries in the South, most of whom will continue to look to economic growth in the North as an engine of their own development. Aid programmes can help with establishing appropriate alternative sources of income and export earnings in those countries. In a very small way this is already happening, as NGOs like Oxfam lend their support to ventures in 'alternative trading'.

Finally, we conclude with rights and entitlement. On pollution there is a view that no country has an unlimited right to make use of the global 'sink'. Much thought has been given to the idea of establishing a worldwide market in tradeable permits, to make use of the global commons for this purpose. In 1995 UNCTAD lent support to a proposed pilot scheme for greenhouse gases. The arrangement could offer a cost-effective response to an environmental problem. But it also generates financial resources for Third World countries, so long as they are allocated an initial surplus of quotas and OECD countries start with a deficit. Polluting activities in the past mean Northern industrialised countries have accumulated a 'natural debt', and this too could be taken into account when allocating permits. That means poorer countries would qualify for a disproportionate entitlement to the available sink. In this context aid could be a misnomer, just as charity misdescribes the 'ethically socially responsible' purchasing by Northern consumers who are prepared to pay more for Third World produce imported under 'fair trade' schemes. Of course, the requirement to make trade-offs is inescapable. If developing countries set high prices to their excess permits, excessive polluters will have an incentive to reduce their demands on the global 'sink'. That would benefit the environment. Poor countries who price their excess permits more moderately may receive in total an enhanced income stream, but only because high polluters continue to exceed their quota, up to the global maximum set by the permits scheme. That is less favourable to the environment. This sort of conflict is typical of aid, which is no stranger to the problems that arise from being directed to serve two or more competing ends.

The problem with people

Very few writers support a global application of 'lifeboat ethics'. Even so, there is a widely held view that some developing countries already face a situation of having too many people for their own national good, or will soon do so. Aid's potential role in helping defuse their 'demographic timebomb' has been an undercurrent in arguments for aid giving for many years, although official aid targeted at this purpose did not really begin until the mid-1960s. An estimate of total spending on family planning in developing countries is $4.7 billion a year, of which 20 per cent comprises external assistance (World Bank's *World Development Report 1992*: 173). Twenty-five years ago international sources contributed 80 per cent of such expenditure. Family planning measures are a relatively inexpensive form of oda and have never received more than 2 per cent, and currently less. The rise of environmental consciousness has brought a fresh prominence to population issues and to the part that aid can play. Even so, objections from Catholic and Islamic quarters to some forms of birth control, the legacy of ill-conceived programmes in some poor countries and an unwillingness to be closely associated with blatantly coercive population measures (as practised in China for instance) all constrain donors and channel their involvement through multilateral and non-governmental organisations. Research by Ness (1989) found that while assistance to population planning has influenced population policy in developing countries, measuring its effectiveness is difficult and it provides no guarantee that fertility will decline.

At approximately 5.8 billion people now, the world's population doubled between 1950 and 1987 and will continue to increase by around 88 million people annually for the remainder of the century. Ninety-five per cent of the increase will be in the developing world and most is likely to occur in urban areas. Annual growth rates above 3 per cent are not uncommon in parts of sub-Saharan Africa (where over half the population of some countries is under 15 years old), but the lower rates in China and India translate into larger absolute increases. A fast-growing population means heavy investment requirements in education, in advance of seeing an economic return. The pressures on scarce physical resources and fragile environments increase. There is a good chance poverty will be exacerbated in at least some of the countries, with attendant social and political consequences, domestic and international. Divergent fertility rates between ethnic groups can provoke inter-communal strife. Perhaps even more important from the point of view of some DAC countries, demographic size could be a significant factor in the balance of power between states. On one estimate, by the year 2025 only the US and Japan among today's established industrial democracies will feature in the top 20 most populous countries (Eberstadt 1991: 128). In other words, there are implications for international security. Eberstadt (1991: 129) inferred: 'one can envisage a fractious, contentious and unhumane international order . . .'

A variety of perspectives on the 'population problem' in developing areas construe it variously in economic, poverty-related, and environmental terms. But in addition, concerns about fertility and birth rates have increasingly taken on a moral dimension, and become entangled with issues central to women-in-development (WID, and subsequently gender-and-development) agendas and feminist agendas. These agendas started to gain prominence in debates on development cooperation at the time of the UN Decade for Women (1976–85). Tinker (1990: 3) claims WID began as a policy concern focused on changing the priorities and practices of development agencies. The theme is certainly not a mere appendage of the population debates; and in gender matters several different intellectual and political communities make distinctive contributions to our understanding of development. Some fairly common ground exists as well, in respect of desiring greater international efforts to help women become more equal with their male partners in taking decisions about family size, and promoting the spread of appropriate information and the means to practise deliberate child spacing. Three hundred and fifty million couples are said to be without access to modern family planning; fertility surveys in 40 developing countries have indicated 20 per cent of births are unwanted (OECD 1990: 111). According to UNICEF, 585,000 women die needlessly each year from causes related to pregnancy and childbirth, and in the worst-affected areas the risk is one in seven.

Thus, oda's objectives have come to include not just improved standards of health for women but also a reduction in gender inequality. In societies where there is systematic oppression of women, aid may be given the mantle of furthering basic human rights. Female-headed households figure disproportionately among the poorest in Africa; and women are reckoned to make up 70 per cent of the world's absolutely poor. They also tend to predominate among refugee populations. Hence, even if oda's main goal should be to meet unsatisfied material needs, or confirm the right to the means to life, women warrant special consideration. Of course, such variables as ethnicity, religion, class and caste interact with gender to produce very diverse situations on the ground. Furthermore, the negative effects of global asymmetries of power and economic opportunities on the life chances of Third World women should not be ignored. Development assistance itself stands accused of having added to the problems women face, for instance by funding development projects and programmes that are gender-blind, and some examples have overtly discriminated in favour of men. Badly designed population programmes have infringed women's basic rights; and in some societies family planning *per se* is said to threaten the status and power which mothers enjoy by virtue of their reproductive function.

The DAC established an Expert Group on Women in Development in 1984; and many aid agencies now acknowledge the proposition that women should be fully integrated into development programmes and the decision-making processes of international development cooperation. There is also considerable agreement that much remains to be done to translate these ideas into practice. Aid directed to women's education and particularly literacy programmes, combined with other steps to improve their socio-economic status and to reduce infant and child mortality rates, will influence the decisions couples make about family size. Primary reproductive (and more general) health care programmes directed at mothers and small children are mounted by many aid agencies. This type of approach is some-times criticised for confirming traditional stereotypes of the woman's place in the home. A largely welfarist bent to aid can be just as limiting as are aid initiatives that concentrate on improving the economic productivity of women (responsible for up to 85 per cent of staple food production in some parts of sub-Saharan Africa for instance), unless the wider social and political structures are addressed. The application of gender analysis to development aid projects and programmes is a step forward. But it will not necessarily deliver the empowerment of women. That is believed to be essential, not just as a necessary means to achieve population restraint. And it will not come about simply as a consequence of fertility reduction achieved through birth control measures.

Progress in many aid agencies appears to be slow. For example, among British NGO projects studied the impact on women is 'quite limited' (Riddell *et al*. 1995: 100). Hirschmann (1995: 1300) found not much enthusiasm for incorporating gender into USAID's Democracy Initiative, and saw signs of 'gender fatigue': 'The lesson after 20 years may be that, at least in the medium term, the objective of institutionalizing WID in the Agency may be a mirage'. WID considerations are still integrated only weakly at best into the EU's aid programme; and probably account for no more than 5 per cent of all oda. The OECD (1996: 409) noted policy-makers have had difficulty in putting WID policy commitments into action in the newest areas of development priority. All the evidence suggests that in the rank order of significant problems with people, gender issues pose a challenge at least as great as does the fecundity of the human race. Demographers agree that rising living standards are usually a precursor of declining birth rates, which means that almost any aid that is genuinely developmental will ultimately help. In contrast there is no such confidence that legitimate feminist concerns have yet to be fully met even in the most advanced of industrial societies.

Conclusions

Many arguments attempt to explain why people in rich countries should provide aid to less fortunate countries. This might be considered a source of strength, but it can also give rise to confusion, even contradiction. Parts of the moral case rest on timeless arguments whose internal integrity may never obsolesce. For instance, Stokke (1996: 77) maintains that from an early stage the promotion of basic human rights has been an integral part of the justification for aid. By comparison, some of the specifics involved in enlightened self-interest and mutual advantage appear to have a more transient appeal. A priority given to interests in the short and medium terms (up to five years) could frustrate the achievement of longer-term objectives. The excitement certain themes arouse at particular times can owe much to events and intellectual developments occurring in the wider scene outside aid and development.

That aid is still around after more than three 'development decades' and continues to attract support suggests that at least some of the arguments are persuasive. Moreover, current debates are injecting a new kind of commitment, by featuring not just the traditional duties and obligations but also the rights of the international community. The UN Charter permits the international community to resort to military force in intra-state disturbances where international peace and security are put at risk. Now, a growing number of voices are proposing there should be a *right* of *humanitarian* intervention, or the less strong 'right of regard', in such circumstances as gross violation of the security of people and intolerable human suffering. The claimed right is not strongly conditional, in the sense that any threats to international peace are secondary, or need not be fundamental to establishing a case. The creation of safe havens for Kurds in Northern Iraq, ostensibly backed by UN Security Council resolution 688 (1991), is often cited as an important precedent. The boundaries between humanitarian assistance and 'humanitarian intervention' are becoming increasingly blurred, particularly in failed states where there is effectively no central authority to erect legal and other obstacles.

Moreover, the idea that the international community has not just a right but a *duty* to promote respect for certain basic rights everywhere, and actively to halt their violation, is also gaining ground. Whereas the claimed right is advanced in retort to oppressive regimes, the onus of duty is canvassed to galvanise support for intervention from countries who can provide material and military help. From its early beginnings the UN was vigorous in pursuing decolonisation goals, but the post-colonial era has not witnessed much enthusiasm for liberating peoples from their home-grown oppression, up until now. For political and diplomatic reasons, the idea of an international obligation to try to ensure minimum *material* standards of life has been much easier to endorse. So for example when, in 1978, US Senator George McGovern mused about an international peacekeeping force to protect Cambodians from the genocidal activities of their own Khmer Rouge government, the West's response varied from indifference to incredulity (the Khmer Rouge had taken power after the US brought Cambodia into its war in Vietnam). Now, with the Cold War behind, sentiment is gradually changing.

Thus, for instance, in 1990 the 35 states of the Conference on Security and Cooperation in Europe stated in the Copenhagen Document that participants have a responsibility to defend and protect the democratic order. Franck (1992: 46) believes democracy 'is on the way to becoming a global entitlement, one that increasingly will be promoted and protected by collective international processes'. He goes on to say (1992: 50): 'We are not quite there, but we can see the outlines of this new world in which the citizens of each state will look to international law and organisation to guarantee their democratic entitlement'. Franck looked to the UN as the enforcement agency, and subsequently the Commission on Global Governance (1995) proposed the UN Charter be amended to allow international intervention in states in the event of petition by non-state actors. Yet despite these straws in the wind, it is still far too early to say whether there will be a clear, new conventional wisdom on the rights or the duties of states to intervene externally and non-consensually, acting collectively through UN agency, separately, or as regionally focused groups (for further discussion see Greenwood 1993; Roberts 1993; Griffiths *et al.* 1995).

Modern times are transitional in many respects, not least in the developing thoughts about security. There is a heightened appreciation of the complexity of the challenges facing humankind and of the issue linkages, even though our understanding of the connections is imperfect and the interpretations range quite widely. Security is acquiring a looser, almost catch-all meaning. Rationales for aid are being adapted to suit. Thus for example some DAC states now openly endorse the UNHCR's (1993: 9) view that the repression of minorities and indiscriminate violence 'can no longer be seen as falling exclusively within the realm of domestic concern especially when they affect other countries by causing an outpouring of refugees'. Increasingly the view is being expressed that the international community is entitled to insist on all states fulfilling certain basic responsibilities in regard to their own citizens. The claimed entitlement is being advanced not just on moral grounds, but as a matter of prudential obligation, and as being in the self-interest of stable and prosperous countries like members of the DAC.

This chapter has located arguments about the provision of aid in the context of much wider debates. But a legitimate question that has yet to be addressed is, why is development assistance still needed, after the efforts of half a century? One answer could be that oda has never received the kind of support that would have enabled it to complete the job, perhaps because not enough people have been convinced by the reasons discussed here and in the previous chapter. A second possibility is that oda might be a blunt instrument for development (see Chapter 6). A third is that the task with which oda is charged is simply too demanding. Indeed, on the basis of the analysis in this chapter we might reasonably conclude that aid's functions have tended to multiply, to increase in difficulty and to escalate out of sight. To substantiate that conclusion Chapter 5 explores the reasons why some countries are thought to need development assistance.

Why some countries need development assistance

Many years ago Huntington (1970–1: 161) said the 'continued quest for a rationale for foreign aid is one of its distinguishing characteristics as an area of public policy'. The observation has worn well. But while Huntington's purpose was to query the benefit donors derive from aid, his remark could just as easily apply to the reasons why some countries apparently need assistance in order to develop well. Those reasons do not explain fully why donors provide aid; and nor should they be confused with the motives behind aid seeking. They cannot even supply a complete explanation of why relatively prosperous countries should provide oda. Nevertheless, they are an important part of the overall picture.

The answer to the question of why some countries need development assistance has brought forward many responses, which have become increasingly elaborate over time. Some reasons have accurately accounted for their contemporary aid practices, while others emerged more as rationalisations during or after the event. Starting out in the 1950s with a heavy emphasis on economic analysis, the development rationale has moved towards an increasingly prominent political content. There are very general themes and many sub-plots and lesser currents. There are variants specific to certain groups of countries, like the countries judged to be most seriously affected by the 1973–4 international oil price rise and its worldwide economic repercussions, and more recently the plight of SILICs in Africa. Individual countries have their own special needs. This chapter is limited to the broad canvass, and singles out four themes: economic gaps, technical assistance, adjustment lending and political reform. The elements overlap in some particulars, and the succession from one to another should be seen not as a series of wholesale switches but as a progressive enrichment of the overall debate.

From economic gaps to technical assistance

The traditional case for development assistance is encapsulated in the so-called two gap theory, elaborated in the 1960s by the economists Chenery and Strout (1966) on behalf of USAID. The argument put very simply is as follows.

Developing countries face two gaps – savings–investment and foreign exchange. Poverty or low average incomes restrict the propensity to set aside resources for saving, to abstain from consumption. However, saving is what makes investment possible, and investment causes the economy to grow and thereby raise income levels. So economic expansion and income growth are held back, which in turn retards saving. There is a vicious circle. An external infusion to the system can raise the rate of investment and help propel the economy on to a virtuous path of self-reinforcing growth, higher propensities to save and invest, and further growth. Aid can be one such infusion, although it is not the only possibility. The more a country offers profitable investment opportunities, the greater are its chances of attracting capital on commercial terms. This helps explain how the US could become the world's largest importer of capital, in the mid-1980s.

The argument is very similar with respect to the balance of payments. Almost by definition a less developed economy is unable to source its requirement for intermediate and capital goods from its own production capabilities. The scope for importing these ingredients of economic expansion and increased productivity is constrained by the capacity to acquire foreign exchange. Aid can alleviate the exchange constraint. As with the savings gap, oda eventually works itself out of a job. The assisted country will then be able to balance its external account in other ways, such as by expanding its earnings from exports and becoming more adept at replacing imported merchandise with local production. In the meantime, aid will have been most beneficial where the principal constraint on economic growth was the foreign exchange gap rather than limited domestic saving (Todaro 1994: 544). Estimates of the exchange gap are customarily taken into account when calculating countries' oda requirements, even now.

The Chenery–Strout model offered no guarantee that oda would produce good results. Moreover, as our understanding of development grew, so the two-gap model came to be refined, and reservations were placed against its usefulness. The aid flows that came about as a result of the model took several forms, but the analysis lent itself to a focus on capital investment in physical projects, which make heavy demands on imports. Later on, the simple dichotomy of developmental (investment) versus non-developmental (consumption) expenditures dissolved, in consequence of the realisation that certain forms of consumption expenditure might be economically productive. But for some years construction projects like roads, railways and power stations were viewed as being of the utmost importance to economic take-off. They consumed large sums of aid.

The general soundness of the whole approach seemed to be confirmed by the success of Marshall aid, during whose relatively short life Western European GNP increased 32 per cent and agricultural and industrial production came to surpass pre-1939 levels, by 11 per cent and 40 per cent respectively (Patterson 1993: 189). However, the Marshall aid programme benefited from circumstances that were not bound to be replicated once the international aid effort turned to developing countries. The programme's sheer magnitude ($13.2 billion, or 5–10 per cent of the US federal budget) was exceptional in relation to the recipient populations, who are estimated to have received an annual average of more than $13 per person in economic aid ($21 including military aid) (Baldwin 1985: 321). Many Third World countries have never received that figure (adjusted for inflation) from all sources combined. US aid to them has not exceeded per capita levels of 'about one-tenth the size of the Marshall Plan effort' (Baldwin 1985: 322), although aid inflows have been higher as a proportion of average incomes in some sub-Saharan African countries. Furthermore, the dominant ideologies of political economy were compatible across the US and much of Western Europe, and this, together with a common commitment to building liberal democracy, underpinned mutual understanding. Europe needed reconstruction, not development. Abundant technical abilities meant high absorptive capacity to put substantial capital infusions to immediate productive use. The same could not be said of many Third World countries in the 1960s and 1970s.

On the one side, domestic capital scarcity soon ceased to be regarded as a sufficient reason for oda. The more advanced developing countries in Latin America were able to attract private finance and official non-concessionary flows. Several East Asian economies began to counter the exchange gap by vigorous export-oriented development strategies. On the other side, doubts surfaced about whether capital shortage was in fact the main constraint on development, particularly in countries displaying managerial, organisational and technical weaknesses of the sort typical of former colonies that had not been well-prepared for self-government. By the 1970s it was apparent that social customs, cultural traditions and political obstacles could all conspire to limit the absorptive capacity for capital, so constraining economic prospects (Schiavo-Campo and Singer 1970: 34). One inference was that the Third World needed a particular form of aid, namely technical assistance, to help create the conditions in which capital transfers would be advantageous. A precursor already existed in the form of the US's Point Four Programme for Technical Assistance, announced by President Truman in 1949. Technical assistance could identify and relax the limits to absorptive capacity for capital and for aid. Accordingly, some economists came to doubt not only the usefulness of the two gap theory in estimating aid requirements but also pessimism over absorptive capacity: 'a good deal of current talk about the "failure of aid", "lack of absorptive capacity", and "waste" amounts to not much more than saying that certain forms of technical assistance have been absent or inadequate or improperly administered or wrongly chosen, and have thus prevented recipients from making better use of a larger volume of capital aid' (Streeten 1972: 64).

Technical cooperation and technical assistance grew in real terms from one eighth of DAC net bilateral oda in the early 1960s to one third by the mid-1980s. They embraced a proliferating range of activities, some more successful than others. In the early years technical assistance advised governments to plan the development of their economies, and even included the preparation by expatriates of detailed national development plans. Later, recommendations concerning how to replace centrally managed with market-based economies came to the fore. The focus on technology transfer for capital projects typical of the early decades has in part given way to an emphasis on providing policy analysis and management skills.

The United Nations' first 'development decade' (1960s) achieved its stated economic target of annual average growth rates of at least 5 per cent. But world poverty and global inequalities continued to increase, in part because declining mortality rates accelerated population growth rates. The record was judged a failure, especially when measured against the high hopes. Aid was deemed to have reached a point of crisis. The Commission on International Development, or Pearson Commission (1969: 4) reported the 'climate surrounding foreign aid programmes is heavy with disillusion and distrust' – a claim that was to be echoed on many more occasions over the next quarter century (recently by Ryrie 1995: ix, for example), with probably no more and no less accuracy. In 1969 a larger aid effort and a more genuine commitment to development both seemed to be required. The UN General Assembly proclaimed the 1970s the second development decade, and adopted Pearson's oda target for donors of 0.70 per cent of GNP. However, by the end of the 1970s the second development decade too was being judged a failure. A combination of economic growth and population increase left the poorest countries worse off, and buffeted by global economic shocks. At the end of the decade there was more poverty, underemployment, malnutrition, illiteracy and poor health than ever, chiefly in rural areas.

As was only to be expected, questions soon began to be asked of the quality and cost-effectiveness of technical cooperation. The costs have been significant but the results seemed disappointing. From the start there were warnings about the limited capacity to absorb even technical assistance. Later there came empirical findings like Lele and Jain's (1992: 601): in Africa such aid 'has made little lasting impact either on agricultural performance or on the development of long-term local capabilities'. In *Governance and Development* the World Bank's (1992: 51) evaluation of its own considerable efforts has taught it that funding expatriate technical assistance is a poor substitute for developing local capability. But that goal has been displaced all too often, perhaps because of a haste to get things done – typical of donor-driven technical assistance. The functions of advising, training and manpower supplementation have often become confused. Reliance on expatriates to carry out operational activities becomes institutionalised, even where there are well-qualified local personnel. The transfer of skills is held back by slowness to adopt new knowledge and to change behaviour. In some countries, investment in high level human capital has been followed by a brain drain – half of all Africa's professional people are said to be working outside Africa. Moreover, local resentment is caused where foreign advisers and consultants (whose fees and expenses can amount to a sizeable chunk of an aid programme, including repayable loans) seem the most visible immediate beneficiaries of technical cooperation, as happened in the early stages of Western assistance to transition economies in Central and Eastern Europe. In Africa, which hosts over 100,000 foreign technical assistants funded to the tune of $4 billion annually (around a third of all oda receipts), some highly educated and professionally qualified indigenous manpower is un/underemployed. Again in Africa, Pierre-Claver Damiba found technical cooperation is a 'politically charged subject', mishandled by governments because 'it is largely perceived, at best, as a free good and, at worst, as something imposed by the donors' (cited in Berg 1993: vii and vi). Sometimes, hard or project-related technical assistance has proved inappropriate to local circumstances. Alternative technology and intermediate technology have long been bruited in engineering circles in the West, but examples of unqualified success have often proved elusive. Anyway, the concepts have never captured the imagination of major donors or the enthusiasm of Third World elites. Satisfactory formulas for technical cooperation have proven rather elusive, and remain so even now, especially with regard to institution-building in the most aid-dependent countries (Berg 1993). The fact that technical assistance has grown so much is itself judged a serious indictment of past attempts to build indigenous capacity to mobilise and manage development resources. According to Moore (1995a: 89) there is now 'something of a crisis in the technical assistance field: conventional methods of delivering technical assistance have recently been authoritatively discredited, yet alternatives are not readily available'.

Adjustment lending

In 1981 the DAC (OECD 1981: 23) advised that donor officers 'almost without exception' have an aversion to attaching policy conditioning to aid, seeing such moves as 'undiplomatic, they ask for trouble, and they make few friends'. The advice became redundant almost as soon as the ink was dry. In the 1980s the World Bank came to the fore as a centre of intellectual influence in development thinking, among many DAC donors. Some like the US, Germany, UK, Netherlands and Canada increasingly keyed their bilateral aid programmes to the approaches of the Bank, although others like Japan and the EU were less committed. Bilaterals entered joint funding arrangements with the Bank and offered parallel financing of its policy-related programmes. They made their own programmes conditional on agreement being reached with the Bretton Woods institutions. The Bank and IMF began to practise an increasing measure of informal cross-conditionality in their relations with borrowers. Paris club reschedulings of official loans became conditional on IMF standby agreements.

The Bank's dissatisfaction with oda's achievements began to show up in a distinctive new pattern of dealings with governments. The Bank first signalled the need for extensive economic policy reform in *Accelerated Development in Sub-Saharan Africa: an Agenda for Action* (1981), although an interest in how the macro-economic policy environment influences development dates from further back. Highly conditional programme assistance for policy reform and structural economic adjustment (and subsequently for sectoral adjustment as well) became pronounced, such that towards the end of the 1980s adjustment lending in more than 70 countries accounted for close to 30 per cent of Bank loans, and nearly 40 per cent of lending to sub-Saharan Africa. A quarter of UK bilateral aid was similarly engaged. Total accumulated advances of policy-based loans by the Bank now amount to around $35 billion; by the late 1980s the average number of primary legal conditions attached to such loans had reached 17, plus a further 28 less precise but still legally binding conditions (Nelson and Eglinton 1993: 42). A high level of involvement in chronically indebted countries was typical. In Ghana, which came to be presented as a success for externally funded adjustment, the government entertained more than 40 World Bank missions in 1987 alone.

The issues have been very well explained in Mosley, Harrigan and Toye (1995). From 1982 on it became clear that many developing countries were unable to service their foreign debts, including meeting obligations to the Bank. This damaged the case for making new loans, even though the Bank claimed the majority of its projects secured satisfactory *ex post* rates of return. The Third World landscape would come to be littered with underutilised and partially abandoned projects funded partly from aid. A reputation for cost over-runs and bad environmental practice was beginning to make large aid-financed schemes difficult to justify. With slowing disbursements, the Bank would face the embarrassing possibility of becoming a net recipient of funds from the developing world. Also, a failure to recover its loans (a situation which the IDA was originally set up to prevent) might upset the Bank's favourable credit rating. Clearly, the Bank's interests were at stake. For, according to Le Prestre (1989: 149), the 'tragedy of the Bank's situation is that expansion is inevitable. The organisation must control its milieu. Had it not expanded, its position as a leading intellectual and financial development institution would have vanished, and the purpose of the institution with it'. Other commentators say US government pressure on the Bank to increase lending, so as to relieve the overextended position of some American commercial banks, was just as important.

The by-now familiar IMF-type stabilisation programmes for countries in deficit had proven unable to offer a sustainable solution. What came to the rescue was the idea that struggling countries need fast-disbursing help with meeting their immediate financial obligations. This must be linked to policy guidance embracing measures that will liberalise the supply side of the economy. The result should be greater efficiency in resource allocation. Thus two objectives would benefit: improved economic prospects and debt recovery. Policy guidance creates opportunities for oda in the form of technical missions, without making demands on the kind of administrative support that more conventional projects require. But most importantly, governments have to be brought to adopt the medicine of structural adjustment programmes (SAPs), and in many cases that means there must be sugar coating on the pill – concessionary assistance in the form of structural adjustment loans (SALs).

The pill is a bitter one not simply because it involves hard choices over the allocation of public expenditure, which must be reined in more tightly. For the standard features include dismantling the raft of controls that keep interest rates artificially low, the currency's value unrealistically high, and the country's producers sheltered from international competition. The denationalisation of state-owned enterprise and other forms of privatisation are fundamental. In exchange, SALs offer to finance recurrent expenditures and facilitate multi-year commitments of oda, so enabling the borrower to maintain imports (and import-dependent economic activities) even while engaging on economic restructuring and trade liberalisation.

As is also true of stabilisation, the process of adjustment and the workings of the freer market-based economy that follows will influence the distribution of opportunities to extract gains from economic activity. Rent seekers with a vested interest in the status quo *ante* should be disadvantaged. Producer groups who were previously undervalued should benefit. For example, agricultural producers will gain from the abolition of state monopsonies in marketing and from the removal of depressive price controls on foodstuffs, which had been widely prevalent owing to governmental sensitivity to urban consumers ('urban bias'). Oda should enhance the political sustainability of the reform process and ease the adjustment phase through to a successful conclusion. Some economists have argued it expedites the economic reform process, enables a 'big bang' approach and so shortens the period of pain; others say it enables a more relaxed approach, spreads the costs over time and lessens the shock. Either way, the Bank (in *World Development Report 1990*: 115) noted the capital inflows can 'play a crucial political role as well as a purely economic one'.

That political role is needed most during the difficult period when groups who believe they will be losers from economic adjustment make opposition, and other groups who might ultimately gain but are uncertain, or are slow to organise themselves politically, fail to give sufficient support (of course, some groups could be both winners and losers). Toye (1992: 87) summed this up in terms of bridging the gap between the arrival of the bad news – the immediate, certain losses, often felt by politically important groups, and the good news – the gains, probably quite diffused, which *might* follow later, perhaps a good deal later. In *Governance and Development* the

Bank (1992: 56) pointed to 'an inherent conflict between the need for quick support of sensitive policy reforms and the need to build understanding of and commitment to the programme. Moreover, greater commitment comes after a programme begins to show results'. The problem is compounded where economic stabilisation and its widely distributed pain accompanies adjustment reforms. Governments can deploy assistance to build supportive coalitions for reform and pacify groups who might otherwise be obstructive, usually in combination with a judicious sequencing of the reform measures and other techniques such as obfuscation, persuasive argument, even coercion.

However, in the 1980s donors did not themselves appear to give a great deal of consideration to the necessary political calculations – such as how much of the assistance should be passed on as consolation payments to the losers, and how much should comprise advance payments to mobilise the prospective winners. The recipient governments were left free to decide the balance between mollifying politically influential groups who were about to suffer downward mobility (not all of whom were affluent) and meeting the needs of the absolutely poor and politically uninfluential social sectors. For they too could be among the immediate losers from adjustment and will not obviously go on to become winners, for example female heads of households in rural Africa. As the decade wore on, Nelson (1989: 17) detected a disparity emerging between, on the one side, the domestic political imperative to shelter the middle class, middle deciles and near poor from the costs of policy reform in adjusting countries and, on the other side, growing international concern (among NGOs especially) about the consequences for the ultra-poor. Later, Haggard et al. (1995) confirmed that politically optimal strategies for executing economic stabilisation and adjustment programmes can be very different from the criteria that would be required to optimise either the economic or the social effects. Only in the 1990s have political economists become more explicit about the need for detailed consideration of the political feasibility of economic policy reform and the implications for designing reform programmes.

Unresolved problems

To this day the Bank adheres to the imperative of structural adjustment for achieving sustainable, poverty-reducing growth, and argued this in, for example, its Adjustment in Africa: Reforms, Results and the Road Ahead (1994). However, the early enthusiasm has attenuated, the approach has been modulated, in the light of criticism from social scientists as well as dismay voiced by recipient governments and some aid organisations. Quite aside from objections that conditionality is an unacceptable infringement of sovereignty and the policy reforms politically damaging to the governments, the critique has been triple barrelled at least: social, managerial and economic.

First, in the 1980s severe censure from UNICEF, NGOs in the North and South and concerned intellectuals in developing countries highlighted increases in absolute poverty which appeared to be a consequence of structural adjustment. According to Lipton and Toye (1990: 100–1) in many cases the SAPs involved 'no published analysis (and in some cases known to us, no unpublished analysis either)' of the effects on the poor. The years came to be known as a lost decade from the perspective of fighting global poverty. As with IMF stabilisation programmes, governments took the line of least political resistance and reduced spending on social programmes and investment, rather than current expenditure on servicing the state. The Bank began to respond in the second half of the 1980s by making some monies available for action programmes for vulnerable groups, and started giving practical support to the idea of safety nets for the poor as well as employment-intensive growth strategies.

Such developments have failed to impress all the critics, some of whom urge the need for very much bolder steps such as asset redistribution. They argue social objectives should not merely be an add-on to economic policy, and instead want poverty considerations to infuse the entire economic policy framework. All economic advice should be tested in terms of the implications for the poor. For example, Watkins (1995a: 82) says the Bank's achievement in incorporating poverty-focused measures into half of all SAL programmes has been reactive, belated and ineffective, and is marred also by its tolerance of governmental non-compliance with social expenditure agreements. Moreover 'there is little to substantiate the claim that adjustment policies are creating a framework for more equitable growth and poverty reduction' (Watkins 1995a: 108). An internal Bank examination in 1996 of 46 of its country poverty assessments conducted between 1988 and 1994 found marked weaknesses and only modest influence on Bank country assistance strategies and poverty-targeted lending. Nevertheless, the shortcomings of adjustment without a human face are acknowledged much more fully, and the importance the Bank now formally gives to human resource development is an advance, even if it is grounded mainly on economistic reasoning rather than social and political analysis. We now understand that SAP measures which degrade the human capital stock will retard economic prospects. We also know that not all governments enthusiastically support poverty reduction agendas, notwithstanding blandishments from the Bank.

Second, in parts SAPs have implied measures that were beyond the managerial and administrative capabilities of some states, given their weaknesses of executive capacity and the underdeveloped condition of market structures. For example, it has proven far easier to devalue currencies than successfully to privatise state-owned enterprises that owe large, unquantified debts, especially where there is no established system of financial markets.

Third, many development economists have questioned the soundness of the economic prescription. Their economic judgement is that programme lending is not technically well founded, and that the evidence of its performance in the field has yet to bear out the Bank's confidence in the underlying analysis. Also, attention is drawn to how the economic difficulties facing developing countries can be compounded by international economic forces for which they are not responsible and over which they have no control, such as the operation of global commodity markets, plus their levels of external indebtedness. Some argue the case for a more active or developmental state than is permitted by the neo-liberalism that underpins typical structural adjustment programmes.

By demonstrating the explanatory power of a bargaining model of the relations between international financial institutions and their clients, Mosley, Harrigan and Toye's (1995) findings were reminiscent of some studies of the IMF, and contrast with models that centre on bureaucratic expertise and political domination. Killick (1984: 226) for instance found: 'The IMF has experienced large difficulties in securing governmental compliance with a number of its key performance criteria . . .' (see also Stiles 1990: 959–74). One of Mosley, Harrigan and Toye's conclusions, repeated later by others (Kahler 1989; Mosley 1992) is that a principal determinant of the SAP prescription offered by the Bank has been the power relationship with the client, not the severity of the economic disease afflicting the country. Countries that might have benefited most from the advice were not all placed under the greatest pressure to reform. Governments that were most likely to adopt the recommendations, either out of desperation or because their leaders were persuaded of the merits of the economic arguments, would have done so anyway. In those circumstances, conditionality could well have been redundant. Even so, assistance that is not needed to supply an inducement to leaders may still be essential if leaders are to overcome local opposition to reform (it buys acquiescence), quite apart from offering a means to shelter poor groups from the possible costs of adjustment. But for middle income countries, who were SALs' earliest recipients, financial transfers without oda's concessionary terms were deemed sufficient to progress the policy reform process anyway.

However, in countries where concessionary finance *is* believed necessary to motivate policy reform, the structure of the bargain can be such as to risk giving encouragement to bad faith. Where strong political commitment is absent, aid inflows might actually undermine the pressures to reform. And in fact governments quite typically defaulted on agreed conditionalities. Overt slippage of around 40 per cent became common. Mosley, Harrigan and Toye (1995) found the Bank routinely tolerated slippage below 50 per cent on conditions applying to earlier tranches, when negotiating subsequent loans. By the end of the 1980s, increased use of tranching and better performance monitoring in advance of further disbursement brought improved compliance rates, but still only around two thirds of all legally binding conditions were being fully implemented during the lifetime of the loans. A complicating factor is the existence of a lag before the full fruits of policy implementation can be expected to appear. Above all, however, is the Bank's interest in maintaining its relationship with clients, in order to continue to make loans. Also, in some cases the strategic or political interest that one or more major subscribers had in supporting a government would enable backsliding. A rigorous application of penalties to all states who show non-compliance seemed out of the question. Any significant discrepancies between the conditionality requirements of the different international financial institutions and other donor organisations would also make the situation worse. All in all, Mosley, Harrigan and Toye identified a number of cases in which they said Davids managed to outpoint Goliath.

And so to political reform

The Bank's initial judgement that structural adjustment programmes need last only around five years proved optimistic. For many countries SALs became almost a way of life. At the end of the 1980s the evidence from sub-Saharan Africa suggested the returns were modest. Successive declines in average per capita incomes and in saving and investment rates proportional to GDP have proved difficult to reverse. In countries accounting for a third of the region's population, 1990 per capita incomes were below 1960 levels. Africa's foreign debt nearly doubled (debt to exports ratio of 91 per cent in 1980 reached 254 per cent in 1994), some social indicators were deteriorating in certain countries, and the share of Bank projects displaying major problems had increased. Yet aid to the region had also increased, both absolutely and proportional to GDP. Hindsight clearly showed the expectations placed on SALs/SAPs were excessive (Schatz 1994; Rimmer 1995: 113).

In particular, policy reform was found to be proceeding too slowly. Among the possible inferences two stood out: ruling elites did not have the interests of society at heart, and/or they lacked the requisite political strength and policy space to initiate change. Regardless of which was uppermost, the political obstacles to economic liberalisation seemed considerable. More specifically, some political leaders proved resistant to making changes that significantly eroded their discretion over resource allocations – the principal instrument of their political survival. Their inclination is to play games with the financial providers, seeking to maximise the inflow of concessionary resources in exchange for the least practical commitment to economic restructuring, beyond what seems inevitable. Neither generous amounts of concessionary assistance, nor high levels of conditionality, were sufficient to guarantee structural adjustment. Even the two provided together could prove inadequate (Kahler 1989: 155). That seemed no less true with respect to generating development than in regard to instigating economic policy reform.

In lands consumed by civil war it has always been apparent that some political transformation is needed before development can become possible. By the late 1980s similar reasoning was beginning to be applied to a much wider range of countries where the state, far from offering solutions to weak economic development, appeared to be part of the problem. Previously, donors had not given enough thought to how to provide oda in ways that would strengthen rather than weaken the domestic political support for the economic reform programmes they profiled in their assistance efforts (Krueger, Michalopoulos, and Ruttan with Jay 1989: 319). Some writers believe this observation is just as true today apropos the social objectives of poverty alleviation, but that is to jump ahead. In 1989 dramatic political events in Central/Eastern Europe and the USSR opened up exciting prospects of political change. Several countries elsewhere, especially in sub-Saharan Africa, also seemed on the verge of political liberalisation, even transition to democracy. Against this background donors started to envisage a political role for aid. The new thinking was not solely a logical deduction from the flawed experience of pressing for economic reform in the 1980s. It was also an opportunist response to unforeseen political developments external to the aid experience and taking place in the Second World especially.

The argument for better governance was first broached by the World Bank in 1989, in *Sub-Saharan Africa: from Crisis to Sustainable Growth*. The Bank defines governance as the manner in which power is exercised in the management of a country's economic and social resources for development. Good governance is synonymous with sound development management and the administrative capacity to implement policy reform – an essential complement to sound economic policies especially for correcting market failure. In *World Development Report 1991* the Bank also noted that democracies are not necessarily better at initiating economic reform, implementing it effectively or surviving the political fall-out. Even so, democratisation could weaken the political influence of groups having the greatest political and material interests in perpetuating unreformed economic policies and institutions, the ones that produce generally harmful economic distortions. And in any case, many countries that had experienced undemocratic rule also exhibited marked weaknesses of governance; many autocracies have delivered economic failure. Thus, Western political leaders went beyond just governance and elevated a broader conspectus of political reforms embracing political pluralism, multi-party elections and respect for human rights especially. Indeed, the Bank is said to have introduced its own agenda as an anticipatory response to the politicians, reflecting the Bank's wish to keep the initiative and to retain the confidence of important subscribers like the US government. For none of these actors was the intention to replace policy dialogue on economic reform. The aim instead was to render it more effective, by encouraging the circumstances in which governments would show greater political commitment, possibly even a greater political capacity, to improved economic management in general and a more faithful implementation of SAPS in particular, especially in sub-Saharan Africa. Nevertheless, it is also true to say that some bilateral donors have come to maintain that democracy and human rights are themselves instrinsic development ends and are aid policy objectives in their own right.

The modern politics of aid harnesses oda to the revised understanding of the development problematic in at least three ways. First, oda is now made conditional on reforms that comply with the new political and governance agendas, in other words second generation conditionality. Second, specialised help is offered to the construction of institutions and practices of good governance including sound policy analysis, and in the form of democracy assistance, for instance help with staging elections. This is another page in the book of technical assistance. In respect of governance it is given the designation 'capacity-building' (and rebuilding). Third, in countries undergoing political transition concessionary financial transfers that provide generalised support to the balance of payments and public expenditure can strengthen the prospects for democratic consolidation. History tells us that economic turbulence of the sort experienced by countries undergoing structural economic change can disturb the social climate. Social stress procures receptive ears to demagogues and others who would fan the flames of intolerance. This applies especially where sub-national identities built on racial, religious, ethnic or class lines provide organising principles for intergroup competition over scarce resources. The economic shocks of adjustment create losers, some of whom will associate their situation with the political reforms. They may try to reverse the direction of change. The more impatient would attempt a direct assault, such as violent insurrection or military coup; the cunning would seek to gain office via the ballot box only to dismantle the democratic framework, in whole or in part – the story of the brief life of the Weimar Republic in Europe in the 1930s.

The 1990s have been distinctive for development assistance. Donors recognise that financial and other support could be critical to countries that are attempting to democratise against a testing economic backdrop, if the interdependent processes of economic and political reform are not both to founder on the rock of rising social discontent. But is democracy essential to good governance, and are market economies and competitive political systems necessarily related? These and other questions are returned to in Chapter 10.

Conclusion

Over time some countries have graduated from a position of seeming to need oda and others have fallen into that situation. And not only have countries experienced divergent trends in their fortunes, but our understanding of the reasons why countries required developmental assistance, and how oda could be of benefit, has also changed. It has become increasingly multi-layered, and is now infused quite explicitly with a political logic. That logic too will not remain stationary.

Generally speaking, Western experts and not the developing countries have been responsible for much of the foregoing analysis. But there are other propositions advanced in developing countries and outside, to explain why assistance is required. One is that their resource base has been badly depleted by imperialist exploitation; another suggests that latecomers to industrialisation are at a competitive disadvantage internationally; and yet another refers to very young countries who just need help in finding their feet. Countries attempting to replace a command economy by free market principles and to substitute democratic government for authoritarian rule face a particularly daunting multiple challenge which, perhaps, merits special help. An almost universally recognised response is that countries need aid because they are poor, reflected in the fact that poverty alleviation is formally stated to be an objective by many aid agencies.

But why are countries poor, and if aid can help, how can it do so? Different answers offered by development theories originating in the North and development practice in the South have interacted with ideas about aid and the lessons of aid practice. However, the marriage has never been complete. Much aid has shied away from allotting due weight to the political weakness of the poor. Yet we now know that ' "doing development" is a complex and difficult undertaking, especially where addressing poverty means addressing power relationships within the community' (Riddell *et al*. 1995: 12). So, while development paradigms that encapsulate ideologies which serve donors' foreign policy objectives have been influential (Stokke 1996: 30), other advances in our understanding have yet to provide equal influence on the principal philosophies, policies and practice of aid.

Aid's record of attainment appears to have been modest in some parts of the world. Mosley, Hudson and Horrell (1987: 636) said the apparent inability of development aid over more than 20 years to provide a net increment to overall growth in the Third World 'must give the donor community, as it gives us, cause for grave concern'. More recently, an inquiry into oda's future observed that although many theories about aid have been elaborated, together with numerous strategies, 'so far the anticipated effects have not materialised' (Pérille and Trutat 1995: 6). Of course there have been many individual achievements, but why can we not be more generally positive in regard to economic development, especially if idealistic reasons best explain the origins and expansion of aid giving, as Lumsdaine (1993) argues? Is it enough to say that giving aid to countries which are selected by virtue of their weak developmental performance prevents a clear separation of responsibility for failure (and success)? Just as significant could be the imperfect nature of economists' mastery of the secrets of growth and of aid's relationship to such probable determinants of growth as saving and investment. And that is matched only by the confusion political science shows when trying to explain why some countries democratise more successfully than others. The economic and the political processes are both ultimately rather mysterious, and there is still a great deal to learn.

Several possible conclusions could be drawn from oda's record of achievement. One is that aid has sometimes been directed to the wrong places and expended on unsuitable causes, perhaps because non-developmental reasons for giving have been uppermost (OECD 1985: 252). Another is that aid has often taken the wrong forms. Thus the right forms now could include debt buy-back and forgiveness, possibly even the employment of DAC aid to redeem debts owed to non-OECD creditors. For an indebted government's obligation to prioritise debt service actually undermines the donors' purpose of highly conditioned aid. It reduces the incentives to undertake politically risky economic reforms and detracts from the gains that could be used to generate public satisfaction through raised consumption and investment. A third is that oda has not placed enough emphasis on the needs and concerns of ordinary human beings – it has forgotten that people should be considered the subjects as well as objects of development (OECD 1996: 4). A fourth possible conclusion is that all aid is fundamentally flawed: not only is there no way of proving aid promotes development, but there is compelling evidence that, on balance, aid as a general approach can never work.

All these conclusions bar the last have support from within the development assistance community. The trend has been to specify the need for oda in ever more wide-ranging, increasingly detailed and more intrusive ways. The view has been taken that in countries where oda has yet to deliver satisfactory results, the extent and nature of those countries' difficulties have been underestimated. Hence, more research is required. Moreover, the functions that have come to be allotted to oda have included helping to establish the conditions that will enable aid to make a better impact. So, in order to improve the reliability of economic returns from development projects, oda came to be directed at reforms to the policy and institutional environments, specifically the removal of distortions in factor and product markets and improvements in the structure of incentives for wealth creation. Once it became apparent that technical assistance programmes could overwhelm the capacity of states to benefit, the next step seemed to be to develop forms of cooperation that would increase the capacity and help recipient governments manage the assistance. Now, the efficacy of structural adjustment lending is to be redeemed by aid for good governance and political reform. All in all, the aid debates have evolved along the lines of a ladder of causation, ascending from projects to policies and to the way in which countries are governed (Cassen et al. 1994: 82). If the Cold War had not intervened at such an early stage and deranged the policies of major donors towards the developing world, the sequence might have occurred in a different order. But that can only be speculated upon. Indeed, Griffin (1991: 647) believes that without the Cold War there would be no aid programmes anyway, because 'it would have been impossible to generate the domestic political support'.

Repeatedly, support for aid has lived to see another day. Aid's proven ability to sustain changes in our understanding of its role in development is actually more impressive than what we confidently know of its contribution to development. Huntington's (1970–1: 162) analysis was prescient: as weaknesses in the rationale for aid have become apparent, so new arguments for it are produced. The one possible lesson that always seemed unlikely to find favour with the aid community is that there should be a dramatic reduction in total oda. From the earliest days DAC reports have pleaded the inadequacy of world aid pledges. Indeed, the excuse 'too little', for periods that are too short, and 'too late' has been a standard explanation of the failures of 1980s aid-assisted SAPs and by 1995 it was beginning to be heard also in respect of democracy assistance and debt relief. And should anyone still be worried about the possibility of there being too much aid, producing aid dependency, there is Hewitt's (1994: 94) advice that dependency is 'more a result of poor quality (i.e. low investment in capacity building) than of excessive quantity'.

Of course, we should always remember that judgements about the overall worth of aid are just that – judgements. The more favourable judgements can find support in examples of aided countries that have performed relatively well, in economic, social and other valuable directions. Nevertheless, aid has its share of trenchant critics. For them, the most pertinent question is not why some countries still need development assistance, but instead, whether any countries need such aid at all. The practice whereby new aid rationalisations have been manufactured once their predecessors were found to be faulty is interpreted as a defensive stratagem, not a vote of confidence. More critical still are arguments that say oda does a serious disservice to the recipient countries, and that its presence there helps explain why they have not enjoyed more development. The case for aid that dwells on shared donor–recipient interests, and the thesis that donor needs (aid as a 'First World consumption good') make aid necessary, fare not much better. For aid is considered harmful even to the principal providers. These perspectives are examined in the next chapter.

Cases for the prosecution

The kings of Siam are said to have ruined obnoxious countries
by presenting them with white elephants that had to be
maintained at vast expense. Receiving aid is not just like
receiving an elephant but like making love to an elephant; there
is no pleasure in it, you run the risk of being crushed and it
takes years before you see the results. Aid is twice cursed: it
curses him who gives and him who receives.

(Streeten 1976: 22)

Root-and-branch critiques of foreign aid either reject almost any justification for aid or require drastic modifications to customary practice. For
convenience they are grouped here into two broad categories, each one
encompassing various shades and tributaries that cannot be explored in
detail. They are designated the cases from the left and the right. In both,
the anti-aid claims are part of much broader sets of beliefs and propositions about the nature of societies and the working of economies, at sub-
national, national and global levels.

The leftist case made the running earliest, and found favour among some
academics and popular writers in the West, Third World political leaders
and intellectuals. But despite making a prominent contribution to aid debates,
its influence on the policies of major donors has been limited. By the 1980s
the rightist case, whose origins resemble more closely think-tank circles in
the US and Britain, came to exert a more pronounced influence on aid policy and debate in powerful circles. The order of succession is no accident:
'The success of neo-Marxism in discrediting the assumption of the benevol-
ent state paved the way down which the new right moved triumphantly in
the 1980s' (Toye 1993: 144). Arguments for the prosecution suggest that aid
does harm, probably more harm than good to the societies that receive
aid. The net effect could be inevitable. On that basis moral arguments for
aid giving would collapse. What is more, countries providing aid may be
judged to be doing themselves harm, so challenging the other reasons for
aid giving. The two prosecutions' conclusions look similar, but the routes

by which they arrive at them are far apart. That much should be apparent from the following abridgements, whose necessary brevity cannot do justice to the relevant literatures, which are both extensive and intricate (see Riddell 1987: Chapters 5, 11–13).

Prosecution from the left

The leftist prosecution is at its most uncompromising in books with titles like C. Hensman's *Rich Against Poor: The Reality of Aid* (1971) and T. Hayter's *Aid as Imperialism* (1971). It centres on the observation that power resources, wealth and status are distributed very unequally around the world. Economic inequality almost necessarily begets political inequality, which in turn serves to reinforce the social divisions. In this milieu, power is exercised in such a way as to ensure aid's benefits in recipient countries are concentrated on relatively privileged groups – the elites, who include senior political figures and their counterparts in the state bureaucracy and armed forces, successful entrepreneurs in commerce, finance and industry, and large landowners. Less privileged groups such as small peasant farmers and landless labourers, the urban unemployed and lower reaches of the informal sector (as distinct from that sector's 'briefcase businessmen'), and those industrial workers who are outside the 'labour aristocracy', receive at most a small share of the gains. They may even be made worse off.

Some accounts focus mainly on arrangements internal to the aid-receiving countries, while others dwell also on the full spread of international linkages between poles of power and wealth – a difference of approach approximating to what Riddell (1987: 131) calls institutional pessimism and structural theory respectively. Either way, the results reinforce inequalities in both domains, domestic and global. The advanced industrial countries exercise structural power through multilateral organisations and international financial institutions – controlling agendas and disseminating their own values and ideas – as well as more directly through bilateral aid. Any suggestions that poverty's principal causes lie in misfortune, or the will of God, or inadequate resources and cultural backwardness are summarily dismissed. Inequality is an inescapable corollary of the capitalist mode of production, which is exploitative of labour and poor societies specifically.

The ruling elites of developing countries have been able to compensate in part for their domestic unpopularity and flawed legitimacy by their receipts of financial and material aid and the means to prosecute internal security, often on aid-assisted terms. Aid helps underpin the status quo in many ways, for example by enhancing the patronage elites use to purchase support from client groups and by funding projects and programmes that will be particularly close to their interests. Aid means governments are able to spend more on 'bread and circuses', the second being an opiate of the masses. For all these reasons, ruling elites are pleased to acquiesce even in those aid relationships that engender foreign domination and do harm to the prospects of national development. From this point many leftist views place aid in an all-encompassing framework of First World domination of the Third World for primarily economic ends, summed up by the category headings of economic imperialism and neo-colonialism (sometimes called imperialism without colonies). The overlap can be considerable with the dependency perspectives on North–South relations that were ubiquitous in the 1970s especially, and with the notion that Third World countries are being *under*developed as a result of their contact with the international capitalist system. In consequence, so-called developing countries are not really enjoying development, but instead are experiencing at best a form of 'perverse growth' (and many do not even experience that), which has very unequal distributive consequences and is determined externally. DAC oda, rather than being a constructive response to poverty, helps perpetuate the underlying systemic causes, of which poverty is an unavoidable manifestation.

Aid's malign role

The ultimate purpose of DAC aid is to help spread capitalism, to the benefit of the dominant economic and financial interests in the international system. These interests may be conceived both as the advanced industrial countries and such transnational entities as business corporations, a majority of whose shareholders are also based in the OECD countries. Aid is 'in a sense a transfer from taxpayers to private firms and banks within the industrialised countries' (Hayter 1985: 8), to the benefit of the owners of capital in the City of London, on Wall Street and the like.

Take for instance international trade. Project aid has been invested in extractive industries around the world to supply commodities to the richer economies, and in infrastructural developments such as roads and ports that will facilitate the export trade. The result is an increase in the global supply of commodities relative to demand, so cheapening the price. The returns to the producers are correspondingly reduced. The terms of trade deteriorate, and developing countries face pressure to devalue their currencies. Also, aid procurement-tying locks the recipients into purchasing imports at inflated prices, which promise super-profits to the producers. This arrangement extends to the maintenance contracts and spare parts for intermediate and capital goods. Aid-funded imports have been responsible for transferring inappropriate production methods, which demand locally scarce factors of production such as capital and energy but do not maximise the demands on the most abundant resource, which usually is unskilled labour. This is because the technologies and equipment have been designed to meet donor country circumstances. Aid conditionalities that impose import liberalisation undermine some cases of local production anyway. Food aid that comprises non-traditional foodstuffs brings about a taste change and cultivates dependence on imported supplies. Typically, the balance of payments constraint on economic growth and development becomes more, not less, severe.

Aid inflows also displace domestic resource mobilisation. By bringing in subsidised capital or its equivalent in goods and services, aid undermines local incentives to save. To illustrate, Ball believed the Rhee government in South Korea in the 1950s 'followed policies designed to encourage the United States to provide more economic aid that effectively reduced domestic savings' (Ball 1988: 265). Rather than translate into domestic investment, indigenous capital saving takes flight in search of more attractive opportunities in developed countries. The affluent lifestyle of expatriate workers who are employed by aid agencies and conspicuous consumption by the principal local beneficiaries of oda exert an unhelpful demonstration effect, raising the propensity for unproductive consumption by the non-poor. A number of economists have tried to confirm that by supplanting or substituting local saving and helping fund uneconomic public investments, aid inflows often increase rather than reduce the savings constraint on growth and development and have an adverse impact on private investment. Griffin as early as the 1970s (and on several occasions since, for instance Griffin 1986) and Boone (1994) are examples. Other economists have disputed such findings. White (1994), who believes aid on balance promotes investment, notes that the investment is not bound to be productive. The conclusion by Cassen *et al.* (1994: 31) is that answers to the classic questions about the relationships between aid and savings, and aid and growth, will have to await more research into single-country cases based on time-series of disaggregated aid flows.

That one of aid's roles has been to facilitate direct inward investment by multinational companies is a further obvious point of regret to many leftists. Donors like the US have a principled objection to providing oda in competition with international private capital. Aid bargains have been made conditional on allowing foreign companies to enjoy access to local investment opportunities, in some agreements even to the extent of identifying the companies. Symptomatic was the Hickenlooper Amendment (1962–73) to the US Foreign Assistance Act, which threatened automatic sanctions on bilateral aid in the event of delays in the payment of satisfactory compensation for expropriated US property. Parallel legislation in 1972 added similar conditions to US approval of multilateral aid offers. From the early 1980s SAL-type conditionalities have required recipient governments to relax exchange controls. This facilitates an outward drain of dividends and profit repatriation. For many years, Third World socialists and economic nationalists alike were highly suspicious of inward corporate investment, laying charges that ranged from the 'super-exploitation' of cheap labour to the destruction of indigenous enterprise, from denationalisation of their economy to decapitalisation of its financial base.

All in all, closer integration into the unevenly developed international capitalist system gears production structures to meeting the interests and demands of producers and consumers in the rich world, instead of the needs of the majority of people in the Third World. By the same token, Wood (1980: 6) bemoaned the fact that in the developing world aid 'systematically undercuts the possibility of state-controlled development and fosters the structural dependence of the state on the processes of private accumulation'.

Political charges

For many years DAC aid and US aid in particular was intended to perform the express functions of stabilising pro-Western governments, containing the spread of communism and limiting the expansion of Soviet influence. Among many such governments with close US ties were a significant number of personal and military dictatorships with poor human rights records, for instance the Somoza dynasty in Nicaragua from the 1930s to 1979. An even larger number were exceedingly corrupt, including the Marcos presidency in the Philippines (1965–86). Large quantities of US military assistance went to military regimes (as did Soviet military assistance). Economic and military support was aimed at strengthening governments' resistance to agendas judged too left-wing. It was even pressed on governments where local desires to end violent class conflict in order to remove the spur to US intervention might have inclined the political leadership to make accommodation with left-wing opponents, for instance El Salvador in the 1980s. Governments who seemed inclined towards substantial redistributive policies, or friendship with the USSR, were penalised. They found their loan applications to multilateral development banks obstructed, and in many cases bilateral support was provided to their political opponents such as the military in Chile's democratically elected government headed by President Allende (1970–3), a professed Marxist. In the 1980s medical and military supplies were freely sent to armed insurgents like Nicaragua's 'contras' and Jonas Savimbi's UNITA (National Movement for the Total Independence of Angola). Here, aid's immediate objective was not stability but the political destabilisation of incumbent regimes. Instability was judged instrumental to the interrelated purposes of projecting US hegemony and safeguarding capitalism worldwide.

The political accusations against aid have shifted in step with the 1980s introduction of SALs/SAPs – seen to be all of a piece with IMF-inspired stabilisation programmes. The assistance conditionalities seemed bound to make life more difficult for governments of almost every shade, from oppressive to more legitimate regimes. Following the IMF's introduction of fiscal and monetary conditionalities in the early 1970s the terms 'IMF coups' and 'IMF riots' were already commonplace (the alternative proposition that these were truly mismanagement coups and riots, occasioned by the unsustainable financial and economic policies that caused governments to apply for financial support, was barely considered). Now, the sovereignty of Third World states appeared to be compromised all the more heavily, in the interests of global capital and the private international banking system in particular. The net impact was predicted to be more political repression. A chain running from financial crisis, to the imposition of stabilisation and SAPs, increased poverty and then greater social unrest seemed obvious to writers like Barratt Brown (1995: 351 and see also pp. 100–2, 112–13), for whom this entire drama made violence and civil war 'inevitable' in a number of countries. Again, an alternative proposition that serious unrest would be even more likely, and the chances of an authoritarian response greater, in the absence of financial assistance, received short shrift. That the costs of not engaging in economic adjustment could ultimately exceed the costs of adjustment also enjoyed little credence.

Of course, some aid is being granted for modest social programmes. But leftists argue this is only because the West has no interest in seeing the authorities become so repressive that they provoke a genuine revolution. For the most part, at least in Africa, the attempt by the World Bank and bilateral donors to encourage a reduction in state activities only creates 'confusion and anarchy, because, while the power of the old rentier elite was undermined, there was no class of large farmers or of local industrialists to create a new centre of power on the basis of a free market' (Barratt Brown 1995: 127). In this way the donors' present declared intentions to help improve governance and promote democratic political reform are undone. In any case the underlying purpose is not to rebuild states *vis-à-vis* markets, but to prevent failing states becoming too problematic for the market. After all, even free markets need an orderly environment. Thus, aid's modern agenda is said to be to arrange for governments to possess enough governing capabilities and a sufficient veneer of legitimacy to implement the economic reforms that are useful to capital and, not least, are thought likely to facilitate debt repayment.

In sum so far, very little aid reaches the poor. The responsibility lies with a system of political economy that aid helps to keep in being. Far from being a solution to the problems of the Third World's poor, aid makes those problems worse. It addresses, weakly, some of the symptoms but not the underlying causes of poverty. Aid perpetuates the apparent need for aid. The political independence of recipients is compromised too. In one of the relatively few books about oda written in the Third World and published in the West Sobhan (1982: 226) said 'Bangladesh's policy-makers continue to wait upon decisions in Washington, London, Tokyo, Bonn and Paris before they formulate their annual development budgets, announce an import policy, formulate a food policy or even decide how many children should be born'.

Possibly, the damage may go even further. Lenin, in *Imperialism: the Highest Stage of Capitalism* (1917) argued that imperialism functions as a life support system for the advanced industrial capitalist economies. It offsets (if only for a while) what Marx predicted would be an inevitable tendency of the rate of profit to fall. Lenin's thesis was updated by Ghana's first president, Kwame Nkrumah, in *Neo-colonialism: the Last Stage of Imperialism* (1965). Aid, an instrument of neo-colonialism, helps prolong the survival in the West of a socio-economic system whose essential nature is to exploit and alienate the working class. Some of the gains are put towards underwriting the social welfare arrangements and other measures that are designed to pacify such people, impede the formation of revolutionary class consciousness, and reward labour leaders who are prepared to align with mere reformers and more conservative forces. Yet capitalism necessarily inflicts relative impoverishment (even if not absolute immiserisation) on the proletariat and the reserve armies of unemployed, who together make up the majority of society, according to Marx. Whatever delays the final crisis of capitalism will postpone the day when the great mass of people cast off their chains, rise above capitalist forms, and accede to economic, social and political arrangements that are infinitely preferable.

The prescription

An extreme position demands that all aid cease until capitalism has been overthrown or the poor have stormed the citadels of power. An exception would be made for the cancellation of outstanding foreign debts – 'a bonfire of the vanities that would bring to an end the era of foreign aid' (Griffin 1991: 678).

However, just as there are many varieties of socialism so there are socialists who accept there is a case for many kinds of oda, even in the current world system. Social democrats in Western Europe have long been among aid's staunchest supporters – the Scandinavian donors are often cited as evidence of the affinity between a commitment to egalitarian social values at home and support for oda. Stokke (1996: 22) calls their aid humane internationalism. Noël and Thérien (1995) found welfare socialist attributes rather than a welfare state *per se* (which might have conservative political origins) contributes a strong statistical explanation for differences in national aid budgets. The belief that aid can promote economic equality between nations, by curbing the power of private capital and advancing the public sector, is found, for example, in Judith Hart's (Overseas Development Minister in a former Labour government in Britain) *Aid and Liberation: a Socialist Study of Aid Policies* (1973). Many socialists have been positive about *inter alia* aid transfers between governments deemed to be socially progressive (as between Sweden and Tanzania before President Nyerere's retirement in 1985); fraternal aid from the USSR to Cuba; properly managed emergency relief; genuine partnerships between NGOs and grassroots organisations sincerely committed to empowering the poor; aid that expresses solidarity with liberation movements opposing colonialism, capitalist imperialism and apartheid; and aid to feminist movements. The 'soft left' has always campaigned for more oda as well as for systemic reforms, such as severing all links between aid and the international arms trade and forcing the Bretton Woods institutions to give much greater priority to the immediate needs of the poor. A sceptical view of where most of aid's benefits have gone to is consistent with believing that intolerable harm would be done to some poor people by the abolition of oda.

Aid defended

An end to aid is very unlikely to effect the kind of thoroughgoing transformation of Third World countries' domestic arrangements that many
left-wing critics desire, although some aid-dependent governments could
be toppled. While some dictatorships have been kept in power with the
help of DAC oda, others have seen their position erode partly as a result
of the aid connections. Comparative studies have failed to reach firm,
generally agreed conclusions about the impact even of foreign military
assistance on the role of the armed forces in politics, and on the existence
of military government and military-dominated regimes. For instance, while
Rowe (1974) argued that US military assistance increased the likelihood of
coups and enabled military governments to remain in office, Schmitter
(1973: 182) found 'the impact of foreign military aid varies, from highly
significant and positive, to indifferent, to highly significant and negative'.
Fitch (1979: 380) on the one hand recognised the institutionalisation of the
coup in Latin American politics was largely due to increasing profession-
alisation of the armed forces, to which the US military assistance programme made a substantial contribution. But on the other hand he also
reminded us that the principal charge made by radical critics of US military
assistance was responsibility for the persistence of conservative regimes,
not military coups. By the 1980s many of these professionalised militaries
had lost confidence in their ability to govern, especially in the management
of economic affairs, having experienced failure in office and damage to
their institution's public and professional standing. US military assistance
to the region is now relatively minimal.

Political repression has never been confined to countries receiving significant Western aid, and among the aid recipients there are states with
liberal and democratic traditions. The thesis that either externally supported
stabilisation or structural adjustment, or both, require authoritarian rule and
must perpetuate authoritarianism, is false on every count (Remmer 1986;
Haggard and Kaufman 1989; Remmer 1990; Healey and Robinson 1992;
Haggard and Webb 1993; Lindberg and Devarajan 1993). Evidence from
mainly middle income countries in the 1980s indicates that consolidated
democracies compare favourably with non-democratic regimes in regard to
stabilisation; and serious difficulties occurred primarily in only some, not
all, countries undergoing democratic transition. Many countries especially
in Latin America and Eastern Europe have now combined the institutionalisation of democratic procedures and economic adjustment. Democracies
can be better equipped politically to execute policies of fiscal austerity and
economic liberalisation owing to their greater legitimacy, especially in the
'honeymoon period' of a newly elected government, and particularly where
the executive can count on reliable support in the legislature. It also helps
if there is an atmosphere of economic crisis, and causal responsibility for
unfortunate consequences can be externalised to a previous regime or international forces. Democratic feedback mechanisms enable fine-tuning of the

policies and their implementation, and the premium that is placed on ruling by persuasion, together with pressures to consult with a range of groups, can improve the chances that economic reforms will consolidate politically after they have been introduced.

In the 1980s especially the Bretton Woods institutions are said to have encouraged governments to initiate reforms in a technocratic manner and delegate key functions to autonomous bureaucracies – the purpose being to generate credibility in the maintenance of the reform process, thereby securing the people's acceptance and compliance. But notwithstanding the alleged bias towards authoritarianism and the fact that some governments adopted repressive measures to shore up their position, events in several countries ultimately took a different pattern. Where stabilisation and adjustment meet significant popular opposition, autocracies that are politically weak can be as sensitive as democracies, and equally prone to make economically damaging populist gestures (Haggard and Webb 1993; Haggard et al. 1995: 43). In democracies, where discontent aroused by economic reforms may be channelled into forms that do not destabilise the polity, governments try to identify and neutralise opposition to change. In contrast, weak autocracies, whose claims to authority often rest on bribing the people with material contentment, can be more inclined to make policy concessions when faced by determined resistance to economic reform. A fear that the most likely alternative would be violent rejection and political overthrow is responsible; for the costs of losing office can compare quite unfavourably with electoral defeat in a democracy. Zambia's one-party state for instance vacillated in applying externally directed conditionalities in the 1980s. Even this did not prevent the regime being terminally undermined by mass discontent that was fuelled by the stuttering reform process (arguably, the circumstances which brought about the conditionalities should be held mainly responsible). Anyway, the interest shown by the 1990s aid agenda in democratisation and human rights surely has to be judged an advance on aid to dictators, even if the motives are not ethically pure.

Needless to say, the consequences for Third World development of incorporation into the international capitalist system are strongly contested, even among Marxists. Warren (1980), rejecting the main burden of dependency thinking, argued imperialism declines as world capitalism grows. Countries like Indonesia and China in the last 20 years have displayed strong economic dynamism concomitant with closer integration into the world economy, regardless of aid. If theories of economic imperialism and neo-colonialism have meaningful application in the final years of the twentieth century, then for many developing countries oda is an insignificant aspect relative to other, more salient features of globalisation like private capital flows. While it is true to say that local cultures and ancient customs have been, and are being, changed the world over, once again, aid's contribution is probably modest compared to other factors whose impact is not contingent on the existence of aid. The way in which aid inflows tend to carry alien ideas (which are then manipulated, transmuted and, possibly, eventually ignored) is not peculiar to capitalist aid. Brautigam (1994) showed how political and cultural ideologies flowed with aid from communist China to African countries, and then changed (towards a greater emphasis on economic performance) in the post-Mao period.

Radical leftists did not show where major initiatives in the developing world to refuse or abandon aid would come from. Collective debt default, mooted by Fidel Castro and others in the mid-1980s, failed to materialise. In any case, the economic viability and social peace of OECD countries would not be troubled much if aid rejection had caught on. The welfare state, far from being bolstered by the profits of aid-engendered neo-colonialism, is currently being trimmed in several countries that are exhibiting growing disparities in income and wealth, notwithstanding economic growth and rising general prosperity. Britain is a prime example. The mood is increasingly to question whether aid is in the donors' interests, not to see it as a prop to existing social relations of production. Fowler's (1992: 25–6) speculation that aid's future as a global system of social welfare may be assured, because the interests of Northern-based capital demand placation of the Third World underclass, could be doubly unconvincing. Indeed, far from underwriting First World prosperity, many LLDCs look like becoming even more marginal to the fortunes of international capital. Such countries may have little choice but to experiment with indigenous pathways to development and greater self-reliance – a course they have neglected in the past, ignoring the urgings of many leftists who recommended it as a deliberate strategy to combat dependence and underdevelopment.

The more deterministic of the negative claims made about aid's effects in a capitalist context have been refuted by the practical evidence. Some aid has benefited some poor people, and the DAC's record here is not demonstrably inferior to aid from communist states. Much aid has indeed failed the chronically poor, and important reasons for this might well be connected with capitalism. But if the abolition of capitalism is truly a necessary precondition for ending dire poverty, then the implications for action are much more profound and far-reaching than the future of aid. In reality, the power of capital, which the left has always warned against, continues to grow, and capitalism looks to be here to stay, for the foreseeable future anyway. On that understanding, there is much to be said for continuing existing inquiries into how oda could be made more beneficial to the most needy.

The tide of political events in the last two decades has moved a long way from a traditional left-wing agenda. The same is true of much intellectual discourse. This does not mean left-wing perspectives on aid and development do not still abound (see for example the journal *Review of African Political Economy* and books published by Pluto Press). And the language of dependence still permeates aid discourse. But the high water mark of dependency theory as a general world view is well past, its logical flaws and empirical weaknesses having been exposed. The 'dependency school' has imploded. Now, some of the central features formerly associated with leftist doctrine are regarded as archaic even by many self-styled socialists. An example is development models that rely heavily on central direction and control. Of course, the ideal of a socially responsible state, which guards the social justice that neither the free market nor civil society have yet shown they can supply, is persistent. But in aid and development, elements of the non-governmental sector, formerly reproached for trading conscience money to suit rich donors, are now presented as strong potential allies of social transformation and the self-determination of the poor. The political debate generally and more specifically in respect of aid has moved on, both within and outside the left. Over the last 15 years very different siren voices have been raised against oda, in keeping with the growing ascendancy of the political right.

Prosecution from the right

The 1980s witnessed something of a sea change in government attitudes towards the state's role in economic affairs, following changes in the political complexion of the executive in major DAC countries, especially the US, Britain and Germany. A neo-liberal agenda displaced the idea of state planning and intervention as a nostrum for renewing economically sustainable growth. Although not a completely new contribution, the rightist case against aid was much more in tune with this emerging ethos. As with the leftist prosecution, it encompasses a range of positions. Toye (1993: 77) observes that for many of what he calls counter-revolutionaries in the field of development economics (who stress the benefits of economic markets and repudiate controls), foreign aid can be countenanced, if it induces recipients to make approved changes in economic policy. Others like Bauer, one of the most widely cited writers on the right, are tempted to condemn aid almost unreservedly (Bauer's thoughts on aid were first published as early as 1966, in an Institute of Economic Affairs Occasional Paper).

Bauer shares with the others the proposition that economic welfare is maximised by the free play of market forces and private enterprise. The state tends to be a dead weight. It is a net consumer of resources. This is a very old idea (Bentham recommended the retort Diogenes reputedly made to Alexander the Great – 'stand out of my sunshine' – as the correct attitude towards government). Unfortunately, according to Bauer aid encourages governments to try to do too much, and so ends up causing harm (see also Ryrie 1995). Bauer singles out aid's politicising effects. First, aid is politically determined by donors seeking foreign policy objectives. Second, and no less important, aid itself encourages the politicisation of economic life in the recipient countries. This, and aid's apparent inability to address the real causes of economic backwardness, mean that 'whatever they (donors) gave, whatever they are giving and whatever they will give is useless' (Bernard Lugan, cited from an interview given with *Paris Match* and reported in Zambia's *Post* newspaper, 10 March 1995). Bauer's own account is even more dire, for aid can be 'worse than useless' (*The Times*, 5 February 1980).

For one reason, aid encourages *dirigisme*, or big government (necessarily bad) and excessive or inappropriate intervention in the economy. After all, most oda goes to governments, so increasing the rewards of public office: power and access to wealth. The bureaucracy expands. Talented and ambitious people are lured away from entrepreneurial activities that would be more productive in economic terms. Rent-seeking behaviour displaces profit-seeking enterprise. Aid flows themselves create bureaucracies just for the purpose of mediating aid relations, and may be funded from oda on both sides.

Furthermore, aid provides opportunities to indulge in policies that are economically irrational but politically attractive. An example is centralised planning. The experience of former communist states now confirms how misguided this can be. But Bauer attacked it even in the years when Western development experts were recommending planning to developing countries as tangible evidence of their political commitment to development – the OECD (1962: 15) said the assessment of aid requirements would 'of course, be facilitated by the formulation of comprehensive development plans by developing countries', a task often conducted as part of technical assistance. In another example of oda's bad effects Bauer mentioned nationalistic postures towards foreign corporate investors; Ryrie (1995) too argues aid has depressed private capital inflows to some countries. Yet these sources can offer so much more than just finance assistance, because of their managerial and technical skills. All these and other features of the dirigiste state are agreeable to Third World political elites because they mean power over society – indeed, capital aid has 'released governments from accountability to their people as taxpayers' (Morton 1996: 51). While not all of the distortionary, growth-inhibiting policies originate with aid, aid encourages their survival by concealing harmful side-effects and underwriting the costs. As donors came to press for neo-liberalism in the 1980s, Third World governments who professed to be unpersuaded of its merits were rewarded with assistance, ostensibly as an inducement to change their behaviour. Failure to implement aid conditionalities (some of them unenforceable anyway) was usually followed by a further round of conditional aid offers.

Third World governments put aid-maximising strategies ahead of wealth creation. They are encouraged to externalise responsibility for their economic failings onto the international community, even when the real causes begin at home. The rich countries are embarrassed into providing aid, and the real causes of economic backwardness go unaddressed. Whereas leftists argue aid undermines the basis of self-reliance, rightists see aid suffocating the spirit of self-help. The International Freedom Foundation (UK) (1990: 5) is illustrative: 'Redistributing money from first world taxpayers to third world recipients merely encourages a psychology of passive dependency rather than a pro-active enterprise mind set'! Aid cannot make development happen in the absence of such preconditions as the right motivations, relevant aptitudes and skills. Where these are present, aid will be surplus to requirements, and could actually pose a threat. Humanitarian relief may be more defensible but is best left to non-political aid charities. And even they risk pauperising their beneficiaries. Evidence culled by a range of investigators suggests even the imposition of well-intentioned humanitarian aid by NGOs can be worse than no aid, when it destroys such qualities as resourcefulness, determination and adaptability in the affected communities, for example refugees (Harrell-Bond 1986: 364). Once again, then, aid is not a solution but a part of the problem. What is more, it can harm the donor countries too.

Not in the donors' interests

Of particular interest here are practices encrusting aid programmes that introduce yet further distortions. In general the effects on recipients have tended to attract most of the attention (especially from the left). It will be helpful to visit these first, before turning to the alleged consequences for donor countries. Receipts of untied aid can lead to overvalued currencies, bias trade composition and challenge production structures in ways similar to the 'Dutch disease' (from the distorting and adverse affects the rise of natural gas production had on the Dutch economy), which comes from the windfall earnings of a natural resource. The country's foreign exchange gap widens in consequence. But, as has already been noted, procurement-tied aid too has disadvantages. A combination of methods increasingly adopted by some donors from the late 1970s onwards consists of mixed or blended credits and associated financing. Here, aid softens the overall terms of a loans package that includes credit advanced on commercial terms. These practices and tying generally can mean a thinly disguised export subsidy to companies and industrial sectors, with the intention of securing international market share. Watkins (1995a: 195–7) cites a World Bank estimate that untying all aid would generate economic benefits to developing countries of up to $4 billion per year. He noted donors were using aid budgets to promote their commercial interests in an increasingly aggressive manner at the very time when developing countries are liberalising their trade regimes, as part of the execution of SAPs. In fact, since the Uruguay round of the General Agreement on Tariffs and Trade (GATT) began in 1986 over 60 developing countries have unilaterally lowered their import barriers, 26 have joined GATT and by 1995 a further 20 were in the process of acceding. But what about the implications for donor countries?

Leftists are not the only ones to criticise the aid procurement practices, and while rightists particularly question whether the donor countries' economic welfare really benefits, their doubts are shared by many other economists. These sceptics argue the practices reduce pressure on business to compete on equal terms. They encourage a redirection of managerial energies towards lobbying the state for help from the aid budget. Such consequences have been overt in Italy for example. In Britain, Toye (1991) drew attention to a coincidence between the concentration on a few companies of orders part financed by the Aid and Trade Provision (ATP) – worth around 10 per cent of the aid budget – and corporate contributions to the funds of political campaign groups associated with the ruling party. Between 1978 and 1985 five firms accounted for more than half of ATP finance, and fifteen firms absorbed 83 per cent. Overall the effects can brake industrial and economic adjustment to changes in the global economy. In theory, economic resources will continue to be employed sub-optimally, although in practice the next most likely alternative could be unemployment. Following the criticisms by Mosley (1987: Chapter 7) and Toye (1991), Morrissey (1993: 80) also finds mixed credits seem not to generate the claimed benefits for donors. Moreover, they tend to displace funds from the normal aid budget and diminish pro-developmental allocations. The aid is biased away from the SILICs and towards countries that prospectively offer good markets for commercial exports, capital goods especially. Some large well-known projects funded in this way cannot be justified as development priorities, even there. Although in the 1990s the OECD has sought to tighten the rules on blended credits and exclude the wealthier developing countries from eligibility, scope remains for donors to avoid and evade the guidelines. The most pervasive general forms of aid tying, which Jepma (1996) found do not benefit donor country welfare in the long run, persist even though the increasing transnationalisation of business firms means governments can less easily 'fix' the producer rent from export subsidies in their own countries.

Rightists, while they may disagree with leftists who maintain that DAC oda serves the systematic imposition of a liberal world trade regime, endorse their view that the current regime is far from freely competitive. However, they do not believe the regime benefits unreservedly the OECD countries, just as they do not agree that a completely free regime would be bad for developing countries by confining their economic participation to a purely static form of comparative advantage. Instead, rightists and others have seen the aid programmes particularly of European countries and Japan to be one side of a tacit bargain. The other side is the economic protectionism these countries maintain, and which retards growth of their own economic welfare in the long run. Here, aid offers weaken a developing country's political resistance to the trade barriers and other, non-aid, distortions of international product and factor markets that are perpetrated by OECD countries in the interests of some particular interests only. Japan's protection of its rice farmers and the EU's CAP are prime examples. A calculation published in 1985 claimed CAP abolition would raise the developing world's income by 2.9 per cent (Ryrie 1995: 24), significantly enhancing the market for Northern exports. In factor markets, developing countries acquiesce in controls on international labour migration (with exceptions for a 'brain drain' to OECD countries totalling more than 1.5 million skilled and professional people), while being encouraged to allow free movement of private capital. While the value of migrant worker remittances already amounts to between one and two times all oda, UNDP estimates indicate that current restrictions deny developing countries at least a further $250 billion in incomes annually.

Protectionism takes many forms, from traditional tariff escalation which discriminates progressively against commodity-based imports as they embody increasing levels of added value, to bogus measures of environmental conservation. The institutionalisation of protectionism illustrates how effective special interests (chiefly producer groups) can be at influencing public policy, especially in comparison with the generalised mass of consumers (who will pay higher prices, and whose freedom of choice is artificially restricted as a result of the measures). An example is the long-running Multi-Fibre Arrangement (MFA) of quotas for developing country textile and clothing exports to Northern markets, whose origins ultimately lie in the Short-Term Cotton Textile Arrangement that was intended to cap Japanese exports, in 1961. The UNDP believes the MFA costs developing countries $50 billion annually (from Watkins 1995a: 137). Similarly, DAC taxpayers underwrite the costs of subsidising their countries' exports by means of procurement-tied aid, which also mainly benefits certain producers in the first instance. In all these cases economic movement towards an optimum pattern of resource allocation is slowed down.

Economics aside, rightists are not alone in pointing out other ways in which aid can do a disservice to donor interests. Many observers note that it can breed Southern discontent. The poll of African and Malagasy opinion leaders (T.G. 1990) held in 1989 found that 55 per cent of respondents regarded aid as a disguised form of exploitation, and 75 per cent thought it primarily benefited donors. Aid is said to encourage developing countries to believe that donors feel a sense of guilt, conveying an admission of causal responsibility for world poverty. To Bauer, the very concept of the Third World is a product of the developed countries' willingness to offer aid. Although that view is somewhat idiosyncratic, it leads us to think seriously about the other consequences for international politics. For example, Sobhan (1982: 7), writing about Eastern Pakistan, shows how the idea that a sovereign Bangladesh could realise a share of aid commensurate with its needs, by establishing *direct* contact with donors, became 'an article of faith with the national leadership'. It encouraged the break away from Pakistan. That unsettled the West's diplomatic relations in the region. While many new states have been established complete with an aid dowry from their former colonial power, some like Namibia and successor states to the USSR and Yugoslavia began life with considerable debts, including debts from past concessionary inflows (as in Bangladesh). We could well expect new and old countries alike to be upset about the harm they sustain from foreign aid interventions that perform badly because the donors gave insufficient forethought, experimented recklessly, or pursued purely selfish ends, or simply made honest mistakes. For the recipients then to be blamed for the failure of aid, as so often happens, must rub salt into the wounds, especially when they are saddled with an obligation to repay loans.

For all these reasons aid dialogues can turn into a source of friction in inter-state relations. In Johnson's (1970: 12–13) words, an 'alleged partnership formed out of the rich man's uneasy conscience and the poor man's resentful need is likely to disintegrate in mutual recrimination – as the aid relationship has indeed been doing'. A reliance on aid has provoked governments to look for ways of demonstrating they are not captured by their principal donor(s), if only to underpin exercises in state-building and garner legitimation at home. This has happened even, and perhaps especially, where aid has been part of the international recognition that quasi-statehood made necessary if domestic political weaknesses were not to prove fatal. Again, the moral is that aid can turn into an irritant rather than always generating goodwill for donors. This seems most likely when donors try to use aid overtly as an instrument of power politics, but is not confined to these situations. Bureaucratic difficulties in aid relations can produce similar effects. Sobhan maintains that Bangladesh's aid relationship with the Soviet bloc bred considerable frustration on both sides, for this very reason (Sobhan 1982: 138). The principle of aid conditioning and the conditionalities themselves provide obvious opportunities for rancour, more so as the conditionalities take on increasingly political dimensions.

To sum up, aid does not always dissolve North–South conflict and it can be a contributory cause. A substantial end to concessionary flows might improve relations. That would not guarantee economic uplift in former aid recipients, but development would probably not be harmed. Moreover, the funding of oda and of aid administration infringes the liberty of taxpayers and poses a disincentive to wealth creation in donor countries. Hence, there is scope for economic welfare to increase on all sides, from a reduction of aid.

Case not proven

The economic case advanced by rightists, having been prominent in recent times, merits several observations, both of the general theory and its specific application to aid.

First, many economists argue that even if theoretical analysis indicates the pure market model of perfect competition would work best for all countries in an ideal world (and not all economists subscribe to this), the underlying economic assumptions are highly limiting. They are far removed from reality and do not reflect the practical conditions in developing countries – conditions which mean that insensitive attempts to enforce neoliberal prescriptions will fail and could cause considerable harm. Moreover, powerful forces in the North have caused the international economy to depart substantially from the free market model of perfect certainty and information, and differences in initial endowments inevitably impact on the outcomes of international exchange and bargaining. The situation seems unlikely to change dramatically, notwithstanding the progressive erosion

of tariff barriers to trade since 1945 and the much increased speed of information flows. The elimination of concessionary flows could worsen rather
than mitigate the prevailing direction of bias, to the disadvantage of many
Third World countries.

Second, while a number of countries have prospered in recent times
without the benefit of substantial oda, any notion that aid must be fatal to
development can be easily refuted. It denies credit where credit is due.
Economies like those of South Korea and Taiwan, which everyone recog-
nises have been among the most successful, were substantial aid recipients
(the former received $8 billion and $5.5 billion in US military and economic assistance between the end of the Korean war and 1983). Other
economic success stories are China and Indonesia, who are major aid recipients. All these countries are generally acknowledged to have a relatively cred-
itable record in tackling absolute poverty, although inequality has increased
markedly in China in recent years. Even Africa has success stories, Botswana
for example. To ignore such accumulated experience is far less sensible
than to seek to learn from the circumstances in which aid can be shown to
have been beneficial.

Third, dirigisme has not been exclusive to aid-receiving countries and
the abolition of oda alone would not guarantee its permanent demise. In
terms of the economic involvement of states, more important than their
size is what they try to achieve, and how they go about it. Rather than
recommend a rolling back of the frontiers of the state, writers like Leftwich
(1994) believe that a more appropriate model for some countries could be
the developmental state – a state that features a strong political impulse to
pursue developmental objectives, and whose institutional structures and
political objectives are developmentally driven. Such states make wise and
effective interventions to correct endogenous (i.e. non-policy-induced)
market failures. The developmental state is given credit for some of the
most successful examples of economic development in the last half century,
notably in East Asia; and Japan appears to be a spokesman for something
like it, in World Bank circles for example. Some commentators believe
worries about regional instability and military threat provided an important stimulus. Nevertheless, there is a general inference that some other
developing countries should take a leaf from this book, even though dis-
carding the less appealing authoritarian traits of certain exemplars.

The state, then, would guarantee basic infrastructures and supply the
essential public goods that private agents who are often wary of long gesta-
tion periods, and alert only to market incentives and particular gain, will systematically underprovide. After all, classical liberals showed no qualms about
acknowledging that government might have to provide non-excludable
public goods, where the benefits cannot be restricted to paying customers,
or where non-payers can be denied access only with great difficulty and at
excessive expense. Aid can help poor governments perform these useful
tasks. The World Bank agrees, and in addition has argued (in *World Development Report 1991* for instance) that sound economic reasons make investment

in people by way of basic health care and education worthwhile forms of public expenditure, and a suitable object of increased international assistance. Market solutions are not bound to satisfy the most minimal of basic needs of the vulnerable and chronically poor. There are good reasons apart from economic ones for public agency to ensure the supply of essential social goods and environmental goods like safe water and proper sewerage, and to provide these if necessary by default of adequate alternative provision.

Fourth, there is the apparent failure of OECD countries closely to follow all of the precepts contained in the neo-liberal agenda. For example, public spending in Britain has risen inexorably in real terms – at an average annual rate of 1.8 per cent since 1979, when a right-wing government came to power – to over 40 per cent of GDP. The equivalent ratio is significantly higher in wealthier economies like Germany and France, and in Sweden government spending is two thirds of GDP. Public sector deficits exceeding 5 per cent are quite common. Indeed, this phenomenon largely explains why gross national saving as a proportion of GDP has fallen from an average of 25 per cent in 1973 to less than 20 per cent in 1993. The gross accumulated public debt of OECD economies has risen from an average of 42 per cent of nominal GDP in 1980 to 71 per cent in 1994 (125 per cent in Italy). On projected trends, by 2030 national debt will double in France and Germany and treble in Japan.

In Britain, an increase in public debt to fund consumption has combined with low public investment and a rundown of state assets to such an extent that the public sector is close to technical bankruptcy (total asset value exceeded by financial liabilities). But among OECD countries state aids to industry are also still in vogue, such as Germany's state-backed guarantees to commercial bank loans. In 1996 the EU gave approval to the British government's plan to offer £71 million to the US-owned Jaguar car company, and in the same year £200 million worth of grants were offered by Welsh development authorities to the Korean company LG, in return for inward investment said to be worth £1.7 billion. In the EU as a whole over £80 billion annually is spent on official support, including around £32 billion of financial help to manufacturing industry. Apparently, more than 50 per cent of the population of the EU receive some kind of financial aid from Brussels (*Financial Times*, 7 November 1996). Of course, one plausible interpretation is that these departures do not render the more pure neo-liberal prescriptions any less sound, and may be economically tolerable only in rich societies. Hence they are not a good guide to others. Even so, neo-liberal platforms do face a credibility problem when preached from relatively successful DAC economies whose argument seems to be 'do as I say and not as I have done' (and, in some respects, continue to do).

Fifth, the burden of aid budgets borne by donor countries should be kept in perspective. Not only do they claim very minor portions of central government spending (in Britain, less than 1.5 per cent) and public expenditure, but the staffing of most bilateral aid agencies is very spartan.

Japan's Overseas Economic Cooperation Fund numbers as few as 330 personnel; at around 1500 persons the staff complement of Britain's Overseas Development Administration is less than Oxfam's and is projected to fall to around 1000 by 1999. As aid budgets are pruned, the savings could just as easily be put towards other, politically more fashionable areas of public spending that are no more defensible in economic or social terms, than be used to effect a slight reduction in 'big government'. In any case, the levying of taxes to finance oda need not always depress economic activity, as people may work harder to achieve their targets for net disposable income. Tax cuts can actually effect a reduction in hours worked where an increasing value is placed on leisure, which is characteristic of most societies as they become more affluent.

Sixth, having come to prominence in the 1980s the rightist critique of aid then lost some of its force, leading Cassen et al. (1994: 192) to conclude: 'if asked whether aid has been a friend or foe of market forces, one would have to answer, on balance, a friend'. This is because the criticisms began to be overtaken by developments in oda and official finance, some of which they accelerated or helped put in motion. Three developments worth mentioning briefly are: donor attempts to explore ways of routing oda through non-governmentalised channels and away from governments; the expansion of mechanisms whereby official and other non-concessionary resource flows can promote development; the design of aid packages and conditionalities that should enhance the working of economic markets, through making states not just leaner but fitter. Take each in turn.

In the DAC's 1987 *Development Cooperation Report* (OECD 1988: 25) there is an admission that aid agencies 'have not always found it easy to translate funding into help for the private sector', especially for small and medium sized businesses. Now, an increasingly favoured route channels oda via NGOs based in the North to NGOs in the South and even to the latter directly (see Chapter 9). Also, oda is offered to governments on condition that they liberate space in the development process for indigenous NGOs, in particular using them to deliver a range of quasi-public services. This signals to government bureaucracies that they too must be cost-competitive, although some commentators believe there is now a danger of pushing the simplistic motto 'NGO good, state bad' too far (Meyer 1992; Edwards 1994). Much concessionary finance that is negotiated in the first instance with public sector institutions is subsequently made available to private entrepreneurs, for example foreign exchange that is conveyed by SALs and sold on at currency auctions. So long as it does not encourage the formation of cosy patron–client relationships the practice whereby financial intermediaries in developing countries lend on the oda can help private entrepreneurship. Successful schemes can be devised notwithstanding Ryrie's (1995: 60–4) conviction that *government* development banks have hampered market-based financial systems and domestic savings mobilisation.

In the first half of the 1990s the World Bank has been served notice especially by the US that its loans must further private as well as public sector initiatives, and do so without crowding out alternative private sources of development finance. This will mean increasing the profile of the International Finance Corporation (IFC), which accounts for around 10 per cent of World Bank group lending, and could lead to budget reductions for the IDA. More analysts may come to share Ryrie's (1995) view that official loans for private sector development on market-like terms, where the recipients could not borrow directly from market sources, offer the most suitable form of multilateral aid to an increasing number of developing regions.

In another example, the European Bank for Reconstruction and Development (EBRD), founded in 1990 with the purpose of stimulating capital flows to projects in Central/Eastern Europe and the former USSR, is permitted to place no more than 40 per cent of its investment in public sector initiatives (the US initially opposed even this amount). The principal subscribers (who include the EU and European Investment Bank as well as governments) agreed to a phased doubling of the authorised capital to £17 billion, in 1996. Although the bank's charter allows a special fund to be created for making soft loans, there is little prospect this will be developed. Instead, pressure is already building from the US especially for the bank to begin planning the graduation of its stronger clients from EBRD loans, into the world of private capital only. Two further illustrations of the general trend was an intergovernmental agreement in 1995 to set up a multilateral Bank for Economic Cooperation and Development in the Middle East and North Africa, and continued US opposition to suggestions that China and India be permitted to borrow from the soft-loan Asian Development Fund. Meanwhile, several bilateral donors like Germany, the US (Overseas Private Investment Corporation) and Britain (whose Commonwealth Development Corporation now has a total portfolio over $2 billion) have their own public development finance bodies. Their aim is to catalyse private sector investment by making non-concessionary advances. However, it should not be forgotten that even more conventional oda to governments can have the effect of reducing the relative economic displacement enjoyed by states *vis-à-vis* markets, by improving the recipient countries' chances of attracting commercial capital into private sector activities – the intention of virtually all donors today.

Then there are the first- and second-generation aid conditionalities of the 1980s and 1990s, which in some countries have prompted substantial economic liberalisation, the elimination of price distortions and divestment of state-owned enterprises. The conditioning of oda, along with assistance to good governance (also intended to further the prospects of economic reform), helps solve the 'orthodox paradox' in its various aspects. That term has been used in different ways to describe a number of puzzles: why should states dismantle an interventionist economic regime that underpins their own pre-eminence and provides opportunities for rent-seeking behaviour by the political elite? How can collective action which implements public policy, a vehicle for state aggrandisement, serve the seemingly contradictory cause of marketisation? Do not some states need to be strengthened first, if they are to be capable of executing the neo-liberal policy agenda effectively? The objective of a more compact state should not be confused with a more feeble state. Similarly, good government is not synonymous with less government. A dynamic private sector and effective performance by NGOs benefits from stable and appropriate legal and financial frameworks provided by a competent public administration, and from government action that remedies market distortions and market failures. There is a '*contradiction* between market relaxation and the contraction of states that are initially small and weak' (Lipton 1991: 23). And van de Walle (1995: 133) argues that in Africa the fine-tuning of SALs/SAPs is much less urgent than the creation of developmental public institutions – 'not only a *sine qua non* of sustained economic growth in the region, but also a key to the consolidation of its new democracies'. Similar news comes out of Russia, where Zhukov (1995: 330) claims the weakness of the state and absence of a modern bureaucracy are probably the most serious obstacles to the success of pro-market democratic reforms. Thus, there can be no abstract formula proving that for all circumstances the downsizing of the public sector is more relevant than the rehabilitation of the machinery of government.

The aforegoing does not constitute an argument for the developmental state in the East Asian mould. However, there is a broadly shared understanding in the donor community that assistance for 'capacity building' is a market-favouring strategy in some instances. This applies not only in brand new states, but also failed or failing states, and overstretched interventionist states as well. Only then can the state become a part of the solution to the economy's problems, instead of being a source of economic problems and a major headache in its own right. Technical assistance as well as aid conditionalities are currently being deployed to this end. Examples include advising on systems of tax collection, where improvements should help finance necessary public expenditures such as on law and order, national security and social safety nets in ways that are non-inflationary, do not create excessive public debt, and do not absorb too much private finance. A good candidate is Pakistan, where only 100,000 registered income tax payers exist in a population exceeding 130 million. Another is Russia, where the federal authorities' tax revenues plummeted to 11.1 per cent of GDP by the first half of 1996, prompting the IMF to withhold the release of tranched loan finance (an estimated capital flight of $60 billion from Russia in the last five years, most of it illegal, adds piquance). In 1994 three Nordic donors suspended balance of payments support to Tanzania in order to encourage the authorities to redress their failure to collect up to $120 million owing in taxes. The ability to collect taxes is a defining feature of the state, and as Morton (1996) argues, the establishment of a tax nexus can be as significant as universal suffrage in leading society to insist on proper accountability by government for its actions. Aid is also helping to establish commercial law, the rule of law and judicial autonomy – institutions that can offer guarantees to private property and help safeguard the environment for responsible investors from influence by organised crime. Strengthening administrative systems against corruption has also become a favourite donor objective. For corruption increases transaction costs of the private sector. It reduces confidence in governments and in their attempts to liberalise the workings of the economy.

Finally, in regard to the diplomatic goals of friendship and goodwill, the fact that aid relations have persisted for so long places the incidence of ill feeling in perspective. For sure there are cases of disappointment, even resentment regarding donors' conduct and a perceived lack of generosity, but more often than not, the web of other and mutually advantageous points of contact survives intact. Anyway, countries that are so aid dependent as to be 'vassal states', Mozambique for example (Plank 1993), have no choice but to evolve a *modus vivendi* with donors. The same could even be said of the donor community when it becomes so embroiled in a country like Mozambique, for there is little scope to abandon the connection in a responsible fashion complete with honour and reputation intact. And in the matter of trade, aid is neither sufficient nor essential to the maintenance of an international trade regime that grants protectionist favours to certain OECD countries. Indeed, in the case of some EU aid to ACP partners the key now is to compensate them for relinquishing their formerly *privileged access* to the EU market (for bananas for example), in the face of accelerating trade liberalisation. Arguably, the power of the G7 countries to determine the global trade regime is eroding anyway, due to shifts in economic activity and trade patterns worldwide (Asia now accounts for a quarter of world trade, for instance), although most SILICs will probably not be the major beneficiaries.

Conclusion

Logic does not allow both the radical left- and right-wing critiques of aid to be valid in their entirety, despite elements of common ground. Their more sweeping claims tend to be mirror images of one another and are mutually exclusive, for instance the contrasting claims about the merits of the market and about oda's effects on state economic involvements (Riddell 1987: 54). Both sets of critiques could be wrong in many respects. Just as likely is that the different perspectives each contain part-truths and offer valuable insights that need to be qualified, in greater or lesser measure. They would then be endorsed by the broad centre ground that cannot be placed in either the leftist or rightist camp. The substantial and well-informed surveys of oda by Riddell (1987) and Cassen *et al.* (1994) for instance show its developmental impact has been so varied that none of the sweeping assertions are wholly convincing. In short, 'blanket theoretical criticisms of aid are unfounded and can be rejected' (Riddell 1987: 177).

Moreover, over the years public policies for oda have adapted in part to some of the criticisms, as well as profited from the advice of its supporters.

Thus Mosley (1987: 107) for example found it was difficult to discover support anywhere, *particularly in recent years*, for the second prong of Bauer's famous proposition that aid does not augment resources, merely centralises power. And according to Cassen *et al.* (1994: 199), the critics who say aid is anti-market 'sound increasingly like prisoners of history'. At the very time in the early 1990s when the volume of aid money was reaching a peak, more countries than ever were moving (at variable rates) away from state-centric strategies of development, including countries in the region that had been most wedded to a command economy. Neither of the general cases for the prosecution has yet finished off oda, and the competing pressures against aid and its developmental intentions have been mutually self-cancelling to some degree. Thus in Britain in the 1980s, the right's objections to state economic intervention helped neutralise the business lobby's designs for a larger but more commercially dominated aid programme (Morrissey, Smith and Horesh 1992). So far, aid has demonstrated a capacity to survive. Apart from anything else, institutional inertia and vested interests in donor and recipient countries have seen to that. The next step, then, is to look more closely at some of these central players.

Third World, Second World: aid's other half

In the vast literature on aid many books give pride of place to donors, their policies, their projects and their programmes. Much of the critical comment too focuses on the Western aid providers. Todaro (1994: 540) rightly notes that considerably more attention has been paid to the motives and purposes of the donors than to why developing countries accept aid. Yet, not only is the aid-receiving universe the more populous and comprised of many more states, but without a market for aid there would be no supply. Although we do not go beyond drawing attention to the skewed coverage, this chapter commences with aid's destination before the principal sources are introduced. First, however, the point should be recorded that although around 20 OECD countries now account for over 95 per cent of all oda, aid from other parts of the world has featured strongly in the history of aid.

Moreover, aid has often been viewed in the West as primarily a feature of North–South relations. But now that must be broadened, to include support by DAC countries to Central and Eastern Europe, Russia included. Even this picture is incomplete, on two counts. First, it masks conflict within the North over such matters as burden sharing between donors, the clash of opinions over the right balance to strike between bilateralism and multilateralism, and the competition between donors for the most highly prized aid opportunities, such as those offering lucrative commercial potential. Second, it does not acknowledge the South–South dimensions, for example competition between developing countries for shares of world aid (which may retard beneficial progress towards greater collective self-reliance), and their cooperation in regional forums and other ventures on aid-assisted joint projects. Furthermore, countries in what used to be called the Second and Third Worlds once provided over a third of world aid.

Partnerships in aid

Today, as many as 180 countries and territories receive foreign aid. In recent years the new additions have easily outnumbered the states who have departed the ranks or are close to graduating. Around 50 of the countries are in sub-Saharan Africa, which has been responsible for an increasing share of total assistance – up from 27.9 per cent in 1982–3 to 35 per cent in 1994 – a real terms increase for most of the period. Asia's proportion was overtaken in the second half of the 1980s, and now stands at around 30 per cent. South Asia's share of bilateral oda halved between the early 1970s and late 1980s, and all oda to that sub-region fell by nearly a quarter between 1990 and 1994, to $4 billion (around $3 per capita), of which 40 per cent comes from the IDA. The sums might decline even further now the region's geo-strategic significance to East–West rivalry has waned. Latin America and North Africa plus the Middle East each take between 10 and 15 per cent of total oda. Europe still furnishes aid candidates, not just in former communist and transition countries and ex-Yugoslavia but also Turkey, where inflows of more than $1 billion in both 1990 and 1991 placed it among the world's leading aid recipients.

In 1994 more than 65 states including some small islands received aid worth less than $100 million, and in at least 15 cases the figure was under $10 million. Total net oda receipts valued at around $1 billion or more went to 12 countries in 1994, most of whom have featured regularly among the leading recipients. They were, in order of receipts: China, Egypt, India, Bangladesh, Indonesia, Ivory Coast, Pakistan, Israel, Mozambique, Ethiopia, Philippines, Tanzania. States of former Yugoslavia can be added, and so can Russia and Poland for official aid. China has been a signal beneficiary of Japan's expansion of its aid programme ever since signing a Peace and Friendship Treaty (1978), and Japan provides around 40 per cent of China's bilateral aid. China's accession to the World Bank in 1980 and the Asian Development Bank in 1986 expanded its access to loans. In the early 1990s Egypt received the most oda of any country, topping $5 billion in each of 1990 and 1991 and benefiting from debt write-offs by several Gulf states. Large and sustained commitments of economic and military assistance to Egypt and Israel give the US a key role in any Middle East peace process and mean that the US has influence vis-à-vis both states. India, once the world's largest aid beneficiary (receiving a third of all development aid in 1960) has seen its proportion decline, from 10 per cent in the early 1970s to around 4 per cent 20 years later. Pakistan too fares less well than before, partly because of the secession of Bangladesh, and notwithstanding the temporary boost its aid inflows from the West received during Soviet engagement in Afghanistan.

Of the 20 or so traditional aid recipients who have witnessed real positive change in their annual aid receipts in 1983–93, more than half are in sub-Saharan Africa (others include Indonesia, Algeria, Bolivia and former Yugoslavia). Some enjoyed an increase amounting to double figures, like

Ghana and Uganda – both rewarded for pursuing IMF and World Bank recommended policies. In 1996 Bosnia was promised $1.8 billion of World Bank and EU assistance for reconstruction, although Serbian non-compliance with the terms of the Dayton peace accord is obstructing full-scale disbursement. Jordan should benefit from King Hussein's decisions to distance himself from the Iraqi leadership and to conclude a peace treaty with Israel, in 1994, as well as setting the Arab world some sort of example in partial democratisation. Apart from India, long-standing aid recipients who have recently been losing ground are Latin American and Caribbean states generally, Afghanistan and Sudan, which in the 1980s attracted considerable amounts of humanitarian relief.

Among high income countries (defined by the World Bank in 1995 as countries which enjoyed per capita GNP greater than $US8626 in 1993), Israel is the most notable aid recipient. Average incomes in Israel are more than 50 per cent higher than the threshold for high income economies, yet until recently aid receipts were routinely over 3 per cent of world oda. US government aid is not the only reason. For instance there were donations by world Jewry to the tune of at least $9 billion between 1950 and 1975. Geldenhuys (1990: 426) contrasts aid to Israel from all sources worth $38 billion in 1952–84 with $2 billion of inward corporate investment. Griffin (1991: 659) calculated per capita aid to Israel in 1987–8 to be 26 times the average of all aid recipients, and more than the *average income* of people in Bangladesh, Tanzania and Zambia.

Middle income countries easily make up the largest number of oda recipients. Many poorer countries have aid receipts that are only a small proportion of world oda and would add very little to their average incomes if distributed evenly among their populations. In half of all LICs per capita aid receipts from all sources in 1991 were less than $50, being above $100 in only four countries (more countries could be found in the middle income range, for example Botswana, Namibia and Papua New Guinea. The last has received more than £5 billion in aid since independence from Australia in 1975, and has consistently been Australia's leading aid partner). Overall, average per capita receipts of aid in the lower middle income economies have tended to be around two and a half times those in the low income countries, although the differential would almost disappear if China and India were excluded from the LIC group.

The extent to which countries are aid dependent varies considerably. Aid dependence can be measured in several ways: by relating aid inflows to GNP and to GDP, to imports, total saving and investment, government revenue and expenditure, the development budget and the availability of key commodities like basic foodstuffs or energy and, even, to technical manpower. For several large-volume recipients like China and India the amount contributes a relatively inconspicuous sum to the nation's economy, although its significance may be much greater in qualitative terms. It may also mean much more to particular sectors or sub-sectors of the economy and to some specific aspects of development, and most of all to the organisations, social groups and individuals who are the main beneficiaries. However, there are usually several countries (five in 1993, all in sub-Saharan Africa) for whom oda represents more than 20 per cent of GNP. A further seven were in the 10–20 per cent range (again, all, bar Bolivia, in Africa). Mozambique holds the record: oda at 111.5 per cent of GNP in 1992–3. At around $80 Mozambique is reckoned to have the world's lowest average per capita income, and for many years to come will bear the legacy of the highly destructive civil war which lasted from constitutional independence (1975) to 1993. For the most part, the highly aid-dependent countries are relatively small LICs and LLDCs in sub-Saharan Africa and groups of islands. There is now a widely held presumption that sustained aid dependence can be self-perpetuating, even though significant inflows did not prevent economic success in East Asian countries. The kinds of oda that are believed to be particularly inclined to create dependence are food aid, open-ended budget support and recurrent cost financing, together with expatriate personnel except when on short-term assignments.

Aid's Southern partners

As Chapter 5 explains, several reasons have been advanced to show why some countries need and could benefit from various kinds of oda, differing between countries and their circumstances and stages in donor thinking. There is no universal agreement that all the arguments are well founded. And in any case, reasons why governments and others seek international help, and accept offers of aid, can be as different again.

For aid seekers, aid's value lies in the expectation that it will enhance their ability to pursue and attain objectives that might otherwise be more difficult, or could lie out of reach. The totality of objectives cannot be encapsulated in a single formula. They will be as varied as a genuine desire to improve society's living standards, concern to minimise the harm done by such shocks as a natural disaster or influx of refugees, and the political kudos that could accrue from being associated with outside sources of support. A government's domestic legitimacy, the country's regional standing and, possibly, its very statehood may be confirmed by external offers of assistance (conversely, aid offers have been made in the search for diplomatic recognition and national security, by Israel and Taiwan for example. Taiwan reportedly offered the United Nations a $1 billion dowry in 1995, to be placed in a fund for developing countries. However, South Africa's decision in 1996 to sever diplomatic relations with Taiwan despite the past financial support given to the African National Congress, and in deference to trade-linked pressure from Beijing, illustrates the limitations).

The political gains from aid offers might have a special symbolic significance to a government that comes into being following a violent breakaway or break-up of an existing state, or where it has provoked disapproval by the manner of its taking power. Similarly, by observing and monitoring competitive elections and underwriting the practical arrangements, the international community could enhance the victor's prospects of political authority. In a different example, the involvement of many Western NGOs in Nicaragua in the 1980s was politically as well as economically important, because the US government had made so very clear its hostility to the ruling Sandinistas. Aid is sought for the purpose of advancing national security directly. For example, US aid covered all but 5 per cent of South Korea's defence budget in 1961. Ball (1988: 291) reckons US military and economic aid in the 1950s and 1960s was essential to that state's survival as a separate entity. For the USSR and many of its clients, and France and its former colonies in West Africa where 9000 French troops remain on station, the donor's willingness to offer military protection to a government (against local insurgents as well as external threats) has often been enshrined in a treaty of friendship, mutual defence pact or common security arrangement, alongside clauses dealing with economic aid and trade. The appetite for patronage resources which can be used to cultivate and retain political support at home is among the other reasons for chasing aid.

State and society both furnish partners to all three sources of foreign assistance – official bilateral and multilateral institutions and northern NGOs (NNGOs). The fast-growing number of indigenous or Southern NGOs (SNGOs) and grass-roots support organisations (currently estimated at 30–50,000) have furnished several prominent aid partners. A well-established example is the Bangladesh Rural Advancement Committee (BRAC), with 1.2 million members and 12,000 staff, which handled loans worth £50 million in 1995. At the receiving end 'opinions about private aid are decidedly mixed' (Sogge 1996: 2) and some SNGOs show impatience at receiving oda via NNGOs. Recent years have witnessed a trend to establish direct funding links with official donors or their offshoots like the Inter-American Foundation, founded by the US government 1971. Aid can influence the balance between state and society and the terms of their relationship, such as by supporting the planning of national development by the state or, alternatively, pressing for economic liberalisation. Recipient governments will see their ability to influence the behaviour of politically important groups altered by the ebb and flow of aid.

A general hypothesis is that the valuation placed on aid will be particularly high where domestic resources are extremely scarce. The same point will apply where the donors are viewed as reliable, permissive and undemanding – a recipient government orientation. For some small LLDCs oda has regularly funded over half of all government spending and three quarters of the development budget. Food aid provided as programme aid for general budgetary support has been a major source of government income. It was equivalent to 40 per cent of government revenue and 10 per cent of gross investment in India for an exceptional period in the mid-1960s. Donor attempts to tie the revenues from commodity aid to identifiable forms of local expenditures may not prevent the commodities being allocated in ways that are politically most advantageous to the recipient government.

In the past governments have probably been able to avoid or postpone difficult decisions about the productive reorganisation of agriculture (in South Asia, especially radical changes to land tenure that would alienate influential large landowners), and to fix price ceilings on basic foodstuffs (in Africa, harming small peasant producers), so reducing the chances of mass urban discontent. In political terms the domestic consequences of food aid allocations in the developing countries have probably been at least as significant as food aid's role in the power politics of North–South relations, although the two spheres are not completely divorced. Bangladesh, especially in the 1970s, is often cited as an example of food aid going to priority groups in the military, civil service, police and other urban non-poor. Large landowners benefited from the labour that was employed on food-for-work programmes upgrading rural feeder roads.

The aid agencies are not monoliths, and neither are the aid recipients unitary actors. Mosley (1987: 91) found over 50 per cent of developing countries do not have any central unit to monitor, much less negotiate, the allocation of aid inflows. In Bangladesh Sobhan (1982: 51–2) found that both 'in terms of intra-bureaucratic power and within the polity' control over aid-funded development projects 'becomes a major source for those contending for state power', leading to a 'built-in drive to seek more and more foreign aid'. The situation may not be very dissimilar among SNGOs. By competing for the available aid the prospects for collective solidarity may be frustrated, even though that would offer more long-run benefit if it mobilised effective pressure for structural change. The kind of aid, and the locii of responsibility for negotiating aid arrangements and positioning of gatekeepers who control disbursement, can have a crucial bearing on the distribution of power: between state and society, and between different social groups and types of social formation; between the public and private sectors of the economy; between politicians (especially the more populist) and bureaucrats (particularly the more technocratically-oriented); often between the state's civilian and military wings, and even between different branches of the armed and paramilitary forces. The balance between the organs of central government and regional or local institutions, and among the various departments and ministries at the centre and the parastatal or other quasi-governmental organisations, will be affected too. Governments have used large aid-funded schemes of economic development to impose tighter central control on localities with disaffected populations or minority groups whose loyalty to the 'nation' is held in doubt. In contrast, the modern aid agenda includes practical support to decentralisation and the deconcentration of administrative functions. This is not tantamount to a devolution of political power; nevertheless, oda going direct to local government impacts on the power structure at that level.

Aid and conditionalities add extra ingredients to what can often be a difficult relationship between, on the one side, spending bodies (invariably expansionary) and, on the other side, the finance ministry and central bank (often predisposed to be more conservative, and usual destination of IMF credits), and between all of these and the economic planning department (aspiring to exercise overall direction). Again, aid's forms will be significant. The finance ministry will warm to programme aid and may even welcome the lenders' insistence on monetary and fiscal policy conditionalities that strengthen its hand against spending departments; oda that takes the form of credits to service overdue foreign debt payments will, however, be non-appropriable. Meanwhile, political leaders may derive some comfort from being able to scapegoat foreign lenders for unpalatable but essential reforms to economic policy that disadvantage political rivals, at least until such time as manifestly beneficial results enable them to reap political credit at home. The project funds that ministries or other public sector development bodies negotiate directly with donors as well as commercial partners advance their autonomy. The development agencies that are sometimes specially created at the behest of donors for the purpose of executing their projects and programmes will complicate the state's own organisational structure. Vital resources like foreign exchange, money for recurrent expenditures and scarce manpower skills may have to be commandeered from other parts and programmes of government. The state becomes fragmented, and fragments acquire a vested interest in resisting the establishment of a supreme authority to deal with all foreign aid. These issues have been detailed by Mosley (1987) in a chapter appropriately headed: 'On the other side of the river: aid from the recipient's point of view'.

The smooth transfer of aid can be interrupted by inter-departmental disputes, but the political fortunes of government figures, entire departments even, may rise or fall in line with their performance in attracting aid and their skill in deploying it to particular advantage. Aid for large single projects can lead to uneven patterns of development that widen regional inequalities and favour (or burden) only the localities that enjoy high political salience. The patchwork quilt of interventions by NGOs further undermines the chances of an even national coverage. In the matter of disaster relief, the standing of the armed forces may rise when they distribute relief supplies efficiently, perhaps impressing poor people who are not accustomed to receiving favours from their government. On the other hand, the standing of organisations and leaders believed responsible for the maladministration or misappropriation of emergency aid will be damaged, like Nicaragua's President Somoza after the 1972 Managua earthquake. Failure to alert the international community to approaching famine in Ethiopia effectively destroyed the domestic authority of Emperor Haile Selassie, in 1973.

The control of humanitarian supplies is also employed as a conventional weapon of war, in situations of internal conflict ranging from Nigeria in the late 1960s through Cambodia in 1979, Sudan and Ethiopia in the 1980s to Bosnia in the 1990s. Governments and local warlords wrangle with international organisations and NNGOs over access to 'humanitarian space', over who shall determine the distribution of supplies. Donor agencies may prioritise respect for need, fairness and efficiency, but local power brokers will object to what they see as 'gunboat relief'. Minear and Weiss in their aptly titled *Mercy under Fire* (1995) recommend that the global humanitarian community should make up its mind to intervene either effectively or not at all. The NGO Médecins sans Frontières withdrew its humanitarian operation from Rwandan refugee camps in Zaire in November 1994, believing with some justification that Hutu militiamen were using the camps to prepare for a resumption of warfare against Rwanda's Tutsis. Other humanitarian agencies, especially UNHCR, continued spending $1 million a day, 'feeding genocidal killers' in the words of a Kigali-based diplomat (*Financial Times*, 4 November 1996). When, in late 1996, Tutsis and Rwandan troops decided the time had come to take decisive military action, the UNHCR was denied speedy access to intervene.

Coordination and other issues

Even where there is the best will in the world, the authorities who receive oda can lack the necessary institutional strength, managerial capability and technical skills to coordinate the inflows and administer them well. One consequence can be that the order of public action is determined by donor initiatives that do not add up to a coherent whole. They transfer the conflicts of interest, the disparities in development ethos, and the coordination weakness of the donors themselves. The local control of domestic resource allocation slips away, as the donors' choices take priority. Uncertainties about future funding levels will also be disruptive. There may be a confusion of signals and a plethora of inconsistent procedural requirements to follow. The overall impact overloads the government bureaucracy and may produce what Morss (1984) called institutional destruction. These and related problems arising from the systemic effects of aid, particularly the obstacles to coordination, have been well known for some time and are summarised by Cassen *et al.* (1994: Chapter 7). They seem most liable to occur in very aid-dependent countries who host many donors, like the approximately 24 bilateral and multilateral agencies and over 60 NNGOs involved with Mozambique. While aid for good governance now aims to improve public sector management and administration, the challenge of managing the aid relationships can itself be a distraction from that end, by distorting the allocation of governance resources. The result could be no less significant for the recipient than are the interruptions to donor disbursements which are just a symptom of the more general problem.

Comparable problems can arise for indigenous NGOs. The most highly regarded SNGOs, who demonstrate the capacity to use substantial sums and deliver outputs that conform to the donors' intentions, will be courted by several foreign suitors. Host governments can experience difficulty in monitoring the activities of foreign NGOs – sometimes likened to unguided missiles. Gordenker and Weiss (1995: 368) quote a UN official saying that coordinating NGOs is 'like herding cats'. In 1980, 95 foreign NGOs were working in Thailand, in a humanitarian crisis whose origins lay outside the country but brought refugee camps inside its border. In the 1984–5 famine in Ethiopia 63 NNGOs were involved in relief operations, acquiring the responsibility for 65 per cent of food aid distribution from official donors who shunned the Ethiopian government's Relief and Rehabilitation Commission.

In the past, India has enjoyed more success than most in centralising external aid relations and imposing its own strategic choices; but now NGOs may be handling as much as a quarter of all aid inflows (Watkins 1995a: 207). SNGO dependency on official aid, either directly or indirectly through NNGOs, for up to 90 per cent of their income is not unusual, and some SNGOs face being overexpanded beyond the limits of their institutional capability. Governments will feel their authority could be undermined as NGOs take over the delivery of services, courtesy of foreign aid. In response a number have developed techniques to exercise cooption, regulation and control. Government-inspired NGOS (GINGOs) and quasi-non-governmental organisations (QUANGOs) are developed with a view to gaining some purchase over aid inflows to NGOs, and to counter excessive SNGO orientations towards the donors. In Bangladesh for example, where foreign funds to NGOs comprise around 12 per cent of all aid inflows, the authorities' refusal to tolerate activities that might threaten the social order has led most of them to move away from organising the poor, adopting more economistic approaches to development instead (Hashemi 1995). Donor attitudes that stress the instrumental role of SNGOs in service delivery, at the expense of community mobilisation, will compound the situation.

The study of aid at the recipients' end reveals how aid serves latent functions in the local political debate. For example, governments have tried to allay their sense of domestic insecurity by launching propaganda campaigns against donor imperialism, even though simultaneously taking vigorous steps to obtain more oda. The governments' political opponents can be no less critical, when seeking to enhance their nationalist and/or socialist credentials. True and false stories of corrupt dealings involving leading politicians, aid and business will circulate, and in recent years have brought down many senior figures in public life in countries in the South and North, East and West. Mention has already been made of the history of aid's contribution to political oppression, through military and security assistance and economic support to dictators. Now, in a number of countries, political activists openly welcome opportunities for aid leverage to further conditionalities of democratic political reform and human rights, against their own government. Although pleas to donors to enforce such conditionalities can be very well founded, they may also reflect personal political and partisan ambitions. The cycle revolves. Thus, as head of the country's 'unofficial opposition' (the Zambia Congress of Trade Unions) in the 1980s, Frederick Chiluba drew the attention of Swedes to the Zambian government's misuse of their oda (conversations with the author,

August 1992), while in the 1990s Zambian critics of President Chiluba's government are also urging international donors to suspend aid, on similar grounds.

Donors outside the Development Assistance Committee

Chapter 2 simulated decision-making for aid allocators, and role reversal invites readers to empathise with aid seekers, compare and contrast the different donors. The bilateral, multilateral and non-governmental categories are distinct, and each contains wide variations. But how distinctive have been the donors from outside the DAC?

By 1994 oda from non-DAC sources was reaching its lowest recorded level, of $1.4 billion or far less than the private voluntary aid of DAC-based NGOs. The situation was not always thus. Arab aid reached a peak approaching $9.5 billion in 1980 (at current 1980 prices), then equivalent to a third of DAC aid. In 1975 aid from all OPEC sources including Iran contributed a proportional high of 40.5 per cent of DAC oda. For part of the 1970s Saudi Arabia was the second largest individual donor in dollar terms, behind the US. Several OPEC members granted aid well in excess of 4 per cent of GNP in the mid- to late 1970s (the figure for Qatar in 1975 reached 16 per cent). The figures would be very much higher when calculated in relation to non-depletable GDP. The aid budgets per capita in Kuwait and the United Arab Emirates in 1977 represented more than 10 per cent of their average incomes. As recently as 1990 Saudi disbursements worth $3.6 billion were exceeded by only a handful of other countries, and at 2 per cent of GNP in 1994, Kuwaiti aid of $550 million outperformed every DAC country.

Another major aid source for many years was the USSR, particularly important to China for capital goods and technical assistance in the 1950s, and coming to an end in 1960 when relations suddenly deteriorated. The methodological and statistical difficulties surrounding the recording and measurement of Soviet aid have not prevented DAC estimates regularly placing it behind only a handful of DAC countries. From the mid-1980s up until 1989 Soviet aid was valued externally at $4–5 billion annually. This represented a comparatively strong performance when judged against donor average incomes, which is one indicator of ability to provide aid. It looks less impressive when related to national economic size. And there is a contrast with DAC countries where the ratio of oda to GNP has tended to covary with the extent of government participation in national economic life.

South–South aid has comprised a polyglot bundle of relationships including as donors at one time or another such countries as Argentina, Brazil, Venezuela, Nigeria and India, some of them pursuing goals of becoming a regional power. Turkey, guardian of the North Atlantic Treaty

Organisation's (NATO's) Eastern flank and sizeable recipient of Western aid over the years, established its own International Cooperation Agency in 1992, and is showing special interest in former Soviet republics in the Caucasus and Central Asia, where it competes for influence with Iran (chiefly offering humanitarian supplies). OPEC aside, China has been the most notable non-DAC source.

China's bilateral aid programme began as early as 1953. By the 1970s it reached around 90 countries, especially Pakistan, and half being in Africa which accounted for half of China's economic aid (a cumulative total of around $5 billion). For some years China aimed to offer an alternative source of inspiration to the USSR and not just the capitalist West, and a distinctive model of development centred on self-reliance, or 'third way'. The relatively generous terms of its aid and a reputation for non-interference in the internal affairs of borrowers suggest its aid was not primarily an instrument of power politics (Bobiash 1992). However, China has consistently used its aid programme (and, now, its importance in international trade) to isolate Taiwan from international diplomatic recognition. The aid programme has more or less stagnated ever since China began to focus its energies on domestic economic modernisation and growth. For some time the ageing leadership's preoccupation with the political succession issue and with charting the country's own direction have precluded expansionary foreign policies in the Third World. But recent indications are that China's profile in international affairs in the twenty-first century could well be considerably more commensurate with its great power attributes and growing economic size. That might mean an expanding aid programme.

OPEC's rise and decline

In the ten years following the 1973–4 oil price rise OPEC members granted $74 billion in aid, equivalent to about 22 per cent of aid from all major donors (Shihata and Sherbiny 1986: 19). The story really begins in 1961 when the somewhat artificial and insecure state of Kuwait founded the Kuwait Fund for Arab Economic Development, which subsequently built a high professional reputation. The rapid increase in oil incomes in the mid-1970s and inability at first to absorb all the revenue explain how member states of OPEC (founded in 1960) could become major donors so quickly. Apart from bilateral aid relations, several new multilateral bodies were founded, such as the OPEC Fund for International Development (1976), joining the Arab Fund for Economic and Social Development and Arab Bank for Economic Development in Africa. They also embarked on cofinancing with DAC donors as well as contributing to existing international organisations; indeed, multilateral channels of all sorts have accounted for over half of total OPEC oda. Now, Saudi Arabia's share of subscriptions and voting rights in the IBRD is exceeded by only five other states.

The OPEC countries' decline as donors in the 1980s is no more mysterious than their rise. Oil revenues fell owing to a real terms price cut and halving of market share for internationally traded oil. Other factors include the rise of very substantial investment programmes at home and for some, such as Kuwait, investment overseas; extravagant consumption expenditure and large-scale arms purchases from abroad; and the diversion of resources and waste occasioned by the 1980–8 Iran–Iraq war. That brought the combatants' aid programmes to an end, and left Iraq owing up to $100 billion to Gulf states. More recently, the PLO's alignment with Iraq during the Gulf war led to retrenchment by Gulf states like Kuwait and Saudi Arabia. The latter had reputedly bankrolled the PLO to the tune of up to $85 million annually, enabling the PLO to maintain a more extensive international diplomatic representation than many fully-fledged states. PLO payments to Palestinian causes of more than $300 million annually prior to 1991 declined to $90 million by 1992.

Most OPEC aid derived from a small group of Arab members (Iran being a notable exception until the revolution in 1979). Hunter (1984: 53) argues it is no less true of these states than any other that their aid programme is first and foremost a tool of foreign policy. Security concerns rooted in the region have been primary determinants. There are also politico-ideological and other objectives including at the pan-Arab level. By contrast with much DAC aid commercial and economic objectives were never important, and procurement tying has been absent. Any concern to compensate poor developing countries for the increased price of their imported oil was much less significant than religious and cultural factors in aid distributions. Arab and Islamic states predominated among the developing countries who were major recipients, especially of bilateral flows. Some lie outside the Middle East, a number like Pakistan originating a sizeable traffic in migrant workers useful to the Gulf states' construction boom. But countries in the front line against Israel – particularly Jordan, Syria and Egypt before President Sadat engaged in dialogue with Israel, visited Jerusalem in 1977 and signed a formal peace treaty with Israel in 1979 – enjoyed the largest aid shares, and together accounted for over half the identifiable aid for 1974–83 (Porter 1986: 46 and 59). General balance of payments and budgetary support was the dominant form in the early years, often channelled through non-institutional channels, so making the end use difficult to trace.

That a number of the objectives ascribed to OPEC aid have not been accomplished is clear from Egyptian President Sadat's historic compromise with Israel. Hunter (1984: 87) believes 'the capacity of the Arab donors to manipulate the foreign or domestic politics of recipients and to impose choices on them has been fairly limited'. The severing of diplomatic relations by many African states with Israel, which itself had established aid relations with many African states in the 1960s, might look like an exception. Between the first Afro-Arab summit in 1977 and 1983 net disbursements of concessional Arab aid were $2 billion. But there were other reasons besides. The first break, by Uganda, was as early as 1972. Many African governments followed soon after because of Israel's occupation of territory belonging to Egypt – an African state and member of the Organisation of

African Unity. Israel's links with the apartheid state in South Africa also caused offence.

The strengthening of the Islamic world, of which Arab peoples are probably no more than one fifth, is another aim that aid diplomacy has not obviously advanced. The coexistence of Sunni and Shiite realms remains an uneasy one. Aid probably prolonged the Iran–Iraq war by underpinning the latter's belligerence with finance and equipment. Unity within the Arab nation has also remained elusive, exemplified in Syria's strained relations with Jordan and Iraq. If anything aid has fuelled the suspicions that exist between the prosperous sheikhdoms and the group of generally larger, more populous and less affluent states who have pursued a more uncompromising policy towards Israel. The former are believed to use their aid to try to deflect criticism of their more conservative stance towards regional politics, a stance that fits with their integration into Western oil markets and links with the 'oil majors', who are fundamental to their financial riches. For example, the containment of Libyan influence in the Arab world has probably been a consistent objective of Saudi aid. Libya's own aid offers did not significantly further Colonel Qaddafi's ambitions to be a leading light in Arab and North African affairs, and they acquired a reputation for being more rhetorical than real.

Other divisions have been evident in the political alignment of Syria and Libya with Iran during the time of the Iran–Iraq war, and most graphically during the Gulf war. Kuwait's considerable investment of aid in relations with Iraq seemed only to whet Saddam Hussein's appetite for territorial acquisition. Saudi aid failed to prevent Jordan and Yemen seemingly siding with Iraq, although several other states may have been persuaded to attach themselves to the international coalition of forces ranged against Iraq, by the prospect of new offers of Gulf aid. Egypt, Turkey, Morocco and Syria were rewarded quite handsomely. Kuwaiti aid rose tenfold in 1990, to reach its highest real terms figure for almost a decade, the major part being disbursed by the government in exile. Kuwait, Qatar and the United Arab Emirates wrote off Egyptian debt of at least $7 billion (OECD 1991: 158). Even so, inter-Arab aid is not the key to security for Gulf states, who look to US-led military protection as the most powerful line of defence. Sudan, which occupies a strategic location, was for many years a major recipient of OPEC and DAC aid, some of it intended to make the country into the 'breadbasket' of the Middle East. That arrangement could be counted an almost complete aid failure. Today, its financial and economic condition are desperate, neighbours view it as a centre of terrorism aimed at spreading Islamic fundamentalism, and the government enjoys good relations with very few states other than Iraq, Libya and Iran.

Aid's contribution to OPEC members' standing in the Third World was never translated into effective leadership of the Third World, or to greater collective self-reliance of the South. A contradiction always existed in that the oil-importing developing countries literally paid a price for OPEC countries' capital surplus. The last 15 years have seen both the power of OPEC and the Third World's political potential, expressed in the Non-Aligned Movement, Group of 77 and United Nations Conference on Trade and Development (UNCTAD), go into steep decline. Communism failed to make extensive inroads in the Middle East or the wider Arab and Islamic worlds, but this cannot obviously be credited to OPEC aid, although it might have been an objective. From a peak approaching $10 billion new oda OPEC's annual aid has fallen to less than $1 billion dollars now, and comes largely from Kuwait and Saudi Arabia. Saudi has faced budgetary pressure in the 1990s, occasioned in part by massive foreign weapons procurement. Per capita incomes have fallen by two thirds since 1981. The full resumption of Iraqi oil exports would restrain world oil prices, and some OPEC producers might see their revenues drop. OPEC itself is unlikely to recover the ability to dictate world oil prices.

Soviet Union: the extinction of an aid power

Although the arms race was the most potent feature of superpower competition between the US and USSR, a less dramatic manifestation took the form of an alms race. That started in the mid-1950s and brought the USSR into a substantial grant equivalent relationship with a few 'special friends'. Cuba, Vietnam, and Mongolia came to account for up to three quarters of the USSR's concessional transfers. Lesser commitments were made to several others such as Afghanistan and Cambodia, and credit arrangements were agreed with many countries in North Africa, Middle East and South-West Asia, particularly India. One estimate is that non-communist developing countries received nearly $50 billion in Soviet military assistance and $10 billion in economic assistance between 1954 and 1981. Another suggests they received $43.78 billion in economic aid in the period 1955–89. Offers (as distinct from drawings) of economic aid reached a high of $6.38 billion in 1988, largely due to credits to India (Dannehl 1995: 7). Military assistance agreements were probably at their greatest in 1977, when they totalled around $5 billion. Other member countries of the Council for Mutual Economic Assistance (CMEA) were also donors, most notably the GDR. At first the GDR sought international diplomatic recognition and later pursued ideological and economic objectives in this way (Howell 1994). By the mid-1980s the USSR was providing up to 90 per cent of CMEA aid. The communist countries did not belong to the World Bank group and were not major contributors to UN agencies.

The formal position of communist states was that aid to developing countries was primarily an obligation of the former colonial powers, for it was they and their capitalist imperialist allies who were responsible for much of the Third World's economic backwardness. Communist states sometimes characterised their own arrangements with developing countries as a genuine form of economic cooperation, and mutually beneficial, rather than aid. Nevertheless, it also suited their purposes to present their efforts as being more generous than Western oda. The bulk of Soviet oda as recorded in the West took the form of credits for large public sector projects in industry and energy, tied to Soviet procurement and technical personnel. The statist bias of the aid reflected the model of political economy of the USSR. Repayment often comprised output produced by these ventures, and also took the form of traditional commodities. Barter trade at subsidised prices was another prominent feature. In addition, more than two million developing country nationals were given technical training at Soviet expense, most of them in their own country. Food aid was given only exceptionally.

In the early years, a large proportion of Soviet loans went to countries on or near the southern border such as Iran and Afghanistan, and also displayed an ideological bias, the goal being world socialism (Arefieva and Bragina 1991: 46–7). Like the US, the USSR too gained access to military bases – indeed, in the course of time access to Cam Ranh Bay (Vietnam) and Berbera (Somalia) changed hands between the two superpowers as the political situation gyrated and with it the structure of foreign alliances and aid relations. However, despite the early preponderance of political, ideological, military and security objectives, the economic interests of the USSR were never very far behind. That is why aid partners later came to include some pro-Western as well as ostensibly non-aligned countries, including Turkey, Morocco and states whose governments suppressed local groups of communist sympathisers. Indeed, whereas Western aid might be thought to have become more ideological in the 1980s, as neo-liberalism came to dominate the economic agenda, so Soviet assistance shed its previous ideological pretensions and ceased to be a device for spreading communism. According to Dannehl (1995), the approach is best summarised as one intended to secure not converts but political influence, trade gains and, even, more altruistic developmental objectives. Roeder (1985: 209) concluded that 'the growing economic rationality' in Soviet economic assistance programmes may, in part, have reflected an emerging recognition that such programmes have only 'limited political value'. He also established that for the 1960s and 1970s Soviet economic aid was less successful than trade dependence in eliciting political compliance from recipients in the non-communist developing world, and that after then trade dependence (cultivated through tied loans) was in decline. The limits to the political influence gained by Soviet military assistance can also be illustrated by two of its major clients: Egypt, which moved into the US sphere of influence after Sadat succeeded Nasser in 1970 and expelled Soviet technicians two years later, and Iraq (awarded $1 billion in Soviet economic credits in both 1983 and 1984 for instance), for Saddam ignored Soviet diplomatic efforts when invading Kuwait and then refusing to withdraw voluntarily.

Soviet assistance to Cuba – estimated to 'have received far more comprehensive, sustained, and massive economic assistance from the USSR than any other developing country outside the Soviet Union's Eurasia orbit'

(Blasier 1979: 225) – has been subjected to the most detailed and extensive examination. This is due to US fascination with Cuba. The aid can be credited with significant achievements. It enabled the central bureaucratic and military authorities in Castro's Cuba to consolidate power. The goals of the 1959 Cuban revolution were not abandoned despite the adversity the US economic embargo posed. The USSR and other CMEA members supplied Cuba with technical assistance and financed Cuba's trade deficits with other socialist countries. They made subsidised purchases of Cuban sugar (in many years taking over half of Cuba's exports) and nickel, and supplied virtually all of Cuba's oil needs (usually at below international prices) plus additional quantities that could be resold on world markets for hard currency (in 1984 for instance Cuba's resales of Soviet oil netted an estimated $550 million). They advanced credits for projects, provided convertible currency backing to the Cuban government's own efforts to raise international bank loans, and deferred and rescheduled loan repayments. And they supplied military assistance. Annual trade subsidies were worth an estimated $4 billion in the early 1980s, equivalent to a quarter of Cuba's economic output. The grand total of all the help has been guessed at around $40 billion for the period 1959–85. By the time economic aid from the former USSR came to an end in 1993, Cuba reportedly owed its former patron well in excess of $24 billion.

Cuba's importance to the USSR was partly strategic. Its potential value as a military base declined after the Cuban missile crisis (1962) and with the advent of long-range inter-ballistic missiles. However, its geographical proximity to the US continued to make it a symbolic thorn in the side, and it remained useful for gathering intelligence. Not only was Cuba a flagship for the socialist path to development in the developing world, but it was also a reliable ally and important to the projection of Soviet power. For instance, Castro publicly supported the Soviets' crushing of the 'Prague spring' in 1968. Cuba became the repository of a considerable Soviet investment of material resources, political commitment and prestige. Thus, the relationship was far more complex than straightforward Cuban dependence. Most observers agree that Soviet pressure caused some changes in Cuba's domestic politics and policies most notably in economic management, and Castro admitted as much (Mesa-Lago 1981: 187). But that the Cuba regime was not a satellite of the USSR was also widely acknowledged, even before it proved that it could outlast the Soviet star.

Aid was a burden on the Soviet economy. Clearly the returns on its aid did not prevent the collapse of the USSR or the retreat of world communism. But neither can these developments be blamed on socialist bloc aid and its weaknesses. Anyway, Russia, like China, has now seen its status transformed from sizeable donor to a notable destination of international aid. In contrast Cuba has been both a substantial aid recipient and significant provider of assistance *at one and the same time* (although now exhibiting *neither* of these characteristics). Cuba's inclusion below represents our token of the developing world as an aid source.

Cuban follies?

Following 1959 Cuba registered impressive social achievements which belie its classification as a Third World country. The same is true of its performance in providing technical assistance, skilled manpower such as doctors, teachers and civil engineers, along with trained military personnel to over 25 countries on three continents, in an effort that peaked between the mid-1970s and mid-1980s.

Cuba's internationalism began in the 1960s with military aid to insurgents in some Central and South American countries, presented in terms of an ideological commitment to solidarity with anti-imperialist and leftist guerilla movements. Castro said any revolutionary movement anywhere in the world could count on Cuba's unconditional help. In the 1980s up to half a million Cuban troops served in Africa, mainly in Angola and Ethiopia, helping socialist regimes combat internal and external threats. Also by the 1980s, Cuba supplied nearly one fifth of all Soviet-bloc economic technicians working abroad in developing countries. There were more doctors from Cuba than the number stationed by the UN's World Health Organisation. Eckstein (1994: 175) contrasts Cuba's record of one civilian aid worker for every 625 Cubans in the early 1980s with that of the US, which sent one US Peace Corps or USAID worker overseas for every 34,704 US inhabitants. Human capital, not finance, was Cuba's comparative advantage in international aid.

Cuba is highly unusual because of the transection of incoming and outgoing planes of aid. Military involvement in Africa cost the country some oda offers that DAC countries would otherwise have made. But Soviet aid leverage does not entirely explain Cuba's willingness to complement Soviet arms to the developing world with its own military and other personnel. Certainly, the division of responsibilities was politically convenient to the USSR, and probably more acceptable to the hosts than large contingents of Red Army troops. But although there is little evidence that Soviet aid to Cuba was a reward for Cuban adventurism, Cuba's overseas exploits probably enhanced its own bargaining position *vis-à-vis* the Soviet bloc. Some of Cuba's initiatives were disapproved of in Moscow. Dannehl (1995: 30) even goes so far as to say the Cuba–Soviet connection in Angola was 'a sort of tail-wagging-the-dog phenomenon'. Moreover, aid's contribution to building friendly ties with Third World states served Cuba's security, by moderating its reliance on the USSR for diplomatic protection and political support. The continuing uncertainty about US intentions after the failed 'Bay of Pigs' invasion in 1961 made it important to accumulate friends, not least in the UN General Assembly.

Other factors explaining Cuba's aid commitment include Castro's ambitions to be a leader of the Non-Aligned Movement (Havana hosted the organisation's sixth summit meeting, in 1979) and of the Third World as a whole. Some economic advantages also accrued to Cuba especially in the form of hard currency earnings, which became more significant as the

exports of manpower came to be placed on an increasingly commercial footing. Thus Eckstein (1994: 194) found 'a fine line evolved between medical
aid provided in a disinterested manner and profiteering from sales of Cuban
medicines'. The defence of left-wing governments overseas also provided
opportunities for young cadres to become socialised into the revolutionary
spirit, so renewing the Cuban government's own revolutionary credentials
and claims to legitimacy at home. Whether the alternative might have been
troublesome unemployment can only be speculated. But while the military
exploits represented the informal influence of the armed forces within the
domestic power structure, they also brought a preoccupation with professional duties, precluding any thoughts of staging a coup.

Around the time of Namibian independence Cuba played a part in the
negotiations. These made significant progress after Cuban forces helped the
Angolan government score a notable military victory over the rival UNITA,
despite the material assistance UNITA received from the US and South
African governments. However, in the foreign policy arena Cuba's aid
efforts were not an unqualified success. Cuba failed to persuade other countries to endorse its support for Vietnam's invasion of Cambodia (1978) and
Soviet military intervention in Afghanistan (1979). In the longer term,
governments professing a Marxist–Leninist orientation have disappeared
from the countries where Cuba once provided support. Cuba's sixteen-
year-long support to the revolutionary Eritrean movement for independence *might* have counted as a success (Eritrea achieved statehood in 1993),
but not after 1975, for Cuba switched its support to the self-styled Marxist
government in Addis Ababa, which was becoming a close ally of the USSR.

Cuba's capacity to provide aid has been much diminished since its own
source of aid and trade favours has evaporated, although some technical
programmes have continued in an increasingly commercialised form. In
1991–3 Cuba's economy contracted by around 40 per cent with a corresponding decline in living standards, and only in 1995 was there a noticeable
improvement. This experience indicates that aid and trade dependence on
the socialist bloc brought vulnerability – something which some of Cuba's
sympathisers often charged was a distinguishing feature of economic dependence on the capitalist West. There is a difference between incidental exposure (of Cuba) to internal political events taking place elsewhere (in the
USSR and other CMEA countries) and the kind of deliberate impositions
on Third World countries that leftists claim are a necessary feature of foreign capitalist interventions. But in terms of the practical consequences, the
significance seems not to be so very great. Substantial aid inflows did not
enable Cuba to progress a self-reliant model of strong and sustainable development. Of course, one reason why Cuba is not more prosperous is the
US blockade 'as expressed by laws, acts of force and intimidation', which
over the years have cost the economy $40 billion, according to Cuba's
trade minister, Ricardo Ruiz (*Financial Times*, 3 May 1996).

One test of how successful Soviet assistance has been will be the extent
to which Cuba's leaders must now compromise their socialist principles

and abandon the conditions they would prefer to attach to closer integration with the international capitalist system. That such integration will come about is surely inevitable, notwithstanding the tightening of the US embargo in 1996, when the Helms–Burton Act sought to stifle inward investment as well as trade (so adding extra-territoriality to US interference in the free working of the global economy). In January 1997 a USAID report held out a prospect of $4–8 billion of international financial support for Cuba over six years if Cuba installed a 'transition government' – one that releases political prisoners, sanctions multi-party elections and excludes Fidel Castro and his brother! President Castro called the offer Machiavellian, adding Cuba's 'freedom and dignity' could not be bought (*Financial Times*, 30 January 1977).

Conclusion

In the West there is a temptation to identify aid with the activities of DAC donors, especially nowadays. That would be a mistake. First, there is a clutch of vital issues surrounding the meaning and the consequences of aid for the countries who get it, and without whom international assistance would not exist. Second, substantial aid has flowed from non-DAC countries, and being a donor has been shown to have attractions even to some less developed countries. Their aid has exhibited some familiar and some unusual features. That claim can be better appreciated only after today's largest sources of aid have been introduced.

8

Major donors

The year in which the Berlin wall fell, 1989, also saw the US lose its hitherto unrivalled position as the world's largest aid volume donor, to Japan. Since then they have exchanged places twice, and Japan's lead now looks unassailable, with oda of $14.48 billion, followed by France ($8.43 billion), Germany ($7.48 billion) and the US ($7.30 billion) in 1995 (provisional data). However, none match much smaller countries who have consistently demonstrated a superior commitment in terms of oda as a proportion of GNP. In 1995 US oda was 0.10 per cent of GNP, the lowest level since accounting was introduced in 1950 and lower than for all other DAC countries, who collectively averaged 0.27 per cent. Denmark, Norway, Sweden and the Netherlands have regularly exceeded twice the DAC average (Norway's performance being over 1 per cent of GNP since the early 1980s until 1995, when changes in accounting methodology substantially increased the GNP representation). These countries seem to bear out the expectation that as a country becomes more affluent, it will devote a larger proportion of its wealth to good international causes. Scandinavian countries together with France have also led in terms of oda per capita of donor population (over $270). Here again the US is much less impressive, at $38 (1993–4) compared with the DAC average of $77. The US and Ireland have often provided less than 1 per cent of the central government budget as oda, but the figures for Denmark and Switzerland for instance have exceeded 3 per cent. The choice of how donor performance is measured can be critical to explanatory theories of donor behaviour. To illustrate, Lumsdaine (1993) highlights aid ratios to GNP and aid per capita in his submission that humanitarian conviction and concern for international justice have been central to the origin and growth of aid. An alternative focus on aid volumes would have given greater weight to the different motives that lie behind much US aid. Even so, Lumsdaine's (1993: 41) analysis, which excludes Soviet and OPEC aid and all military aid, acknowledged that probably around one third of aid can be attributed to direct donor self-interest.

Mosley (1981: 253) found in respect of DAC donors outside the top five that, moving forward from the 1960s and outwards from the special case of donors who are ex-colonial powers, 'to consider the case of aid donors not constrained by historical commitments to specific less developed countries', the explanatory power of the recipient-need model of aid allocation increases. The Scandinavian countries especially with their social democratic traditions and pacific internationalist outlook are usually thought to approximate most closely to the more idealistic versions of aid giving, or Stokke's 'humane internationalism'. Along with the Netherlands they have been relatively generous, and are believed to draw on moral principles committed to confronting poverty and furthering social justice on a global scale. A commitment to multilateralism has been evident. Norway, Sweden and Denmark tend to be among the leading contributors to UNICEF and UNDP and, on a per capita basis, to UNHCR. Humane internationalism has also meant targeting bilateral aid on a carefully selected group of poorest countries including some whose governments claimed Marxist credentials.

Nevertheless, hard-nosed financial and commercial considerations have been gaining ground for years as even these countries seek to come to terms with economic pressures and public spending constraints (Hook 1995: Chapter 5; Stokke 1995 and 1996). For example, in January 1995 the Swedish government announced a four-year freeze on oda. Except for Norway, participation in EU development cooperation might further weaken the Scandinavians' distinctive approach to aid. Canada, once entitled to be judged part of the same set, probably no longer qualifies because of significant retrenchments. Moreover, the objectives of humane internationalism should not be considered in isolation from what donors perceive to be in their own long-term interest. Their stance is explained at least in part by the logic of economic diplomacy and self-evident appeal of internationalism to small states, who lack the military muscle or the political and economic wherewithal to pursue their national interests by more nakedly powerful means. The countries provide evidence to support the hypothesis that ideals furnish a more reliable basis for a sustained commitment to sound oda than does the absolute primacy of national and sub-national interests, but idealism on its own appears not to be enough.

The last couple of decades have seen some significant differences in aid trends among DAC countries, with no close correspondence emerging between aid disbursements and GNP rate of growth. The real terms commitment of some countries such as the US and Britain is reducing, Italy's rapid expansion of the 1980s has come to an end, and in the early 1990s Spain and Portugal registered large increases but from a very low base (and recorded considerable reductions in 1995). France has steadily increased its budget throughout much of the period, and more strongly so than Germany which in the 1990s has faced large unforeseen costs of integrating the former GDR, including additional demands on public spending, inflationary pressures and increased unemployment.

France, with the highest oda/GNP ratio (0.55 per cent in 1995) of all G7 countries, remains one of the most enthusiastic to expand its own and the EU's aid programmes. Hook (1995: Chapter 3) interprets this as being all of a piece with France's enduring pursuit of national prestige and cultural nationalism, encapsulated in the self-proclaimed '*mission civilisatrice*'. French aspirations to remain a sizeable world power with a special position in North–South relations are well known. France's accounts of its oda have at times been contentious because of the inclusion of very substantial resource transfers to France's Départements d'Outre-Mer and Territoires d'Outre-Mer. Hook (1995: 56–7) shows that Reunion, Martinique, New Caledonia, French Polynesia and Guadeloupe have been among the foremost beneficiaries; and Algeria alone, prior to independence, received assistance equivalent to 0.7 per cent of France's GNP. The Overseas Departments have been excluded from DAC figures for French aid since 1992. Other leading destinations comprise over 20 francophone states in Africa (15 of whom were once direct dependencies). In total the 15 franc zone countries received 79 per cent of French oda in 1992 (Schraeder 1995: 555). This pattern brings trade advantages to France – the CFA zone has been called a 'private hunting zone' for French business – and serves the desire to maintain a long-standing regional sphere of influence. Technical and cultural assistance have been marked features of French oda. Around a quarter is devoted to educational spending, compared to under 3 per cent of US aid, and compares with the more than half of Japanese aid that goes to production and economic infrastructures like energy and transport projects.

The wealth and self-confidence generated by the German economy up to reunification facilitated a large aid programme extending to over 100 partners. They exhibit a geographical spread that befits Germany's position as the world's second largest trading nation (after the US), unfettered by prior claims from former imperial ties. German aid has enjoyed a high procurement ratio without relatively high procurement tying, although mixed credit financing (linking aid and commercial loans) has been significant. Important factors in the 1960s were the Cold War and preventing the GDR gaining recognition (the Hallstein doctrine), following on from an initial phase of war reparations. In 1991 the government formulated new guidelines incorporating human rights, economic marketisation and the rule of law. National security interests along with a growing corporate investment stake in the former Soviet bloc, especially Poland and Russia, are now major considerations. Down all the years, Israel has been given special consideration. Turkey, which in the years preceding the mid-1970s sent many guest workers – two million Turks now live in Germany – has also been favoured. Overall, Germany's substantial aid programme can be seen against the background of constitutional constraints on the country's licence to participate in international peacemaking and related military activities, although in recent years there has been some easing of the constraints, despite domestic political opposition.

In the rest of this chapter only three countries are profiled, very briefly. Japan, the world's largest creditor country since 1985, is the largest donor and largest bilateral donor to around 34 countries, although at 0.28 per cent its oda/GNP ratio is relatively low. The fifth medium-term target is for total net disbursements of $70.75 billion, in 1993–7. The US, the greatest cumulative source of aid – roughly $500 billion in 1992 dollar terms (Bandow 1992: 75) – is central to the story of aid by virtue of its dominant economic and political role after 1945 (Hook 1995: 24), even though in 1995 it was only fourth-largest donor. Also included is Britain, whose aid programme has often been said by government spokespersons to be world-renowned for its technical excellence and strength of development expertise. The EU is also included, as a growing aid presence with hybrid credentials – a multinational rather than a pure multilateral, or what Hewitt (1991: 136) called (at a time when the EU numbered twelve countries) 'little more than a thirteenth bilateral programme'.

Japan

An abiding popular perception ties Japan's policy towards aid (called economic cooperation in Japan) into a national prioritisation of self-regarding economic objectives, or Japan Inc. The reality is more complex, for several reasons. Over time the programme has become less dominated by narrow and straightforward commercial and economic interests, although these continue to be important; and the oda remains highly geared to promoting economic growth in the recipient countries. Since 1978 Japan has been reducing its tying of bilateral aid procurement, to under a half now (over 95 per cent of yen loans are untied). The actual procurement share has fallen, from 67 per cent in 1986 to 29 per cent in 1993. The forces behind Japan's doubling of its share of world oda between 1972–3 and 1992–3 (from 9.2 per cent to 18.9 per cent) blend the political with the economic, and come from outside the country as well as from within.

Aid policy in Japan has been largely the preserve of a weakly coordinated and complex government bureaucracy. Eighteen ministries and agencies with different mandates and priorities have all played a part, most notably the Ministry of International Trade and Industry, Ministry of Foreign Affairs, Ministry of Finance, and Economic Planning Agency. Implementation is by the Japan International Cooperation Agency and Overseas Economic Cooperation Fund. Traditionally there has been a strong interpenetration by businessmen and bankers; and the political culture as determined by the Liberal Democratic Party, which controlled the government without interruption from the mid-1950s up until 1993, emphasised economic objectives. No significant oversight was exercised by the legislature in this policy area, and there are no strong traditions of public lobbying or of NGOs in voluntary fund-raising and project implementation.

Japan's aid has attracted a growing body of scholarly attention (for example Koppel and Orr 1992; Rix 1993; Yasutomo 1995). There are differences in interpretation, but the following factors are agreed to have been at work. Up until the mid-1960s reparations to South-East Asian countries which had been invaded by Japan comprised at least half of the aid. Non-reparations aid began in 1958 (to India), followed by an expanding programme of loans to East Asian countries vital to Japan's economy. Their significance lay in their raw materials, their market for Japanese capital goods and technology, and the opportunities for investment in infrastructures that would enable the commodities to be shipped out. These countries offer destinations for corporate and commercial bank finance from Japan, and occupy strategic locations relative to sea lanes in the region, particularly the Malacca Straits.

The rise of OPEC and instability in the Middle East in the 1970s led Japan to extend assistance to Arab states, to secure its oil supplies. Japan continued to benefit from US military protection provided under a mutual security treaty of 1952. The US has continued to provide security even after its partial military withdrawal from Indo-China following the Vietnam war, which left 100,000 US troops still stationed in East Asia including 47,000 in Japan, even in 1995. In return, Japan diversified its aid towards countries that bordered areas of conflict with the USSR and Afghanistan and Cambodia, in response to US encouragement. By 1979 that meant extending loans to countries like Turkey and Pakistan 'in which it is very difficult to identify either short- or long-term Japanese foreign policy goals' (Orr 1988: 748). Japan also began building closer financial and trade ties with China. China's modernisation programme announced in 1975 promised enormous economic opportunities. By 1993 Japan had become China's largest trading partner, surpassing even Hong Kong. US strategic thinking also supported giving assistance to China, as a counterweight to the USSR. Stability in China predicated on its enjoying economic development, and a harmonious relationship between the two governments, have come to occupy a central place in Japan's own strategic thinking about regional stability and peace, which are essential to its own security. There is a latent fear of China as an expansionist power. The growth of aid to China has meant Asia consistently taking over 60 per cent of Japan's bilateral aid, with well over half going to East and South Asia.

However, relations with the US have continued to be central to Japan's outlook on the world, for another reason. From the 1960s on the US pressed Japan to increase its global oda. By the 1970s a growing US trade deficit with Japan (coming to account for over a third of Japan's total trade surplus) began to assume political importance. A prominent theme in domestic US politics asserts that Japan has not practised fair trade, most notably by maintaining obstacles to US penetration of Japan's domestic market, for example for automobiles and rice (Japan's farmers enjoy disproportionate political influence), as well as by excessive state support to Japan's export drive, including such means as tied aid in the early years. This has brought discord to intergovernmental relations. Japan's expansion of its aid budget has been a contribution to issue management in the increasingly high politics of trade diplomacy with the US, especially in the 1980s, by which time the US was clearly wanting to reduce its own share of the global burden of oda. Aid seemed tailor-made for Japan's circumstances as an increasingly prosperous country yet unable to exert more conventional forms of military or political leadership in international affairs. The reasons are foreign resentments of Japan's past adventurism in its near abroad (a 'Greater East Asian co-prosperity sphere' was pursued by military means in the 1930s and up to 1945), constitutional bars (Article 9 of Japan's US-drafted constitution permits military force to be used only in self-defence), and the anti-militarist sentiment prevalent in Japanese society. Nevertheless, the US government has never accepted that Japan should view its aid as a substitute for defence spending, and urges Japan to be more active in promoting regional security by various means. Japan's defence spending of $56 billion in 1995 was probably second only to that of the US.

Aid could also help reduce trade friction with the US by developing other export outlets for Japan, so lessening its trade concentration. In fact, the US share of Japanese exports has declined in ten years from 40 per cent to under 30 per cent in 1994. Aid has also been part of Japan's political management of its persistent trade surpluses with some Asian states; in 1993 Japan's trade surplus with East Asia, which now takes 40 per cent of Japanese exports, exceeded that with North America for the first time. And US exports to Japan have risen by one third in the last three years. Before long Japan's annual trade surplus with the US ($45.6 billion in 1995) could be overtaken by China's trade surplus with the US (around $40 billion in 1996), as happened for the first time on a monthly basis in June 1996. Within 20 years China could supplant the US as Japan's main trading partner.

By the 1990s real terms appreciation of the yen (38 per cent between 1985 and 1995) began to cause concern to countries holding large amounts of Japanese concessionary loans, as well as yen-denominated commercial credit. In ten years the total debt owed by China, Thailand, Malaysia, Philippines and Indonesia to official bodies in Japan doubled and debt service increased more than fivefold. The kind of prolonged economic recession and financial malaise Japan experienced during the first half of the 1990s might be expected to weaken support for aid giving in most donor countries. But Japan's preference for making loans rather than grants and traditional suspicion of debt forgiveness could bind it into further replenishments of the aid lines, if only to underwrite debt servicing and to remain a net donor. In time the programme might also be rededicated more strongly to the task of securing exports, so as to help offset the increasing trend for Japan's own manufacturers to seek cheaper locations abroad and export products back to Japan (up to a third of Japan's imported manufactures now come from Japanese-owned plants). Japan's economy is undergoing a sustained structural realignment. The trade and current account surpluses (denominated in yen) have been falling since 1992, largely due to accelerating manufactures imports. In the year up to mid-1996 the currency fell 25 per cent in value against the dollar – a trend that will reduce Japan's lead as an aid donor, in dollar-denominated terms and, perhaps, lead to a revival of bilateral trade tensions with the US.

Taken as a whole, Japan's aid has been called a key to the country's search for status as an accepted member of the world community (Yasutomo 1989; 1995). The recipients number over 150 countries and territories. But Japan is far from being an aid leader in the sense of pioneering the evaluation of aid or prioritising poverty alleviation. It has not obviously shared other DAC members' enthusiasm for attaching economic conditionalities, and was not the first to introduce the conditionalities of Western-style liberal democracy and human rights. Traditionally, Japan has tried to avoid complicating its aid relationships in these ways, preferring to seek 'kudos from the simple fact of giving, rather than by manipulating aid to achieve kudos' (Rix 1993: 175). Japan was the first donor to re-establish aid 'business as usual' with China after the Tiananmen Square 'massacre', one year later. Since 1992 and the government's adoption of an oda Charter, the allocation of aid is supposed to be sensitive to recipient criteria governing: the development, production and transfer of weapons of mass destruction; military expenditure; efforts to introduce a market economy; democratisation and respect for human rights; as well as compliance with environmental concerns. On human rights, Takagi (1995: 107–9) says Japan has now firmly identified itself with the West. Others, like Arase (1993: 942–5) have not been persuaded. They note the Charter contains deliberate loopholes and failed to specify implementation procedures. Japan has been criticised for appearing to shield governments in China, Myanmar and Indonesia from Western pressure on democracy and human rights. China's programme of nuclear testing in 1996 was not welcomed in Tokyo, but the government responded with only token sanctions affecting $88 million of grant aid, leaving untouched subsidised credits worth more than $2 billion annually. Subsequently, China's signature of the UN global nuclear test ban paved the way for a resumption of the grant aid.

The dramatic expansion of Japan's oda has not been accompanied by a master plan setting out an overriding goal. It has been criticised for outpacing the government's capability to administer the flows well, and in some cases for exceeding the capacity of recipients to use the aid wisely. In the 1990s, however, there is closer and more critical scrutiny by domestic opinion-formers, in part owing to heightened concern over unseemly relationships between Japanese business, money and politics generally, and because of the potential for aid waste and misuse in particular. Thus, 1995 saw Japan's Fair Trade Commission for the first time impose fines on 37 companies for forming illicit cartels to share out contracts funded from tied aid.

In the future Japan's policies towards aid could be affected by how the country adjusts to the greater uncertainties brought into economic and political life by the bursting of the 'bubble economy' in 1990 (renewed growth in 1996 is largely due to government spending), and the ending of the Liberal Democratic Party's assured monopoly on office. It is too early to say whether the 'iron triangle' of political, administrative and business circles will prove resilient; but so long as there is weak supervision by politicians, the influence of bureaucratic politics will continue to prevail. One possibility is that instead of continuing to expand the bilateral programme, international financial and development institutions will be invited to raise more loans from Japan's private sector capital market. That would strengthen the country's growing presence in multilateral forums, which has already been displayed in an increasing contribution to international peace assistance (as in the sending of Self-Defence Force personnel to Cambodia for UN peacekeeping duties, which was sanctioned by legislation in 1992). The prominent roles played by Sadako Ogata, UN High Commissioner for Refugees since 1991 and Yasushi Akashi, UN special representative in Cambodia (1992–3) and then to former Yugoslavia, are also significant.

A characteristic of Japan has been to make selective concessions to DAC peer group pressure over such aid quality issues as tying, as well as by increasing the total budget. This is said to illustrate a generally reactive approach to foreign policy, which responds to the anticipated concerns and expectations of others. New and beneficial implications for oda might follow in the future. But other considerations might exert a different effect, including the political elite's aspiration to Japanese permanent membership of the UN Security Council. That might indicate a policy of continuing to target East Asia (with loans that have only weak effective conditionalities), and China in particular, so as not to disappoint expectations and put accumulated goodwill at risk. Better relations with Russia over the disputed Northern Territories/Kuril Islands would be another useful requisite. That may not be impossible, notwithstanding animosities dating back to the last century and the failure so far to sign a peace treaty from the end of the Second World War. After all, basically good economic relations exist between Japan and China despite the existence of a parallel dispute involving the Senkaku/Diaoyu islands in the East China Sea. Substantially increased Japanese financial support for Russia has been continually called for by other G7 members. The aid programme will also continue to bear witness to narrower economic interests, notwithstanding the Ministry of Foreign Affairs' growing concern to display commitment to a stable international economic and political order more generally.

The future shape of Japan's aid programme cannot be predicted precisely, but the already large contribution being made to international development and peace assistance seems bound to feed ambitions to take a greater role on the world political stage. That should ensure that the total oda programme, up 9.4 per cent in 1995 to $14.48 billion, will remain relatively substantial, notwithstanding fluctuations in the yen's international value.

United States

In 1960 the US provided nearly two thirds of all grant and grant-like contributions of international development resources, and over half of total official flows of long-term financial resources to developing countries. Between 1962 and 1989 it transferred $175 billion in economic assistance and $104 billion of military assistance including $66 billion in grant form, to well over 100 countries (Hook 1995: 126). Scholars agree that a consistent and dominant theme has been a close linkage with successive US governments' understanding of national security interests, defined primarily in political, territorial and military terms (McKinlay and Little 1977; Lebovic 1988; Zimmerman 1993; Hook 1995). For Zimmerman (1993: 55) 'the primary purpose of US economic assistance is to support the diplomatic processes that promote overall US foreign policy objectives'; and Conteh-Morgan (1990: 2) claims aid 'became a cornerstone of US global power projection'. Another striking feature of the literature is the criticism for taking too short-range a view of US interests. Thus, while its aid has thrust the US into the affairs of a good many countries, the actual contributions to overseas development and to long-term US foreign policy goals are judged to be highly variable and, in some cases, probably negative on both counts. Of course, the fact that the US emerged the victor from the Cold War, and that some observers believe the US is currently the only superpower, are both undeniable. What has yet to be established with any great conviction is the approximate measure of US aid's contribution to these achievements, and whether something more could have been achieved, possibly at less cost.

The period of Marshall aid and aid to Greece and Turkey up to 1952 opened the era of aid on a scale not since repeated – over $13 billion in economic aid and more than half as much again of military assistance. Together they accounted for 15 per cent of US federal spending and over 3 per cent of GNP, in 1949. The pattern of combining development and military assistance was to become an enduring and distinctive feature of US aid. They are particularly difficult to separate out in the case of the Economic Support Fund, a mechanism that grew rapidly in the 1980s to account for more than half of all US bilateral economic assistance, ahead of the Development Assistance programme. The purpose is to facilitate political stabilisation of strategic states friendly to the US.

The origins of the European Recovery Programme and the motivations that lay behind it include the desire to halt communist inroads into Europe, by helping to rebuild war-shattered economies, especially Germany, and the establishment of export outlets for US manufacturing, which had expanded enormously during the war. The reorientation of aid towards countries bordering China and the USSR in Asia in the mid-1950s also had much to do with the goal of containing communism, spurred on by the Korean war (1950–3). For a while 'economic aid was classified as defence support' (Ball 1988: 247), and not until the late 1950s did the US begin to make a clear distinction between economic development aid and support for security goals.

Ten years of the Mutual Security Act as the legal basis for US aid came to an end with the Foreign Assistance Act, in 1961, and the United States

Agency for International Development (USAID) was set up to administer development aid. Although reflecting President Kennedy's more idealistic outlook on world affairs, the new Act still required among other things that aid promote the foreign policy, security and welfare of the US. The stabilisation of anti-communist regimes remained uppermost as an object-ive in the mid-1960s, as it had been for most of the 1950s. The Alliance for Progress launched by the Kennedy administration in the early 1960s aimed to promote broad based socio-economic change in Latin America, and to bring more popular involvement in the benefits of change. A major object-ive was to prevent other countries following the example set by the Cuban revolution in 1959. At the height of the war aid commitments to South Vietnam came to account for up to half of all US oda, and military support continued right up until US military withdrawal in 1972; Thailand and Cambodia too shared in economic assistance with major security object-ives. In the US the debacle of its role in Vietnam, coupled with the emer-gence of large and persistent budgetary and trade deficits, dealt a serious blow to support for aid, which has never really recovered. Even so, the US was still supplying a third of all economic aid to developing countries in the early 1970s.

President Carter hoped to bring a more ethical dimension to foreign aid policy, in the shape of a linkage with the human rights record of countries. His intention was frustrated by his administration's political weakness, and by overriding considerations of *realpolitik* that were brought back to the fore as Soviet power once again caused alarm. Soviet military incursion into Afghanistan (1979) was a trigger that renewed fears of a long-term design on the oil fields of the Middle East and Iran – lost to US influence with the fall of the Shah. Perhaps Carter's most notable legacy was the Camp David peace accord brokered between Israel and Egypt in 1978. In the following years Israel, already a major partner, and Egypt came to account for around 45 per cent of all US bilateral development assistance. The Reagan years reconfirmed the connection between aid policy and tra-ditional foreign policy concerns. The radical politics of the New Jewel Movement in Grenada (1979–83) spurred the US to devise new funding initiatives as well as a preferential trading arrangement with the region, in the form of the Caribbean Basin initiative (1982). Much larger sums were pledged to Central American governments besieged by left-wing guerillas and popular movements. A determination to undo the regional and domestic standing of Nicaragua's Sandinistas gave a particular tilt to the programmes of economic and military assistance.

The principal means by which the US sought to reassert its global reach in the 1980s, in the face of relative economic decline, was not aid but a large-scale programme of military refurbishment. An increasing propor-tion of aid took the form of military assistance and military sales, which together with the Economic Support Fund totalled almost two thirds of US aid by the mid-1980s. Berg (1991: 69) says that of the $15 billion aid budget in 1989, only $3.9 billion plus half as much again allocated to multilateral institutions 'is more or less unambiguously "development aid" '. The 1980s also saw a hardening of attitudes against the multilaterals, whose conformity to US policy preferences and usefulness to US objectives came to be doubted more and more. Oda's share of aid began to recover under the Bush administration, although nearly half of the more than $15 billion budget remained committed to military assistance and security-related economic aid.

The politics of US aid cannot be understood without some reference to the domestic institutional setting. Unlike Britain, where power lies predominantly with the executive, and Japan, where the Liberal Democratic Party was politically supreme for so long, the separation of powers and weak party discipline allow members of Congress considerable influence over public policy. Congressional representatives, ever mindful of the cycle of election campaigns, pay close attention to constituents' views. The presidency is generally conceded to have extended the executive's role in foreign affairs, occasionally drawing the country into military engagements without first seeking Congressional approval. But aid is one aspect of foreign policy where legislators have been determined to retain influence, most notably through exercising the power of appropriation for the federal budget. A reaction to the so-called 'imperial presidency' of the 1970s gave an additional push. Invariably, restrictions are attached to the proposed aid expenditure and high levels of 'earmarking' are made to suit the demands of Congressional members. They seek some economic benefit to their constituents or the satisfaction of more value-based demands. The former category includes farmers and defence contractors; the latter includes pro-life and 'ethnic' lobbies – not just pro-Israel but also, for example, pro-Greece (whose supporters insist Turkey's claims on security-related assistance must be counterbalanced), and pro-Poland. Needless to say the various groups do not always see eye to eye, and logrolling and coalition building are essential to getting legislation passed.

The law-making process as described, along with the influence exerted over aid by several public sector bodies – not just USAID but the State Department and Defence Department as well as the Treasury and Department of Agriculture – mean the final programme is anything but unified and well coordinated. Although expert witnesses say US oda has displayed strengths such as in economic policy evaluation and was for long a pioneer in aid quality (Cassen et al. 1994: 206), the developmental content of US aid in all its forms now looks less distinguished. In 1992, 33 different goals were set for economic aid by US law. One of USAID's 'major handicaps is that it does not control its own destiny' (Zimmerman 1993: 39; see also Hoben 1989). The fact that aid's political supporters have long emphasised how aid is good for America has made the programme vulnerable to international political and economic developments (most notably the retreat of communism and collapse of the USSR) that now make the benefits appear less obvious. Of course, oda's predicament could also be said to be a function of the democratic nature of the US polity. Other features of the political system that have been well exemplified in the aid arena are legislative scrutiny of policy administration, and investigative journalism. An outstanding illustration is the exposure (eventually) of the 'Iran–contra affair' – the undercover funding of Nicaraguan contras from the proceeds of arms sales to Iran, done without Congressional authorisation. There were political consequences in that President Reagan's second term proved much less successful than the first, in the domestic arena.

The nadir of communism creates a major problem for aid's defenders in the US, some particularist self-seeking interests apart. A maturing of the peace process in the Middle East could depress US aid further if it weakens the geo-strategic claims made by Israel and Egypt, claims that have been dented by the removal of Soviet influence in the region. Conventional wisdom borne out in public attitude surveys maintains that US government aid is perennially unpopular with large swathes of the electorate. The situation is not helped by the fact that the dollar is no longer king and US manufactures are challenged in Europe and Asia-Pacific, whose economic rise has benefited from US military protection and economic assistance in the past. On first taking office the Clinton administration sought to persuade Americans that US security and economic interests justified an aid programme couched in terms of building democracy, fostering sustainable economic development, protecting the environment and stabilising population growth worldwide. But the initiative was undermined by the 1994 Congressional elections which brought Republican Party majorities to both Houses of Congress. Persistent pressure to reduce the federal budget deficit, which dates back at least as far as the passage of the Gramm–Rudman–Hollings Act in 1986, culminated in an agreement in January 1996 to eliminate the deficit by 2002. Coming on top of a 28 per cent real terms fall in US oda in 1995, this has meant *inter alia* significant cash terms reductions in USAID's budget and in peacekeeping expenditures which qualify as aid. But the bilateral programmes to Israel and Egypt still enjoy special protection, accounting for 35 per cent of US aid.

Neo-isolationism has rarely been completely absent from the US, and one possible scenario sees it gaining ground. There is a suggestion that, following the end of the Cold War, the US is no longer 'bound to lead'. Some US commentators like Carpenter (1991) believe US interests are not fundamentally affected by Third World poverty or violent conflict around the world, except in such key regions as their own 'backyard' – the Caribbean and Central America. Tonelson (1994: 127) for example argued the human rights situation elsewhere does not have, and never did have, any noticeable effect on US national security, and so should be of no concern. Such a perspective worries that US interventions will simply entangle the country in events it cannot control, and at significant expense but with little opportunity for gain, especially if there is no clear-cut mission statement of objectives or plausible exit strategy. An oft-cited illustration is the failure to bring peace throughout all Somalia, where local warlords remained *in situ* after the complete withdrawal in 1995 of a 30,000 strong international force of peacekeepers – the US marines pulled out in 1994, having run up operational costs of over $1 billion. In addition to UN peacekeeping efforts, contributions to the UN's general budget, where the US is over $1 billion in arrears, have become especial objects of attack by some Republican Party figures and others who demand substantial reductions in the organisation's running costs. In early 1997 President Clinton proposed to increase the budget for foreign affairs and aid, abetted by a warning from the newly appointed Secretary of State, Madelaine Albright, that the country would be very unwise to unilaterally disarm its diplomatic armoury. But the last words can go to Kansas Congressman Sam Brownback (as reported in the *Financial Times*, 19 May 1995), if only because of their rich irony: 'I think we ought to cut the foreign aid budget. I wish there was a lot more of it to cut'!

Britain

Britain's planned aid budget is £2.046 billion (£1 = $1.62 in February 1997) for 1997–8. At $3.18 billion in 1995, the programme was the sixth largest, and well under half the size of the German and French programmes. Recent times have seen two very energetic and able ministers (Chris Patten 1986–9, followed by Lynda Chalker) head the Overseas Development Administration (ODA), whose declared purpose is to improve the quality of life of people in poorer countries by contributing to sustainable development and reducing poverty and suffering.

However, the casual observer might be forgiven for thinking that if Britain's overall approach to aid since the earliest days had to be described in one word, confusion would be a strong candidate. For example, just how do we reconcile one of the most highly publicised moments – the 1991 commitment of up to £234 million on Malaysia's Pergau hydro-electric dam project – with the founding proposition that the aid programme has a moral basis and must not be used to gain military sales – a proposition spelled out in the 1965 White Paper, *Overseas Development: the Work of the New Ministry*. The British government provided its largest ever cash sum for a single scheme under the Aid and Trade Provision to the Malaysian project, knowing full well the project could not be justified on economic development grounds and would be environmentally damaging. Malaysia is an economically dynamic middle income country. Large orders associated with the project accrued to some major British companies, but the deal was not obviously a good one for the British economy. The fact that a 'conditional linkage' existed with British export orders for arms with a potential value over £1 billion has been formally acknowledged, and formed part of a protocol between the two governments in 1988. However, perhaps this instance in which the ODA's political superiors chose to override its own professional advice was exceptional. For not every day is the Foreign Secretary found by a High Court ruling to have acted unlawfully, as subsequently happened in this case.

The objectives of Britain's aid programme have been much speculated on over the years. Official pronouncements have consistently maintained that more development objectives are entirely compatible with serving political, industrial and commercial interests important to Britain, or in Patten's (1987: 2) words, 'We should not be coy about the extent to which to do what is right can also be to do what is good for Britain'. As a nation Britain has to trade to survive. A persistent theme has been that by helping promote prosperity abroad aid serves stability, which in turn is good for international trade as well as Britain's security. Another constant has been the refrain that, even if the size of the programme fails to impress its critics, the overall quality shines (Seers and Streeten 1972; Burnell 1991a: 11–14). Thus Douglas Hurd, Foreign Secretary, told an audience at London's Overseas Development Institute (February 1995) that 'overseas aid is one of the things we are good at, and it is good for us'. Britain's position as a major source of private capital flows to the developing world (currently the fourth largest) is also sometimes offered as a relevant pointer.

Byrd (1991) argues aid's value as a foreign policy tool has never been as significant to Britain as to the US. Britain has adopted a more pragmatic approach, notwithstanding the 'special relationship' in transatlantic links that has harmonised the broad thrust of foreign policy and brought close military cooperation between the two countries, ever since the 1940s. But a sequence of leitmotifs can be traced back in time. The 1990s have seen the Foreign and Commonwealth Office (FCO), of which the ODA is a part, claiming to be in the van of countries pushing for the observance of human rights, democratic legitimacy and good government. In 1990 Hurd (1991: 17) remarked that his proposal to link aid to progress in these matters would have 'been greeted by uproar' if made three or four years earlier. Nowadays, social goals in health, education and population matters are also presented in a prominent light.

Former periods send different messages. The late 1980s saw the ODA regaining its morale as a development force, having stabilised the real terms budget, asserted its professional commitment and acquired, in global environmentalism, a newly fashionable string to its bow. This followed a very inauspicious start to the decade. On 20 February 1980 the minister responsible (Neil Marten) informed the House of Commons that henceforth, political, commercial and industrial considerations would be given increased weight in decisions on aid allocation. In reality, aid policy's subordination to such considerations was already well established (Burnell 1991a: 20–2). But in addition the ODA's budget and staffing were singled out by the new government for disproportionately large cuts, at a time when other countries like Finland, Italy and Japan were extending oda targets. Britain's performance proportional to GNP fell from a high of 0.59 per cent (for total official resource flows) in 1961 to an oda low of 0.28 per cent in 1987 (comparable to the current figure). As a proportion of public expenditure oda fell from 1.25 per cent in 1979 to under 0.8 per cent in 1993–4. The constraint which used to be identified as aid's adverse impact on the balance of payments has now been replaced by the desire to contain public spending, which seems to have become an enduring public policy wish.

The policy directives given to aid in the early 1980s set back the previous Labour government's notification that an increasing emphasis in bilateral aid would be given to the poorest groups in the poorest countries, outlined in a 1975 White Paper. Perhaps that aim was too ambitious at the time. Probably not enough was known about how to prioritise the poorest effectively. It was also undermined by the encroachment of structural adjustment concerns, in the 1980s. Even so, an interest in the poorest aligns closely with the humanitarian tradition that has always been claimed as a major feature of Britain's aid (see for instance Healey and Coverdale 1981), and it comports with what opinion surveys reveal is the main basis of public support for aid in Britain, namely poverty alleviation. An affinity also exists with the political commitment to maintain ties with Commonwealth countries, many of whom are LLDCs. This historical background to Britain's aid, which can be said to date from the first Colonial Development Act (1929), accounts for the fact that until recently around two thirds of the bilateral budget has regularly been allocated to Commonwealth countries and Dependent Territories. But the proportion has been falling even as the Commonwealth has grown (to 53 countries in 1996), and from time to time there have been other prominent recipients, many suffering from major disasters as in Ethiopia, Sudan, Mozambique and Bosnia.

Overall, the *ad hoc* manner in which Britain's aid has evolved since the 1950s, in pursuit of multiple objectives and producing a wide dispersion of resources among more than 150 recipient societies (plus more than 50 multilateral agencies), is all of a piece. It fits with the country's difficulties in adjusting its world role, and focusing its foreign policy energies, following the end of empire. The reduction in Britain's international displacement as a volume donor matches its relative decline both economically and as a major power. There will be more changes to come. Budget limitations (the planned aid budget for 1997–8 incorporates a nominal 5 per cent reduction) will exacerbate the conflict between more traditional destinations and the EU's growing interest in other regions. For around 55 per cent of the ODA's allocated expenditure is now routed through multilateral channels, and Britain's EU contribution is half as much again as its combined subventions to all other multilaterals. The multilateral commitment will continue to grow; forecasts indicate that in 1996–7 40 per cent of Britain's total aid allocation for the year could be committed to the EU alone (Foreign Affairs Committee 1994).

Sooner or later a decision had to be taken to sharpen the geographical focus of whatever monies remain for bilateral allocations. And in 1996 the Minister identified 26 preferred countries in Africa and South Asia. Over the next few years the top 20 will take around 75 per cent of the bilateral programme. China could well remain a significant partner for commercial reasons and due to its geopolitical importance. India too offers commercial advantages, as a large and growing economy, but will not regain the special aid relation with Britain that saw her receive more than 20 per cent of gross aid disbursements and over a third of bilateral disbursements in 1970 (the figures now are under 5 per cent and 15 per cent respectively). In the 1980s alone British aid reaching India was more than £1 billion, but for the last eight years India's largest donor has been Japan. South Africa, where Britain has substantial commercial and investment interests and where 40 per cent of the population lives below the poverty datum line, could also become a prominent partner. Some African countries like Zambia, with fewer economic attractions, could lose out if they relax economic policy reform and halt progress towards democracy and good government.

All things considered, Cassen's (1991: 205) characterisation of the aid programme provides a fitting conclusion, for what at first sight might confuse becomes much easier to understand when viewed as yet another example of 'a thoroughly British compromise'. But even compromises are not static. There has been change. According to Lady Chalker (author's interview, 10 June 1996) the most significant change in Britain's aid over the last 20 years is the close attention the ODA now pays to results. The most significant constant is the pressure on resources, which itself is said to be a force for inventiveness.

European Union

The EU (EC prior to 1993) is sometimes said to be the world's largest source of oda, and it now supplies over half the world total. This is correct only after aggregating the budget for development cooperation of the EU, which is a sort of collective bilateral programme, and the member states' own bilateral programmes. Their average proportional contribution to GNP of around 0.38 per cent enables EU states to compare favourably with the DAC average. They also comprise the largest group of shareholders in the World Bank and IMF. While the EU's own development cooperation has been responsible for only around a sixth of the members' total aid effort, it has grown considerably, to $7.5 billion in 1995, and is now ahead of all but a handful of countries (half of whom are EU members). Continued growth and a rising share of some members' aid budgets can be expected from EU enlargement, and the 1992 Edinburgh meeting of the European Council decided to increase the budget ceiling for aid outside the Lomé Convention by 60 per cent in real terms, by 1999.

EU aid consists of funds disbursed through its own budget for such items as food aid, aid to certain countries in Asia, Latin America and the southern Mediterranean region, Central/East European countries, and cofunding of NGO activities. The European Development Fund (EDF) accounts for over 40 per cent of all aid expenditure administered by the EU, and is financed directly by the members and disbursed outside the EU budget, under the Lomé Convention. The Lomé Conventions (Lomé IV runs from 1991 to 2000) and their forerunners, the Yaoundé Conventions (which began in 1963), form contractually binding agreements with the associated Africa, Caribbean and Pacific (ACP) countries. This arrangement has often been said to make a distinctive contribution to international aid relations, one of true partnership. Lomé covers trade and aid relations between the EU and the now 70 ACP countries. The qualified membership of South Africa is anticipated soon (providing it can satisfy Spain's demands for access to its fishing grounds in return). Two grant aid funds (STABEX and SYSMIN) are intended to compensate for sudden declines in ACP country export earnings of key commodities, but both have fallen far short of their objectives. The Directorate General VIII (DG for Development Cooperation) is the body in the European Commission responsible for Lomé aid and most food aid. The rest is managed by DG I (External Relations) and the European Community Humanitarian Office, created in 1992.

The development of EC policy towards development cooperation was 'never part of an overall plan: it was incremental, piecemeal and partisan' (Hewitt 1993: 310). Why does the EU have an aid programme? This is best answered in terms of how it came to acquire the commitment. The reason was France's desire to maintain close political, economic and other ties with former colonies, overseas dominions and Dependent Territories, and her interest in sharing the cost with other European countries. At the Treaty of Rome (1957) France insisted on enshrining the special relationship, which came to be known as EurAfrica. The ambit of associated states subsequently widened in parallel with EC expansion, and Africa remained at the core. Notwithstanding their extensive poverty, Britain's former colonies in Asia were not granted equal status in terms of aid and market access. Their claims on aid would have been large, and their potential to challenge European producers in markets for labour-intensive manufactures was feared.

The EC/EU's relationship with Africa has been explained by Hewitt and others in reference to three main supports: the legacy of colonialism bequeathed by some of its principal members (although the EC/EU itself is free of the stigma of imperial exploits); a belief in the economic complementarity of the two blocs, especially in the 1970s when the West wished to safeguard established sources of raw materials; and an assertion that Europe has more to offer than the US and USSR. The Lomé arrangement was advanced as a new model of North–South cooperation, offering aid without strings and guarantees in the form of multi-year agreements. The EDF gave Europe an aid presence autonomous of the two superpowers, so promoting Europe's claim to an independent seat of power in world affairs. EC/EU institutions have a vested interest in expanding the development cooperation and aid effort, and enhancing the organisation's profile in as many countries as possible – aid administration 'gave Community institutions a much coveted foreign policy function to perform' (Grilli 1993: 54). Thus, the programme serves the process of state-formation in the EU simultaneously with giving support to recipients' own state-forming activities. Perhaps because the overriding political objective of Lomé has been to further EC–ACP relations (Lister 1988: 135), the EDF in particular acquired a reputation for endorsing projects without first fully establishing their economic justification. The developmental- and cost-effectiveness of EU aid has been much criticised, particularly in Britain, partly because it takes an increasing share of a total aid budget which government policy seems unlikely to expand (Foreign Affairs Committee 1994).

The policy objective of development cooperation was incorporated for the first time by the Treaty on European Union (Maastricht Treaty, Title XVII) which came into force in 1993. The aims are to foster sustainable economic and social development, alleviate poverty, consolidate democracy and promote human rights and the rule of law. The EC's original posture to cultivate an appearance of equal partnership with the ACP and non-interference (illustrated by its aversion to making policy-based SALs, for most of the 1980s) has undergone revision. And in 1995 provisions relating to democracy, good governance and human rights were strengthened, despite long-standing ACP resistance (Lomé III in 1984 first included reference to human rights). The EU has acted unilaterally to suspend aid in a few countries on human rights grounds, but in 1995 agreement was reached that this would be done only after consultation. Nevertheless, it was also decided that the release of the final 30 per cent of monies earmarked for a country would be made conditional on how the first tranche is used. Thus, together with a late conversion to structural adjustment lending (responsible for a quarter of Lomé IV allocations), the current zeal to promote democracy means the EU is becoming a much less distinctive donor, to Africa especially. Similar effects can be expected from the refinement of a more demanding 'contract approach' to relations with recipients. Nevertheless, in development cooperation as in other matters, the EU's own performance has failed to exhibit to everyone's satisfaction such essential features of good government as accountability, transparency and openness.

Historically, the management of the EU aid budget has been a weak point and the allocative process has been haphazard at best (Grilli 1993: 350). The EU lacks the technical capacity for development policy analysis, and has never shown a strong commitment to monitoring and evaluating project spending, or checking the contribution made to policy objectives, which remain somewhat cloudy anyway. Not much EU aid has benefited the poor (Independent Group on British Aid 1989). The procedures for making aid applications have been called excessively bureaucratic, and the organisation tends to be inflexible once it has determined its position. On occasions the response time in humanitarian emergencies has been lamentable. Some critics say the EU should withdraw from aid delivery and employ the best national programmes instead. That is unlikely to happen, in spite of the desire some member states have to renationalise their aid budgets. The Commission has not yet demonstrated the authority and capacity to coordinate the national aid programmes, although the Maastricht Treaty does establish the principle of complementarity between EU and member state policies towards development cooperation.

Aid remains a valued instrument of the member states' foreign and commercial policies, and government aid bureaucracies have their own entrenched interests. As befits the differences of national interests and ideological shading among EU states, the governments remain divided over the future content and distribution of EU aid. Members' individual interests have always intruded, most notably the bias towards francophone Africa in the first three Lomé conventions. So far, the ambiguous character of EU development cooperation – neither bilateral nor fully multilateral – has been a reflection of the EC/EU's indeterminate political status as only a part-formed polity. Total synergy between the EU and members' bilateral programmes could remain a chimera, although much may depend on how far political integration progresses, at least in the 'fast-track' states.

In 1989 the European Commission assumed responsibility for coordinating OECD aid to Hungary and Poland, beginning with the PHARE (Poland Hungary: Assistance for the Restructuring of the Economy) programme. That was subsequently extended to other countries in Central and Eastern Europe and so far almost $1 billion has been disbursed. It came to be flanked by the TACIS programme set up for former Soviet republics in 1991. These new aid destinations now take more than double the EU funds set aside for Asia and Latin America. Another region of great interest to states like France and Italy is North Africa, especially following Algeria's descent into lawlessnes in the early 1990s and growing Islamic militancy there, in Egypt and Tunisia. Under the heading 'strategic challenges in the Maghreb' the OECD (1994: 18) noted the labour force in the Maghreb is growing at 5 per cent a year and will double by the year 2010, and unemployment is already between 20 and 30 per cent in urban areas, being particularly severe among young people. The 'political context is fragile. Ecological pressures are unsustainable and particularly critical as regards water resources. Emigration pressures continue to build, fed by the demographic contrast between this region and Western Europe'. EU countries host over five million immigrants from the Southern Mediterranean. Hence, the region is a focus of considerable interest. Special technical and financial cooperation arrangements go back to the 1970s, but they are now being intensified. Morocco, Tunisia and Israel have association deals with the EU. There are plans to create a Euro-Mediterranean free trade zone encompassing 12 Southern rim Mediterranean states, where in November 1995 the EU pledged $6 billion to aid education and cross-border infrastructure projects.

Pagni (1990: 17) noted 'the long-fostered illusion that Europe had a "debt" to the ACPs is disappearing'. Europe's stake in stability and good relations with Russia beckons (see Chapter 11). The EU's most recent enlargement to the North has brought in countries who as donors are well known for their recipient orientations and poverty goals. But the next round of EU enlargement, to the East, will not bring much extra money to DG VIII, and it will place large additional and competing strains on total EU resources (although the Commission's most recent thinking claims the EU budget will not have to be increased in real terms for the next ten years, because the timetable of accession for new members is lengthening). The EU is expected to make a leading contribution to the rehabilitation of former Yugoslavia, the largest recipient of EU aid in 1993–4. In 1991–5 the ACPs were allotted nearly half of all EU aid, and in 1992 sub-Saharan Africa received almost 70 per cent of EU disbursements. But from now on these countries could find it difficult to retain such preferential treatment. The 1995 financial protocol to Lomé, which granted Ecu 14.6 billion (1 Ecu = £0.8) for ACP states for 1995–2000, exceptionally did not increase real terms funding. In the future, ACP countries might have to think less in terms of EU aid and more of the trade possibilities an expanding European single market could offer (the single market could actually depress bilateral aid if it means procurement tying becomes illegal). However, for some ACP countries an improvement of export production capabilities may well require first an effective application of more oda. For all the countries, the margin of price preference available under Lomé is likely to be eroded by global liberalisation, spurred by GATT and its successor, the World Trade Organisation (WTO).

Conclusion

In world aid there has been a marked pattern to bilateral allocations, with sub-Saharan Africa accounting for the largest share of oda from Britain, France and the EU, and Asian countries receiving three quarters of Japan's aid between 1970 and 1990. Asia still receives more than half of Japan's aid and regularly provides around eight of the top ten recipients; although for some years Japan (like Germany) has been allocating more aid than Britain to sub-Saharan Africa. Egypt and Israel ensure around half of US aid goes to the Middle East and North Africa, and Central America has been another favoured US destination. At their peak, OPEC flows favoured 'front-line' states in the Middle East, and Soviet aid concentrated on a yet different group of countries. When these two sources abandoned Egypt the US became its principal donor. Also, some aid recipients who enjoy close relations with a certain donor, especially the former colonial power, have seen their interests given special representation in multilateral forums like the Bretton Woods institutions, such as in discussions over eligibility for debt relief. Their 'patrons' have also shown a tendency to be more cautious than others in applying economic and political conditionalities and aid sanctions for non-compliance.

The reasons for being a donor can be distinguished analytically from the reasons for adopting a particular pattern of aid allocation, but the two sets will usually interact. The global pattern has come about not as the result of deliberate application of some rational criteria concerning the distribution of need, proven oda effectiveness or developmental performance. Instead, it is a product of historical and geopolitical factors and it reflects the mixtures of commercial, strategic, political, developmental, humanitarian and other motivations particular to countries individually. The pattern has evolved over time and will continue to change, in accordance with the evolution of the financial and economic strengths of donors and developments in local, regional and world politics. But through all, it is worth bearing in mind that the politics of implementation temper the importance of policy-making; and the field observations of Tisch and Wallace (1994) illustrate the significance of Morrissey, Smith and Horesh's (1992: 88) conclusion (made apropros Britain) that 'the aid policy process confirms the hypothesis that policy cannot be made in advance of implementation'.

Aid policy has been driven by concerns that take their particular character from donors' individual circumstances; the Burmese economist Hla Myint (1967: 183) was right to say we cannot blame the people of the developing countries if they sometimes find it hard 'to distinguish the "crypto-philanthropists" who hide altruism under a mask of national self-interest from the "neo-colonialists" whom they suspect of hiding national self-interest under the mask of altruism'. A feature common to much of the literature about individual donors is that a lack of vision is detected. This can mean several things, such as the absence of sustained long-term thinking or of one dominating sense of purpose. Also, it means aid programmes can turn into by-products of how a number of government departments and agencies – not themselves responsible for development cooperation – pursue their own objectives, and the balance of power among these actors. The foreign ministry is usually the overseer; and aid agencies have not usually been the lead organisation even in the recent growth area of humanitarian operations with a peacekeeping dimension (Randel 1994: 339).

A lack of vision also implies that a sense of moral purpose does not really capture the essence of aid policy, at least for the largest volume donors, notwithstanding the involvement of many high-minded people on the operational side of oda. In the Nordic region, corporatist-style structures of governance have reinforced the favourable influence on public attitudes of redistributive policies at home, so enabling public policy to draw on the idealism found among NGOs. Elsewhere, NGO representation tends to be weaker. And in Britain, where the Minister for Overseas Development is not assured a seat in Cabinet, the office is held at the time of writing by a non-elected politician. Access to top tables in government has to be shared with and mediated via others who will exact a price in return for giving their support – 'there are an awful lot of people who think they should have a hand in how the aid programme should be spent' (Ryrie 1986: 7). Just as in aid-receiving countries, individual components of the total bureaucracy of government will seek influence over the aid programme so as to promote their own organisational interests vis-à-vis the other actors. This is not an environment obviously conducive to maximising aid's developmental efficacy, with all its social and environmental ramifications. Nevertheless, the main donors from outside the DAC have not delivered a demonstrably better prospectus. Far from breaking the mould, the South's most dramatic contribution – OPEC aid – 'generally followed the established pattern of the traditional donors' (Hunter 1984: 264). And the former USSR, China and Cuba are better known now as candidates for concessionary inflows than as major donors. They have come to be overshadowed not just by the multilateral institutions, but by the non-governmental organisations as well.

Large and little

Multilateral bodies and non-governmental agencies complete the organisational map of principal aid suppliers. The claims that one or both of these groups make a specially valuable contribution to aid are reviewed in this chapter.

Multilaterals

In international affairs multilateralism refers to the coordination of relations among three or more states on the basis of generalised principles of conduct. In aid, multilateral organisations supplemented $41.3 billion of bilateral oda with a further $18.4 billion of multilateral oda, in 1994. True multilaterals draw their membership and some income from aid-receiving countries as well as the main donors. There is no single organisational model: some, like UN bodies, have almost universal membership; in others, for example OPEC funds, recipients may not be subscribers and are not represented on the governing bodies, and these are not acknowledged universally as true multilaterals. Some multilaterals are regionally-focused, others have a world-wide remit.

DAC states disburse on average around 20 per cent of their oda through multilaterals not including the EU. The EU's inclusion obviously produces a considerably higher figure for EU countries – the EU accounts for a quarter of all multilateral oda. Some donors fund more than 60 multilaterals. In budgetary terms the major ones include the International Development Association (IDA), which provides interest-free loans to countries meeting the low income threshold (currently 79 countries), at a nominal administrative charge, with a ten-year grace period and maturity of up to 50 years. Since 1960 the IDA has approved loans totalling over $90 billion. In 1994 IDA loans boosted total new commitments by the World Bank to over $20 billion, although the IBRD actually made negative net disbursements. After the IDA ($5.6 billion) there are several large grant-disbursing departments and autonomous agencies (the latter indicated by ⋆) of the United Nations, the largest being the World Food Programme ($1.39 billion in 1994) and UNDP ($1.24 billion) – followed by others like the Food and Agriculture Organisation⋆ (FAO), UNICEF, WHO⋆ and UNHCR, all dating from the 1940s. As well as having a specific clientele, a unique feature of UNICEF's mandate allows it to operate in areas whose rulers do not have UN recognition. In addition there are numerous international research organisations like the International Institute for Tropical Agriculture.

White and Woestman (1994: 541) found that, on average, multilateral aid is slightly harder (less concessional) than bilateral aid, chiefly because the IDA provides only loans. There are also international financial institutions lending on terms that in the main are not sufficiently concessional to count as aid. These include the IBRD, IFC and regional development banks such as the Asian Development Bank, Inter-American Development Bank and African Development Bank, which have their own Funds for providing soft loans. The IMF traditionally provides short-term loans to countries in deficit on their external accounts, to enable them to correct the imbalances without resort to measures that disturb the international monetary system or international trade. The IMF is not intended to be either an aid or development organisation. However, it established a Structural Adjustment Facility in 1986 (enhanced in December 1987) to refinance 'hard loans' with virtual interest-free loans, for countries with annual average per capita incomes below $865 and experiencing problems with their external accounts; implementation is carried out jointly with the World Bank. In 1994 the IMF made concessional net disbursements of almost $1 billion, and only a few of its 30 LIC borrowers faced completely non-concessional terms.

Donors, recipients, and aid's developmental and humanitarian objectives can all benefit from multilateralism, in different ways. Multilateral channels offer donor governments several possible attractions. International prestige has been one incentive; another is the political gains that can come from demonstrating solidarity with other donors and the strengthening of diplomatic ties. There is no iron law whereby small donors channel a higher proportion of their aid through multilaterals than do larger donors, but governments with only modest aid budgets and restricted competence in development cooperation can take advantage of the multilateral infrastructure. In particular they can share in its greater bargaining power when negotiating terms, conditions and conditionalities with aid seekers. Ireland places over half of its aid with multilaterals, chiefly because of EU claims, and Denmark and Luxembourg are rather similar. Although it is possible for a small donor to spread its aid too thinly across too many multilaterals, a country can use multilateral participation as a way of capping bilateral aid commitments. Bilateral approaches by aid seekers will simply be redirected. Even for large donors such a strategy might mitigate any harm to goodwill that could be caused in countries awarded a low priority in the bilateral budget. Multilaterals can also help donors like Japan with rapidly growing aid budgets and limited experience in some sectors to make the most effective use of their expenditures, especially in unfamiliar countries. Multilateral contributions are close to 30 per cent of Japan's oda, underscoring its aversion to direct intervention in recipient states. Peer review and exchanges among members should cause lessons in good practice to become widely known and they can then be incorporated within bilateral programmes.

By acting collectively donors might hope to safeguard their foreign policy interests from the onus of initiating aid conditionalities that recipients find anathema. Recipient resistance to bilateral conditionalities can be more easily deflected where their conformity with multilateral conditionalities can be shown. Moreover, donors may be able show support for a cause which they might feel unable, or unwilling, to support by acting singly, for political as well as financial reasons. For example, domestic opposition in the legislature or ruling party could prevent the foreign ministry pursuing a particular bilateral aid initiative, such as aid to a government whose ideological or political features are disapproved of but which holds geostrategic importance. Pressure from a foreign power provides a different kind of example. In the early 1980s some European governments who wanted to support the development efforts of Nicaragua's Sandinistas, contrary to US government wishes, sent aid through an EC programme. Certain expenditures like some types of family planning programmes or efforts to counter AIDS can be considered too sensitive to proceed on a government-to-government basis, or might risk jeopardising good diplomatic relations, and will be routed via multilaterals and NGOs.

Reality check on multilateral virtues

Multilaterals comprise a diverse assortment of organisations differing widely in their mandates, stated purposes, resources and capabilities. This makes generalisation difficult. Bilateral agencies vary too, in their developmental commitment, professional and technical competence. Some have accumulated superior insights in respect of specialised activities and countries that share certain characteristics. There are no grounds for believing that every multilateral is more effective than every bilateral, in developmental terms or in the estimation of aid partners. To illustrate, African and Malagasy opinion-leaders have judged EC aid to be inferior to bilateral aid and the UN's specialised agencies (T.G. 1990: 12–13). Negative views about EC aid were expressed by 69 per cent of responses, in a 1253-strong sample drawn from seven countries. The commitment to rigorous self-evaluation of their effectiveness has been very patchy among multilaterals – strong in the World Bank, weak in several UN agencies. The absence of comprehensive data and methodological difficulties also impede clear-cut comparisons of performance between multilaterals and bilaterals, since both groups harbour such a variety of very different examples. The point should be borne in mind in what follows.

Money and politics

A long-standing presumption holds that multilaterals focus more single-mindedly on developmental and welfare goals than do official bilateral aid agencies. The latter may even be under a statutory obligation to factor donor and sub-national interests into their decisions on aid. Put differently, multilateral aid is oriented more to recipient needs. This shows up in a greater allocative bias towards LICs and LLDCs. Multilaterals are less likely to react quixotically to partners who suddenly shift their domestic politics or foreign policy alignment in ways unacceptable to a principal bilateral donor. The World Bank's (*World Development Report 1990*: 129) claim is fairly typical, and unsurprising: 'Bilateral donors are frequently criticised for providing aid for political, strategic and commercial reasons . . . Multilateral agencies generally give more weight to developmental criteria . . .' However, in reality the picture is less straightforward.

Take the commercial angle. Donors can and do seek to profit from multilateral aid. Thus for instance Britain was reckoned to receive export orders worth 170 per cent of its contributions to multilateral budgets, in the late 1980s. Multilateral aid spending is not tied to one source, and competitive bidding for tenders should drive down costs and ensure value-for-money. But over time, aid recipients may bear extra costs as a result of failing to standardise their sources of procurement. They may suffer from an incompatible mix of technologies introduced by multilateral financing. The EU is exceptional in that procurement is limited to suppliers from EU and ACP countries. EU food aid has been shown to have chronic weaknesses including over-concentration on expensive dairy products, idiosyncratic country allocations, poor programming and inadequate staffing (Independent Group on British Aid 1989: 41). The awarding of procurement contracts even by multilaterals can be politically influenced, as has frequently been alleged of EU development cooperation.

Second, far from being situated outside politics, multilaterals are exposed on both sides. Malek (1991: 145), who is an economist, considers 'all the rhetoric about the de-politicisation of aid and transfer of aid resources from bilateral to multilateral agencies, since the latter are not politicised (or less political) is factually baseless and superfluous'. Multilaterals may be unable to avoid entanglement in the domestic and regional politics of recipients. There is no permanent guarantee to the recognition proferred by multilateral aid – Taiwan was excluded from the UN in 1971 (at Beijing's insistence), despite being in receipt of UN technical assistance. Major subscribers exert pressure through the power of the purse. This is a form of 'active multilateralism'. It may be dedicated to achieving political objectives of donors as much as their developmental agendas. At the very least the intention can be that a donor's bilateral preferences gain the appearance of multilateral endorsement. An illustration is Japan's lobbying of the World Bank to soften its sanctions imposed (as a result of US pressure) on China after the Tiananmen massacre (1989). World Bank consideration of new loans to

China was deferred for a year, and then resumed shortly after. Political horse-trading takes place. Thus Yasutomo (1995: 167), who approximates China's importance to Japan with Russia's significance to the West, connected G7 endorsement of Japan's wish that aid to China be resumed with Japan's own (reluctant) endorsement of G7 assistance efforts to Russia.

Swedberg's (1986) claim that the World Bank and IMF have been routinely subject to political pressure derived from Western security and ideological positions geared to the Cold War situation, directed from within and without and especially by the US, chimes with what close observers have said more recently. For instance Mosley, Harrigan and Toye (1995: xxxi) say it is difficult for the Bank to resist politically motivated pressure over loan allocations. Gibbon (1992: 135) argues that not only has Bank lending always been political in the sense of being linked to the promotion of specific kinds of economic policy, but also, 'political considerations have always been present in decisions about who to lend to, how much they should receive, and on what terms'. Lady Chalker (1990: 358) refers to 'creative tension' between the governments' representatives on the executive board and multilaterals' top management. International disputes in high politics such as Arab–Israeli confrontation have intruded in the forums of several multilateral organisations. In the mid-1980s the US, Britain and Singapore withdrew from the UN Educational, Scientific and Cultural Organisation (UNESCO – not chiefly a financing agency), some say because its African Director-General had the temerity to criticise cultural imperialism; others say because they objected to managerial incompetence and a communist bloc-inspired inclination towards media censorship. UNESCO lost almost a third of its funding.

Major subscribers will not all speak with one voice on every issue. Moreover, cohesion among multilaterals is impeded by divisions within governments over their approaches to international affairs, for instance between the foreign affairs establishment (dominant in the UN as a political body), finance ministry (lead representatives in the multilateral development banks) and the more specialised interests involved in the UN's technical and operational work. At home, political wrangles, difficult executive–legislative relations, or just the alternation of parties in office can all disrupt a member state's behaviour in and towards multilateral bodies, affecting their work adversely. Thus USAID withdrew funding from the International Planned Parenthood Federation and the United Nations Fund for Population Activities in the mid-1980s, following intense campaigning by 'pro-life' campaigners. General hostility towards the UN and the involvement of US troops in UN peacekeeping especially has caused US government support to falter – at the UN's fiftieth anniversary in 1995, US subscriptions were $1.3 billion in arrears. The US is normally assessed for a quarter of the general budget. Dissension between governments over the apportioning of dues is not uncommon in the multilaterals. This applies particularly when a country that has been a major contributor decides the costs must be redistributed, yet opposes a corresponding reduction of its voting rights or political influence in the organisation, as has happened in the World Bank from time to time.

Multilateral aid can be just as political due to circumstances at the recipient end. This is because development work cannot be confined to purely economic logic and technical detail. Even deciding arrangements for distributing humanitarian assistance often involves much more than selecting the most logistically convenient route. That multilateral aid can have political effects in the recipient country is undeniable, notwithstanding any attempts by the institution to deflect donor politics. In any case, a country's political situation and government behaviour may have to be taken into account before being able to assess whether assistance will serve the multilateral's objectives. A well-known fact is that Article IV of the World Bank's Charter requires that economic considerations alone shall be relevant to its loan deliberations. Interference in the internal political affairs of countries is prohibited. However, aspects of the social situation and political risks that might affect the economic viabilities are legitimately considered in the Bank's decision-making process. Nowadays, it is also considered legitimate to raise the human rights situation and military spending in dialogue with recipient governments, because of their possible economic consequences. Similarly, EC/EU aid, 'once depicted as a model of political neutrality and non-interference in the internal affairs of the recipient countries, is now becoming distinctively more political', in regard to its conditionalities (Grilli 1993: 341). Indeed, the fact that multilaterals like the IDA are not beholden to donor commercial lobbies, and so can give preference to programme aid over project-linked aid, means they are freer to seek influence over borrowers in respect of their policies. To repeat, it is the leverage potential that is part of the multilaterals' attractiveness to donors, who can hide under their skirts. The encroachment of multilateralism, together with increased aid coordination by major multilaterals, means aid seekers face a narrowing of choices and less freedom to manoeuvre. Their bargaining position is made weaker.

The comparative advantage of multilaterals in policy dialogue is not just due to their financial resources. As membership organisations they may enjoy close and continuous relations with representatives of recipient governments, some of whose negotiators may have worked for one or more of the multilaterals in the past. Multilaterals' officers who hail from the Third World may enjoy a confidence and trust not normally extended to bilateral agencies other than historic allies. Bonds of personal friendship and mutual understanding in this international epistemic community are functional for reaching agreements. But none of this means developing countries have comparable power to shape the multilaterals' policy agendas, especially where voting rights are weighted in accordance with subscriptions, as in the World Bank group. OPEC's decline has accentuated the imbalance. To illustrate, the voting structure of the governing council of the UN's International Fund for Agricultural Development (founded in 1976 and enjoying a good reputation) had to be reconsidered in 1995. The original tripartite basis whereby OECD, OPEC and other developing country groups each enjoyed equal voting rights increasingly jarred with the growing preponderance of OECD funding. Another recent case involves the recapitalisation by non-African members of the African Development Bank, where 24 countries are in arrears. At stake is the survival of the soft-loan African Development Fund, bereft of funds for over two years. At one point it seemed that the quid pro quo for $2.6 billion in new pledges would be a transfer of shareholding out of Africa. Instead, it now seems that in future decisions will require a two thirds majority. DAC countries source more than 90 per cent of the funds of the universal multilaterals. The headquarters of all the most important bodies will continue to be in the developed countries. That the IMF and World Bank both came to be pilloried in the 1980s by countries dependent on their financial support suggests their reputed advantage over bilaterals in talking to borrowers is not simply due to greater acceptability: in principle, their superior financial clout is what enhances their 'powers of persuasion'.

Finally, inter-organisational relations among multilaterals are not unusually beset by bureaucratic politics, and by conflicts over turf and resources. This has been particularly noticeable among some of the more than 20 aid-disbursing UN agencies and departments, and among their heads, evident even in moments of humanitarian crisis (Kent 1987). The UN Secretary-General has authority to designate a lead agency in emergencies, but he is only '*primus inter pares* (first among equals), with the emphasis on *pares* rather than *primus*' (Minear and Weiss 1995: 146). Similarly, disagreements between the World Bank and IMF over what might look like doctrinal matters, such as different perspectives on Third World debt, can be bound up with institutional rivalry and competition for standing and seniority. These political manifestations will hinder the execution of mandates and can thwart the achievement of formal organisational goals. Like other organisations, multilaterals fall prey from time to time to clashes of personality and other internal breakdowns, even in the upper echelons. Some lose direction or are distracted by informal objectives. Such traits form the basis of perennial criticisms levelled at various UN bodies, where overlapping mandates, blurring of institutional boundaries and susceptibility to the competing foreign policy interests of members all provide a recipe for systemic mismanagement. By 1995 some UN organisations seemed to be in danger of losing significant portions of their funding. The US announced an intention to withdraw from the UN Industrial Development Organisation (UNIDO) on 1 January 1997 and to default on arrears and current contributions, notwithstanding their legally binding nature. The Commission on Global Governance (1995) recommended the disbandment both of UNIDO and the United Nations Conference on Trade and Development (UNCTAD) – the conscience and advocate of the developing and disadvantaged countries, according to UN Secretary-General Boutros Boutros-Ghali. While UNEP's valuable work in advance of the 1992 'earth summit' and its contribution to the debate on global climate change are widely acknowledged, a perception exists now that even this body presently lacks dynamism; in 1996 the US government halved its financial contribution, to $18 million, and in February 1997 the US, Britain and Spain decided to withhold their contributions pending acceptable reforms.

Centres of excellence

Several positive claims about multilaterals can be combined under the rubric of centres of excellence. First, unlike bilaterals, which cannot develop a competence across the full range of activities that aid finances, multilaterals can be repositories of wisdom, concentrate experience and draw on all the talents, pooling the internationally available technical expertise. The importance of this is obvious in such specialised areas as, say, crop and disease control research. The recruitment of staff from developing areas should bring unique perspectives and vital local knowledge.

However, peak organisations can also become inward-looking, and the development of a 'house view' may impede smooth adjustment to new knowledge and to changes going on in the world outside. One consequence can be that when new lessons are finally absorbed, there is a fundamental paradigm shift. Something like this has been said of the succession of themes taken up by the World Bank, starting out from capital projects in the 1950s, through basic needs and rural development (1970s), structural adjustment (1980s), good governance and now the resurrection of a focus on poverty. Although insiders may be able to detect a groundswell for change well in advance, to outsiders like modest clients, the final turn of the tide can appear abrupt. They sometimes express bewilderment. They could well be unable to adapt their public programmes, policy commitments and institutional practices as suddenly as the multilaterals seem able to reformulate their advice. Lele and Nabi (1991: 356–7) say the repeated 'waves of new themes' turn multilateral agencies increasingly towards employing generalists and away from specialists, which further reinforces their vulnerability to yet more new fads.

A second positive claim is that multilaterals are well placed to provide coordinating mechanisms. These are needed to bring order out of the chaos created by the plurality of bilateral and non-governmental aid agencies. The World Bank is an example, for it regularly chairs consultative group meetings of donors and aid consortia for more than 40 countries. The UNDP has been organising round table meetings since 1972. However, traditionally there has been resistance to coordination from many aid agencies, who wish to maintain control over their resource flows so as to pursue their own policy objectives, and who might fear that loss of control would weaken their oda's developmental effectiveness. Moreover, as has already been noted of UN family members, the record of coordination among multilaterals is itself deficient. The UN Disaster Relief Office, established by 1972 to mobilise, direct and coordinate relief activities of the UN system is a notable failure, so much so that in 1992 it was absorbed into a newly created Department of Humanitarian Affairs (DHA). The DHA has yet to demonstrate it can do much better. There has been a persistent failure to develop agreed guidelines and a clear division of labour among the UN's departments and specialised agencies; the case for identifying a clear mandate for rehabilitation assistance is a pressing example. By dividing the monies among the different bodies (rather than, say, building up UNDP to pre-eminence), and making nationality an important consideration in key appointments, the members have also weakened the system.

A third claim is that the international nature of multilaterals gives them a comparative advantage in mobilising financial resources on a large scale, including, in the case of the banks, the ability to borrow from capital markets around the world. Thus they are better placed to help tackle the very large challenges, for example post-communist transition in Russia. Multinational and regional development schemes can also make financial demands well beyond the capacity of even the largest bilateral donors. Multilateral involvement provides a useful opportunity to demonstrate international solidarity with attempts at cross-border economic cooperation that have political significance, an example from the 1980s being the Southern African Development Coordination Conference, which ranged Africa's 'front line' states against apartheid.

However, Tendler's (1975) early observation about the World Bank, repeated by other commentators many times since (and about other organisations too) bears repetition. Size often seems to be accompanied by an undue emphasis on moving the money, which tends to displace the formal goals of the organisation. Like some other weaknesses found in multilaterals, this trait has shown strong resilience. Detection has not proven to be a prelude to resolution. Time will tell how far James Wolfensohn will be successful – on becoming the World Bank's President in 1995 he is reported to have said (*Financial Times*, 16 September 1995) that Bank officers should achieve promotion not in accordance with how many loan proposals they get approved by the board, but instead on 'how many smiles we put on people's faces'!

The 'giantism' in multilateral projects (agricultural, especially irrigation schemes, as well as industrial projects) which has been encouraged by having large budgets to spend, has also been much criticised, on a variety of grounds including financial, economic, social and environmental. Occasionally it has led to ventures that were too complex to be managed effectively, like the integrated multi-sector rural development programmes fashionable in the 1970s. The developmental potential of small-scale producers and micro-projects gain less support, for they fall below the financial threshold, and call for excessive staff time relative to the loan size required. Also, a number of UN bodies as well as multilateral development banks have been much criticised for spending too much on themselves, in the form of remuneration and expenses. The most graphic account, Hancock's (1989) *Lords of Poverty* appeared to receive subsequent confirmation by the lavish commissioning of the London headquarters of the European Bank for Reconstruction and Development (EBRD), during the presidency of Jacques Attali (1990–3). That phase in the EBRD has now passed, but Hancock's (1989: 183) notorious assertion that so-called aid is 'inherently bad, bad to the bone, and utterly beyond reform' owes a good deal to shortcomings of managerial and operational accountability in large multilateral organisations. The World Bank is certainly not the only example, but is particularly notable because of its large financial and policy-related involvement in developing countries and its ability to withstand bad debts of a magnitude that could seriously undermine some ordinary banks. Hancock exempted the voluntary aid agencies, which have fewer resources, even though their critics believe they are no more accountable as organisations.

Even so, at the present time multilaterals are not uncommonly experiencing great difficulty in raising enough finance to pursue their objectives; and Cassen et al. (1994: 216–19) argue their work will become *less* effective if their funding is reduced. While the existence of a formula for burden sharing and peer group pressure can lead to an increase in members' all-round contributions, it can also have the opposite effect – the funding spiral goes into reverse. The IDA, which depends on government donations, just escaped this consequence in 1996, when it received a $3 billion emergency replenishment without the benefit of US participation. At one point in 1996 the Asian Development Fund looked as though it could run dry before replenishment became due, owing to the US government's reluctance to make good its arrears until East Asia's wealthiest 'dragon' economies offered increased contributions. Total arrears at the UN topped $3.7 billion in 1995, and the regular budget has been subsidised by transfer payments from funds supposedly earmarked for peacekeeping operations. More than 130 members are in arrears. As total real terms commitments by governments to development and peace assistance stagnate or go into decline, the competition between multilaterals for funds can only intensify. In an illustration from 1995 the British government attempted to persuade EU partners to maintain IDA funding levels by trimming contributions to the EDF, if necessary. The argument was used that non-EU countries could be pressured into sharing in the funding of the IDA, in contrast to the EDF. Inside some donor countries the bilateral share of the aid programme is the easiest to defend politically. There, the possibility exists that if multilateral contributions were increased markedly, the impact on public support for oda could be adverse.

Finally, apart from aggregating resources, engaging in an impressive range of specialised activities, and providing collective goods like policy analysis, the multilaterals can be presumed to offer the most appropriate organisational response to the growing number of challenges that are of an increasingly global or transnational nature. International relations are revolving more and more around such issues. The pattern is less and less for nation states to behave singly or in very small groups. Almost everywhere, forces and trends that could seem abstract and difficult to comprehend to the ordinary citizen now appear to be shaping important aspects of people's lives. The anxieties to which this can give rise help explain why the relatively comfortable idea that small is beautiful exerts a powerful appeal. That idea has served the NGOs for aid and development well, by endearing them to bodies like the World Bank, UNICEF and UNHCR. They invite NGOs to help implement their spending decisions, such as in matters where grass-roots contact is thought desirable, even essential. The drawing of favourable comparisons of NGOs with examples of multilaterals became virtually *de rigueur* in the 1980s. The multilaterals suffered from the more public nature of the political and other controversies that have surrounded their performance, while NGOs benefited from the fact of having emerged into the limelight comparatively recently, and seemingly without taxpayers' support.

Non-governmental agencies

The global data for NGOs are notoriously imperfect, but at roughly $6 billion the grants they provide annually for relief and development work from privately raised resources are greater than the net oda disbursed by the World Bank group, and compare favourably with other UN agencies. Aid from NGOs approximates to around 10 per cent of all oda (up from 0.2 per cent in 1970). In addition NGOs collectively spend more than half as much again in monies provided by official sources – at least $5 billion and possibly approaching $9 billion in 1993 (Hulme and Edwards 1997: 6). These amounts fluctuate from year to year in accordance with the incidence of Third World disasters, because NGOs are used extensively by many bilateral and some multilateral agencies for distributing food and other humanitarian supplies. Nevertheless, oda provided to NGOs for non-emergency activities overseas has been increasing (from 0.7 per cent of oda in 1975 to at least 5 per cent now) as a matter of policy. All the figures understate the true worth of the expenditures, if claims about the superior quality of what NGOs do are correct.

Mapping the landscape

While most NGOs are relatively small, some are absolutely large (BINGOs, or big NGOs). For example Oxfam has an annual income exceeding £100 million, 840 retail outlets and partnerships with 3600 organisations in over 70 countries. Catholic Relief Services (United States) and the International Committee of the Red Cross (ICRC) have both handled around $500 million in one year, or more than the aid budget of some DAC states. Other well-known NGOs are Médecins sans Frontières (France), Danchurchaid, Trocaire (Ireland), and Misereor (Germany). In the US private and voluntary organisations (PVOs) collectively raise aid of around $2.6 billion annually – exceeded by the official budgets of only five countries and the US. The average DAC figure for private grants proportional to GNP (0.03

per cent) is bettered in several countries whose oda ratio is unimpressive, including the US, Switzerland, Germany, and Ireland whose proportional voluntary aid performance is treble the average.

The more than 3000 development-related NGOs in the OECD countries encompass a wide range of organisational and technical proficiencies. Some are highly specialised, others are multifunctional (Burnell 1991b, Chapters 3 and 4). Not all are funding agencies. Only some station officers overseas and are operational in developing countries – Save the Children (SCF) has been a notable example, although it is rapidly moving away from that role. Others like Christian Aid prefer to work exclusively through local partners. Many prefer to work with non-governmental bodies, some work routinely with governments, SCF for example. Most have one home base, a few have branches in several Northern countries, and some such as the Red Cross movement are truly international networks. Many make use of volunteer workers; some have become increasingly professional. Around 200 of the larger NGOs account for more than three quarters of the voluntary funds. They are unevenly distributed, barely figuring in Japan where there is no comparable tradition to Judeo-Christian charity or Muslim almsgiving. A few well-known charities in Europe have been involved with poor countries for longer than their government's machinery for development cooperation. This is partly due to missionary-related activities dating from the early days of imperial expansion. The majority of NGOs possess charitable status, which in most countries brings certain benefits including privileged tax treatment and a generally favourable disposition among the public.

Strengths and weaknesses

Although the 1980s, especially media coverage of famine relief in Africa, brought a dramatic increase in public awareness of NGOs, their reputation as development organisations was already building. To some extent this was due to growing criticism of official bilateral and multilateral oda. *The Economist* (16 March 1985) headline was typical: 'Do-gooders in sandals often do more good than international civil servants'. The NGOs' standing also benefited from the fact that little was known about how effective they really were. This remains a shortcoming, particularly in respect of ignorance about their overall impact on the lives of poor people (as distinct from the performance of individual projects and programmes). Indeed, Smillie (1993: 19–20) argues that even in cases where there have been attempts to evaluate performance, opportunities to learn from the results and exchange findings are still being neglected.

The NGOs' reputation embodies a number of claims. At their maximum these suggest NGOs *must* be better at doing certain things, especially at the very local level. This is because of organisational and other characteristics ascribed to them and which are unavailable to official structures. It is claimed that they are: flexible (due to their being relatively small); non-bureaucratic (staffed by highly dedicated people); innovative (unlike public servants, for whom rules on accountability incline towards risk-aversion); participatory (they work with people at the grass-roots); and relatively cost-efficient (they do not seek a profit and are run on tight budgets, yet are willing to engage on personnel-intensive tasks). Also, NGOs' field presence and contacts with local partners mean they are well placed to know about social needs and to monitor human rights, a function whose value has come to be appreciated more and more by OECD diplomatic cadres.

The above list is impressive, and hints at features attractive both to right- and left-wing critics of official aid. The former look to NGOs to erode old-fashioned public administration socialism in the provision of welfare and to be a seedbed of micro-enterprise and grass-roots capitalism. The latter see in NGOs and especially local community groups vehicles for the empowerment of poor people, by organising against privileged vested interests and structural inequalities. Such NGOs are far preferable to state agencies captured by domestic elites and foreign capital. In reality, the picture is much more mixed than either representation (see Burnell 1991b: Chapter 4) and there is evidence to suggest both sides could be disappointed. By the late 1980s the heightened profile and increased resources of NGOs began to attract closer scrutiny, Chris Patten's comment being indicative: 'the ODA has earned the right to ask the same questions about their quality of performance as they ask of it' (author's interview, 1 March 1989). Careful criticism of NGO performance has emerged from NGO staff ranks. That is healthy. It also indicates that substantial room for improvement exists. Take for instance speed of response in humanitarian crises. While it is said the UN often fails to make a prompt response even when given an early warning, NGOs have on occasion intervened prematurely. Also, some have fairly rigid views about what they should be doing and how. This limits their adaptability. Spokespersons admit the claims about participation are overblown. They acknowledge great difficulty in bringing sustained improvements in the conditions of the very poorest people. An obsession with growing bigger, and the phenomenon of too much money chasing insufficient worthwhile projects (and too few good local partners), have been detected and remarked upon. In a fieldwork-based comparison, Marcussen (1996: 279) found NGO and multilateral projects barely differed in respect of quality, scope and flexibility, local participation and reaching the poor. The detailed evaluation by Riddell *et al.* (1995) of the development impact of Swedish NGO projects funded by oda also proved disappointing, even where NGOs achieved their own internal objectives. Very similar findings have been reported in other studies (cited in Edwards and Hulme 1996: 963; see also Hulme and Edwards 1997). The frequent failure of the benefits to outlive the involvement of NNGO aid is especially worrying.

Not all of the features in respect of which NGOs are said to be distinguished can be easily reconciled in practice. For example, innovation means risk-taking which can be inappropriate for the vulnerable poor. Equally there is an overarching uncertainty about the nature of the contributions NNGOs can, and should, make to the worlds of aid and development. Social scientists have theorised stages in NGO evolution, often criticising those NGOs (probably the majority, especially the larger American PVOs) that have not moved far along the continuum. For example, Korten (1990) identifies four generations of development-oriented NGO – relief and welfare (dominant in the 1950s/60s), community development, sustainable systems development, and people's movements. He says most NNGOs are still confined largely to the first two stages. But their aim to assist in terms of improving material conditions, through tranferring productive technologies and suitable tools, is now out of step with more 'progressive' ideas of social mobilisation and empowerment, even consciousness-raising. NNGOs are urged to concentrate more on the collective organisation of poor people to gain greater control of their lives, through challenging the socio-economic and political structures that are held responsible for their impoverishment. The support of institution-building among SNGOS is said to be superior to financing discrete development projects. Some NNGOs endorse these 'progressive' approaches even while continuing to employ fairly traditional messages in their appeals for donations at home.

Finally, a significant component of recent thinking about NGOs has focused on how they might influence the deliberations, policies and decisions of governments, intergovernmental forums, and powerful transnational bodies like large companies and commercial banks. The suggestion is NGOs should scale up their impact by emphasising 'demand-side' activities more than delivering aid, which will always be relatively small-scale and highly localised. Clark (1992: 193) for instance urged NGOs to 'manoeuvre' into a closer relationship with the international institutions (he subsequently left a senior position in Oxfam for the World Bank). Indeed, Sogge's (1996) call to replace the more typical voluntary aid agencies by true citizens' associations expressing international solidarity for empowering the poor restates quite an old view: namely, that voluntary agencies should move away from decision-taking on projects, even fund-raising, towards greater lobbying, policy advocacy, and efforts to inform and mobilise public opinion about Third World needs (see Lissner 1976). In principle a small measure of influence over matters like Paris club initiatives for debt relief could deliver far more of value to the Third World's poor than any number of NGO-sponsored development projects. There have been successes. In the 1980s the NGOs led official bodies to greater consideration of environmental concerns and the needs and entitlements of women. They kept the flame burning for poverty as a priority issue. Even so, some NNGO representatives remain cautious about how far NGO advocacy can be successful in the future, and on what sorts of issue. Some are even more sceptical in regard to NNGOs attempting to influence government policies in developing countries directly, rather than by setting examples through practical work. The objection is not just to forming close relations with governments, but that NGOs would be departing from ground where their comparative advantage is strongest. Moreover, helping the poor to become their own advocates is less paternalistic and potentially less stifling than acting as advocates on their behalf. In any event, NNGOs that maintain practical involvement in overseas work lend authenticity to their messages, and should gain in authority as advocates representing the Third World. Unobtrusive lobbying in the corridors of power may have to be given preference over open campaigning which, although closer to what some people call development education, is more likely to come into conflict with the restraints of charity law (Burnell 1992).

Some are born beyond politics, some seek to become political, and others have politics thrust upon them

Charitable status imposes legal constraints on political activity. For instance in Britain, charitable objects must not be political in the sense of seeking public office, bringing pressure to bear on the government or disseminating 'propaganda'. Political activity is permitted only if it is demonstrably ancillary to, and directly furthers the achievement of, the organisation's declared charitable object(s). Thus advocacy may be permissible, but the manner and tone should be restrained. Non-charitable NGOs interested in Third World causes, the London-based World Development Movement (WDM) for example, are under no such legal restraints, and are allowed even to be partisan in terms of party political alignment.

A commonly held view is that a peculiar virtue of voluntary agencies lies in their being apolitical or non-political. Some charities abjure politics altogether. An example is the International Red Cross Movement. This consists of the ICRC – concerned primarily with victims of conflict and fundamental human rights – and the League of Red Cross and (in Islamic countries) Red Crescent Societies. The League and its constituents help people harmed by natural disasters and refugees outside areas of conflict. The Movement's principles require that no discrimination be made as to nationality, race, religious beliefs, class or political opinions. The Red Cross may not take sides in hostilities (not even with the UN), nor engage at any time in controversies of a political, racial, religious or ideological nature. Unlike some NGOs, the ICRC will not normally take advantage of military escort when operating in conflict situations, for fear that its credentials could be jeopardised. The national Red Cross societies should not allow governmental interference to distract them from the Movement's principles, although in some countries their conduct has proved controversial.

There is also the belief that NGOs for aid and development are political and must be political if they are to have a chance of achieving their ends. Even the ICRC must make political judgements. Human well-being and development are about resources and opportunities. These can be intensely political matters, especially in the midst of scarcity. Economic inequality translates into political inequality; dominance is exploited for the purpose of maintaining and extending material privilege. The idea that powerlessness precludes a substantial long-term improvement in the material condition of the poor seems to be widely endorsed among the more vocal officers of many NNGOs. Similarly, a lessening of political inequality would be viewed as a desirable long-run effect of measures that in the first instance address other objectives, such as better primary health, improved access to education and greater economic self-reliance. The long march from disaster relief to pressure group-type activity has been halting and slow, with no little slipping back. But the aim would undeniably bring political activity more overtly to the fore. The asymmetrical relationship between NNGOs and SNGOs has always been inherently political anyway. The NNGOs' preference for the language of 'partnership' and 'cooperation' over 'customer'/ 'provider' exchange barely conceals the power advantage they enjoy in most cases. For, as Sizoo (in Sogge 1996: 196) observes, the fact that NNGOs have an interest in spending their budget seems hardly ever to be openly acknowledged, and is not usually manipulated by SNGO partners in negotiations over the transfer of funds. The problematic of how NNGOs should relate to Southern counterparts has sharpened with the latters' explosion in numbers (an estimated 30,000–50,000 SNGOs and grass-roots support organisations), their articulate contribution to critical debates about the NNGO–SNGO relationship and about how NNGOs relate to their own governments, and the breaching of the NNGOs' gatekeeping function vis-à-vis official funders. For all these reasons Smillie (1993: 14) believes NNGOs are 'in trouble'. However, the most common inference is not that redundancy is just around the corner. Instead of succumbing to a gradual 'hardening of the arteries' (Hulme and Edwards 1997: 278), NNGOs should think more carefully about what they try to do in the future, and resolve what is being called their crisis of identity.

Most NGOs know that from time to time they may wish to benefit from the good offices of governments. First, take the government at home, which could restrict NGOs' freedom to pursue their objectives, as the US government obstructed harmless PVO assistance to private groups in Nicaragua, in the 1980s. The NGOs have much to offer government in exchange, including the advancement of good relations between nations. They can put a kindly human face on foreign aid and promote positive public perceptions, even where moral or unselfish reasons do not supply the chief reasons for government oda policies. Abroad, NGOs operate in terrain that may be politically awkward for official donors, where the authorities do not permit even the FAO and WFP freedom to operate, and in crisis-ridden countries whose administrative structures have lost the capability to distribute humanitarian relief. To illustrate, in 1984 NNGOs channelled emergency supplies to areas of famine-stricken Ethiopia controlled by anti-government forces, using supply lines in Sudan. NGOs have facilitated arms-length funding from official sources to Palestinian projects in the Israeli Occupied Territories and to black groups in apartheid South Africa. Where a declared aim is to encourage transition to democracy, as in the 1990s, NGOs can be employed to channel resources to local civic action groups and social movements that are challenging authoritarian regimes. Direct subvention from donor governments would be more easily subject to control here, if not forbidden outright. In sum, NGOs can be useful intermediaries and valuable buffers. Donor governments are insulated from the risk of unexpected political embarrassment.

In the US, where the government fostered PVO growth in response to social problems in Europe at war's end in 1945, and where there is a PVO tradition of receiving substantial income from government sources, some PVOs have been unashamed vehicles of the government's foreign policy endeavours. Superpower politics has impacted on government–PVO relations in a manner not so evident in other DAC countries (see Linden 1976; Sommer 1977: Chapter 7; Smith 1990: 25). The war in Vietnam and support for the Nicaraguan 'contras' provided instances, and Smith (1990: 209) maintains public policy-makers use PVOs as 'useful instruments for finessing opponents, partially placating dissidents in their own ranks or introducing new agendas into policy debates when their own options or leverage on these fronts are limited'. PVO and NGO programmes can be used to satisfy domestic lobbies without government having to account too closely for the way resources are used.

However, NGOs can also attract displeasure at home. For example, they may impede good diplomatic relations if the authorities overseas believe they are *agents provocateurs*, say in their work with minority groups, the poor and oppressed. On occasions they press their own government to exert political pressure abroad, including on oda partners. The criticisms they sometimes voice of their own government's aid programme and of its foreign policies can also complicate intergovernmental relations. An example is the controversy stirred by the legal challenge brought by the World Development Movement (WDM) against the British government's funding of Malaysia's Pergau dam. Attacks on the quality of oda can weaken the relevant minister's hand when negotiating resources with the Treasury, as can the seemingly insatiable nature of NGO demands to increase the budget (author's interview with Chris Patten, 1 March 1989).

NNGOs will need to consider their relations with the authorities overseas, and not only if they wish to influence public policy. Elliott (1987: 63), a former head of Christian Aid, said NGO relations with developing country governments are 'often sensitive, sometimes difficult, always a matter of concern'. More recently, relations are said to have improved in countries that have abandoned authoritarian rule. This does not extend to Myanmar, where in 1995 the ICRC announced steps to withdraw because of obstruction by the military government. Any government can legally deny foreign NGOs access to society, and some have banned named agencies and personnel. They can impose conditions on the relationships their citizens are allowed to form with NNGOs. Many require that all aid transfers be registered and obtain official sanction. Governments also control the use of resources such as information, the time of public servants and other services vital to the success of NGO endeavours.

Antagonism has existed in some countries where the activities of NNGOs have disturbed politically influential vested interests. In places they have been judged a threat to sovereignty and national security; UN agencies have to be more respectful, and are more shy of behaving in clandestine ways. NNGOs working with refugee communities that harbour 'freedom fighters', terrorists and criminal elements face particular difficulties. Efforts to improve the position of women can provoke especial resentment, and may be interpreted as cultural imperialism, or offensive to prescribed religious beliefs. Foreign NGOs can be an irritant when they attract international attention to circumstances a government would rather not have scrutinised, child labour for example. In the extreme, they will be sandwiched between a suspicious host and a distrustful government in their home country, as happened to Oxfam at the outset of the Cambodia emergency in 1979. A profusion of project and programme initiatives promoted by a multiplicity of NNGOs may be considered potentially subversive in a different way, by deranging national strategies for development. Cernea (1988: 41) noted that 'more than a few governments (at the political level) and numerous government agencies (at the technical level) oppose formal NGO involvement' in schemes receiving World Bank funding. Even today there are countries where the legal and political environment for local NGOs is not particularly friendly, notwithstanding efforts by the international donor community to persuade governments to be more relaxed.

Overall, the chances are that voluntary aid agencies and developing country governments will cooperate easily on some things, and on others will find agreement to be much more difficult. The presence of NNGOs may be valued by government as a source of international credibility, especially if they are willing to work with its own programmes. NNGOs sometimes make international representations on behalf of their Southern hosts and seek to persuade official donors to be more generous. Government officials could be relieved that NGOs take on some of the burdens of service provision. But there will also be resentment if NNGOs and indigenous groups funded from abroad threaten to become competing structures to the state, better resourced and possibly more popular. At the same time, astute political entrepreneurs will exploit NGO-funded initiatives in ways that advance their careers. There have also been numerous instances where the personal security of aid workers has been seriously threatened. The salience of this problem has increased as NNGOs have become more central to the international community's pattern of response to complex emergencies, characterised by lawlessness and endemic violence. In the 1990s what Michael Aaronson (1995: 4), chief executive of Save the Children, calls 'emergency relief with a strong political flavour to it' has accounted for a sizeable proportion of the voluntary agencies' activities, notwithstanding their preference for longer-term development work. One consequence has been an increase in reported incidence of trauma and stress among NNGO workers – a darker side to the human face they bring to aid. A second effect is to intensify the questions raised about the funding nexus that has developed between official bodies and NGOs, and the implications this has for what the NGOs try to achieve.

The nexus with official funding

A corollary of the political liberalisation and democratisation that have occurred in a number of countries in the 1990s is that more space should open up for NGOs, foreign as well as indigenous. This means more opportunities. At the same time, the funding relationship between official bodies and voluntary agencies has become considerably more important, and is now well entrenched. The view is often put forward that this can also bring constraints and distortions.

Government funding and cofunding of NGO activities goes beyond humanitarian relief operations, to include development projects and programmes. In the 1970s rural projects taking place in the context of basic needs strategies of development provided a launching pad for NGOs, after years of being largely ignored by many official donors, especially multilaterals. From then on a variety of financial arrangements have been installed in all main DAC countries. The sums involved vary quite significantly. On average DAC governments disburse around 1.5 per cent of their oda through NGOs, but there is wide variation from under 1 per cent for Britain (where NGOs accounted for £185 million of ODA expenditure in 1994–5) to over 10 per cent for Canada and Switzerland for example. Close to 30 per cent of the bilateral aid budget of Sweden's International Development Authority is earmarked for NGOs (Riddell *et al.* 1995: 26). The trend is for NGOs to draw an increasing share of their income from official sources, which now account for around a third of the total. In the US, where PVOs obtaining government finance are legally obliged to raise at least 20 per cent of their income from private sources, grants and contractual revenue from public sources account for up to 80 per cent in some cases. As well as funding block grants and NGOs' own development projects or programmes, official donors also employ NGOs as contractors for their own proposals. Now, NNGOs and SNGOs are said to be involved in around half of all projects funded by the World Bank, in operational and consultancy-type roles. There is far more confidence in NGOs than in the official structures of some developing countries to deliver aid fairly and efficiently. A contrast with Soviet assistance was made by Bartsch (1988: 12), who said the remoteness from local needs and inability to engage in grass-roots projects was 'at least partly related to the absence of non-governmental aid organisations in the Soviet Union'.

What do NGOs get out of official funding, apart from increased resources? One possibility is greater flexibility, if they are enabled to advance the sort of activities that do not attract private donations. Also, government backing can raise an NNGO's international standing and open doors in the developing world, as well as enhance its chances of levering funds from multilaterals. A working relationship with official sponsors may encourage

NGOs to professionalise their general approach, with beneficial consequences for their effectiveness (it can also endanger the established consensus on intra-organisational values, if there has been a strong egalitarian tradition). Funding and cofunding links have brought opportunities to advise official donor organisations and influence the administration of public policy toward development cooperation.

For at least a decade, however, a number of warning voices in both the Northern NGO community and the South have been saying no lunches are free, even if the dangers associated with government funding lie mostly in seduction, not overt control (Kent 1987: 98). Government sponsors may seek to introduce politically determined agendas for development coopera-tion. They have their own preferred expenditure headings and country priorities. At the very least their understanding of development and devel-opment guidelines may well not coincide with NGO ideals. Currently there is a concern that NGOs are being coopted into the state-reducing bias inherent in much Western official thinking (Edwards 1994; Watkins 1995a: 214). This means a commitment to delivering services rather than to build-ing local NGO and community institutions, social mobilisation and social transformation (Edwards and Hulme 1995; 1996; Hulme and Edwards 1997). Quantifiable short-term outputs take precedence over less easily measurable, longer-term process outcomes. Official sponsorship can also mean admin-istrative and particularly auditing requirements that are onerous, especially for small NGOs. The imposition of financial accounting procedures that extend upwards to the funders overshadows the development of account-ability to the Third World's poor.

Some newer NNGOs have started out life as virtual quasi-non-governmental bodies; and in competing with them for resources longer-established NGOs could unwittingly turn themselves into executing agents too. The special virtues that were once ascribed to the NGO sector will come to look increasingly mythical. Rather than become more like watch-dogs *vis-à-vis* donor governments or perform the function of critical advo-cacy, NNGOs risk acquiring a kind of establishment status, but without any great power to shape the public policy process. Abroad, the appearance of losing their independence may endanger their relations of trust; some SNGOs resent what they see as the imposition by NNGOs of managerial models of cooperation that conform to donor government preferences. The host authorities will become more wary both of NNGOs and their local part-ners. It becomes more likely that SNGO claims to a voice in public affairs will be discounted, owing to their growing financial links with foreign gov-ernments, directly or indirectly through NNGOs. But the continued flow of official subventions to NGOs can be no more guaranteed in the future than are private donations. They will be exposed to the vagaries of foreign policy, changes in government and intergovernmental relations, possibly even the exercise of conditional aid cut-offs. These are but some of the fears.

However, the extent to which there must be a trade-off between public funding and the autonomy of NNGOs should not be exaggerated. Among countries, between different NNGOs of the same nationality, and even inside individual NGOs there are differences of opinion about how serious these problems have (or will) become. While the size of NGOs and where they get their money from may be significant, so are the other influences colouring the relationship with government. Thus, for example, in Britain both the ODA and most NGOs reckon relations are generally satisfactory. That state of affairs could continue in spite of the increasing importance of government funding. Similarly in Sweden, a longer and greater financial dependence of some NGOs appears not to have infringed their operational independence (Riddell *et al.* 1995). In any case there was no golden age of total autonomy in the past, and NGOs' future usefulness to governments could remain contingent on their not being de facto adjuncts of the state. NNGOs may believe a distinctive identity is essential to keeping their popular support, but the preservation of their integrity need not be contingent on displaying a confrontational attitude towards government anywhere.

These days few OECD governments can realistically aspire to cultivate a growing corpus of increasingly financially dependent development NGOs. That scenario would run counter to the almost ubiquitous trend for private finance initiatives to be sought in what once were public sector preserves. Indeed, while a concern about how much public money they should accept will continue to circulate among NGOs, there is a no less pertinent (but less often posed) question for governments: how far should they go in giving support to NGOs? There is a belief that as NGOs are encouraged to grow and become more capable in administering large flows of aid, so the ruse of handing them more of the responsibility for addressing recipient needs will be easier to accomplish. In a growing number of crisis aid interventions, NGOs say they are increasingly being put 'in the front line' of diplomacy, and are taking the place of a more considered approach by the international community to devising long-term solutions to difficult problems. They acquire responsibilities without power. The ethnic conflict in Burundi, Rwanda and Eastern Zaire is an example. Gordenker and Weiss (1995: 365) cite the view of Omaar and de Waal that NGO involvement in expanded relief operations funded by governments is but one side of a coin – the other side being official disengagement from development efforts in poor countries offering little strategic or commercial benefit. Perhaps for not much longer is the NGOs' role primarily to complement, or even to supplement, oda. From having been regarded by the DAC as useful allies in mobilising public support for increased development assistance, NGOs now risk being interpreted as substitute providers of genuine aid. Put differently, donor governments will feel more free to devote the bulk of (reducing sums of) oda to the promotion of donor interests, feeling safe in the belief that moral responsibilities have been devolved to the NGOs. This stratagem has been called the privatisation of aid. It might look attractive from the point of view of developing close relations between ordinary people in the North and the South, far better than elite level bargains struck between states. However, a contrary view regrets what is construed as a weakening of the principle of public responsibility. Past experience suggests that where voluntary fund-raising for international emergencies is hugely successful, the achievement can be double-edged. On the one side, it demonstrates a significant level of support for aid from the public. On the other side, it is said to strengthen the case for leaving real aid increasingly to individual charity and the private sector. And where changing norms concerning relations *between* societies will lead, redistributive arrangements *inside* DAC countries could follow soon after, so undermining the welfare state even further.

Conclusion

The crystal ball is hardly any easier to read for NGOs than it is for multilateral and bilateral agencies, and making generalisations is equally hazardous. The three sets of actors are becoming thoroughly intertwined. This means occasions both for tension and for fruitful cooperation among them will continue to arise. Currently, the range of tasks NGOs have formerly undertaken is being overlaid with yet a further set of expectations, exogenously determined. The NGOs' origins outside government and their traditional overseas connections have made them candidates for enlistment in the challenge to develop civil society in emerging democracies. This is but one of the many aspects in which the tide flowing towards political liberalisation and democratisation is adding distinctive new characteristics to the politics of foreign aid in modern times.

The modern politics of aid

Aid cannot be proven to have become more, or less, political with the passage of time. Just as there has never been an identity of political purpose among the different donors, so the politics has taken on fresh aspects and new combinations. In the modern politics of aid, donors link oda to a bundle of aspirations embracing democracy and such properties as accountability, legitimacy, the rule of law, human rights, transparency and good governance, also sometimes referred to as good government. The linkage takes two forms: political conditionalities attached to aid allocations and disbursements, and support for specialised projects and programmes like those currently receiving around $400 million annually from USAID (a total of more than $1 billion since the mid-1980s) for 'democracy assistance'. This chapter explains why the modern politics of aid came about when it did and examines the reasoning behind it, and reviews some principal problems.

First, however, it should be noted that the modern politics of aid is not entirely new. Beginning around the turn of the decade, it is already halfway into the average lifespan of big ideas in aid. And there have been precursors. Previous decades saw the US in particular and others including Sweden, Norway and the Netherlands formally incorporate such objectives as human rights, participation and even democracy into government aid policy, for example the US Alliance for Progress in the early 1960s. The 1961 US Foreign Assistance Act required the military budget of aid recipients to be taken into account, and the addition of Title IX in 1966 authorised the direct promotion of democracy. Between 1976 and 1979 Congress passed 25 pieces of legislation linking foreign policy and human rights. The Reagan administration in the 1980s sought to connect the anti-communist anti-Soviet goals of foreign policy and a mission to promote the *idea* of democracy. The US's quasi-autonomous government-funded National Endowment for Democracy began work by 1984.

Of course, aid has always had political objectives, conditions and strings. But the declared intention in the 1990s to employ aid for the purpose of engineering systemic political reform, involving institutions as well as policies, the very conduct of government and the organisation of the political process, is striking. So much so that Baylies (1995: 328) says a 'strongly coercive element is particularly characteristic of the new aid regime'. Equally significant is that most of the previous initiatives did not go far beyond rhetoric, even for the European donors. In the US they tended to be quickly overtaken by national security considerations, as happened to the Alliance for Progress, or were resisted by USAID and derailed in the foreign affairs bureaucracy, like President Carter's personal commitment to human rights. The very goals were misappropriated to serve other ends, as in the support given to oppressive right-wing regimes in Central America, in the name of preserving freedom from communist dictatorship.

During the era of decolonisation, national self-determination dominated the rights agenda in international politics. The diplomacy of good relations between the ex-colonial powers and their former colonies inhibited any firm practice of continued political mentoring. Apart from which, ideas of human rights were contested as part of the ideological struggle between the capitalist West and socialist Eastern bloc. Diplomatic means to advance the rights of individuals around the world were stifled. Vincent (1986: 132) claimed there was a freemasonry of diplomacy which gave precedence to the mutual accommodation of the interests of governments; he conceded it seems natural for democracies to prioritise national security in their foreign policies. Similarly, Jackson (1990: 196) maintained 'live and let live' has been the religion of international relations. These perspectives now look somewhat old-fashioned. Something else that is different now is that *all* of the main donors (who are all DAC members) and many multilaterals seem to embrace *broadly* similar themes. Almost all world oda falls within the orbit of what is said to be today's donor consensus on oda. But of course, there is no uniformity of practice. Indeed, that donors display different emphases between such headings as democracy, human rights, governance and their various components indicates there is some disagreement over what they are trying to achieve and a degree of confusion over the reasoning behind the objectives.

Origins of the modern politics of aid

The World Bank's declaration of interest in governance in *Sub-Saharan Africa: from Crisis to Sustainable Growth* (1989) arose from dissatisfaction with the record of adjustment lending. But it was Western political leaders who raised enthusiasm for linking aid to democratic considerations and human rights. In June 1990 Britain's Foreign Secretary called for good government and political pluralism in Africa, and France's President Mitterrand spoke likewise to a Conference of Heads of State of Francophone Africa.

Shortly after, the Heads of State and Government of the Organisation of African Unity declared their support for democracy, human rights and the rule of law. A revised version of Commonwealth aims taking account of this new climate was agreed at the Commonwealth Heads of Government meeting in 1991. At the time no provision was made for enforcement procedures, but in 1995 Commonwealth heads agreed to suspend Nigeria for human rights abuse, and set the government a two-year deadline for the reintroduction of democratic rule.

The end of the Cold War and popular revolutions in Central/Eastern Europe highlighted that dramatic political reform is possible. The collapse of Soviet power released the West from former restraints: no longer could risk-taking in the management of political relations with the South redound to the benefit of the communist bloc. At the same time, courageous men and women in a number of Third World countries were calling openly for an end to their own experience with authoritarianism. The timing may have owed much to the events in Europe, but the provenance of these demands for political reform was unmistakably endogenous, and usually was fuelled by growing frustration with the economic mismanagement and impoverishment in their societies that long predated the fall of the Berlin Wall. Third World voices for change could be said to give authorisation to the donors' new aid initiatives, particularly in their support for basic political freedoms. In this way, local and external factors interacted. The combination caused a second 'wind of change' to start blowing across sub-Saharan Africa. Of course the origins of what Samuel Huntington called the 'third wave' of democratisation, which began in Southern Europe and Latin America, lie further back, in the 1970s: the modern politics of aid was not responsible for that. Instead it was an opportunistic response to later developments in the USSR. The moment was also politically opportune for the 'aid industry' in DAC countries, where exposure to what seemed to be diminishing public support was beginning to cause concern. The enthusiasm for famine relief in Ethiopia in the mid-1980s had been followed by anticlimax, and by the 1990s reports of a renewed bout of aid fatigue which were featuring regularly in the media, especially in Britain.

Aid fatigue – a diversion

There is nothing novel about the claim that aid fatigue exists and is on the increase. The Pearson Commission (Commission on International Development) detected aid weariness on all sides in 1969. In donor countries the malady has been diagnosed at frequent intervals ever since, especially by journalists.

However, little effort has been invested in specifying what aid fatigue is and who suffers from it most – politicians, aid administrators, NGOs, the electorate, or the attentive public? What counts as evidence for its existence, and can it be measured? Should any significance be attached to the kinds of support for Third World causes and the examples of development cooperation that do not show up in aid figures? Over the years most of the claims about donor fatigue have ignored the performance of non-DAC donors. Some DAC countries like Japan and Italy must be exempted for some years anyway, having increased their oda in real terms or proportional to GNP; others like Sweden and Norway have consistently exceeded the UN's target.

Customary usage leaves the term aid fatigue very unclear (Burnell 1991c). The reference point in many instances is reducing oda budgets (no distinctions being made between real and nominal terms, or absolute and proportional changes). But what extent of time and magnitude of change should trigger the diagnosis? Sometimes, variations in aid's volume are accorded less significance than oda's inadequacy relative to the imputed needs (which are usually assumed to be increasing). Occasionally, what is being referred to is a failure of imagination or the lack of foresight which prevents donors responding to warnings of an impending disaster until it is too late to take precautionary steps. A yet further angle is the way governments treat aid and other public expenditures differently. Hence Oxfam director Frank Judd's plea for a humanitarian equivalent of Norman Schwarzkopf, the US General who seemed to be granted virtually unlimited access to resources for fighting the Gulf war. Other accounts of aid fatigue invoke not just budgetary indicators but a perceived tilt in donor concerns towards non-developmental objectives like national security and commercial interests. That means aid fatigue would be a misdiagnosis where a reducing aid volume is overcompensated by improvements in aid's developmental and humanitarian quality.

The confounding of aid fatigue with speculation on the reasons for its existence is also a common mistake. Many such reasons have been advanced, some of them barely compatible. This suggests our understanding of the phenomenon is plastic over time. If, as some analysts suggest, the end to the rivalry with communism and Soviet power lies behind Western aid fatigue in the 1990s, then different explanations must apply to earlier bouts of the malaise. Perhaps they were different strains. The following litany of explanations drawn from several countries is illustrative. One: aid fatigue increases when donor countries experience economic difficulties and the sense of personal insecurity rises. Two: the overall context of public affairs is important, chiefly intensifying pressures on other objects of public expenditure such as health care and education. Three: while most people are uninterested in foreign affairs anyway, societies go through phases when they become more inward-looking. The post-Vietnam 'syndrome' in the US, the rise of Quebec separatism in Canada and current European preoccupations with the future of the EU are examples, although in the US Roper (1979) argues general apathy towards international affairs actually blunted the potentially damaging impact of negative public perceptions of aid. Four: SALs/SAPs in the 1980s dismayed aid supporters, who came to think oda might be making Third World poverty worse. The same point applies in respect of the repayment of foreign debt.

The list continues with special reference to voluntary aid. Five: from time to time good causes other than foreign aid become fashionable, and will compete strongly for donations, for instance in the 1980s environmental conservation. Six: growing 'compassion fatigue' lessens charitable giving all round. It may be due to 'compassion confusion' – the bewildering proliferation of fund-raising appeals that has followed government attempts to shift the burden of welfare provision from state to market and NGOs. Seven: in Britain in the early 1990s some right-wing politicians claimed people were being alienated from aid by certain voluntary agencies that were becoming too politicised, that is to say too left-wing. Eight: the mass media, which plays a central role in focusing interest and shaping attitudes among the public, has never given enough publicity to the need for development assistance, which is not deemed to be as newsworthy as disaster relief. This has long been depicted as a problem for the more development-oriented NGOs. But its impact became more serious in the late 1980s as a result of 'image fatigue', caused by the heightened sensationalism of the media's coverage of emergencies. The NGOs' determination to exploit the fund-raising potential of well-publicised disasters shares responsibility. The effect has been likened to poisoning the well – no longer are people so easily shocked into giving support. Since the last great Ethiopian famine even media coverage of disasters is said to be more parsimonious. Nine: Allen (1986) identified a persistent and endemic failure to explain why poor countries are poor and why they continue to be so vulnerable to disasters, even after humanitarian operations. Aid is marketed in donor societies like a consumer product. Yet the public's appetite for consumer products is typically fickle. The shelf-life is short. Education in how international politics and capitalism in particular, not 'acts of God', create problems for the South would produce more lasting support for forms of development cooperation that have enduring value.

Finally, there has been half a decade of steady erosion of confidence in aid's effectiveness with respect to *all* of its objectives, donor- and other-regarding, developmental and non-developmental, among governments and donor publics alike. Many Americans have long doubted that aid is cost-effective in winning friends and influencing people. Almost everywhere the end of the Cold War brought the genuine misgivings that aid and development experts have about oda's developmental efficacy into sharper relief. Against this background, the well-known abuse of aid by corrupt, sometimes oppressive and often incompetent regimes could prove to be too much for aid to bear. In Britain, Lady Chalker (*Sunday Times*, 18 August 1991) mused that many people who understand the economic and moral arguments for development aid 'became rightly repelled by taxpayers' money being spent to reinforce brutish and self-serving regimes'. Aid was in danger of losing support. Society may not be against the principle, but looks for reassurance that official aid especially will clean up its act.

Aid fatigue might be an unwelcome diversion from oda's legitimate tasks, but all the same something had to be done to assure claims on resources, particularly public resources. In these circumstances the new political agenda offered a welcome chance to present a reinvigorated message on aid's behalf, although it has not stopped some of aid's supporters drawing a very different conclusion. That conclusion argues extra hurdles are being set for traditional aid seekers in order to make it easier for donors to justify running down their programmes, or, alternatively, to facilitate the redirection of aid to post-communist states. In other words, it is the politicians and not the public who suffer most from aid fatigue; the real danger is that their fatigue will undermine public support for oda, most notably in Europe (Hewitt 1994: 90).

There is one more important piece to the jigsaw explaining the modern politics of aid: an intellectual reversal concerning the relationships between economic and political development.

Economic and political development

The relationships between economic growth and development on the one side and political change on the other have long fascinated social scientists. In recent years, the connections between the willingness or ability of governments to engage in economic liberalisation and the nature of the political system have added to the interest. The theorising has been both deductive and inductive. The theories diverge over how far they control for the influence of additional variables such as sociological forces, and in their sensitivity to individual considerations of time, place and circumstance. On many of the issues the jury is still out. Also, there have been some premature judgements; and the outset of the 1990s saw a judgement reversed, with significant implications for international aid.

In a famous article Lipset (1959: 75) wrote about the social requisites of democracy:

> Perhaps the most widespread generalisation linking political systems to other aspects of society has been that democracy is related to the state of economic development. Concretely, this means that the more well-to-do a nation, the greater the chances that it will sustain democracy. From Aristotle down to the present, men have argued that only in a wealthy society in which relatively few citizens lived in real poverty could a situation exist in which the mass of the population could intelligently participate in politics and could develop the self-restraint necessary to avoid succumbing to the appeals of irresponsible demagogues.

Lipset's study embraced only a restricted group of countries, and he acknowledged that the conditions against which democracy arose in the West might be unique and historically determined. He did not specify sufficient conditions either for the spread of democracy or for the stability of democracies. Nevertheless, the notion of a firmer, almost causal connection between economic progress and democratisation gained ground afterwards and was even given a label – the wealth theory of democracy. The more refined versions stipulate a minimum level of development before democracy could be viable, and postulate a lag before the political effects of economic progress would fully appear. Generally speaking, the influence of theories of development on aid policy should not be exaggerated. Even so, the view that economic development would ultimately lead to democratisation was embraced by the US aid establishment from the earliest days. Conversely, poverty and hunger were held to be breeding grounds for communism and other 'totalitarian' forms of government.

However, the political transformation of Central/Eastern Europe at the end of the 1980s was not due in any straightforward way to economic development, but instead occurred as the economies were beginning to stall. Furthermore, it was clear by then that many developing countries were not enjoying significant economic progress. Only half registered a discernible upward trend in average per capita incomes over 1950–85. In the 1980s the average growth was a meagre 0.1 per cent. Fifteen countries in sub-Saharan Africa actually registered an average annual decline over 1965–88; in Bangladesh, real per capita incomes in the late 1980s barely exceeded those in the late 1960s. Clearly, new thinking was required, and Western political leaders determined that political liberalisation or democratisation might be needed first if there was to be any sustained economic uplift. Also, the idea that a symbiosis exists between political and economic freedoms, and between political pluralism and a market-based economy, seemed especially alluring. The dismantling of authoritarian interventionist government and an end to arbitrary rule could bring a more secure environment for private property. The rule of law and predictable enforcement of contracts are an encouragement to private enterprise to invest in wealth creation, secure in the knowledge there would be no predatory dictatorship or self-indulgent military regime to appropriate an undue share of the benefits. In Collier's (1991) phrase, democratisation would introduce 'agencies of restraint' against distortionary economic policy regimes. At around the same time, the lesson was being drawn from India and Botswana that democracies are less prone to famine. Democratically elected governments will strive to secure the food entitlements of vulnerable groups. They are also less likely to indulge in mass abuse of human rights, which disrupts economic activity in many ways, for instance by producing a refugee exodus.

The result of all these influences is that aid policy began linking allocations and disbursement to progress in respect of political conditionalities, and offering specialised assistance to political reform. The agenda embraces *inter alia* multi-partyism, free and fair elections, human rights and the rule of law. Britain and Germany have placed market economics in the same basket. The World Bank's focus on governance prioritises reform of the public sector, for increased efficiency and effectiveness and reduced corruption. The political and economic (or first generation) conditionalities overlap and intersect in such policy thrusts as improving value-for-money from the public service and the privatisation of state-owned enterprises. At the same time, official donors as well as voluntary agencies are professing support for the healthy development of civil society. The concept of civil society is much debated among theorists. Here it means the largely auto-nomous public realm that exists between the family or household and the state, and where citizens join together in pursuit of shared goals. Ideally it means a plurality of diverse and law-abiding civic associations and NGOs, internally accountable, existing in harmony with one another and willing to cooperate among themselves. At its best civil society is mutually sup-portive with democracy, the civic associations serving a variety of func-tions for the body politic that go well beyond just delivering social and economic services. In reality, however, civil societies also have exclusionary components with closed recruitment and hierarchically structured bodies that can prove highly problematical for democracy.

Inevitably, the modern politics of aid soon began to acquire a sceptical press. Indeed, it provided a springboard for political scientists to occupy a more central place alongside development economists, in critical examina-tions of aid. Many questions have been raised, few of them satisfactorily answered (see for example *IDS Bulletin* 1993; Burnell 1994; Moore and Robinson 1994; Baylies 1995; *IDS Bulletin* 1995; Stokke 1995; Crawford 1997). A rash of difficulties have been uncovered, most of them yet to be resolved.

Disputed logic

The idea that all good things go together, including good governance, democracy, human rights, economic development and an absence of pov-erty, is an attractive one. So too is the belief that variables that are often paired like multi-party competition and political accountability, or account-ability and sound economic management, or the rule of law and liberal democracy are exclusively and positively related. However, the empirical evidence is incomplete, at best. There is little support for the thesis that progress normally takes place smoothly and uniformly on all major fronts. The history of the world shows a variegated path that includes chaos, oscillation and not a few reversals along the way. There are times when trade-offs have to be made between certain values or desirable objects. And the various parties to aid relationships are not bound to agree on which choices are the right choices.

Nobody seriously believes liberal democracy is a sufficient condition for economic prosperity let alone societal contentment. After all, some entrenched Third World democracies have shown a persistent appetite for international aid. There is much more disagreement over whether democracy is a necessary condition, or a precondition, for sustained economic develop-ment. The literature outlines at least three positions (see for example Healey and Robinson 1992; Moore 1995b). Przeworski and Limongi (1993: 60–1) note that most of the pre-1987 studies found in favour of non-democratic regimes: authoritarianism seemed to be good for economic performance. Growth is sought by authoritarian regimes because it improves their legitimacy. In contrast, political competition leads elected governments to pursue irresponsible economic policies. They pander to populism and/or make economically costly concessions to politically well-organised special interest groups. Thus democracy might be a luxury that only rich societies can truly afford.

Przeworski and Limongi also observe that most quantitative studies post-1987, of conditions favouring economic progress, find in favour of democracy: they invite us to ponder whether the prevailing ideology influences the use of statistics! Now, democracy is seen to be functional for economic development, or at minimum the two are compatible. There is a 'new political economy' which says public officers are essentially self-serving. So, democratic accountability is necessary if the common weal is to be promoted. Jeremy Bentham argued thus many years ago.

A third position is sceptical or agnostic about the connection between type of political regime and economic performance. For one reason, the evidence is inconclusive. For another, there is no meaningful basis for making comparisons. The conventional categories of political regime each embrace cases that are very dissimilar in important respects. For example, 'authoritarian' states range from those with strong capabilities to some that are grossly incompetent and politically weak. Democratically elected governments number the politically strong and the very fragile. These and other factors like social cohesion, political stability, the ruling ideology of political economy, and quality of leadership can all make a crucial difference to the economic performance, just as non-economic factors like political culture and degree of national unity might impact on democratic sustainability. While the nature of the people in power can be as significant as how they came to power, the former will not be determined by the latter alone. Authoritarian examples of a developmental state have been impressive in East Asia but might work well only in that region, say for cultural and social reasons. Developmental democracy might be able to offer more in some other regions, like Central/Eastern Europe (see Sørensen 1993: 27–31).

Moreover, as was argued in Chapter 6, it is not only authoritarian regimes that can secure necessary bargains between powerful interest groups, and withstand economically disruptive social pressures, when effecting policies for economic liberalisation. However, it would be wrong to conclude that the introduction, or maintenance, of market-based policies depends on the presence of a competitive political system. Certainly, if democracy is assumed to be the only political system whose preservation depends on the existence of economic freedoms and a market economy (either directly or through some mediating forces), then democracy might be judged the most reliable security for a liberal economy. That is to say, successful democracies will incline towards embedding their own essential conditions. But of course success is not guaranteed. And while there is much evidence to corroborate Barrington Moore's (1966: 418) famous aphorism 'no bourgeois, no democracy', there is no truth in the inverse proposition of 'no democracy, no bourgeois'. All things considered, then, donors would be unwise to invest too much faith in. the magic of the political market, even for the limited purpose of enterprise-driven growth, let alone the elimination of poverty.

Donor credibility

What exactly do the donors set out to achieve by means of the modern politics of aid, and why? The answers are not self-evident. Professionals in development cooperation were caught unawares. So sudden was the introduction of the new politics of aid by the foreign policy establishments that some bilateral aid agencies were still trying to clarify their ideas, and work out how best to operationalise the substance, several years later. Democracy causes particular difficulties: universal agreement on its meaning remains elusive, even though the idea has been in contention since the time of the ancient Greeks.

Donors differ in terms of the specifics of their agendas. As has been noted already, unlike the World Bank's approach to governance some bilaterals take up more obviously political matters, but they differ on the relative weights to accord to the specific elements. The US openly preaches a model of democracy that carries many of the attributes of American politics, for example the lobbying by interest and pressure groups and checks on executive power. Britain's ODA has dwelled on legitimacy and good government; by 1993 the French government's approach, increasingly coloured by a determination to defend French economic interests and resist the incursion of Anglo-Saxon influences in Cameroon and Rwanda for instance (Schraeder 1995: 552–8), was giving greater weight to political allegiance to France. Moreover, whilst all donors appreciate that governance and political reforms *can* be instrumental for economic prospects, some also place an intrinsic value on such non-economic policy objectives as certain human rights.

The consequences which donors envisage could follow from the modern politics of aid and the form in which they expect to draw benefit are not fully transparent. Speculation on their motives leads to various estimates of how long the present phase of aid will continue before donors become disinterested or, possibly, dissatisfied with the results. Judgements about this can have an important bearing on how much cooperation aid seekers will extend to the donors in the meantime. There have been several attempts to make sense of the motivations.

What is in it for the donors?

One version proposes the thesis that as democracies proliferate, so the prospects for international peace are strengthened. By exporting democracy the West will enhance national security, relatively cheaply. For this reason

Diamond (1992) believes *realpolitik* dictates that the US promote democracy abroad. Eberstadt (1991: 129) argues security 'is a matter not only of power but of the ends for which – and the means by which – power is exercised'. Russett (1995: 120) provides a representative exposition of the 'pacific thesis' – the 'spread of democratic norms and practices in the world, if consolidated, should reduce the frequency of violent conflict and war'. Certainly, throughout their history democracies have practised self-defence and have even commenced military aggression, for instance the US towards Grenada (1983), Libya (1986), Panama (1989) and Haiti (1994). But apparently democracies are not aggressive towards one another. In the more than 100 wars since 1945, costing a total of over 20 million lives, none is said to have been between democracies. Russett believes this is due to the very nature of democracies, being unusually sensitive to war's consequences for civilians as well as to international opinion. Keohane, paraphrased in Holm and Sørensen (1995: 12), makes a similar inference when he says the extent to which hot peace or worse – international anarchy – replaces the Cold War will depend crucially on the global incidence of pluralist democratic institutions.

The above reasoning does not convince everyone. Sceptics distinguish causality from mere coincidence, and say the stability of relations among democracies in modern times could owe more to other factors like their anti-Soviet ideological alliance. A different argument is that peace has obtained among democracies because, up until now, these countries in the main have been economically developed. Strange (1994b: 216) maintains rich countries are aware that survival depends on competing successfully more for market shares than for territory, and that 'national interests can be better and more economically served by bargaining than by battling'. However, poor democracies might see the world otherwise, so rendering violent conflict over power resources including economic assets more probable; and some researchers claim emerging democracies are more war-prone than established democracies. If time-honoured concerns of territory, state sovereignty, national identity and national security do remain flashpoints, then the spread of democracy could be a less effective strategy for pursuing world peace than integrating developing countries more tightly into the world economy, rendering the economic costs of being belligerent more prohibitive. Finally, while democracies might value peace, there are pathways of democratisation which can jeopardise good relations with other states, especially neighbours who feel threatened in some way.

A different reading of US behaviour says Americans are possessed of a missionary zeal to spread what they sincerely believe are fundamental universal values. Also, if the distinguishing feature of the US among nations is its commitment to freedom, as Americans like Diamond suppose, then by advancing freedom's cause around the globe US prestige will be enhanced. Other interpretations applied to more donors also centre on self-interested reasonings. For example, political and governance reforms that pave the way for economic development serve international trade and investment,

which should benefit DAC economies. Finally, we should remember political conditionality is a means to try to exercise power. Power is highly prized
in its own right, regardless of the contribution it makes to national security and prosperity; and power is said to be an object of aid conditionality
just as it is of aid. Ake (1995: 40) expresses a view from Africa: 'The West,
through political conditionality, lends ambiguous support to democratization in order to seize an unexpected opportunity for consummating Western
hegemony'. This has echoes of a familiar goal, even if the present manifestation is not physical force, or simply economic domination, but power in
the realm of ideas.

Pragmatism versus consistency

Perhaps the search for some long-range vision or strategic rationale that
could lend overall coherence to the modern politics of aid is too ambitious. Probably, the objectives are still evolving and no single key exists.
Indeed, the charge that not even donor agents fully understand the motives
is fuelled by evidence of donor inconsistency. The promotion of democracy and human rights does not fit aid's earlier record, which often supported undemocratic and oppressive regimes. Of course, that might be
considered so much water under the bridge. But even donor credibility
couched solely in terms of recent behaviour is questionable. Good governance provides a good illustration, where Landell-Mills and Serageldin (1991:
15–16) draw attention to the indirect complicity of aid agencies in corrupt
financial practices initiated by their own country's suppliers: the 'financing
of unwarranted "commissions" by export credit agencies is but one example'.
The fact is the nostrums of the modern agenda are not being applied consistently by DAC donors when considered all together or taken singly,
whether behaving towards aid recipients as a group or individually. Donor
countries are also at variance in their domestic affairs. Just as aid agencies
have seemed indifferent to political reform in the past, so DAC government ministries with responsibilities for trade, non-concessional capital flows
and national security are not marching wholly in step with the new aid
agenda. Furthermore, the way relations are being conducted with some
friendly countries where aid leverage is not available, for example the Gulf
sheikhdoms, is patently incongruous with the spirit of modern aid politics.

There are at least two points here. First, not all donors are singing from
an identical hymn sheet. Second, as is true of almost all relations, the nature
of aid relationships continues to be strongly coloured by the relative bargaining strength of the recipients. Take each point in turn. It would be
difficult for Japan to be completely insensitive to some of the claims made
about Asian values by its regional partners in aid, trade and investment.
These governments argue the importance of an ordered society and of
obligations to the community – ideas that should not be surrendered to the
more individualistic construction of civil and political liberties familiar in
the West. DAC circles consider the human rights agenda to be the most

suitable component of second-generation conditionality, for there exists something like an international human rights regime. But some of the features could be culture-specific, relative to levels of economic achievement and not well suited to universal application. Thus, some Asian voices argue that external pressure to conform is a Western conspiracy aimed at slowing their countries' burgeoning economic performance (see Tang 1995: 6). The rights would undermine social cohesion, and state forms that have contributed strongly to development will become less stable.

In reality, of course, there are not one but several Asian perspectives on human rights. Some correspond quite happily to prevailing norms in the West, where human rights conceptions have themselves been changeable. The reification of state sovereignty as a bulwark against the infiltration of alien ideas about rights itself has Western origins; and in any case some traditional values in East Asia have been placed under threat by deliberate choices to pursue industrial modernisation, market practices, technological progress and high material consumption. The activities of human rights campaigners in these countries lend some credence to universalist claims about rights. No less relevant is the voluntary assent the states have given to the (non-legally binding) Universal Declaration of Human Rights (1948) and various other international and regional declarations, treaties and covenants on rights, which may be no less binding than are the Geneva Conventions (1949) and Additional Protocols (1977). Naturally there are mavericks, but by definition they are exceptions. For instance China, which has not signed the International Covenant on Civil and Political Rights (adopted by the UN General Assembly in 1966), has rebuffed an invitation from the UN Human Rights Commission to file human rights reports on Hong Kong, after regaining sovereignty in 1997.

The uneven application of political conditionality as between countries holding different degrees of commercial, strategic, diplomatic, political or other advantage reflects the fact that donors pursue multiple policy objectives, just as with the ends of aid. Aid has taken on a new politics but the old politics has not gone away. Crawford (1997) illustrates several cases of the dog that did not bark – countries like Sri Lanka and Egypt exempted from political aid sanctions. The situation may be reinforced in non-aid domains such as preferential trading arrangements. Thus, in 1994 commercial considerations persuaded the US government to step back from taking China's human rights into account when deciding to renew China's most favoured nation trading status – a focal issue in US Congress–executive relations. Human rights were relegated below disputes over intellectual property rights and nuclear non-proliferation; and by late 1996 the Clinton administration was giving priority to improving relations with China's leaders. Anyway, the practice of maintaining oda to governments judged to have a persistently bad human rights record is often defended on the grounds of avoiding double jeopardy for needy social groups, who would be vulnerable to aid cut-offs. Van Tuijl (1994) shows how the Indonesian government not only severed aid ties with the Netherlands, in 1992, but also took reprisals against local civic groups, after the Dutch government suspended oda (a tiny fraction of total aid to Indonesia) in protest at the East Timor massacre in 1991. Dutch aid to local groups worth $15 million annually was jeopardised.

In the few countries where development assistance has been withdrawn on human rights grounds, such as Sudan and Myanmar, the donors' willingness to continue to consider cases of humanitarian relief is contestable. Clearly, a denial of such relief could be said to obstruct the basic right to the means to life. More usually, oda channels are kept open even if aid transfers are reduced, in the hope that dialogue will be served. NGO routes will be explored for administering most of the aid including for poverty alleviation, so as to avoid handing propaganda coups to the government. Where practicable and prudent, help might be given to human rights groups. Despite the application to Africa of a theoretical model of development that runs from political reform to improved economic prospects, the inverse sequence which follows more closely on Lipset's reasoning (democratisation through development) is still being applied to China, by Japanese commentators for instance, so justifying continued oda. Economic stagnation in China would be politically destabilising for the country and the region. In contrast further economic development will create domestic pressure for democratic reform, if only because of increased exposure to outside influences, and the greater consumer choice which accompanies a prospering market economy will generate demands for increase of political choice. In the long run these arguments might hold true, but in the meantime there is a possibility that the signals being broadcast by donors look confused, and could be misunderstood. Donor credibility is dented even further by such practices as the granting of export licences for the purchase of counter-insurgency instruments to military or military-backed governments, as was alleged against France when French aid to Algeria was increased following the military's annulment of the democratic process in January 1992. Onlookers in other aid-seeking countries could be forgiven for being cynical, or bemused – a parallel exists with respect to economic management (see page 118).

In principle, legitimate grounds exist for believing political conditionality should be applied flexibly. After all, there are relevant differences in the circumstances of aid recipients. Moreover, donors face a real dilemma over which to view as being the more significant: an increase in the shortfall of democracy and good governance, or the absolute size of the democratic deficit. What counts most, the nature of the trends or the baseline situation? The tools to measure change are not yet adequate to the task of rigorously fine-tuning conditional aid offers. Guidelines exist, like the UNDP's Human Freedom Index of 40 indicators. But Patten's (1989: 13) remark bears repetition, that 'it is immensely, inordinately difficult to calibrate in a precise way that avoids grotesque humbug' the distribution of aid according to countries' records on human rights – or, for that matter, many other features of the political reform agenda.

In practice, however, the flexible application of political conditionality can also be a weakness if it comes to look like discrimination on non-relevant grounds, and geared more to the particular interests of donors than to some independent general principle. The result is that donors are accused of hypocrisy and double standards, even more so when they blatantly deviate from their stated principles at home. On human rights Tomasevski's (1993: 122) verdict is that aid's record is 'inherently arbitrary', and in regard to good government more generally Moore and Robinson (1994: 153) found 'little basis on which the aid donors can validly claim to have been acting ethically in implementing a policy that ultimately can only be justified in ethical terms'.

The limits of conditionality

Kenya (1991) and Malawi (1992) provided early instances of collective donor action to withhold or suspend new aid so as to apply pressure for political reform and improvement in human rights. But before long a consensus began to emerge that, outside of a few exceptional circumstances, threatening severe aid sanctions in the event of non-compliance with political condition-alities might not be very effective.

This conclusion was extrapolated from economic conditionality's mixed performance in the 1980s, and then seemed to be confirmed as a record of political conditionality began to assemble. The reasons held responsible in the case of first-generation conditionality were rightly deemed capable of thwarting the intentions of political conditionality too. Indeed, the possib-ilities for failure soon began to look even greater. For criteria for assessing recipient compliance with economic conditionality seem clearer and more precise, the objectives being fewer, more specific and easily measurable. Also, the World Bank's willingness to organise concerted action on these (and governance) matters is very much greater, so making for a better coordinated and therefore more effective application of pressure (Stokke 1995: 61–2).

However, there is also a valid comparison with economic liberalisation in that the chief impetus for democratisation, especially democratic consolida-tion, must come from within the society if it is to be sustained. No amount of external conditionality can create or substitute for a domestic political com-mitment to make reforms, either economic or political. In certain instances aid conditionality has helped spur the initial stages of political liberalisation, where a relatively weak authoritarian regime decides to remove some restric-tions on freedom without fully intending to initiate far-reaching democratic reform. Political conditionality has even helped bring about democratic transition, when employed in combination with assistance to well-grounded pro-democracy initiatives taking place in the country. But beyond demo-cratic transition, a number of commentators now think political condition-ality's role is minimal. Within limits, specialised assistance can take over and help to further the process of democratic consolidation, although the chances are that the all-important civic culture of democracy will still take a long time to grow, and may not be amenable to official encouragement. Some analysts go even further. They believe not only that democratisation must be driven from inside the country (rather than come about as a result of external pressure), but also that democracy has to be produced from the 'bottom-up', or grass-roots, instead of being an elite-led or 'top-down' phenomenon. That is, if the end product is to be truly democratic and locally 'owned'.

The idea that democracy (or the political circumstances conducive to democratisation) can be foisted on a country from outside is unconvincing. Germany and Japan since 1945 may be singled out in support of the idea, but they are unusual. They do show that foreign actors can be midwives, and that military occupation need be no hindrance. But donors who employ political conditionality must have an acute grasp of the disposition of key political forces in a target country, if they are to be successful. A detailed grasp of why indifference, suspicion or outright opposition could greet their reform agenda may be even more essential in regard to their political preferences than in respect of their preferred economic policy reforms. Too unsophisticated an approach could fail to distinguish between, say, vested political and/or pecuniary interests in the status quo; a sincere judgement by local politicians that their country is not yet ready for major political changes; some principled objection to Western-style concepts of democracy; and misunderstandings owing to shortcomings in donor–recipient communication. One possible outcome of political conditionality is the emergence of democrats for convenience and not by conviction, among the governing elite. They go no further than introduce the most minimal institutional reforms acceptable to donors, formal acknowledgement of the right to form opposition political parties and an electoral timetable for example, in order to remain eligible for aid. Full civil and political liberties remain in abeyance, and the constraints on executive power are barely effective. What Gills et al. (1993) call low-intensity democracy may prevail. Even these achievements may last barely longer than the aid leverage that brought them about, and do little to improve the economic and social prospects of the country. There, and where donors market democracy principally as a passport to economic prosperity, the political reform process will be shallow-rooted. If it fails to deliver the promised benefits in terms of economic development, the changes will unravel. Even more counter-productive would be where a heavy-handed application of political conditionality strengthens anti-democratic elements, who manipulate populist, nationalist and anti-imperialist sentiments to their political advantage.

A further reason for the reducing confidence in political conditionality has been a growing realisation that the conditions required for the threat of sanctions to be invoked, and once implemented to have the desired effect, are quite demanding. The lesson is borne of experience. The case of Indonesia following the East Timor massacre was instructive. The government's retaliation against Dutch aid was viewed in Indonesia as the apogee of decolonisation. It tells us that good coordination among donors and multilaterals is vital, notwithstanding the constitutional reluctance of the multilaterals to join action that is deemed political. In contrast to the Dutch some bilateral donors simply placed more weight on their national interests, particularly their commercial ties with Indonesia. The value of cross-conditionality is another lesson. Effective conditionality may be contingent on there being a level of aid dependence greater than exists in Indonesia or, say, Nigeria, where in 1995 a military government sanctioned executions including the writer Ken Saro-Wiwa, knowing there would be international condemnation. Both countries have bargaining strengths in the form of their oil exports, domestic markets that include sizeable government procurement, and inward investment.

Thus, political conditionality is not a panacea for the abuse of human rights. It has limited potential in countries whose regimes are indifferent to the expressive dimension of threatened sanctions, impervious to the economic costs or insensitive to the misery such costs might cause the populace. The same is true where the military or para-military forces act in ways beyond government control, where the chief culprits are terrorists or insurgents, and where civil order has collapsed. Conditionality is problematic where central government jurisdiction does not extend to the internal affairs of self-governing provinces and municipalities. In any case, aid sanctions are morally questionable where bad living conditions are made worse for the most vulnerable groups. The Kurds in 'safe havens' and the people of Iraq, more than 20 per cent of whom now live in extreme poverty, could be cited as an example. They have suffered from the obstacles to implementing UN Security Council Resolution 986. That authorises Iraqi oil exports of $2 billion every six months but only if revenues are earmarked for specific purposes that include purchase of humanitarian supplies of food and medicines, and compensation to the victims of Iraqi aggression against Kuwait. Conditionalities are pointless where they actually stiffen a government's resolve and make it even more oppressive. Moreover they cannot touch countries that receive little or no aid, which means most donor countries.

The introduction of conditionality only where there is a reasonable chance of it being effective might be one way to try to preserve the instrument's credibility. But this would be at a cost of drawing attention to the instrument's limitations; and in any case we lack the necessary predictive power to be very successful. Crawford's (1997) comparison of four significant donors and 29 recipients shows political conditionality has been ineffective in some very aid-dependent countries, even while exerting a positive influence in some less dependent countries (although making a significant impact in only two cases). To reduce all the reasons to insufficient donor commitment would be simplistic. We cannot deny there is a real dilemma where sanctioning disreputable government would frustrate socially beneficial developmental achievements, by stalling aided projects and reducing the pressure from programme lending to enact sound economic policy reform.

Although donor public opinion can require that aid sanctions be threatened even in these circumstances, in practice political sanctions have been applied more sparingly than was originally expected. They tend to be introduced after other steps to secure compliance have been tried and failed, and usually in a graduated fashion, invoking full suspension only as a last resort. For the most part 'positive conditionality', or the promise of substantial extra rewards for compliance – something that might have been presumed to form part of a balanced package of sticks and carrots, so maximising the donors' power potential – never really materialised. For by 1993 the prospect of a real terms contraction of donor aid budgets was becoming apparent, and aid flows even to Africa were starting to be affected.

So, funds drawn from within aid budgets for the support of governance initiatives and other political reforms, or democracy assistance, are now widely seen to offer a potentially more fruitful approach than political conditionality, in most circumstances. But even here, there are constraints set by how flexible aid agencies can be in reallocating resources away from more conventional objects.

Reservations about specialised assistance

Assistance is being offered to a kaleidoscope of projects and programmes involving state and civil society. Some of the descriptions are familiar, merely being given new labels. Others are more innovative, and donors as well as recipients are at an early stage on the learning curve. Examples include assisting with multi-party elections (for which purpose the UN received requests for help from 52 states between 1992 and mid-1994), which can range from supplying ballot boxes and election monitors to funding voter education; giving advice on legal frameworks and processes to protect womens' rights and minority groups; giving encouragement to the development of the private media; and in the World Bank's portfolio, capacity building in policy analysis, public sector management and sound financial accounting. Civic associations and NGOs are being provided with technical advice, equipment and even funds. But, beyond a recognition that civil society's role and *modus operandi* in a democracy should depart from how it behaves when trying to bring down authoritarian rule, there is much confusion over what it is for and what it should do. Some alternatives are: collaborate with and strengthen the state's ability to get things done; countervail the state and exert opposition; be a source of demands on the state; advance the economic market; check the adverse social and moral consequences of unregulated economic markets; be a school for democratic citizenship, force for social integration and training ground for future political leaders; provide a *summum bonum* of its own.

It is perhaps too early for the effectiveness of the newer forms of specialised assistance to political change to be studied in detail and over a meaningful stretch of time. However, there is a presumption that they should perform best where there is a domestic political tide already running in favour of reform. They may be much less effective where the need for external involvement looks to be greatest, that is to say where the political climate is hostile to reform. Specialised assistance faces an uphill task where it gains access only because donors apply political conditionality to their oda. It cannot substitute for and cannot create a local commitment to political reform and better governance. It must be wise to local circumstances. To illustrate, advice on the installation of competitive elections should heed the risks of encouraging a 'winner-takes-all' mentality (a possible consequence of 'first-past-the-post' systems), a recipe for instability in very divided societies. There, political competition can easily turn into violent conflict, as happened in Kenya when President Moi was pressed into agreeing to hold multi-party elections, in 1992. Donors risk opening up a Pandora's box if they force the pace of change too hard or push inappropriate institutional changes. The increasing phenomenon of failing states posts a warning. Bad government may be preferable to a slide towards ungovernability – which damages the very economic objectives that help explain the donors' interest in political reform. Vietnam is just one test case: while some donors are restive at the modest pace of economic reform and of aid disbursement, others value the country's political stability, and advise against provoking anti-reform elements in the administration to block all further progress.

The challenge of a double transition – from state-led to market-based economy and from authoritarianism to democracy – is especially daunting for any society. Few if any successful precedents can be identified in the West, especially for the telescoped timescale that aid donors now seem to expect. Many countries in Africa and some former Soviet republics are less well placed to take on the challenge now than they were in former days, in several significant respects. Population pressures are greater, and average living standards have fallen. Large financial, economic and environmental problems have accumulated. Inequalities have increased. The democratic architecture will become just a facade if social and economic discontents – exacerbated by attempts to comply with economic conditionalities and to service international debt – induce widespread voter apathy, cynicism or indifference towards the democratic process. By any reckoning *poor* democracies can be fragile. Indeed, Przeworski *et al.* (1996: 50) argue that democratic consolidation is an empty term, in as much as the chances of a democracy surviving hinge on its enjoying economic development, not the length of time since it was first introduced. Against this background, a carefully selective approach to political conditionality and specialised assistance look prudent, if unheroic, especially because of the problem with accountability.

The accountability of states, both political and bureaucratic, features high on the donors' agenda. But their involvement in indicating economic, political and other measures to recipients, and their strictures regarding the kinds of programmes and projects they might be willing to support, together with the relevant conditions, muddies the waters. Clientelistic patterns of relationships with donors are difficult to avoid, as aid-seeking governments and civic associations, or SNGOs, frame their declared intentions partly in accordance with what they believe will attract funding and satisfy the donors' policy and procedural requirements. Local consultation may be minimal, the veneer of authenticity thin. The chances of appearing unresponsive to the electorate and of failing to represent local views and interests are compounded in the presence of painful economic measures that originate in aid conditionality. The opacity of aid agencies' internal decision-making processes provides an additional complication for establishing lines of accountability.

Aid conditionality is not proscribed in international law, but the feeling that it can turn into an improper intervention in the internal affairs of sovereign countries is difficult to resist. Indeed, the recipient states have been variously described as subject to 'supervision', 'tutelage', even 'co-governance'; and they are now tantamount to 'local government' (Fowler 1992: 26) in the global political order. Comparable views are being expressed about positive assistance. It has always made sense for donors to reflect on the politically optimal strategies for governments who are seeking to consolidate essential economic reforms; now, we cannot dismiss the possibility that their meddling may become intrinsic to a recipient country's political scene. What really transpires in the black box of discussions between representatives of donors and recipients is still a mystery to the outside world. But there is a suspicion that donors find themselves tempted to try to succour and to maintain the requisite amount of political support (and the organisations) necessary for the success of their political and governance proposals (Moore 1995a: 95).

Already, some of the foreign assistance to party building has been intentionally partisan, under the guise of levelling the playing field between democracy's more and less fervent supporters (Carothers 1996: 35–44). Donors could be drawn in anyway, whether they like it or not. For competing groups and personalities among the local political elite will endeavour to manipulate (intentionally non-partisan) democracy assistance to their particular advantage. So, in one way or another donors become party to the domestic political drama. They will be causally implicated in the course of events (Burnell 1994: 491, 498–501). The principle of accountability is undermined, irrespective of whether the specific consequences do or do not conform to the donors' aims. The damage is compounded when donors do not acknowledge their share of responsibility for the outcomes, especially outcomes that prove embarrassing politically, such as when political forces they have backed subsequently turn renegade or projects they have funded then cause an infringement of rights (as with the forced and uncompensated eviction of communities from lands that are flooded by major dam schemes). Exit and the threat of exit are significant instruments for enforcing supplier accountability in many market situations, economic and political. But highly aid-dependent countries cannot be expected to see exit as a viable option, either with or without the exercise of voice. They have no formal political or juridical means to make donors liable for an ill-judged interference in their political or economic affairs. Ideally, donors should employ a *modus operandi* in aid relations that exemplifies the very qualities, values and beliefs they hope to spread as part of their commitment to reform, accountability included. This ideal could be unattainable in regard to the aid seekers who are most vulnerable to the realities of power and influence in international affairs and aid specifically.

There have already been some failures of specialised assistance and there will undoubtedly be more to come. Serious setbacks will store up 'aid fatigue' in the future, and could produce more aid disillusionment among recipients too. Aid disillusionment has taken on different personas over time, just like aid fatigue. Indeed, its very existence may be questioned among the majority of the Third World's people. They probably harbour no well-developed views of aid at all. They have been allowed no part in the decision-making processes, and many of aid's benefits will seem remote. They might even be ignorant of how features of international aid could impact adversely on their surrounding circumstances. Thus, for instance, David Williams (in Legum 1970: 55) said about the very first UN Development Decade that although we have heard a lot about aid disillusionment, 'I never find anything like disillusionment, for the simple reason that the vast mass of the poor have never heard about the Decade at all. They are not in a position to be disillusioned about it. They are not conscious of playing any kind of a role in an exciting international experience'. Even so, it would be difficult to deny there is dissatisfaction at the burden of foreign debt in developing countries, and objections to aid's economic conditionalities, or 'adjustment fatigue'. To these must now be added the possibility of growing resentment towards detailed political interference, particularly where it seems to have no good material effect. There will be great uncertainty about judging when some of the new democracies have become truly consolidated and in no further need of external encouragement; indeed, the challenge for some years to come could be the prevention of democratic 'hollowing out' or reverse. If the donors' agendas for political reform and governance prove to be rolling programmes, which reveal new sets of benchmarks for democratic 'deepening' one after another and never seem to end, then reform fatigue will bring a new aid disillusionment, among recipient country elites at least. Where the polity is genuinely participatory, the chances are the resentment will be felt much more widely.

Widening the debate

The modern politics of aid has been criticised for not going far enough on at least three counts.

First, the donors' enthusiasm for democracy is confined largely to a minimalist procedural model centred on competition for votes in elections that are not blatantly unfree and unfair, chiefly at the national level. This falls short of many models including those that emphasise participatory values and, perhaps, privilege the local arenas that often matter most to ordinary people, where their participation can impact on decisions having a significant bearing on their day-to-day lives. Democracy is of course a contested (some say essentially contested) concept, but a defining feature in many accounts is an equal distribution of power and influence. In short, democracy is a condition of political equality. This has no obvious place on the donors' agenda. Indeed, they are portrayed as giving emphasis to the liberal over the democratic, in their version of liberal democracy – they ignore the claims of civil society to be protected by government against private capital, indigenous or international. Put differently, donors take a stronger interest in negative liberty, especially freedom from state regulation of economic affairs, than in the exercise of positive freedoms by ordinary people, meaning equal capabilities and empowerment for short. An example typical of Latin American experience is Matear's (1996: 258–60) finding that donor policies towards pro-democracy NGOs in Chile shifted from supporting empowerment-type activities to market values, once the country had turned back from military to elected civilian government, in 1989. Few NNGOs could honestly claim to cultivate extensive and deep roots in their own society, let alone strong credentials for furthering truly participatory development abroad. Many seem content to work with SNGOs whose own compatibility with democratic values is questionable, and who lack accountability to the people they purport to represent. Indeed, the established commitment of a notable Sri Lankan NGO to participatory and decentralising values has been assaulted by the centralising, managerialist relationship brought by a consortium of Northern donors, including NNGOs (Perera 1995).

Second, donors make assumptions about human rights that are not universally accepted. Some people contest the idea of universal human rights; others agree on the substance but not on the reasons why they are rights; yet others argue the way rights are specified, and the approach taken to implementing them, should reflect local conditions. Again, the NNGOs are not exempt from charges of practising a form of imperialism in respect of their own values and beliefs, religious or developmental; an African view, from Yash Tandon, sees the private aid agencies not as radical but as 'the advanced guard of a new era of Africa's recolonisation' (in Sogge 1996: 182). Writing about Niger's proposed *Code de la Famille*, Villalón (1996) highlights the difficult moral and practical issues when donors seek to have their understanding of human rights enforced in a Muslim society, the majority of whose members would use democratic procedures to reject that understanding.

By concentrating largely on the civil and political liberties of individuals and freedom from violation of personal integrity, donors are accused of doing little to promote the idea of social and economic rights. They have made no attempt at all to sell the idea of 'third-generation' rights, such as the collective right to development. Their selective approach to rights is unsurprising. After all, they are capitalist countries. Some like the US have not ratified the 1966 International Covenant on Economic, Social and Cultural Rights (indeed, as of 1995 the US had not ratified the International

Conventions on the Elimination of Racial Discrimination and on the Elimination of All Forms of Discrimination against Women). The donors might retort that all their oda is aimed at improving social and economic well-being. But that could remain unconvincing when set against the increase in poverty attributed to donor-designed SAPs, now becoming evident in post-communist societies of the former Second World just as it did in Third World countries in the 1980s.

Another possible retort is that socio-economic *rights* are ideals, related to the level of developmental achievement. They lie beyond the present economic situation of many developing countries. To insist on rights that could impose unsupportable economic burdens would be irresponsible. This kind of argument has been applied in defence of, for example, bad conditions of employment and the use of child labourers (who may number 250 million worldwide). It contrasts with the view associated with China that certain needs including economic survival and material well-being must take priority over civil and political liberties. According to Clark (1991: 224) the idea that democracy is more valuable than economic reform 'may appear imperialistic' but is 'very much in keeping with the view of many African grassroots NGOs . . .' However, that view could yet prove perishable. Many Africans are beginning to lose confidence in their country's recent attempts at political reform. Some are suffering even greater economic hardship than before. Herein lies the origin of the view that, having helped to set political change in motion, the donors should now undertake an obligation to meet popular aspirations for material progress, 'without which democracy will surely fail' (Kpundeh 1992: 78). To the extent that adoption of the donors' neo-liberal economic agenda is held responsible for the persistence of great poverty and socio-economic inequality, their professed concerns to strengthen civil society and advance democracy will be judged insincere.

In fact, the donors' commitment to a worthwhile form of democracy will probably remain in question as long as the following propositions seem valid: they remain reticent about social and economic rights; they appear to set greater store by formal institutional and procedural norms than underlying socio-economic realities; oda does not demonstrably improve on its former record of poverty alleviation. Indeed, according to leftists there is a clear sub-text to the modern politics of aid, namely to vanquish the last remnants of socialism. Political pluralism is advocated chiefly because it provides a means to embed neo-liberal economic reforms while making them appear less like the product of external imposition. The good governance discourse 'merely marks a new phase of surveillance and control on the part of international capital . . .' (Baylies 1995: 335); the crusade for democracy is 'an integral aspect of the economic and ideological restructuring accompanying a new stage of globalisation in the capitalist world economy' (Gills et al. 1993: 4). While the benefits of 'bourgeois democracy' are necessarily modest and enjoyed mainly by the few, even these benefits have yet to be realised in most Third World political transitions. Furthermore, such 'democracy' no longer has a guaranteed future even in its heartland in the West. This is because of concern about the growing economic strength of East Asian countries, China particularly. Where their economic perform-ance is seen to draw on politically illiberal aspects of 'strong government' (rather than, say, the specific educational, industrial and wealth distribu-tion policies), the example could prove tempting to the dominant socio-economic formations and governments in the West, as they struggle to maintain international competitiveness and keep their class interests intact. The rights of organised labour are already being eroded in a number of EU countries and there are parallel pressures in South Korea, for example.

   In this summary so far, the criticisms of the modern politics of aid dwell on a failure to go much beyond elitism and managerialism, notwithstand-ing the gestures towards civil society. Indeed, the particular forms of 'demo-cracy' that are being exported are considered unsatisfactory even for their countries of origin. Instead, DAC governments are urged to identify more with the political and economic plight of the poor. Attention and resources should be refocused downwards, at the level of the community and below the central state. In contrast, the third and final point goes above the level of the state, and criticises the disinterest of the main OECD powers in applying canons of democracy and good governance to the multilateral and other international bodies which they usually dominate. UN Secretary-General Boutros Boutros-Ghali (1995: 10) said: 'Today, democracy in the international community of states remains at a very rudimentary stage'. There always have been criticisms by Third World sympathisers of the Bretton Woods institutions for their bureaucratic style and lack of open-ness, and for having voting regimes weighted against the great majority of members. Now, perhaps more striking is the growing chorus of concern directed at the United Nations, said (by Watkins 1995a: 218) to be the one global institution that could yet play a decisive role in world poverty reduc-tion in the years to come.

   The UN is not a world government. The General Assembly does not pass laws, and proposals that seats be filled by election could well be imprac-tical. Even so, the privilege that is vested in a handful of countries by virtue of permanent membership of the Security Council, and their possession of a veto power, have come under increasing scrutiny. On the one hand, cri-ticism has been directed at the manner in which the UN has been used to further American foreign policy objectives, in the Gulf war for instance. On the other hand, the post-Cold War atmosphere has seen a more positive approach to decision-making by the Security Council, and a useful increase in UN-sanctioned peace-related activities. These developments could be harbingers; and interest has revived in reconfiguring the UN to take on a more expanded role in world affairs. Many suggestions for reform have recently come forward from bodies like the Commission on Global Gov-ernance (1995), such as the termination (or restriction) of the permanent members' veto, and expansion of the Security Council to include in the permanent membership some large developing countries; alternatively, the abolition of permanent membership has also been suggested. Another idea, from the Independent Commission on Population and Quality of Life (1996), is that the Security Council should be authorised to discuss matters relating to global economic and social security, as well as other threats to peace. Many of the proposals are fanciful, and will be forgotten as the UN's fiftieth anniversary recedes. A democratic UN is not in prospect. Together with economy drives, nothing more than marginal adjustments to the power structure is likely to happen in the near future. That assessment would seem to be supported by the ease with which the Security Council seat formerly occupied by the USSR passed straight to Russia, whose claims to receive foreign aid are considered in the next chapter.

To Russia with love

The start of the 1990s saw post-communist countries formerly at the core of the Second World begin to enter the lists as aid recipients of DAC member states. By 1995 they comprised 12 Newly Independent States (NIS) of the former USSR and ten Central and Eastern European Countries (CEECs) that had formerly belonged to the Soviet socialist bloc, excluding the former Yugoslavia. Four NIS states including Russia and all the CEECs bar Albania were dubbed 'countries in transition' and they are considered eligible for official aid, which meets oda's requirement of concessionality but does not count towards the UN aid target of 0.7 per cent of donors' GNP. The rest are likened to developing countries and may be considered for oda. So far, the total flow of concessional transfers to all of the countries has been relatively modest. Official aid may well have peaked in 1994, at $7.8 billion, or 0.04 per cent of average DAC GNP, divided fairly evenly between the NIS and CEEC groups (OECD 1996a: 8). Russia and Poland have each accounted for almost one third of the total. The bulk has come from Western Europe in the form of bilateral and EU flows. Prior to 1994, when the US's contribution jumped, Germany was easily the largest single donor to both Russia and Poland and was supplying almost half of the concessionary flows to CEECs and NIS, as well as a substantial proportion of officially guaranteed export credits. Now, the US and Germany combined account for two thirds of current disbursements. In addition, private international foundations have provided over $500 million inclusive of humanitarian aid and assistance to civil society initiatives, with the Soros Foundation being notable in Hungary for example.

Much larger 'aid' figures for Russia especially have been bandied about in the context of G7 agreements and summit meetings of the World Bank and IMF (Russia joined the IMF in mid-1992). Multi-donor packages valued at $24 billion and $43.4 billion were announced in 1992 and 1993 respectively. However, these included items like official trade credit and loan guarantees,

IMF standby loans and rouble support packages and, especially, debt deferrals and IMF rescheduling. Highly concessional flows have been smaller than private investment and export credit, worth over $14 billion in 1992 for instance, although over the period 1990–4 aid has been more stable than other official transfers and private flows. The EBRD is not an aid agency and sees its priority as being to encourage corporate investment in the region. Like the World Bank, it raises funds from the international capital markets. Its loans are secured at market rates. However, the EBRD charter is unique in incorporating express politico-economic objectives: the purpose shall be to foster the transition toward open-market economies and to promote private and entrepreneurial initiative in Central and Eastern Europe, with a commitment to applying the principles of multi-party democracy, pluralism and market economics. By 1996 it had approved 368 projects in 24 countries, over two thirds of them in the private sector.

The disbursement of official financial resources of all kinds has tended to be considerably less than the headline figures. For one reason, reaching agreement with the IMF and then complying with IMF conditionalities have both been problematic for Russia and the Ukraine especially. Confidence that financial stability had finally been achieved in Russia began to build only towards mid-1995, although President Yeltsin then began to make large spending pledges in advance of the 1996 presidential election. Problems of ensuring financial accountability and bureaucratic difficulties bedevilled operations like the distribution of food aid in Russia in the 1991 winter, and the EU's technical assistance to the Commonwealth of Independent States (TACIS) programme to former Soviet republics. On both sides some of aid's earliest supporters have been disappointed by the international community's efforts. Wolf (1996: 14) argues that around 1991–2 Western politicians and bureaucrats 'with the vision of accountants' were mesmerised by the former USSR's indebtedness, and missed the vital moment to underpin reform by providing non-inflationary financing to the Russian budget. Lavigne (1995: 238) believes 'Eastern recipients often feel that Western assistance is dominated by a collusion among private lobbies and political interests'. But while one viewpoint maintains the aid has been inadequate, another sees aid as a poor alternative to more comprehensive forms of international economic and financial cooperation. The worry is that aid could bring about a situation comparable to Third World dependency. There has been a lingering suspicion in the West (evident in for example the World Bank's *World Development Report 1996, From Plan to Market*) that large-scale support might have the unintended effect of relieving the pressure to carry out economic liberalisation and industrial reorientation away from military production. After all, communist China introduced a thriving market eonomy without the benefit of massive aid. Nevertheless, the aid case has many strands, some applying throughout the DAC and extending to much or all of the former Soviet bloc, and others being more specific to certain DAC countries and locating a narrower set of possible recipients.

Traditional security issues

The last half-century of East–West tension punctuated by Cold War makes the security rationale paramount, although geopolitical forces provoking instability and violent conflict in Eastern Europe actually date back much further. At the outset the stakes seemed high if, as a result of extending aid to the former Soviet bloc, the West could win over its arch-competitor for international power and influence, and render its greatest military rival a probable enemy no longer. In the US Allison and Blackwill (1991: 93–4) argued investment in the democratisation of the former USSR would offer more to international peace than the $5 trillion they estimated the US had spent worldwide (and the over $10 trillion the West has spent, in 1996 terms) on containing the Soviet military challenge. Later, others were to argue that Russia's internal strains and economic collapse were destroying its power capabilities anyway (Rosefielde 1993).

At the beginning of the 1990s especially there was much talk of a peace dividend that would follow the abandonment of superpower rivalry. This seemed to promise the West improved public finances and higher consumption standards all round, notwithstanding the costs of restructuring industry away from research, development and manufacturing associated with military procurement. Also for a time there were visions of a US–Soviet partnership shaping a 'new world order'. That term and the vision died with the Gulf war and the disintegration of the USSR, although not before the value of improved relations had been amply shown by the agreement reached in the UN Security Council over how to respond to Iraq's invasion of Kuwait. Even today there remains considerable scope for Moscow to hinder the West's preferred responses to regional or international crises and its foreign policy goals. Russia's involvement in diplomatic manoeuvres over Bosnia arguably shows this (for Russian opinion is more sympathetic to the Serbs), as does Russia's proposal to sell nuclear reactors worth $1 billion to Iran, contrary to US wishes. Russian refusal to allow the UN Security Council to bless the US's response to an Iraqi military incursion in Kurdish areas in September 1996, and resistance to the incorporation of former Warsaw Pact states into NATO's military structure, are even more significant. Possibly, aid could help make Russia more accommodating on these and other issues.

Japan has its own interests of *realpolitik*, namely the objective of recovering the Northern Territories (Kuril islands) situated off the coast of Northern Japan and taken by Russian forces at the end of World War II. For the time being, however, the Russian military's attachment to the strategic value it places on the islands and the provincial governor's opposition to change rule out initiatives to exchange territory for aid. The growing Russian nationalism made apparent in the December 1993 general elections to the Federal Assembly also weakened Yeltsin's political position, and made a deal very unlikely. The suspicion reportedly shown by Yeltsin towards Japan's offer of aid to victims of the Sakhalin earthquake in June 1995 is indicative. In fact, Japan has shown rather more enthusiasm to assist the five Central Asian Republics, and, for instance, argued their case for oda-eligibility to fellow DAC states.

Unsteady aims, uncertain times

There is much disagreement over precisely what kinds of change in the former Soviet bloc, especially in the former USSR and Russia in particular, would be of most benefit to the security and other foreign policy interests of OECD states. Views have ranged from the desirability of complete frag-mentation of the former states system to the need to retain a strong centre capable of imposing order in the region. The uncertainty complicates think-ing about whether assistance is at all appropriate, and about what kinds of assistance and to which countries and which institutions. For example, should the West target Russia's 'near abroad', the equivalent of the US's 'backyard', hoping to secure these areas from Russian designs, and thereby contain Russia's future might? Or would that so alarm Russian national-ists and activate old suspicions that there would be a return to East–West enmities? In Russia, are regional and local bureaucracies more trustworthy partners than the central authorities? Should assistance be directed to the public sector, with the risk of confirming old patterns of power, or instead to the emerging private sector notwithstanding its proneness to a form of gangster capitalism? Which of these courses is least likely to undermine the domestic mobilisation of resources for productive investment? The right choice of moments to send positive signals of support and to deliver sub-stantial material help has been just as difficult to discern, because of the volatile nature of events in the former USSR and Russia especially. Critical junctures for providing support met setbacks like Russian difficulties in meeting deadlines for interest payments on foreign debt (of over $130 billion), and, from December 1994, the war in Chechnya (not least because of its financial consequences).

The 'pacific thesis' of democracy provides little reassurance in the con-text of the events taking place in a number of post-communist states, espe-cially the former USSR, where the territorial geography hangs in the balance and societies are enduring heavy costs of economic dislocation. Insensitive diplomacy by aid agencies and particularly the Bretton Woods institutions could so easily arm reactionary tendencies. In Russia, old-style communists and nationalists alike resent the loss of superpower status. Political opponents of Yeltsin have portrayed the economic shock and social impact of liber-alisation as an externally-driven conspiracy aimed at disabling the Russian state and destroying the Russian Federation. Yet the absence of financial support would be interpreted by political opponents as a sign of weakness of the Yeltsin government, or, 'If the West does not provide the money, the whole reformist wing of the government loses its influence and import-ance' (Sergei Aleksashenko, Deputy Finance Minister, in *Financial Times*, 18 January 1995).

There have been many imponderables such as the constant friction in executive–legislature relations, the military–industrial establishment's determination to retain control over resources, growing indications of the generals' presence in the power structure (as evidenced by the prosecution of the war in Chechnya, responsible for over 40,000 Russian casualties), and the shifting relationships between the authorities in Moscow and the provinces. There have been frequent reshuffles of personnel in key government posts especially in regard to economic management, the pro-reform wing seeming to be progressively eroded, up until the 1996 presidential election. Foreign Minister Kozyrev's resignation in the same year was received as an uncomfortable omen by the West. Doubts about the political survival of Yeltsin have been ever present, and success for the Communist Party's presidential candidate Gennady Zyuganov, who campaigned on the themes of nationalism and return to a planned economy, looked possible until the second ballot. Even Yeltsin's victory did not resolve the leadership issue, due to his poor state of health. All in all, the political scene has been and remains a picture of great and continuing uncertainty.

So, it is easy to see why Zbigniew Brzezinski (1994), who was National Security Adviser to President Carter, argued that premature support for Russia could have unintended effects. He hypothesised an incoming regime that would seek to reverse the recent tide of history, by reviving the centralising and imperialist ambitions of pre-Soviet Russia. He recommended that support be given instead to the other NIS and CEEC states. Prominence was given to the Ukraine (the largest aid-recipient country after Russia and Poland), energy-dependent on Russia and containing in Crimea longings for unification with Russia, yet occupying key buffer territory between Russia and the West. Brzezinski premised that geopolitical pluralism in the region is a necessary precondition for the emergence eventually of a stable democratic Russia – a Russia unlikely to pursue expansion by aggressive means. In fact Russia has indeed set about rebuilding close ties with many former Soviet republics. For example, there has been an agreement partially to reunify armies with Kazakhstan (1995), and a 'union treaty' was signed with Belarus in 1996. Also in 1996 the parliament voted to annul the 1991 treaty dissolving the USSR.

Ranged against Brzezinski's thesis is the argument that chronic political instability in Moscow could be an even greater threat to regional peace and global security. Something like this view was advanced by President Gorbachev's Foreign Minister, Eduard Shevardnadze. He predicted the disintegration of the USSR would destabilise world order. To preclude such a chain of events he called for Western support, material and symbolic. These pleas proved incapable of preventing the dismemberment of the USSR into 15 independent states and the abandonment of the Warsaw Pact. However, that such a fate for what President Reagan once called the evil empire might enhance Western security is only one of the possibilities. Concerns exist about what might follow the collapse of the order that was maintained by Soviet power within and beyond its borders, the breakdown of central command structures in the former Red Army, a weakening of the political controls previously exercised over the military by communist ruling parties in the region, and the potentially explosive force of ethno-nationalism.

Around 25 million Russians live outside the Russian Federation. They comprise significant minorities in several of the new independent states, for example 34 per cent of the population of Latvia, 30 per cent in Estonia, 22 per cent in Ukraine. The UNHCR (1993: 122) estimates that 72 million former Soviet citizens live beyond the boundaries of the republics of their ethnic origin. The potential for violent conflict soon became reality in the Caucasus as well as former Yugoslavia. Of course not all of the societies at risk are of close concern to Western Europe, but there have already been some unwelcome consequences, such as large-scale movements of refugees. There have been increased demands on the budgets for humanitarian aid. For instance, by 1995 EU aid was accounting for half the state budget of Georgia, chiefly providing vital food supplies. International aid workers have faced high personal risks in the conflict zones, exemplified by the murder of six Red Cross workers in their beds, in Chechnya in December 1996. Political settlements are usually followed by requests for reconstruction assistance, as in Bosnia where average annual incomes have fallen to around $500. Bosnia is said to need more than $5 billion over the next three years alone. The exposure of fault lines within NATO over the best way to respond to the conflict there could have lasting consequences for the sense of unity and trust in the Western alliance. Some of these costs might have been avoidable *if* substantial international support for the USSR had materialised from 1989 onwards and *if* it had helped the 'centre' to hold. We will never know. But once Soviet disintegration got under way, it became increasingly difficult to predict what the centre would look like. Events proceeded to move too fast for durable analysis, let alone for DAC country policy-makers and aid officials to take timely action on informed advice.

The nuclear and other security dimensions

The USSR is reckoned to have amassed around 45,000 nuclear warheads. The idea that aid could be exchanged for the liquidation or transfer of some of this stockpile, and for agreement to mutual arms reduction, is an appealing one. However, such arrangements could not eliminate the danger of an accidental nuclear strike. Threats to employ such weaponry, even their actual use, cannot be wholly discounted when a nuclear state suffers such serious internal disruption that its external relations are destabilised as well, including in this case Russia's relations with former Soviet republics and other allies. The case for aid, then, must be predicated on practical contributions to political stabilisation and to ensuring effective systems of control over and within the armed forces, in Russia especially.

In Russia, financial and economic distress are more than usually hazardous if they impair the state's ability to maintain adequate storage conditions for nuclear material (spread around 900 sites), or if they lead the government to approve the export of nuclear materials and technology or other sensitive technology (Russia's *conventional* arms exports reported as $3 billion in 1995 were an 80 per cent increase on 1994; the US Congressional Research Service puts the figure at closer to $6 billion). The possibility that nuclear scientists may market their know-how to the highest bidders who could include 'pariah states', and, perhaps, connive in smuggling plutonium or weapons-grade uranium, is another worry. So, offers of Western aid have been made in return for promises to tighten safeguards against such contingencies. Reassurances were agreed at the nuclear safety summit of major leaders held in Moscow in 1996. In January 1994 Ukraine surrendered its warheads in exchange for promises of around $1 billion worth of nuclear fuel needed to power its civilian nuclear reactors, and disarmament assistance, to be provided by the US and Russia. The EU and some bilateral donors have also pledged assistance to help Ukraine convert from armaments manufacture. The retraining of military personnel, missile dismemberment and improvements to the safety of nuclear reactors in other parts of the former USSR are also being funded by Western countries.

Along with military aggression and nuclear anarchy, a third possible threat to security comprises incidents like the Chernobyl explosion in 1986. The rationale for advancing technical support for the maintenance, upgrading, and closure of unsafe civil nuclear power stations in countries lacking the necessary means is self-evident. The Ukrainians obtained promises from the G7 of $1.8 billion in credits and $450 million in grants towards the costs of decommissioning the remaining Chernobyl plant, by the year 2000; another $1.5 billion is needed to renew the concrete sarcophagus on the damaged reactor. The USSR built more than 50 nuclear reactors including 15 of the Chernobyl design. There are more countries with nuclear reactors in Eastern Europe than in any other region. Nuclear reactors produce approximately one third of total electricity in the Ukraine, Slovenia, Bulgaria and Czech Republic and one half in Slovakia. These levels of dependence make external help vital to the speedy introduction of alternatives. In the meantime the EU's TACIS programme is funding the installation of an early-warning monitoring system for accidental radiation leaks, in Belarus and Ukraine.

There are other transboundary environmental issues in which Western European countries have a close interest, such as atmospheric pollution from old-fashioned coal-fired power stations and steel and chemical plants in countries like Poland. Again, financial and technological assistance could hasten progress; it helps explain why Austria has mounted the largest aid effort proportional to GNP (0.14 per cent). Aid could also be offered to persuade Russia to halt its production of CFCs, which are still illegally entering world markets. There are reckoned to be 700,000 ecological migrants in former Soviet territory, and this can be seen as another potential source of social and economic instability that might have harmful international consequences.

Security in today's enlarged sense is applicable in other ways too. For example, one effect of the dramatic economic changes under way in post-communist states has been an exodus of migrant workers seeking employment in Western Europe. Germany has been in the front line, at a time when it has been grappling with its own economic, employment, social and budgetary problems arising from reunification. The influx has given rise to increased tensions in some German towns. The violent response shown by a small minority of local people, awakening fears of a revival of neo-Nazism, has brought embarrassment to many Germans and to the authorities. Aid that would improve socio-economic conditions in the countries of origin, or simply fund a stricter enforcement of border controls on every side, can look very worthwhile. The same is true of practical support to efforts in the former Soviet bloc to contain mafia-type activities and narcotics trafficking, in which Russians are thought to be heavily involved. These activities have an international impact, the theft of luxury automobiles in Germany and their transport eastwards through the Polish corridor being a highly publicised example.

Following German reunification, a special reason for Germany to maintain goodwill in Moscow has been to hasten the withdrawal of Warsaw Pact troops from the territory of the former GDR, which housed three quarters of the more than 500,000 Soviet forces stationed in Eastern Europe. In the early days a constraint on repatriation was a shortage of suitable accommodation for returning soldiers in Russia. As the special payments by Germany arising from reunification come to an end, German aid to Russia will probably decline.

Economic, financial and social arguments

The economic case for aid to former CMEA members has several strands interwoven. First is the belief that a successful transition to market economies would add vitality to the global economy, so benefiting the OECD economies too. Western assistance can speed the development of market-supporting institutions. Russia's 150 million-strong population and the 400 million people of the NIS and CEEC countries combined offer a huge prospective demand for internationally branded goods and services, not just from Western Europe which is the main trade axis (as early as 1991 South Korea offered the USSR aid tied to the procurement of a variety of its own consumer manufactures like televisions and sports apparel). The abundance of materials such as oil and natural gas in Siberia, an educated if not highly trained workforce that is already familiar with the discipline required by industrial organisation, and a willingness to work for relatively low wages, all indicate good investment opportunities to international capital. More immediately, ex-communist countries offer a greenfield site for Western consultancies. Various DAC countries have devised aid initiatives to exploit the commercial opportunities. For example Britain's official 'Know-How' funds for bilateral technical assistance were set up to promote

British expertise in such areas as financial services, and have spent £230 million since 1989. Of the £69 million disbursed on technical cooperation with transition economies in 1994–5, over half related to Russia and Poland.

The dismantling of centrally planned economies and rapid liberalisation pose economic, financial and technical challenges. They also generate considerable social costs, especially concentrated where large but uneconomic industrial plants are closed, or heavily restructured, in what have been 'company towns'. Large numbers of people have experienced dramatic changes in their living conditions. Workers who were highly unionised now experience a loss of job security. Consumers have faced steep price increases for basic items that were previously heavily subsidised and whose supply has been disrupted. For example, retail consumer prices increased by over 10,000 per cent in Armenia and the Ukraine in 1993 and by over 2000 per cent in six other NIS economies. Pensioners have seen the value of their state pension plummet, and most families are affected by uniform deterioration in public services like medical care and education. The majority of CEEC and NIS economies recorded yearly GDP falls in 1990–4, on average over 10 per cent annually in half of the countries. In Russia 1996 GDP was probably less than half the 1989 level, and real industrial production virtually halved in five years. In some countries a collapse of civil order was a major factor; more generally macro-economic reforms have been a precipitating factor; and in cases like Ukraine, prior to 1994, responsibility can also be attached to a slowness to respond to the collapse of intra-regional trade caused by abandonment of the CMEA. Against this background international assistance can offer to play a combination of economic roles: rewarding governments that have boldly initiated macro-economic stabilisation and liberalisation and helping their societies to consolidate the reforms, as in Poland; and inducing the more cautious governments to follow suit, by offers of conditional support.

However, the great variety of economic and social conditions displayed by the former Soviet republics and Central/Eastern European countries means no one case for development aid and no one kind of assistance could be appropriate everywhere. In some countries, favourable resource endowments and the possibilities for considerable productivity gains in agriculture and industry auger well for the economic prospects. There, aid looks like an economically sound investment. Indeed, concessionary transfers might be thought to be unnecessary, especially for capital projects that merit the interest of the IFC, EBRD and foreign multinational corporations. The stock of foreign direct investment in the CEECs and former Soviet republics in Central Asia increased by 60 per cent in 1995. Former Eastern bloc countries now account for one fifth of US investment in Europe. The three Baltic republics together with Hungary (which is now host to well over $10 billion of foreign direct investment) fall within the World Bank's classification of upper-middle income states. And in 1996 Poland and the Czech Republic became candidates to join the OECD. However, even for countries where notable social and economic achievements and market economy features existed prior to transition, the justification for programme loans during the most demanding years of structural economic reform remains strong, even if the argument for high concessionality is relatively weak. Financial institution building and infrastructural investment will remain priorities for some years to come, with domestic savings mobilisation now being seen by the EBRD as one of the most difficult of the challenges still outstanding in most transition economies.

In most cases an argument can be mounted that economic assistance could contribute, directly or indirectly, to multiple goals. The successful passage to political liberalisation and democratisation may be posited as two such goals of economic transformation, and 'there is no higher strategic interest for the West in this decade than the successful democratization of Russia and the other former East bloc countries' (Diamond 1992: 34). All this would be endangered if the social costs of economic transition were allowed to become excessive. Great social need is particularly evident in parts of the former USSR, including Armenia, Azerbaijan, Georgia, Kazakhstan, Kyrgyzstan, Tajikistan, Turkmenistan and Uzbekistan. Per capita GNP in the majority of these republics in 1992 ranged below $3000 – half of the average incomes prevailing in at least five of the CEECs. Absolute poverty has increased markedly since 1989. More than half the population now live below the official poverty line in the five Central Asian republics, as do over a quarter of Russia's population, where average male life expectancy fell by six years between 1990 and 1994 (and similarly in the Ukraine). Thus, quite aside from emergency relief, there is ample scope for aid to be directed at alleviating poverty and improving the satisfaction of basic needs. The arrival of Western NGOs, who are providing around $0.5 billion annually, is symptomatic. Some examples have drawn considerable local interest in donor countries, such as the concern shown by Christian church groups for orphaned children in Romania. So far, however, the geographical distribution of all aid including that from multilaterals has not been at all correlated with poverty criteria.

Finally, economic progress would also improve the chances of there being repayment of at least some of the foreign debt contracted by the former communist states. Again, Germany has a special interest, for up to 40 per cent of the entire Soviet foreign debt involved West German banks and the former GDR. The need to apportion responsibility for the inherited liabilities of the USSR (itself owed considerable sums by such states as Cuba and Vietnam) has been an obstacle, but Russia has assumed responsibility for over $100 billion of foreign debt. Following international agreements to reschedule official and commercial debt in 1996, Russia looks set to be admitted to the Paris club of creditor nations in the near future.

Other political arguments

Political arguments for assisting former Second World countries include helping to advance capitalism, democratisation and the future of the European

Union. The successful conversion of former communist countries to capitalism may be seen as one more confirmation of the triumph of the West. More disappointing would be an anti-capitalist reaction more comprehensive than just the occasional electoral success of parties calling themselves communist, and failed transitions. So too would be the entrenchment of what Rosefielde (1993: 359–60) calls kleptostroika – a degenerate form of state socialism, in which a corrupt and politically well-connected oligarchy appropriates the country's major industrial assets for itself, without pioneering new enterprises or bringing in a competitive market economy comprehensively opened to international investors. By late 1996 just such a narrow group of clans, who had provided considerable financial backing to Yeltsin's re-election campaign, seemed to be consolidating their position in banking, commerce and key sectors like telecommunications.

However, the victory of capitalism looks the more solid for having come about from within former communist countries, rather than being produced by external imposition or as a quid pro quo for Western aid. And the identification of capitalism as a Western trademark is in any case unconvincing, now that its most successful exponents in recent decades are in East Asia. So, in terms of the global pursuit of ideological hegemony the West may have more to gain from the degree to which economic marketisation in former Soviet-bloc countries spreads the growth of liberal democracy. Liberal democracy definitely is a patent of Western civilisation, and, in some accounts, of Western Christendom specifically. Capitalism is not a sufficient condition for liberal democracy to exist. Nevertheless, according to Lindblom (1977: 162), 'political polyarchies' are 'not only without exception market systems but specifically are private enterprise systems'. Hence the inference drawn by Diamond (1992) and others that support given to the capitalist development of the former socialist countries would be a sound investment in democratisation.

The security gains and the enhanced prestige of the established democracies apart, democratisation provides its own justification for lending support to the former Second World. Currently, the reform of the main instruments of government, capacity building in governance and the development of the economic institutions that underscore stable political pluralism are all objects of foreign assistance. The general weakness of civil society, which is notable in many ex-communist countries, also means there are many opportunities extending to the provision of equipment, advice and training sessions to new political parties. The National Endowment for Democracy in the US and Britain's Westminster Foundation for Democracy have been active in this field. Over 50 per cent of projects funded by the latter's budget (half of which is directed through Britain's political parties and half allocated to all-party and non-party projects) have been in Central/Eastern Europe and former USSR.

As is true also of their economic marketisation, countries in the region that consolidate democratic forms will be setting examples for other emerging democracies, and for societies with less benign regimes. They might consider this a fitting sequel to the inspiration that was sent out in the early days of democratic transition. To illustrate, a signal moment in the developments that propelled Zambia back to plural politics came in December 1989. Frederick Chiluba asked in public, why should Africans continue to imitate models of socialism and the one-party state that were being abandoned by their inventors in Central and Eastern Europe? The question was a telling one, enthusiastically received by compatriots. Now, the vindication both of liberal democracy and capitalism in the former communist world might even bolster confidence among Western societies. For there is evidence of increasing dissatisfaction with their own social and political institutions, as manifest in waning public trust in elected politicians, increase of job insecurity, unemployment, relative deprivation and crime, and the growing vulnerability of national economies to such uncontrollable forces as international financial speculation.

The future of Europe and beyond

The future of the EU now seems inseparable from developments in the rest of Europe. Most CEECs have signalled a firm desire to join the EU at the earliest available opportunity. In several cases plans for their integration into the single market are well advanced, and by mid-1996 ten had signed association agreements (so-called 'Europe Agreements'). Hungary, Poland, Romania, Czech Republic, Slovenia, Slovakia, Latvia and Estonia (and Turkey, with whom a draft customs union accord was negotiated in 1995) had applied for EU membership. A lengthy delay could sour relations. But the present disparities between these countries and the economic conditions, institutional norms and standards of performance inside the EU will have to be reduced first. Otherwise, the calls made on EU structural funds and the CAP could be overwhelming, notwithstanding proposals to make those arrangements less generous. Also, on entry the new members might incur too great a shock of sudden adjustment. The EU has identified 2005 as the earliest feasible date for completion of procedural formalities, for accession of the most eligible applicants. Aid in the intervening period will help prepare the way, buy time during which internal reforms can be made to EU arrangements, soften the disappointment over the wait, and help reduce the period of probation for some. The EU is sponsoring pre-accession programmes designed to facilitate eventual harmonisation in legislative and regulatory matters; and the EBRD is looking to fund schemes that improve transport and communications links between Eastern and Western Europe. Needless to say, in seeking to qualify, the candidates for EU membership must continue in a democratic direction. There are precedents for offering economic assistance conditional on enacting the political reforms required to meet criteria for full EU membership, for instance in the management of Portugal's path to accession.

Enlargement to the East is the main option, now that few countries elsewhere in Europe remain outside the EU. EU widening could help reduce the existing tensions over how far and how fast the organisation should develop into a federal state. As a source of dynamic, the strategy of widening offers a partial alternative to deepening, and will eventually create such a large and diverse membership that complete agreement on further political integration seems improbable anyway. At that point a form of 'variable geometry', 'structured flexibility' or multi-level arrangement might win common approval, benefiting harmony overall. As a general principle, the presence of cross-cutting cleavages can be an aid to harmony. In the case of the EU the established divide between Britain and the Franco-German alliance over political integration is overlaid by joint Anglo-German enthusiasm for enlargement to the East (although there is also strong disagreement over the issue of qualified majority voting in the Council of Ministers and the veto rights that states individually should retain in an enlarged collective body). The shared interest in EU expansion eastwards contrasts with the greater interest shown by France and other Southern European members in relations with the Maghreb, as well as France's greater determination to persist with the Lomé Convention. EU expansion might also help contain Germany's propensity towards dominance in Europe. The revitalisation of Russia could have a similar effect. The containment of Germany should benefit peace and security in the region. As an economic project, enlargement is made more essential for Europe by the emergence of other regional trade blocs, examples being the North American Free Trade Agreement (NAFTA) and the Asia Pacific Economic Cooperation forum (APEC). The US, Japan, China and the other 15 members of APEC account for around half of world output and half of world trade (excluding trade within the EU); and East Asia alone is growing in regional self-sufficiency, with half of its trade being within the region.

Looking beyond just the European land mass, there are further issues in high politics. One is the expansion of NATO – a Western goal notwithstanding Russian objections (which Russian defence minister General Rodionov downplayed in November 1996). The two processes are not formally connected, but delay in the accession of former CMEA countries to the EU could affect the timetable for bringing the majority of former Warsaw Pact territories within the security framework of Western Europe (currently Poland, Hungary and the Czech Republic seem likely to gain accession to NATO before EU membership). Under President Clinton the US has pursued a policy of more positive engagement with the authorities in Moscow than was apparent under his predecessors, although attitudes among the American public towards committing substantial concessionary flows could remain tinged by the legacy of Cold War hostilities. Of course, the US and EU are both allies and competitors for power; and economic forces will pull the US more closely to the Pacific rim, just as the EU's 'near abroad' will be pushed further and further to the East. But Huntington (1993) has posited a different basis for analysing the coming alignments. He says that following the end of ideological confrontation between East and West, the clash of civilisations will be as portentous as economic competition between trading blocs of nations. He identifies major divisions between Christendom and Islam, and between Western and Asiatic cultures. The West's interest is said to lie in gaining the attachment of its closest neighbours, principally the Eurasian power of Russia. For Europe, this would mean building on the pulls of affection exerted by common elements of culture and a shared past, common threads in religion and race – historical directives that vie with the moral obligations to former colonies in the Third World.

Needless to say, Huntington's article, which proposed that Russia must choose between being part of the West or becoming leader of a distinct Slavic–Orthodox civilisation that could come into conflict with the West, is highly controversial. Moreover, some commentators take more notice of Russia's reviving diplomatic friendship with China (evidenced in the 'strategic partnership' agreed by the two governments in April 1996), which will become concrete in the shape of increased trade in Russian arms. Another possibility is that Russia will not join a stable prosperous West but instead decline into becoming a large annex to the 'zone of conflict' – a synonym for a struggling and unstable South. Clearly, the stakes are high for everyone. So high that it is tempting to believe there must be a role that international aid can play, in influencing the outcome constructively. But what kind of role, to what end, and can aid be truly effective?

Observations

One of the first reactions in the West to the events unfolding in Eastern Europe in the late 1980s was that these societies need help in building democratic structures and market economies. Assistance could contribute a pool of wisdom and practical support; it would steady confidence (see for example Rollo 1990: 10). An immediate objective for the US was to keep the Strategic Arms Reduction Treaty (START) negotiations with the USSR on track. These were completed in 1991 (although by 1996 the Russian parliament had still not ratified the 1993 treaty, START II, which limits each country to 3500 strategic nuclear warheads). In 1992 former President Nixon called on the US government to devise an equivalent to the Marshall Plan for the development of the former Soviet republics and their conversion into democracies. Similar pleas came from the left (Griffin 1991: 679–80). Others also advised that the strategic aim of Western policies should be to enmesh Eastern Europe in an ever-deepening network of political, economic and social interdependencies (Hyde-Price 1994: 245).

However, the parallel with Marshall aid was never sound, and aid's potential effectiveness in regard to former Second World countries has not been straightforward. They are attempting not simply to rebuild but to transform their economies. Some are trying to construct new states at the same time. While the handicap of economic and social turmoil in the region could be advanced as a ground for extending help, it may also mean that substantial assistance would be premature, except for pressing humanitarian needs. These reservations apply particularly to those former Soviet republics where 'the economies are not robust; and there appears to be little tendency towards co-operation at any level of government' (Patterson 1993: 191).

In the beginning the period for which assistance might be required looked lengthy and the total bill potentially formidable. The DAC members knew the countries in transition were entering unchartered waters, and they have been unsure about the prospects. The dearth of reliable information about the true nature of their economic situation recommended caution; estimates of their absorptive capacity and needs have varied widely, being continually revised. Unlike the Marshall Plan, the post-communist societies are treating with several possible bilateral donors, few of whom are in expansive mood. Above all they have to maintain a *modus vivendi* with the Bretton Woods institutions. Concessionary transfers cannot solve all the problems, and may not even be necessary for project investment in the countries that are increasingly being served by private international financial and capital markets. For much of the region the EBRD now judges the phase of declining output is over and the growth prospects good. By 1996 twelve of the CEEC and NIS economies were registering growth; increasing income inequalities are another noticeable feature. In Poland four consecutive years of growth have virtually restored the economy to its pre-transition size. Even in Russia, where the state has halved its share of GDP (in part through the privatisation of 14,000 companies), the stock of foreign direct investment has risen by a third in 1995, to over $4.4 billion. The IMF agreed a $6 billion standby loan in 1995 and, in early 1996, a further concessionary $10.2 billion loan for the following three years. Also in 1996 the Paris club conditionally agreed to comprehensive rescheduling of more than $40 billion of former Soviet debt, leading the way to a successful Russian debut in the international bond market. However, economic activity remains severely depressed.

Significant differences exist among the post-communist countries. For example, in many CEECs pro-democratic sentiments are probably stronger than in the former USSR and could prove more resilient if there is protracted economic disappointment. Aid must be considered on a case by case basis. Specialised assistance including technical cooperation for economic marketisation and democratisation, including for the building of civil society, is particularly apposite when tailored to local circumstances, and together with project assistance now accounts for over half of all the official aid. Debt cancellations could also be appropriate, but the governments should not be encouraged to accumulate large new foreign debt, especially for the purpose of underwriting institutional reforms that will deliver returns only slowly. Previous experience in the region posts a warning. The Paris club agreed in 1991 to cancel up to 55 per cent of Poland's $33 billion debt (which explains why Poland has been the destination of a major share of all official aid to the region), but would not want a similar need to arise again. Now, Hungary's foreign debt of over $30 billion is the highest per capita in the region. Another lesson is that the symbolic importance of assistance which makes well-timed gestures of solidarity should not be underestimated, especially in countries where the balance of political forces for and against reform remains fluid.

Not all DAC governments have perceived their interests identically, as has been shown by Germany's greater urgency manifest from early on in the drive to secure Soviet agreement to full German reunification. Initially, the US government seemed most interested in introducing conditions into its support for change in the USSR that would further isolate Cuba, rather than seize the larger importance of the events that were taking place (Eckstein 1994: 95). Like Japan, the US initially opposed Russian membership of the EBRD. The Gulf war too was a major distraction. So, no second Marshall Plan was launched, notwithstanding the growing commitment to support President Yeltsin that has been very evident under the Clinton administration. In any case it is not easy to divert substantial resources quickly from within aid budgets, particularly if there are sound commercial or political grounds for maintaining existing programmes. The international gatherings that meet from time to time have failed to achieve donor consensus over allocating the new burdens of support. For example, as regards Ukraine, in 1994 Germany, Japan and the US were reported to be willing to provide balance of payments support, on condition the EU also participated. The US wanted to reward Ukraine for having signed the Nuclear Non-Proliferation Treaty as a non-nuclear state. However, Britain and France demanded there first be a firm commitment by the Ukrainian authorities to a full-scale programme of macro-economic reform, agreed with the IMF. And EU states could not agree among themselves over how far the European Commission should submit a policy position of its own. Everywhere, the Bretton Woods institutions have been able to enjoy a fulcrum position, but in Russia their preoccupation with fiscal and monetary matters is perceived to have served democratisation badly (Zhukov 1995).

Future historians will mull over whether the West should have taken bolder initiatives in the epoch-making years early on. Affirmants may take their cue from Andrei Kosyrev (1992: 9–10), who said history 'has witnessed many times how the domestic problems of Russia made that state a dangerous and unpredictable participant in international affairs'. However, even if Kosyrev's plea for support had fallen on more receptive ears, the best way to help the situation develop in ways agreeable to DAC governments has been far from obvious. Both the case for aid and decisions on its composition would still need regular updating. Zubok (1995: 116) has said: 'Most of the direct effects of the outside world on Russia are either ambiguous or downright ruinously counterproductive'. In reality, the outside world cannot foretell Russia's future, and has not evinced clear agreement on the shape it would like the wider region to take. So far in the 1990s Russia has lived up to Gogol's famous metaphor (in *Dead Souls*) for Russia's past – of a ramshackle troika, gathering pace in erratic and uncontrolled flight. Probably, nothing that would have been feasible in the matter of international assistance could have significantly diverted the troika from its path.

The Second World and the Third World – love's labours lost

The consolidation of DAC aid to the Part II countries has coincided with a real terms decline in the oda available to the rest of the world. The gravest fears voiced especially in Africa that there would be a substantial diversion of aid away from Third World countries cannot be dismissed as groundless, but nor are they conclusively confirmed. We cannot know what would have happened if the USSR had survived intact. We can presume that the sooner the post-communist economies are rejuvenated, the sooner they will provide growing export markets for the Third World and, possibly, become significant donors once again. Of the total net receipts of external resources by NIS and CEECs in 1990–4 less than a third ($31 billion) have been official aid. And the World Bank's calculation (*World Development Report 1996*: 136) is that in 1990–5 the NIS and CEEC economies in transition have absorbed only 15 per cent of all capital flows to developing and transition economies (compared with sub-Saharan Africa's meagre share of 9 per cent). In any case, the issue of aid diversion raises much more than just financial considerations. The aid disbursements in the CEEC and NIS so far are probably of much less significance than the political and psychological impact of the end of the Second World and the transformed political relationships between East and West. These developments, together with emerging realignments in international trade and commerce as well as non-concessional resource flows, increase OECD countries' bargaining power *vis-à-vis* some of their long-standing oda partners. The evidence lies in the apprehensiveness felt within the Third World, the more assertive posture taken by donors and the steps a number of aid-seeking governments have already taken to accommodate, or to deflect, the new approach.

Similarly, the evaporation of aid flows from the socialist bloc seems less important for the sums involved than as a symptom of much more fundamental changes in global political and economic affairs. In comparison with Africa, China together with certain East Asian and Latin American countries were always likely to be stronger competitors for the 1990s upsurge in foreign direct investment flows, regardless of happenings in the Soviet bloc. Moreover, not only did the USSR play no part in the Bretton Woods institutions or supply direct flows of corporate investment, which are of growing importance to many developing countries, but it offered large-scale assistance to only a few countries. These programmes were always likely to go into decline, or become more commercialised and geared increasingly to Soviet economic needs. From the mid-1980s former clients in Southern Africa were advised to seek economic assistance elsewhere; and in 1988 the State Committee for Foreign Economic Relations (responsible for aid) was merged with the Foreign Trade Ministry. The pricing of oil exports was switched to convertible currency, 'friendship prices' to special friends were withdrawn, and Soviet loans shifted from a non-repayable to repayable basis (Mesa-Lago 1993). Yeltsin called for all Soviet assistance to be greatly reduced, in May 1990. The writing was on the wall, even before the change of political regime.

For a few countries, greater significance attaches to the contraction of the former Soviet economy and the CMEA's dissolution than to the changes already pending in Soviet aid by the 1990s, or DAC aid diversion from the Third World. Cuba carried out 85 per cent of external trade with the CMEA in 1985–8 and 71 per cent with the USSR. More than 90 per cent was on a non-convertible currency or barter basis. In 1989–90 the USSR could not honour export commitments for a range of items to Cuba particularly. Soviet oil output fell by a quarter in 1989–91. By 1992 all trade subsidies had come to an end, and the value of Cuba's trade with the former Soviet bloc fell to 7 per cent of its 1989 value. The end of Soviet arms sales on credit was another important development, but so were the much more sweeping revisions to Soviet foreign policy that were afoot well before the collapse of the USSR.

The USSR traditionally gave political support to many more countries than the handful of most favoured aid partners. The situation was bound to be affected as improved relations with the US became a priority. Cuba's strategic value diminished, and by the late 1980s the Soviet government concluded, on the basis of political as well as economic cost-benefit analyses of its aid, that policy reforms were overdue in some of its most favoured allies. Cuba was pressed to begin liberalising its economy. And, following discussions with the US in 1991, Gorbachev announced the withdrawal of 11,000 Soviet military and other advisers stationed in Cuba. Not long before, Vietnam's decision to withdraw its 150,000 troops from Cambodia by 1990 had been made in the context of increasing reluctance by the USSR to continue with annual pledges of support, formerly contributing up to a quarter of the government's budget and estimated to be worth $2 billion over five years (Soviet arms supplies have been valued at over $1 billion annually during 1981–8). Vietnam's occupation of Cambodia had been a major obstacle to Soviet attempts to improve its relations with both the US and China. Of course, there are some societies for whom it is the disintegration of the USSR that has been most profoundly influential, bringing economic and social crisis. Examples include Mongolia and former Central Asian Republics. While the Soviet collapse threatened to make some Third World governments less secure (because they lost Soviet guardianship, or because their strategic importance to the West now evaporated), the effect has elevated the regional status and relative power potential of some other states, like Turkey and Iran.

The DAC countries now virtually determine the total world figures for concessionary resources, without having the same need as before to purchase Third World loyalties. This is more significant than just aid diversion, and so is the political message that is spread by the retreat from one-party communist rule and socialist economics. The West has gained, as a source of models of economic and political development. Sir Winston Churchill is reputed to have said democracy is the worst system on offer, apart from all the rest. Now, a similar verdict might be applied to capitalism as well, by default of plausible examples of accessible alternatives. No longer is there a second superpower to sponsor a plausible choice. A greater combination of economic and political lore than ever before is being embodied in DAC oda and aid conditionalities. So, if 'progressive' social forces in the Third World are to avoid surrender to notions that the West has 'first of all moral superiority, but also superiority with regard to insights into what could be in the best interest of the South' (Stokke 1996: 75), then they must fall back on their own intellectual and moral resources. If more authentic ideas of development come to be explored as a result, that would be no bad thing. For while the sea-changes introduced in this chapter have brought some established oda recipients to make modest political adjustments, there are far fewer signs that great inequalities in the distribution of social and economic goods are being significantly reduced.

Conclusion: change and continuity

Making sense of foreign aid today necessitates a familiarity with its past. Aid has undergone marked changes over the last 50 years. So have the economic and political environments with which aid interacts, at the international, national and sub-national levels. Our understanding of those environments and how they interact, and of aid itself, have also changed. The following changes have had significant consequences for aid.

One: a major redistribution of power in the international system, in particular the disappearance of the communist bloc. Two: a worldwide shift in ideology of political economy away from state-led arrangements and towards markets. This enshrines the importance of incentives to wealth creation and underscores that individuals and societies have a responsibility to look after their needs without constant resort to government help. Three: a meshing of involvement by non-governmental and hybrid organisations with government in many areas of public policy and collective provision. For example, in Britain charities' income from government grants and fees for providing contracted services increased over 40 per cent between 1992 and 1996. Four: increasing differentiation within the South. The Third World as a monolithic place of undifferentiated countries, all highly dependent and poverty-stricken, has shrunk, revealing a sizeable core of seriously indebted least developed countries. Eighty-nine countries are worse off in income terms now than a decade ago, over half being in sub-Saharan Africa, in contrast to the 'emerging economies' of Asia, Latin America and elsewhere. Five: the UN system has come to be enveloped by a growing sense of malaise, epitomised by official US opposition to Secretary-General Boutros Boutros-Ghali taking a second term of office. The difficulties have accompanied a growing awareness that new opportunities for an enhanced role in international affairs should be possible in the present disorderly condition of world affairs, which has earned the label post post-Cold War world. Familiar understandings of security have been set adrift, to be compounded by a host of other actual and potential sources of fear. The border between the domestic and the international arenas has shifted. Indeed, according to some analysts it no longer exists, for the two spheres have become so thoroughly entangled. Finally, and specifically in regard to aid, many donors now claim that democracy, human rights and good governance have special importance. At the same time, as people look increasingly to the next millennium, aid is being talked about more and more as a transitory phenomenon of the twentieth century.

Together, these developments raise fundamental questions about what aid is for and the forms in which it should be provided, about what aid should be expected to achieve and how far it deserves our support. However, the issue of who will lead the response looks like becoming more acute. As a donor the US, for so long the largest aid power, may well continue to experience decline in its relative weight. Japan still seems reluctant or unable to take on global leadership pretensions, intellectual or political, although some observers claim to detect recent signs of initiative, even assertiveness. The EU will be distracted by issues concerning widening and political deepening of the Union, for some years to come. Also, divisions will persist over the strategic direction of its aid allocations. There are internal problems at the World Bank too, whose president, James Wolfensohn, detects a culture of cynicism and despair. He draws attention to a 'glass wall' existing between employees and top management. While some of its critics like Ryrie (1995) recommend that it withdraw from subsidised lending, the Bank's own vision of its future role in a globalising economy dominated by private capital flows remains unclear. In contrast, there has been no shortage of (conflicting) ideas about the contribution the NGO sector should attempt to make to international development cooperation. But for all practical purposes NNGOs are subject to large exogenous forces over which they have little or no control. Indeed, according to Edwards and Hulme (1995: 226–7), NGOs have already spent too much time criticising others and not enough time 'putting their own house in order'. They offer no 'magic bullet' in respect of development problems, and apparently none are seriously trying to work themselves out of a job.

Changes

Most catalogues of recent events that have significantly changed the world give a high place to the disappearance of the USSR and Central/East European transformations. Aid's contribution was marginal. Aid power could not save the USSR from its economic and other weaknesses, although the rival aid efforts of the West raised the cost of competing for superpower parity. Nevertheless, the East–West changes have had major implications for North–South relations generally and aid specifically. One such is a closer focusing of attention on aid's developmental effectiveness. Other developments that have influenced aid, and are not themselves primarily the product of aid, include the economic trajectories that have enabled Japan to over-take the US as a donor, and political developments inside countries like Vietnam (now the second largest recipient of IDA assistance, after India), Cambodia (pledged more than $1.5 billion since 1991), South Africa and Nicaragua. Their governments are now accepted almost universally as can-didates for aid, and the same is true of the fledgling Palestinian Authority. Also in the South, the growth in numbers and size of SNGOs can only partly be explained by aid inflows, and yet SNGOs are becoming increas-ingly important to aid administration.

Changing parameters in oda

For all oda's faults and a lengthening awareness of its limitations, aid has not become any less highly sought after. On the contrary, more countries than ever are recipients, being drawn from North, South, East and West. These days, the sun does not set on foreign aid. Globally, the demand continues to outstrip the supply. Supply is under increasing pressure from competing claims on resources. The DAC remains committed to the view that the most aid-dependent countries still need more assistance. But the vocabulary of development cooperation has changed 'with breathtaking speed' (OECD 1990: 1). Western donors began to feel freer to introduce a growing raft of political conditionalities. The regime of politeness in diplomatic rela-tions, which was once called the white man's burden in a post-colonial climate, has been broken. Lady Chalker exemplified the new robustness when she openly criticised the Kenyan government's human rights record, immediately prior to receiving an audience with President Moi. Kenyans reproached her for being 'impolite and contemptuous' (*Financial Times*, 2 August 1995). Oxfam's willingness to criticise African governments for showing lack of initiative, in *Multilateral Debt: the Human Costs* (1996), is also indicative. Of course, some NGOs would also say they have travelled in the opposite direction: they insist they are committed to partnership for empowerment, instead of merely dispensing aid for development. Equal respect is their house rule. Nevertheless, there is probably much greater congruence between NGO themes and the developmental understandings circulating in many official aid agencies than used to be the case. Almost all now say gender issues, the environment and human rights should be on the agenda, even though there are disagreements over how to operationalise the substance, and doubts about one another's sincerity, as well as a shared recognition that the actual achievements to date leave much room for fur-ther progress.

More than ever before oda must be viewed as part of a larger set of financial, economic and other relationships. The variety of dealings that con-tain some concessionary element has grown, for example extensions to debt relief schemes that fall short of debt cancellation. Also, the international community's non-oda financial interventions, as in Mexico in Decem-ber 1994 and IMF loans to Russia, have assumed enormous significance

(1996 saw the members agree to a $55 billion emergency credit line for the IMF). As Strange (1994a: 211) has argued in the context of the global political economy, there is more to welfare than foreign aid: aid is just one of several kinds of resource transfer, and resource transfers are not the only form in which welfare is provided. So, on the one hand, the relative importance of the DAC's formal demarcation of oda as a distinctive and special phenomenon begins to weaken. On the other hand, the idea of foreign aid is being purified, to the extent that military assistance has declined. That trend may be of more value to Third World peoples (especially where past external intervention fomented inter-state and intra-state conflict) than the foregone oda they are possibly now being denied, as a result of aid diversion to the post-communist countries.

In any case, there are now more doubts about the entitlement of all developing countries to be considered eligible for oda, as their economic and financial profiles differentiate. Wider themes to do with their integration in world commerce and trade and private resource flows take on greater significance. Oda as presently construed is only one of several possibilities, even though we now tend to think of money as much as merchandise when we identify what makes the world go round. The contrast between the Brandt report (Independent Commission on International Development Issues 1980) and the report of the Independent Commission on Population and Quality of Life (1996) illustrates both points nicely. For whereas Brandt proposed that increased aid be funded by taxes on trade, so the more recent report recommends a global charge (0.01 per cent) on international financial dealings. It is estimated that this would raise $150 billion annually – enough to pay for the priorities concerning poverty, the environment, reproductive rights, women and children agreed by four major UN conferences between 1990 and 1994.

Aid and development

That development poses a multidimensional challenge is widely accepted, as is the lesson that development in places like sub-Saharan Africa is not easy, speedy or cheap. There is said to be more consensus among DAC members than ever, on a cluster of primary requisites that includes governmental transparency and accountability, private enterprise and environmental sustainability. This may be true at a very general level. But the claim that there is also a growing convergence of views among donors and recipients merits greater qualification. It fails to explain why 'the christmas tree' effect – the overloading of aid relationships with multiple conditions and conditionalities – has become so pronounced, often magnified by the burden of informal cross-conditionality as between the Bretton Woods institutions for example. The 1980s saw 'an unprecedented degree of external intervention in internal economic policies' (OECD 1991: 65), and by the 1990s 'almost every political issue under the sun now intersected with one aid policy or another' (Gibbon 1993: 45). At times the conditionalities work at cross purposes, create negative externalities and render wholehearted compliance impossible, by making contradictory or mutually incompatible demands. The chances are that donors are increasingly overreaching our understanding of how economic, social and political systems work and interact with one another. Yet, tightening aid budgets could lead aid agencies to become less tolerant of recipient performance slippage on conditionalities, unless donors' self-regarding policy objectives make them indulgent.

Oda's purpose and modalities have acquired an increasing number of different guises, as the construction of physical infrastructures has been overlayered by structural economic adjustment and political reform. The chances of making meaningful comparisons of cost-effectiveness become increasingly remote. Carlsson *et al.* (1994: 1) say our knowledge of aid's economic contribution is 'at best ambiguous or, more commonly, non-existent'. However, economists have probably devoted more resources to the study of oda than any other group of social scientists. No less perspicacity could be required to traverse the learning curve in regard to, say, democracy assistance. So, how much more true of such assistance must be Riddell's (1987: 126) studied conclusion about economic development aid, that trying to 'prove that aid does or does not assist recipient economies is akin to trying to locate the end of the rainbow'? Political forms of aid like democracy assistance have recently gained in recognition because of the enthusiasm of Western politicians and the relatively modest demands they make on cash. Democratisation and human rights especially now vie as developmental objects of aid in their own right. But, inevitably, they look vulnerable to the canard which equates worth with demonstrable and positive *quantifiable* returns. And after all, two of Africa's most trumpeted success stories of orthodox stabilisation and structural adjustment – Ghana in the 1980s and Uganda in the 1990s – owed little to liberal democracy. The chances are that donor patience with at least some of today's political enthusiasms could soon start to wear thin, and not only because the number of embarrassing failures will inevitably grow. (In an example from July 1996, Burundi's Major Buyoya staged a military coup and proscribed political parties, after having enjoyed the confidence of the US government.) The fact is the pace of demands to see tangible results is quickening in respect of all manner of human endeavours. Urgency could well be a watchword of the twenty-first century.

Democratisation itself will always be an unfinished process. At some future date it may be deemed too slow, uneven and unreliable an instrument of oda's economic and social goals, especially where it appears to make economic reform more, not less, problematical. In the old saw, the voters' power to get rid is not a power to get right. New development nostrums will come along. The possibility should not be discounted that emerging trends might resemble recent history put into reverse. First, a retreat from some of the most patently ethnocentric of political demands, like effective competition between political parties, through reducing occasions to insist on neo-liberal economic policy reform, and, eventually, back to basics. By basics we mean investing in physical infrastructures – very necessary in rapidly urbanising Asian economies, former Soviet republics and run-down SILICs alike – and promoting enterprise at the micro-level (microcredit schemes for the poor are now very fashionable in development circles), together with community-based programmes that tackle social deprivation, chiefly in conjunction with NGOs and grass-roots organisations. The large project-oriented approach always favoured by Japan, whose main aid partners have led the world in terms of economic growth, could regain some of its former lustre. Also, the draft *World Development Report 1997* (*Financial Times*, 28 June 1996) indicates that Japanese scepticism about the appropriateness of rigorous neo-liberalism for all developing countries no longer appears quite so heretical (ironically, evidence is growing that Japan's and South Korea's own economic requirements might now have outgrown their home-grown models of developmental or state-guided capitalism and active state involvement in industrial development). The Bank pays compliment to 'activist government', which adds value to the market, and calls for an agile state.

Finally, in the countries where the democratic genie, having escaped from the bottle, continues to roam free, incoming aid's effectiveness and distributional consequences will probably be subjected to more local scrutiny than was previously the case.

Agenda inflation

Today, aid projects and programmes have to satisfy the critical demands not just of a much greater number but a much wider range of professionally involved constituencies. For this reason the chances of aid initiatives being deemed an unqualified success are even further reduced. Moreover, the development and aid agendas have both expanded and become less well focused. There is increasing talk of the need of a holistic approach. Our understanding of the kind of solutions oda can offer and of how aid can best be delivered are fluid; and the evidential basis for thinking aid will work is very incomplete. The frank admission that (OECD 1969: 121) 'we have only a vague idea of what we are doing' comes to mind. Around the time of the Brandt Commission's ruminations a DAC report remarked that the 'mutual benefit claims have been too sweeping, facile and indiscriminate, and in the process the thesis has been discredited in some policy quarters' (OECD 1979: 17). Aid's future usefulness will continue to be called into question if it is set goals that are so large and disparate as to be unfeasible, and capable of defying not simply oda but the best efforts of all interventionist devices available to the international community. Just such a criticism has been levelled at the World Bank, said to be a prime candidate for the 'Ministry of Everything Else' (see Mosley, Harrigan and Toye 1995: xxxv).

The post post-Cold War world has seen the rise of new disorders and new uncertainties, making the arguments for security more complex. By itself political stability is no absolute guarantee of security; and the meaning of security has succumbed to conceptual stretching. The idea that aid's purpose should be global system maintenance seems more appropriate now than ever before, even though it is not a new idea and it still lacks clear definition. The reasons are obvious: the growing permeability of national frontiers, heightened awareness of economic and environmental interdependence, and an enlargement of the basket of concerns that are now keenly thought to pose some sort of threat. To one degree or another all are said to be connected with poverty, directly or indirectly. The elevation of 'human security' as a primary object of aid can be seen in this light. And it is proposed that security and the quality of life everywhere would benefit from greater human security in the developing world (OECD 1995: 7 and 1996: 12). Put differently, there is an expansion of functions being wished upon aid. Additional expectations are being encouraged, if only as a strategy to defend oda's claim to resources. The ploy's merit is doubtful. For at a time when world oda is actually falling in real terms, the effect squeezes oda and it is role defined more narrowly in terms of poverty alleviation. In short, there is a scissors effect.

The recent profile of the UN can be seen against this background and the increasing number of people affected by disasters. Kent (1987: 9–11) noted an increase in the size and frequency of disasters even before the idea of complex emergencies became fashionable, with the incidence of conflict and state failure in the 1990s in such places as the Horn of Africa, Bosnia and Central Africa. UNICEF identified 40–50 countries suffering disasters, ten being complex emergencies, in 1993, and it claims around 90 per cent of all deaths in modern conflicts are civilian (including two million child casualties and another five million left disabled, in the last decade). War (mainly intra-state wars) occupied around 50 countries in the mid-1990s (Macrae, Zwi and Forsyth 1995: 670–1); and globally, around 300 million people are now reckoned to be suffering from the effects of disaster and war. The UN Security Council never vigorously addressed humanitarian issues during the Cold War (Minear and Weiss 1995: 5), but more lately has perforce increased the international community's endeavours in humanitarian assistance, and resorted to relatively unconventional delivery methods. On occasions military forces have become centrally involved; and humanitarian aid is being directed to achieve peacemaking as well as peacekeeping goals (Randel 1994: 332). The UN's commitment of personnel to peacekeeping operations rose from 10,000 in five operations in 1987 to more than 70,000 in eighteen operations in 1995. The annual cost increased twelvefold to $3.3 billion, out of total budgeted UN expenditures of $8.3 billion (excluding the specialised agencies).

Of the oda channelled through the UN, the proportion spent on emergencies has risen from 25 per cent to 45 per cent. Post-conflict peace building exercises such as the demobilisation of combatants are also being undertaken more frequently, a relatively successful example being the UN Observer Mission in El Salvador (1992–5). Increased commitments to peace enforcement might yet lie in store, if not for the UN then for other intergovernmental bodies with a regional role such as NATO and the Economic Community of West African States (whose military arm has sought to stabilise Liberia, for example). Some analysts urge caution, noting from the confusion surrounding the movements of Rwandan refugees in Eastern Zaire in November 1996 that military-backed intervention must be prefaced by good intelligence, clear objectives and a sound strategy for eventual withdrawal. They are alarmed by the possibility that the UN, a supposedly neutral force, might become associated with one side in a conflict. However, others are more interested in seeing the UN equipped to use force to 'neutralise whoever or whatever is threatening the security of people' (Mortimer 1995). A consequence would be to politicise further the humanitarian relief work both of UN agencies and NGOs working alongside. The UNHCR too is said to want an expanded mandate, to cope with refugee emergencies or large, sudden movements of desperate people in difficult conditions, which it says have been a hallmark of the 1990s (UNHCR 1993: 83). The talk is of a more proactive role that would combine relief work with human rights protection and poverty-focused development programmes – the essential ingredients of a sensible approach to disaster preparedness and preventive diplomacy, as well as peace building. Crisis prevention is assumed to be cheaper than cure. Emergency aid and distress relief including food aid and refugee expenditure more than trebled between 1988 and 1993, to reach around one tenth of oda. Strategies for peace through development are in competition for resource commitments with peace assistance, even for shares of oda, although UN peacekeeping operations do not themselves count as oda. This is at a time when new kinds of claim on aid are emerging and the total pot seems unlikely to grow.

Budgets under pressure

A combination of circumstances is placing aid funding under pressure. There is a concerted drive across OECD countries to reduce public sector deficits and public borrowing, formulated in response to an increasingly competitive international economic environment (Japan is an exception, where a renewal of economic growth has been brought about by expanding the fiscal deficit). This is good for world interest rates but bad for aid. In Europe an additional factor comprises attempts to meet Maastricht treaty criteria for participation in European monetary union, including lowering general government annual net borrowing to below 3 per cent of GDP. Also, attention has been distracted by reasons that are country specific, such as ructions in the party system and government in Italy, where aid has been tarnished by corruption scandals (the oda programme, which fell by over 45 per cent in real terms in 1995, has been said by the Foreign Minister to be in a state of semiparalysis). While in the past cross-national surveys have revealed a positive correlation between the political acceptability of aid spending and relatively generous social welfare programmes at home, now governments are looking to economise social spending as well as to reduce employers' non-wage employment costs, in many countries such as Germany, France, Sweden, Britain and the US (Norway is an exception). The projected increases in the cost of state pension arrangements are causing particular concern. The absence of a popular enthusiasm for retrenchment provides no defence of the budgets for development cooperation. If anything, their position becomes more exposed. However, although budgetary considerations have replaced balance of payments ones in government thinking towards aid restraint, oda cuts offer more a domestic political gesture than a substantial contribution to sound public finances. Indeed, the oda budgets' principal security lies in the smallness of their share of public expenditure. Nevertheless, the hope that oda might benefit from the 'peace dividend' delivered by the end of the Cold War is now known to have been misplaced, even though spending on military research and development has more than halved worldwide since 1987. Instead, aid's aura is now defensive, faced by what Ryrie (1995: 27) detects to be a mixture of indifference, cynicism and outright hostility in the Anglo-Saxon world – countries where 'aid fatigue is giving way to terminal sleeping sickness' (Watkins 1995b: 517). Even in Japan, where aid used to be called the sacred area in the government's budget, the 1990s have witnessed a marked increase of critical attention.

There is an old argument that donor commitments to aid would be more steadfast if based more exclusively on humanitarian and developmental grounds, geared to the needs of people who are poor or in distress. In reality, oda's standing has been weakened by doubts about its developmental effectiveness and by an accumulation of evidence in the field that excess assistance can be as harmful as insufficient practical help. Over time the theories purporting to explain weak development have moved from accounts whose prescriptions call for what only donors can provide (more and improved concessionary transfers) to steps developing countries must take for themselves, in particular compliance with the recommendations that donors dispense. Where there was once a presumption that a failure to secure good results meant more aid should be provided, now that inference is less easy to draw, and it is being drawn less often and on a more discriminating basis. Thus the DAC Development Ministers and Heads of Aid Agencies in their May 1996 deliberations on future strategy for development cooperation emphasised outcomes rather than volume of inputs. Poor countries where oda's developmental results remain unimpressive, and who have low political or commercial salience to donors, could find themselves disadvantaged. Advances in information technology and international media make it more difficult for their governments to conceal emergencies like impending famine, as well as speed the worldwide transmission of good (and bad) stories about initiatives in aid and development. On the one hand, failure by the international community to intervene becomes more difficult to justify – no longer is ignorance a valid excuse. On the other hand, bad publicity of the sort that was attracted by the dismal train of events inside Somalia, Bosnia and Rwanda highlights shortcomings in the steps taken by the international community, the UN included. Where there is manifest failure of political resolve or sheer incompetence, there is a risk of public disaffection even from humanitarian relief (which is usually no more than a second best solution, anyway). Hence the argument that a greater Northern commitment to cultivating a sympathetic, well-informed awareness of the international, among domestic publics, is more pressing than ever before; for there is little doubt the canvass of global integration will tighten, probably irreversibly, in the years ahead.

What leadership?

Leadership and coordination are not synonymous. But they do bear a family likeness, and poor coordination is often attributable to an absence of leadership. Coordination can mean a variety of things, ranging from consultation and the pooling of information to centralised control. Deficient coordination among donors and aid agencies and between donors and recipients is a perennial and vexed issue. Ross (1990: 332) concluded it had persisted for so long that 'we might be tempted to throw up our hands'; Cassen *et al.* (1994: 242) reserve some of their harshest words for aid coordination 'where it finds donors and recipients sadly wanting, though making belated efforts to improve'. Donors dislike the kind of coordination that significantly reduces the freedom to pursue their own policies and objectives in their own way. Recipients understandably feel threatened by what might look like donors ganging up. Even in regard to international relief operations, there seems to be no obvious maestro suitable for all seasons (Minear and Weiss 1995: 203). Among NGOs too competition for turf and high profile activities are remarked upon. A homogenised approach is not appropriate to all kinds of aid anyway. For example, democracy assistance should be provided in a manner that advertises the virtues of pluralism.

Nevertheless, cooperation if not coordination has increased, partly because of pressure on resources. Moreover, the DAC has steadily accumulated a large body of evidence about what does not work well for development. It produces guidelines and monitors members' performance in increasing detail, and has begun to publish the results of peer group evaluations. Teamworking and the sharing of experience among donors are said to be more prevalent. The World Bank too has acquired some of the characteristics of principal actor. The rise of policy dialogue and conditional programme lending in the 1980s accentuated this development and its significance, which has been further extended in the 1990s with the Bank's willingness to communicate political memoranda from donors to recipients.

The progress notwithstanding, donor coordination remains 'ineffectual in many cases' (Hewitt and Killick 1996: 155). The Bank's appetite for the mantle of supreme coordinator has always been in doubt, despite its leading role in economic policy analysis. Important donors like Japan, Norway and the EU have not mimicked the Bank's approach in the past, and other donors too have not conformed fully (Hewitt and Killick 1996: 148–9). The Bank probably lacks the administrative resources; and it cannot supply *political* leadership. If there are to be guidelines about where the responsibilities for leading and enforcing collaboration lie, then they must come from the major governments, principally the industrial powers (Nelson and Eglinton 1993: 96). In any case, the emergence of regional banks like the EBRD and the quadrupling of private international capital flows to the developing world since 1990 have eroded the Bank's position somewhat. Now, IDA annual net disbursements of around $5 billion are dwarfed by the total flow of financial resources to all developing countries, although they remain important to the beneficiaries, especially countries beyond the positive effects of globalisation. With aid coordination, as with other aid ideals, the goalposts seem intangible and are liable to move. According to some analysts, the idea of better coordination between donors misconstrues the problem anyway, and nothing short of substantive programme partnership with aid recipients will do.

Generally speaking, the changes identified so far in this conclusion have not been part of some grand design, let alone the product of Southern pressure and bargaining power. What is more, some things have not changed very much.

Continuities

Like the international economy and global politics, the world of aid too is in transition, although to what, we cannot know. But many of the threads present in the past still linger on. They have an air of timelessness. Not all of them hang well together. For example, alongside the numerous allegations against aid agencies of bureaucratic inertia and unnecessary procedural delay, there is a frequent repetition of the misplaced emphasis on moving the money (and hence the temptation to favour those countries and channels that demonstrate results). This might seem surprising in the present financial climate. But there can be a connection as Parfitt (1996: 58) shows in his interpretation of the EU's late conversion to SALs as a ruse to defend aid budgets, by improving the notoriously slow rate of disbursement. Hook (1995: 22) maintains that the existence of tensions between the national interests of donors and the collective standards of a desirable oda 'regime' has been, and remains, one of the defining features of aid. The aid literature discloses other continuities, like the susceptibility to swings of fashion and a proneness to failures of institutional memory, even among NGOs. Of course, there have also always been disagreements among commentators, and variations in national performance. Thus, Lady Chalker identifies the aid monitoring and feedback from the field as being primarily responsible for the improvements in British aid over the last 20 years (author's interview, 10 June 1996).

Power, or persuasion?

Power has to be exercised from time to time if that eminence of abilities which defines power is to be demonstrated and preserved. The question which asks, 'Why have it if you don't use it?' is complemented by the maxim, 'Use it or lose it'. Occasional displays of domination become a functional requirement of dominance. Aid is and always has been a power resource. The application of aid conditionality can be valued as an exercise in power for its own sake, as well as a means to achieve other objectives. However, the political relationship of aid has never been straightforward and unidirectional. Dominant socio-economic strata and their political representatives on the recipient side have long since learned to select the concessions to donors that will make least compromise of their own original aims and interests. Principal among these are the retention of their own power and privileges. For example, measures of economic liberalisation have been embraced where judged important to that purpose and, even, turned to advantage, as in Latin America. In contrast, from West Africa to East Asia the implementation of open, transparent government and the institutionalisation of genuinely free and fair political competition face stronger resistance. Moreover, although some recipients have seen their bargaining power weaken and can no longer work both sides of the street – socialist East as well as capitalist West – others continue to exploit divisions among donors. Thus Gibbon (1993: 36) believed it would not be entirely cynical to argue that the World Bank's influence over other donors 'has increased in proportion to the increasingly comprehensive demonstration of the hollowness of the influence of donors generally over recipients'. Kenya is illustrative. For many years now President Moi has been able to play what opposition politician Kenneth Matiba (*Financial Times*, 25 July 1995) calls a 'cat and mouse game with aid donors', helped as much as hindered by the proliferation of competing demands figuring on the donors' agendas. Kenya illustrates the aid stop-go cycle, of steps forward, steps backwards in economic and political reform, which is the most that conditionality has seemed able to achieve.

So, we continue to be reminded that there are limits to aid power, just as there are limits to oda's potential as a force for development. Democratic political philosophy maintains that in the long run, persuasion could be the most efficacious form of power. The same has been said many times specifically in relation to development cooperation. Persuasion means reasoned argument. Agreement based on shared understandings and commonly held belief is a proper object of persuasion. As an approach by donors, this is not the same as seeking compliance. Furthermore, it should not be confused with what Douglas Hurd has called in respect of politically conditioned aid, 'helpful pressure'. Neither is it identical with the idea of exchange that is contained in most bargaining relationships. For optimal effect, aid should not be presented as the carrot, as a bribe, an inducement or reward offered in return for accepting the donors' advice. Indeed, there is a step even beyond the hollow notions of persuasion that are a euphemism for one-way transfers of know-how (the role model of donors as consultants who always know best). The further step is to engage in joint efforts to identify problems and to respect one another's contributions to mutually agreed solutions. This involves a recognition that in principle both sides can learn.

The proferred relationship of dialogue is not simply proactive or react-ive, but interactive; it is not reducible to donor pressure or donor purchase of the final outcome. But why has it come to be offered as one of the main conclusions to be drawn from the history of aid and conditionality? Answer: because it offers the most promising basis for achieving local ownership of policies, programmes and projects that are appropriate and will work. The need for ownership – itself now considered one of the principal lessons of the last decade or so of aid practice – means local acceptance of respons-ibility for ensuring implementation takes place, an acceptance of stakehold-ing in sustainability. Indeed, the very idea of partnership between donors and recipients is said to mean both sides caring fully about the results of development cooperation, working together to effect positive and durable outcomes (author's interview with Lady Chalker, 10 June 1996). A practical illustration comes from health care policy in India, where local medical purists who had been dedicated to a high cost, high technology provision of service came round to a more socio-economic approach that favours rurally focused preventative medicine. Lipton and Toye (1990: 71–2) say this was a result of 'mutual learning and exchange of knowledge, not arm twisting', in the dialogue with donors. The merit of this kind of collabora-tion is not a new discovery. The moral has been there all along. But only now is it being argued as if it were a new conventional wisdom. In the past, humanitarian aid no less than development assistance has been widely faulted for failing to respect the point (see for instance Harrell-Bond 1986; de Waal 1989). The point still seems a long way from being enshrined through-out customary practice, even though 'capacity development' (autochthonous) now substitutes for 'capacity building' (from outside) in up-to-the-minute jargon about the objects of aid. A need to continually relearn old lessons and to apply them for real seems to be one of the most prominent and enduring features of aid. Perhaps there have been too many lessons, some of them contradictory and bound to confuse. Hence mistakes are repeated.

However, there is no escaping a familiar dilemma concerning the way aid or its potential availability structures perceptions and situations. Finan-cial help can easily become identified by aid seekers as the principal benefit to be secured from engaging in dialogue with donors. This has been shown in the case of SALs/SAPs (Gordon 1992: 40). The aim of dialogue, under-stood to mean persuasion by donors, is frustrated in this case. Perhaps dialogue should be divorced from the prospect of aid, and *ipso facto* from the possibility of aid sanctions – especially if Knorr (1973: 170) was correct in saying recipients may still feel aid is coercive even when there are no obvi-ous strings attached, and when donors neither intend to coerce nor realise they are producing that effect. Goran Ohlin's observation (cited in Hewitt 1994: 70) that the 'logic of foreign assistance is fundamentally incompatible with the logic of self-determination' echoes that view. But there is a dilemma here, for without the prospect of assistance, the chances of there being dialogue are much less promising. 'No aid, no dialogue' could be an over-statement, but aid does buy for donors the chance of a hearing, though not a guaranteed outcome. Furthermore, some poor countries do need external assistance first, if they are to acquire the analytical, professional and tech-nical skills to engage in dialogue on anything approaching more or less equal terms, and if they are to engage in designing programmes of action and put them into practice, acquiring 'ownership' in the process. Other requisites could include a stable infrastructure of political parties, civic asso-ciations, and community organisations without whom society as a whole cannot fully participate in the process, and all of which *might* benefit from international encouragement and applications of material support.

In any case, there are circumstances where aid's purpose must be to alter the structure of incentives facing the domestic forces who are ranged against desirable change. That includes the decision makers and politic-ally influential groups whose attachment to particular interests impedes action for society's wider good, or who cannot be expected to prioritise the greater global well-being (as in environmentally beneficial but econom-ically costly initiatives). Here, dialogue alone would not be enough. Equally, an unadorned transfer of resources is not sufficient to satisfy donors' most legitimate requirements such as financial accountability, let alone advance all their enduring commercial, political, security and other self-regarding aims. Therefore, although we will hear much more about the merits of persuasion and recipient ownership of aid solutions, the interface between aid recipients and even selfless donors will continue to be coloured by influ-ence, pressure and asymmetrical power. Aid conditionality may be coun-terintuitive to true partnership, but we do not predict that conditionalities or conditions will soon be a thing of the past. True reciprocity will remain a chimera. Aid recipients cannot require that the strictures spelled out in aid's conditionalities should be faithfully observed in the donors' internal affairs.

Does aid have a future?

And lest we forget, one more thing that has not drastically altered is the existence of mass poverty in a world of growing affluence. The proportion of people living in poverty has barely decreased – 29.4 per cent lived on under $1 a day in 1993, compared with 30.1 per cent in 1987 (World Bank figures). Nearly 90 countries are now worse off than they were ten years ago, according to the UNDP's human development index. Third World poverty is more intensively studied and almost certainly better understood now than before. However, the processes of aid policy-making and imple-mentation have not obviously become *very* much more participatory for poor people, notwithstanding NGO aspirations and the growing interest shown by some official agencies.

Of course, participation is a hurrah word and protean of meaning. It has been called a human right, even a basic need. Many aid analysts and development practitioners argue that a lack of participation by the poor in problem analysis, planning and executing aid initiatives reduces their likely effectiveness. This has been said both of official and non-governmental levels. To illustrate there is the message Chambers (1979: 3) has repeated many times, for outside experts to 'step down off their pedestals, seek out the poorer people, and sit down, listen and learn'. Hence, appropriate attitudes are as crucial on the aid-providing side as anywhere else. However, there is also much agreement that it is very difficult to bring about the effective participation of the very poor in particular, and 'the skills needed for encouraging participatory processes may be quite different from those of articulate doers and achievers' (OECD 1991: 57). It all takes time. And in doing development, the quick fix that provides a permanent solution tends to be rare; more usually, it proves to be shortlived. That too is a lesson we have to keep relearning, even though it sits uneasily with rapid appraisal techniques and the demand for visible early results, which are characteristic of the present age.

We can safely assume the poor, even the destitute, will still be with us for some time to come. Yet, tackling poverty appears to be what most of aid's supporters among the general public believe is its principal justification. And as 'expressed in the rhetoric, poverty alleviation has always been the most prominent single objective set for aid by most if not all donors' (Stokke 1996: 86). In the past, world aid distribution has stubbornly refused to give overall priority to the poorest countries. Present indications would suggest that poverty is moving up some aid agencies' practical agenda – although how far aid can help is contentious: the evidence that social conditionality can be effective is scant, and as yet a full-blown third-generation aid conditionality is difficult to discern. Nevertheless, it is simply too early to conclude that aid has gone from 'big business' (Mosley 1987: 3) to 'sunset industry' (Hawkins 1996). Foreign aid has sported many faces and undergone considerable changes over the last half century, but the smart money must presume that it will survive in some form well into the next.

References

Aaronson, M. (1995) Our independence is very important to us, *The Courier, Africa–Caribbean–Pacific–European Union*, 152: 2–5.

Adamson, P. (1975) Weakest in the water, *New Internationalist*, 29: 11–12.

Aiken, W. (1977) The right to be saved from starvation, in W. Aiken and H. La Follette (eds) *World Hunger and Moral Obligation*, Englewood Cliffs, NJ, Prentice-Hall.

Ake, C. (1995) A view from Africa, in H. Holm and G. Sørensen (eds) *Whose World Order?* Boulder, CO and Oxford, Westview.

Allen, R. (1986) Bob's not your uncle, *Capital and Class*, 30(Winter): 31–7.

Allison, G. and Blackwill, R. (1991) America's stake in the Soviet future, *Foreign Affairs*, 70(3): 77–97.

Ampiah, K. (1996) Japanese aid to Tanzania: a study of the political marketing of Japan in Africa, *African Affairs*, 95(378): 107–24.

Angelopoulos, A. and Fagen, M. (1994) *The Third World and the Rich Countries: Proposals to Combat the Global Economic Crisis*, Lanham, MD, University Press of America.

Arase, D. (1993) Japan's policy toward democracy and human rights, *Asian Survey*, 33(10): 935–52.

Arefieva, E. and Bragina, E. (1991) Changing approaches to development strategy and development assistance (USSR), in R. Feinberg and R. Avakov (eds) *US and Soviet Aid to Developing Countries: from Confrontation to Cooperation?* New Brunswick, NJ, Transaction Publishers.

Ayoob, M. (1995) The new–old disorder in the Third World, *Global Governance*, 1(1): 59–77.

Baldwin, D. (1985) *Economic Statecraft*, Princeton, NJ, Princeton University Press.

Ball, N. (1988) *Security and Economy in the Third World*, London, Adamantine Press.

Ball, N. (1992) Pressing for peace: can aid induce reform? Washington, DC, Overseas Development Council, Policy Essay no. 6.

Bandow, D. (1992) Economic and military aid, in P. Schraeder (ed.) *Intervention into the 1990s: US Foreign Policy in the Third World*, Boulder, CO and London, Lynne Rienner.

Barnett, M. (1995) The new United Nations politics of peace: from juridical sovereignty to empirical sovereignty, *Global Governance*, 1(1): 79–97.

Barratt Brown, M. (1995) *Africa's Choices: After Thirty Years of the World Bank*, London, Penguin.

Barry, B. (1973) *The Liberal Theory of Justice*, Oxford, Clarendon Press.

Bartsch, J. (1988) New trends in Soviet aid, *OECD Observer*, 151: 11–12.

Bauer, P. and Ward, B. (1996) Two views on aid to developing countries, Institute of Economic Affairs, London, Occasional Paper 9.

Baylies, C. (1995) 'Political conditionality' and democratisation, *Review of African Political Economy*, 22(65): 321–37.

Bentham, J. [1789] (1948) *An Introduction to the Principles of Morals and Legislation*, W. Harrison (ed.), Oxford, Basil Blackwell.

Berg, E. (1991) Recent trends and issues in development strategies and development assistance (US), in R. Feinberg and R. Avakov (eds) *US and Soviet Aid to Developing Countries: from Confrontation to Cooperation?* New Brunswick, NJ, Transaction Publishers.

Berg, E. (1993) *Rethinking Technical Cooperation*, New York, United Nations Development Programme: Regional Bureau for Africa.

Blasier, C. (1979) COMECON in Cuban development, in C. Blasier and C. Mesa-Lago (eds) *Cuba in the World*, Pittsburg, University of Pittsburgh Press.

Blasier, C. and Mesa-Lago, C. (eds) (1979) *Cuba in the World*, Pittsburgh, University of Pittsburgh Press.

Bobiash, D. (1992) *South-South Aid*, Basingstoke, Macmillan.

Boone, P. (1994) The impact of foreign aid on savings and growth, Centre for Economic Performance, LSE, University of London, working paper no. 1265.

Bose, A. and Burnell, P. (eds) (1991) *Britain's Overseas Aid since 1979*, Manchester, Manchester University Press.

Boutros-Ghali, B. (1995) Democracy: a newly recognized imperative, *Global Governance*, 1(1): 3–11.

Box, L. (1994) Crisis management in Dutch international development, in A. Hewitt (ed.) *Crisis or Transition in Foreign Aid*, London, Overseas Development Institute.

Brautigam, D. (1994) Foreign assistance and the export of ideas: China's development aid in The Gambia and Sierra Leone, *Journal of Commonwealth and Comparative Politics*, 32(3): 324–48.

Brzezinski, Z. (1994) The premature partnership, *Foreign Affairs*, 73(2): 67–82.

Burnell, P. (1991a) Introduction to Britain's overseas aid: between idealism and self-interest, in A. Bose and P. Burnell (eds) *Britain's Overseas Aid Since 1979*, Manchester, Manchester University Press.

Burnell, P. (1991b) *Charity, Politics and the Third World*, Hemel Hempstead, Harvester Wheatsheaf.

Burnell, P. (1991c) Aid fatigue: concept and methodology, Department of Politics and International Studies, University of Warwick, Working Paper no. 51.

Burnell, P. (1992) Charity law and pressure politics in Britain: after the Oxfam inquiry, *Voluntas, International Journal of Voluntary and Non-Profit Organisations*, 3(3): 311–34.

Burnell, P. (1994) Good government and democratization: a sideways look at aid and conditionality, *Democratization*, 1(3): 485–503.

Burns, W. (1985) *Economic Aid and American Policy Toward Egypt 1955–1981*, Albany, NY, State University of New York Press.

Byrd, P. (1991) Foreign policy and overseas aid, in A. Bose and P. Burnell (eds) *Britain's Overseas Aid Since 1979*, Manchester, Manchester University Press.

Carlsson, J., Kohlin, G. and Ekbom, A. (1994) *The Political Economy of Evaluation: International Aid Agencies and the Effectiveness of Aid*, Basingstoke, Macmillan and New York, St Martin's Press.

Carothers, T. (1995) Recent US experience with democracy promotion, *IDS Bulletin*, 26(2): 62–9.

Carothers, T. (1996) *Assessing Democracy Assistance: the Case of Romania*, Washington, DC, Carnegie Endowment for International Peace.

Carpenter, T. (1991) The new world disorder, *Foreign Policy*, 84: 24–39.

Cassen, R. (1991) Afterword, in A. Bose and P. Burnell (eds) *Britain's Overseas Aid Since 1979*, Manchester, Manchester University Press.

Cassen, R. and associates (1994) *Does Aid Work?*, 2nd edn., Oxford, Clarendon Press.

Cernea, M. (1988) Nongovernmental organisations and local development, Washington DC, World Bank Discussion Paper no. 40.

Chalker, L. (1990) Britain's role in multilateral agencies, *Development Policy Review*, 8(4): 355–64.

Chambers, R. (1979) Editorial, *IDS Bulletin*, 10(1): 1–3.

Chambers, R. (1983) *Rural Development: Putting the Last First*, London, Longman.

Chambers, R. (1988) Sustainable rural livelihoods: a key strategy for people, environment and development, in C. Conroy and M. Litvinoff (eds) *The Greening of Aid*, London, Earthscan.

Chenery, H. and Strout, A. (1966) Foreign assistance and economic development, *American Economic Review*, 56(4): 679–733.

Clark, J. (1991) *Democratizing Development: the Role of Voluntary Organisations*, London, Earthscan.

Clark, J. (1992) Policy influence, lobbying and advocacy, in M. Edwards and D. Hume (eds) *Making a Difference: NGOs and Development in a Changing World*, London, Earthscan.

Collier, P. (1991) Africa's external economic relations: 1960–90, *African Affairs*, 90(359): 339–56.

Commission on Global Governance (1995) *Our Global Neighbourhood*, Oxford, Oxford University Press.

Commission on International Development (1969) (Pearson Commission) *Partners in Development*, New York, Praeger Publisher.

Conroy, C. and Litvinoff, M. (eds) (1988) *The Greening of Aid*, London, Earthscan.

Conteh-Morgan, E. (1990) *American Foreign Aid and Global Power Projection*, Aldershot, Dartmouth.

Cooper, R. (1979) Developed country reactions to calls for a New International Economic Order, in A. Hirschman (ed.) *Toward a New Strategy for Development*, New York, Pergamon Press.

Crawford, G. (1997) Foreign aid and political conditionality: issues of effectiveness and consistency, *Democratization*, 4(3) (forthcoming).

Dannehl, C. (1995) *Politics, Trade and Development: Soviet Economic Aid to the Non-communist Third World, 1955–89*, Aldershot, Dartmouth.

del Rosso Jnr., S. (1995) The insecure state: reflections on 'the state' and 'security' in a changing world, *Daedalus*, 124(2): 175–207.

de Waal, A. (1989) *Famine That Kills*, Oxford, Clarendon Press.

Diamond, L. (1992) Promoting democracy, *Foreign Policy*, 87: 25–46.

Domínguez, J. (1978) *Cuba: Order and Revolution*, Cambridge, MA, Harvard University Press.

Domínguez, J. (1984) Limitations and consequences of Cuban military policies in Africa, in I. Horowitz (ed.) *Cuban Communism*, 5th edn., New Brunswick, NJ and London, Transaction Books.

Eberstadt, N. (1991) Population change and national security, *Foreign Affairs*, 70(3): 115–31.

Eckstein, S. (1994) *Back from the Future*, Princeton, NJ, University of Princeton Press.

Edwards, M. (1994) International non-governmental organizations, 'good government' and the 'new policy agenda': lessons of experience at the programme level, *Democratization*, 1(3): 504–15.

Edwards, M. and Hulme, D. (eds) (1995) *NGO Performance and Accountability: Beyond the Magic Bullet*, London, Earthscan.

Edwards, M. and Hulme, D. (1996) Too close for comfort? The impact of official aid on non-governmental organisations, *World Development*, 24(6): 961–73.

Eldridge, P. (1969) *The Politics of Foreign Aid in India*, London, Weidenfeld and Nicolson.

Elliott, C. (1987) Some aspects of relations between the North and the South in the NGO sector, *World Development*, 15(Supplementary Issue): 57–68.

Falk, R. (1995) *On Humane Governance*, Oxford, Polity Press.

Fitch, J. (1979) The political impact of US military aid to Latin America, *Armed Forces and Society*, 5(3): 360–85.

Foreign Affairs Committee (House of Commons) (1994) *Monitoring of the European Community Aid Programme*, HC 111, London, HMSO.

Fowler, A. (1992) Distant obligations: speculations on NGO funding and the global market, *Review of African Political Economy*, 9(55): 9–29.

Franck, M. (1992) The emerging right to democratic governance, *American Journal of International Law*, 86(1): 46–91.

Geldenhuys, D. (1990) *Isolated States: a Comparative Analysis*, Cambridge, Cambridge University Press.

Gibbon, P. (1992) Structural adjustment and pressures towards multipartyism in sub-Saharan Africa, in P. Gibbon, Y. Bangwa and A. Ofstad (eds) *Authoritarianism, Democracy and Adjustment*, Uppsala, Scandinavian Institute of African Studies.

Gibbon, P. (1993) The World Bank and the new politics of aid, *European Journal of Development Research*, 5(3): 35–61.

Gills, B., Rocamera, J. and Wilson, R. (1993) *Low Intensity Democracy: Political Power in the New World Order*, London and Boulder, Pluto Press.

Gilpin, R. (1987) *The Political Economy of International Relations*, Princeton, Princeton University Press.

Goldgeier, J. and McFaul, M. (1992) A tale of two worlds: core and periphery in the post-cold war era, *International Organisation*, 46(2): 467–91.

Gonzalez, H. (1984) Bloc voting at the United Nations or US foreign aid?, *Inter-American Economic Affairs*, 38(1): 78–84.

Gordenker, L. and Weiss, T. (1995) Pluralising global governance: analytical approaches and dimensions, *Third World Quarterly*, 16(3): 357–88.

Gordon, D. (1992) Conditionality in policy-based lending in Africa: USAID experience, in P. Mosley (ed.) *Development Finance and Policy Reform: Essays in the Theory and Practice of Conditionality in Less Developed Countries*, Basingstoke, Macmillan.

Goutier, H. (1996) Relief and expectancy, *The Courier, Africa–Caribbean–Pacific–European Union*, 155: 3–7.

Greenwood, C. (1993) Is there a right of humanitarian intervention?, *World Today*, 49(2): 34–40.

Griffin, K. (1986) Doubts about aid, *IDS Bulletin*, 17(2): 36–45.

Griffin, K. (1991) Foreign aid after the cold war, *Development and Change*, 22(4): 645–85.

Griffiths, M., Levine, I. and Weller, M. (1995) Sovereignty and suffering, in J. Harriss (ed.) *The Politics of Humanitarian Intervention*, London and New York, Pinter.

Grilli, E. (1993) *The European Community and the Developing Countries*, Cambridge, Cambridge University Press.

Haggard, S. and Kaufman, R. (1989) Economic adjustment in new democracies, in J. Nelson and contributors *Fragile Coalitions: the Politics of Economic Adjustment*, Washington, DC, Overseas Development Council.

Haggard, S. and Webb, S. (1993) What do we know about the political economy of economic policy reform?, *World Bank Research Observer*, 8(2): 143–68.

Haggard, S., Lafay, J. and Morrisson, C. (1995) *The Political Feasibility of Adjustment*, Paris, Organisation for Economic Cooperation and Development.

Hancock, G. (1989) *Lords of Poverty*, Basingstoke, Macmillan.

Hardin, B. (1992) *Africa–Dispatches from a Fragile Continent*, London, Fontana.

Hardin, G. (1977) Lifeboat ethics: the case against helping the poor, in W. Aiken and H. La Follette (eds) *World Hunger and Moral Obligation*, Englewood Cliffs, NJ, Prentice-Hall.

Harrell-Bond, B. (1986) *Imposing Aid: Emergency Assistance to Refugees*, Oxford, Oxford University Press.

Hart, J. (1973) *Aid and Liberation: a Socialist Study of Aid Policies*, London, Victor Gollancz.

Hashemi, S. (1995) NGO accountability in Bangladesh: issues of legitimacy and accountability, in M. Edwards and D. Hulme (eds) *Non-Governmental Organisations – Performance and Accountability: Beyond the Magic Bullet*, London, Earthscan.

Hawkins, T. (1996) Crisis worsens, *Financial Times*, 20 May.

Hayter, T. (1985) Aid: the West's false hand out, *New Socialist*, 24: 7–11.

Hayter, T. (1989) *Exploited Earth: Britain's Aid and the Environment*, London, Earthscan.

Healey, J. and Coverdale, A. (1981) Foreign policy and British bilateral aid: comment on McKinlay and Little, *British Journal of Political Science*, 11(1): 123–7.

Healey, J. and Robinson, M. (1992) *Democracy, Governance and Economic Policy: Sub-Saharan Africa in Comparative Perspective*, London, Overseas Development Institute.

Hewitt, A. (1991) 1992 and its effects on European aid, in M. Malek (ed.) *Contemporary Issues in Development Aid*, Aldershot, Avebury.

Hewitt, A. (1993) ACP and the developing world, in J. Lodge (ed.) *The European Community and the Challenge of the Future*, 2nd edn., London, Pinter.

Hewitt, A. (ed.) (1994) *Crisis or Transition in Foreign Aid*, London, Overseas Development Institute.

Hewitt, A. and Killick, T. (1996) Bilateral aid conditionality and policy leverage, in O. Stokke (ed.) *Foreign Aid Towards the Year 2000: Experiences and Challenges*, London, Frank Cass.

Hirschmann, D. (1995) Democracy, gender and US foreign assistance: guidelines and lessons, *World Development*, 23(8): 1291–302.

Hoben, A. (1989) USAID: organizational and institutional issues and effectiveness, in R. Berg and D. Gordon (eds) *Cooperation for International Development: the US and the Third World in the 1990s*, Boulder, CO and London, Lynne Rienner.

Holm, H. and Sørensen, G. (eds) (1995) *Whose World Order?* Boulder, CO and Oxford, Westview.

Hook, S. (1995) *National Interest and Foreign Aid*, Boulder, CO and London, Lynne Rienner.

Howell, J. (1994) The end of an era: the rise and fall of GDR aid, *Journal of Modern African Studies*, 32(2): 305–28.

Hulme, D. and Edwards, M. (1997) *NGOs, States and Donors*, Basingstoke, Macmillan.

Hunter, S. (1984) *OPEC and the Third World: the Politics of Aid*, London, Croom Helm.

Huntington, S. (1970–1) Foreign aid for what and for whom, *Foreign Policy*, 1: 161–89.

Huntington, S. (1993) The clash of civilisations, *Foreign Affairs*, 72(3): 22–49.

Hurd, D. (1991) Evidence presented to Foreign Affairs Committee, *UK Policy towards Southern Africa and the Other States in the Region*, HC 53–II, London, HMSO.

Hyde-Price, A. (1994) Democratization in Eastern Europe: the external dimension, in G. Pridham and T. Vanhanen (eds) *Democratization in Eastern Europe*, London and New York, Routledge.

IDS Bulletin (1993) Good government?, 21(1).

IDS Bulletin (1995) Towards democratic governance, 26(2).

Independent Commission on International Development Issues (1980) (Brandt Commission) *North–South: a Programme for Survival*, London, Pan.

Independent Commission on Population and Quality of Life (1996) *Caring for the Future: Briefing Summary*, Oxford, Oxford University Press.

Independent Group on British Aid (1989) *Real Aid: What Europe Can Do*, London, IGBA.

International Freedom Foundation (UK) (1990) *Freedom Bulletin*, 16.

Jackson, R. (1990) *Quasi-states: Sovereignty, International Relations and the Third World*, Cambridge, Cambridge University Press.

Jepma, C. (1996) The case for aid untying in OECD countries, in O. Stokke (ed.) *Foreign Aid Towards the Year 2000: Experiences and Challenges*, London, Frank Cass.

Johnson, H. (1970) *The 'Crisis' of Aid and the Pearson Report*, Edinburgh, Edinburgh University Press.

Judd, F. (1991) 'From charity to justice', public lecture at University of Warwick, 15 October 1991.

Kahler, M. (1989) International financial institutions and the politics of adjustment, in J. Nelson and contributors *Fragile Coalitions: the Politics of Economic Adjustment*, Washington, DC, Overseas Development Council.

Kegley, C. and Hook, S. (1991) US foreign aid and UN voting: did Reagan's linkage strategy buy deference or defiance?, *International Studies Quarterly*, 35(3): 295–312.

Kent, R. (1987) *Anatomy of Disaster Relief*, London, Frances Pinter.

Killick, T. (1984) *The Quest for Economic Stabilisation: the IMF and the Third World*, London, Heinemann.

Kinoshita, T. (1993) The end of the Cold War and Japan's financial contribution to international development, in S. Murshed and K. Raffer (eds) *Trade, Transfers and Development*, Aldershot, Edward Elgar.

Knorr, K. (1973) *Power and Wealth*, London, Macmillan.

Koppel, B. and Orr, R. (eds) (1992) *Japanese Foreign Aid: Power and Policy in a New Era*, Boulder, CO, Westview Press.

Korten, D. (1990) *Getting to the 21st Century: Voluntary Action and the Global Agenda*, West Harford, CT, Kumarian Press.

Kosyrev, A. (1992) Russia: a chance for survival, *Foreign Affairs*, 71(2): 1–16.

Kpundeh, S. (1992) *Democratization in Africa: African Views, African Voices*, Washington, DC, National Academy Press.

Krasner, S. (1985) *Structural Conflict: the Third World against Global Liberalism*, Berkeley, CA, University of California Press.

Krueger, A., Michalopoulos, C. and Ruttan, V. with Jay, C. (1989) *Aid and Development*, Baltimore and London, Johns Hopkins University Press.

Landell-Mills, P. and Serageldin, I. (1991) Governance and the development process, *Finance and Development*, 28(3): 14–17.

Lavigne, M. (1995) *The Economics of Transition*, Basingstoke, Macmillan.

Lebovic, J. (1988) National interests and US foreign aid: the Carter and Reagan years, *Journal of Peace Research*, 25(2): 115–36.

Leftwich, A. (1994) Governance, the state and the politics of development, *Development and Change*, 25(2): 363–86.

Legum, C. (ed.) (1970) *The First UN Development Decade and its Lessons for the 1970s*, New York and London, Praeger.

Lele, U. and Jain, R. (1992) Aid to African agriculture: lessons from two decades of donors' experience, in U. Lele (ed.) *Aid to African Agriculture*, Baltimore and London, Johns Hopkins University Press.

Lele, U. and Nabi, I. (eds) (1991) *Transitions in Development: the Role of Aid and Commercial Flows*, San Francisco, CA, ICS Press.

Le Prestre, P. (1989) *The World Bank and the Environmental Challenge*, London, Susquehanna University Press.

Lessnoff, M. (1986) *Social Contract*, Basingstoke, Macmillan.

Lindberg, M. and Devarajan, S. (1993) Prescribing strong medicine: revisiting myths about structural adjustment, democracy and economic performance in developing countries, *Comparative Politics*, 25(2): 169–82.

Lindblom, C. (1977) *Politics and Markets*, New York, Basic Books.

Linden, E. (1976) *The Alms Race: the Impact of American Voluntary Aid Abroad*, New York, Random House.

Lipset, S. (1959) Some social requisites of democracy: economic development and political legitimacy, *American Political Science Review*, 53(1): 69–105.

Lipton, M. (1986) Introduction: aid effectiveness, prisoners' dilemmas, country allocations, *IDS Bulletin*, 17(2): 1–6.

Lipton, M. (1991) The state–market dilemma, civil society and structural adjustment, *Round Table*, 317: 21–31.

Lipton, M. and Toye, J. (1990) *Does Aid Work in India?* London, Routledge.

Lissner, J. (1976) *The Politics of Altruism*, Geneva, Lutheran World Federation.

Lister, M. (1988) *The European Community and the Developing World*, Aldershot, Avebury.

Lumsdaine, D. (1993) *Moral Vision in International Politics: the Foreign Aid Regime, 1949–1989*, Princeton, NJ, Princeton University Press.

McKinlay, R. and Little, R. (1977) A foreign policy model of US bilateral aid allocation, *World Politics*, 30(1): 58–86.

McKinlay, R. and Little, R. (1978) A foreign policy model of the distribution of British bilateral aid 1960–70, *British Journal of Political Science*, 8(3): 313–32.

McKinlay, R. and Little, R. (1979) The US aid relationship, *Political Studies*, 27(2): 236–50.

Macrae, J., Zwi, A. and Forsyth, V. (1995) Aid policy in transition: a preliminary analysis of 'post'-conflict rehabilitation of the health sector, *Journal of International Development*, 7(4): 669–84.

Malek, M. (ed.) (1991) *Contemporary Issues in Development Aid*, Aldershot, Avebury.

Marcussen, H. (1996) Comparative advantages of NGOs: myths and realities, in O. Stokke (ed.) *Foreign Aid Towards the Year 2000: Experiences and Challenges*, London, Frank Cass.

Matear, A. (1996) *Desde la protesta a la propuesta*: gender politics in transition in Chile, *Democratization*, 3(3): 246–63.

May, R., Schumacher, D. and Malek, M. (1989) *Overseas Aid: the Impact on Britain and Germany*, Hemel Hempstead, Harvester Wheatsheaf.

Mesa-Lago, C. (1981) *The Economy of Socialist Cuba*, Albuquerque, University of New Mexico Press.

Mesa-Lago, C. (1993) The economic effects on Cuba of the downfall of socialism in the USSR and Eastern Europe, in C. Mesa-Lago (ed.) *Cuba after the Cold War*, Pittsburg, University of Pittsburg Press.

Meyer, C. (1992) A step back as donors shift institution building from the public to the 'private' sector, *World Development*, 20(8): 1115–26.

Miller, M. (1995) *The Third World in Global Environmental Politics*, Buckingham, Open University Press.

Minear, L. and Weiss, T. (1995) *Mercy under Fire*, Boulder, CO, Westview Press.

Moore, B. (1966) *Social Origins of Dictatorship and Democracy*, Boston, Beacon Press.

Moore, M. (1995a) Promoting good government by supporting institutional development?, *IDS Bulletin*, 26(2): 89–96.

Moore, M. (1995b) Development and democracy in cross-national perspective: a new look at the statistics, *Democratization*, 2(2): 1–19.

Moore, M. and Robinson, M. (1994) Can foreign aid be used to promote good government in developing countries?, *Ethics and International Affairs*, 8: 141–58.

Morrissey, O. (1993) The mixing of aid and trade policies, *World Economy*, 16(1): 69–84.

Morrissey, O., Smith, B. and Horesh, E. (1992) *British Aid and International Trade*, Buckingham and Philadelphia, Open University Press.

Morss, E. (1984) Institutional destruction resulting from donor and project proliferation in sub-Saharan African countries, *World Development*, 12(4): 465–70.

Mortimer, E. (1995) A duty to meddle, *Financial Times*, 25 October

Morton, J. (1996) *The Poverty of Nations: the Aid Dilemma at the Heart of Africa*, London and New York, I.B. Taurus.

Mosley, P. (1981) Models of the aid allocation process: a comment on McKinlay and Little, *Political Studies*, 29(2): 245–53.

Mosley, P. (1985) The political economy of foreign aid: a model of the market for a public good, *Economic Development and Cultural Change*, 33(2): 373–94.

Mosley, P. (1987) *Overseas Aid: its Defence and Reform*, Hemel Hempstead, Harvester Wheatsheaf.

Mosley, P. (ed.) (1992) *Development Finance and Policy Reform: Essays in the Theory and Practice of Conditionality in Less Developed Countries*, Basingstoke, Macmillan.

Mosley, P., Harrigan, J. and Toye, J. (1995) *Aid and Power*, 2nd edn., Vol. I, London, Routledge.

Mosley, P., Hudson, J. and Horrell, S. (1987) Aid, the public sector and the market in less developed countries, *Economic Journal*, 97(September): 616–41.

Murshed, S. (1993) The environment and North–South interaction, in S. Murshed and K. Raffer (eds) *Trade, Transfers and Development*, Aldershot, Edward Elgar.

Myint, H. (1967) *The Economics of the Developing Countries*, 3rd edn., London, Hutchinson.

Nelson, J. (1989) The politics of pro-poor adjustment, in J. Nelson and contributors, *Fragile Coalitions: the Politics of Economic Adjustment*, Washington, DC, Overseas Development Council.

Nelson, J. and Eglinton, S. (1993) Global goals, contentious means: issues of multiple aid conditionality, Washington, DC, Overseas Development Council, Policy Essay no. 10.

Ness, G. (1989) The impact of international population assistance, in A. Krueger, C. Michalopoulos and V. Ruttan with C. Jay, *Aid and Development*, Baltimore and London, Johns Hopkins University Press.

Noël, A. and Thérien, J. (1995) From domestic to international justice: the welfare state and foreign aid, *International Organisation*, 49: 523–53.

Nye, J. (1992) What new world order?, *Foreign Affairs*, 71(2): 83–96.

Olsen, G. (1996) Public opinion, international civil society and North–South policy since the Cold War, in O. Stokke (ed.) *Foreign Aid Towards the Year 2000: Experiences and Challenges*, London, Frank Cass.

Opeskin, B. (1996) The moral foundations of foreign aid, *World Development*, 24(1): 21–44.

Organisation for Economic Cooperation and Development (OECD) (various years) *Development Cooperation Reports*, Paris, OECD. [Reports usually published in the title year, but published in the year following for Reports 1961, 1986, 1987, 1993, 1994, 1995].

Organisation for Economic Cooperation and Development (1996) *Aid and Other Resource Flows to the Central and Eastern European Countries and the New Independent States of the Former Soviet Union (1990–4)*, Paris, OECD.

Orr, R. (1988) The aid factor in US–Japan relations, *Asian Survey*, 28(7): 740–56.

Pagni, L. (1990) From Lomé I to Lomé IV, *The Courier, Africa–Caribbean–Pacific–European Union*, 120: 17.

Parfitt, T. (1996) The decline of Eurafrica? Lomé's mid-term review, *Review of African Political Economy*, 23(67): 53–66.

Patten, C. (1987) *Idealism and Self Interest: Britain's Aid Programme*, London, Overseas Development Administration.

Patten, C. (1989) Evidence presented to Foreign Affairs Committee, *Aid Policy*, HC 447, London, HMSO.

Patterson, L. (1993) A 'Marshall Plan' for the former Soviet Union: ideological, economic and political considerations, *Arms Control*, 14(2): 181–97.

Perera, J. (1995) In unequal dialogue with donors: the experience of the Sarvodaya Shramadarna movement, *Journal of International Development*, 7(6): 869–78.

Pérille, J. and Trutat, J. (1995) Does aid have a future?, *The Courier, Africa–Caribbean–Pacific–European Union*, 152: 6–8.

Pinto-Duschinsky, M. (1991) Foreign political aid: the German foundations and their US counterparts, *International Affairs*, 67(1): 33–63.

Plank, D. (1993) Aid, debt and the end of sovereignty: Mozambique and its donors, *Journal of Modern African Studies*, 31(3): 407–30.

Porter, D., Allen, B. and Thompson, G. (1991) *Development in Practice: Paved with Good Intentions*, London, Routledge.

Porter, R. (1986) Arab economic aid, *Development Policy Review*, 4(1): 44–68.

Przeworski, A. and Limongi, F. (1993) Political regimes and economic growth, *Journal of Economic Perspectives*, 7(3): 51–69.

Przeworski, A., Alvarez, M., Cheibub, J.A. and Limongi, F. (1996) What makes democracies endure?, *Journal of Democracy*, 7(1): 39–55.

Randel, J. (1994) Aid, the military and humanitarian assistance: an attempt to identify recent trends, *Journal of International Development*, 6(3): 329–42.

Rawls, J. (1973) *A Theory of Justice*, Oxford, Oxford University Press.

Remmer, K. (1986) The politics of economic stabilization: IMF standby programmes in Latin America, 1954–84, *Comparative Politics*, 19(1): 1–24.

Remmer, K. (1990) Democracy and economic crisis: the Latin American experience, *World Politics*, 42(3): 315–35.

Riddell, R. (1987) *Foreign Aid Reconsidered*, London and Baltimore, James Currey/ Overseas Development Institute and Johns Hopkins University Press.

Riddell, R., Bebbington, A. and Peck, L. (1995) *Promoting Development by Proxy*, Stockholm, Swedish International Development Authority.

Rimmer, D. (1995) Adjustment blues, *African Affairs*, 94(374): 109–13.

Rix, A. (1993) *Japan's Foreign Aid Challenge: Policy Reform and Aid Leadership*, London and New York, Routledge.

Roberts, A. (1993) Humanitarian war, the new United Nations and peacekeeping, *International Affairs*, 69(3): 429–49.

Robinson, M. (1995) Strengthening civil society in Africa: the role of foreign political aid, *IDS Bulletin*, 26(2): 70–80.

Roeder, P. (1985) The ties that bind: aid, trade, and political compliance in Soviet–Third World relations, *International Studies Quarterly*, 29(2): 191–216.

Rollo, J. (1990) *The New Eastern Europe: Western Responses*, London, Royal Institute of International Affairs and Pinter.

Roper, B. (1979) The limits of public support, *Annals of the American Academy of Political and Social Science*, 442(March): 40–5.

Rosefielde, S. (1993) What is wrong with plans to aid the CIS?, *Orbis*, 37(Summer): 353–63.

Ross, D. (1990) Aid coordination, *Public Administration and Development*, 10(3): 331–42.

Rowe, T. (1974) Aid and *coups d'etat*: aspects of the impact of American military assistance programmes in the less developed countries, *International Studies Quarterly*, 18(2): 239–55.

Rural Advancement Foundation (1994) *Conserving Indigenous Knowledge: Integrating Two Systems of Innovation*, New York, United Nations Development Programme.

Russett, B. (1978) The marginal utility of income transfers to the Third World, *International Organisation*, 32(4): 913–28.

Russett, B. (1995) *Grasping the Democratic Peace*, Princeton, NJ, University of Princeton Press.

Ryrie, W. (1986) Managing an aid programme, *IDS Bulletin*, 17(2): 7–13.

Ryrie, W. (1995) *First World, Third World*, Basingstoke, Macmillan Academic.

Schatz, S. (1994) Structural adjustment in Africa: a failing grade so far, *Journal of Modern African Studies*, 32(4): 679–92.

Schiavo-Campo, S. and Singer, H. (1970) *Perspectives of Economic Development*, Boston, Houghton Mifflin.

Schmitter, P. (ed.) (1973) *Military Rule in Latin America*, Beverly Hills, Sage.

Schraeder, P. (1995) From Berlin 1884 to 1989: foreign assistance and French, American, and Japanese competition in Francophone Africa, *Journal of Modern African Studies*, 33(4): 539–67.

Seers, D. (1972) What types of government should be refused what types of aid?, *IDS Bulletin*, 4(2/3): 6–19.

Seers, D. (1980) Muddling morality with mutuality, *Third World Quarterly*, 2(4): 681–93.

Seers, D. and Streeten, P. (1972) Overseas development policies, in W. Beckerman (ed.) *The Labour Government's Economic Record*, 1964–70, London, Duckworth.

Sellar, W. and Yeatman, R. (1961) *1066 and All That* (First published 1930), Harmondsworth, Penguin.

Sen, A. (1981) *Poverty and Famines*, Oxford, Clarendon Press.

Sengupta, A. (1993) Aid and development policy in the 1990s, *Economic and Political Weekly*, 13 March.

Shihata, I. and Sherbiny, N. (1986) A review of OPEC aid efforts, *Finance and Development*, 23(1): 17–20.

Singer, P. (1977) Famine, affluence and morality, in W. Aiken and H. La Follette (eds) *World Hunger and Moral Obligation*, Englewood Cliffs, NJ, Prentice-Hall.

Slote, M. (1977) The morality of wealth, in W. Aiken and H. La Follette (eds) *World Hunger and Moral Obligation*, Englewood Cliffs, NJ, Prentice-Hall.

Smillie, I. (1993) Changing partners: Northern NGO, Northern governments, in I. Smillie and H. Helmich (eds) *Non-governmental Organisations and Government: Stakeholders for Development*, Paris, Organisation for Economic Cooperation and Development.

Smith, B. (1990) *More than Altruism: the Politics of Private Voluntary Aid*, Princeton, NJ, Princeton University Press.

Sobhan, R. (1982) *The Crisis of External Dependence*, Dhaka and London, The University Press and Zed Press.

Sogge, D. (ed.) (1996) *Compassion and Calculation*, London and Chicago, Pluto Press.

Sommer, J. (1977) *Beyond Charity: US Voluntary Aid for a Changing Third World*, Washington, DC, Overseas Development Council.

Sørensen, G. (1993) Democracy, authoritarianism and state strength, *European Journal of Development Research*, 5(1): 6–34.

Spero, J. (1990) *The Politics of International Economic Relations*, 4th edn., London, Allen and Unwin.

Stiles, K. (1990) IMF conditionality: coercion or compromise?, World Development, 18(7): 959–74.

Stokke, O. (ed.) (1995) *Aid and Political Conditionality*, London, Frank Cass.

Stokke, O. (ed.) (1996) *Foreign Aid Towards the Year 2000: Experiences and Challenges*, London, Frank Cass.

Strange, S. (1981) Reactions to Brandt, *International Studies Quarterly*, 25(2): 328–42.

Strange, S. (1994a) *States and Markets*, 2nd edn., London, Pinter Publishers.

Strange, S. (1994b) Wake up, Krasner! The world *has* changed, *Review of International Political Economy*, 1(2): 209–19.

Streeten, P. (1972) *Aid to Africa: a Policy Outline for the 1970s*, New York and London, Praeger.

Streeten, P. (1976) A first aid lesson, *New Internationalist*, 35: 22–3.

Streeten, P. (1984) Basic needs: some unsettled questions, *World Development*, 12(9): 973–8.

Swedberg, R. (1986) The doctrine of economic neutrality of the IMF and the World Bank, *Journal of Peace Research*, 23(4): 377–90.

T.G. (1990) The image of EEC aid: a painful truth, *The Courier, Africa–Caribbean–Pacific–European Union*, 122: 12–13.

Takagi, S. (1995) Human rights in Japanese foreign policy: Japan's policy towards China after Tiananmen, in J. Tang (ed.) *Human Rights and International Relations in the Asia Pacific*, London and New York, Pinter.

Tang, J. (ed.) (1995) *Human Rights and International Relations in the Asia Pacific*, London and New York, Pinter.

Tendler, J. (1975) *Inside Foreign Aid*, Baltimore, Johns Hopkins University Press.

Timberlake, L. and Thomas, L. (1990) *When the Bough Breaks: Our Children, Our Environment*, London, Earthscan.

Tinker, I. (1990) *Persistent Inequalities*, Oxford, Oxford University Press.

Tisch, S. and Wallace, M. (1994) *Dilemmas of Development Assistance*, Boulder, CO, Westview.

Todaro, M. (1994) *Economic Development*, 5th edn., London and New York, Longman.

Tomasevski, K. (1993) *Development Aid and Human Rights Revisited*, London, Pinter Publishers.

Tonelson, A. (1994) Jettisoning the policy, *Foreign Policy*, 97: 121–3.

Toye, J. (1991) The Aid and Trade Provision of the British overseas aid programme, in A. Bose and P. Burnell (eds) *Britain's Overseas Aid since 1979*, Manchester, Manchester University Press.

Toye, J. (1992) Interest group politics and the implementation of adjustment policies in sub-Saharan Africa, in P. Mosley (ed.) *Development Finance and Policy Reform: Essays in the Theory and Practice of Conditionality in Less Developed Countries*, Basingstoke, Macmillan.

Toye, J. (1993) *Dilemmas of Development*, 2nd edn., Oxford, Basil Blackwell.

Tucker, R. (1975) Egalitarianism and international politics, *Commentary*, 60(September): 27–40.

United Nations High Commissioner for Refugees, *The State of the World's Refugees 1993*, Harmondsworth, Penguin.

Uvin, P. (1992) Regime, surplus, and self-interest: the international politics of food aid, *International Studies Quarterly*, 36(3): 293–312.

van de Walle, N. (1995) Crisis and opportunity in Africa, *Journal of Democracy*, 6(2): 128–41.

van Tuijl (1994) Conditionality for whom? Indonesia and the dissolution of the IGGI: the NGO experience, in A. Clayton (ed.) *Governance, Democracy and Conditionality: What Role for NGOs?* Oxford, INTRAC.

Villalón, L. (1996) The moral and the political in African democratization: the *Code de la Famille* in Niger's troubled transition, *Democratization*, 3(2): 41–68.

Vincent, R. (1986) *Human Rights and International Relations*, Cambridge, Royal Institute of International Affairs and Cambridge University Press.

Warren, B. (1980) *Imperialism: Pioneer of Capitalism*, London, New Left Books.

Watkins, K. (1995a) *The Oxfam Poverty Report*, Oxford, Oxfam.

Watkins, K. (1995b) Aid under threat, *Review of African Political Economy*, 22(66): 517–23.

Watson, R. (1977) Reason and morality in a world of limited food, in W. Aiken and H. La Follette (eds) *World Hunger and Moral Obligation*, Englewood Cliffs, NJ, Prentice-Hall.

White, H. (1993) Aid, investment and growth: what prospects in the 1990s?, in M. Murshed and K. Raffer (eds) *Trade, Transfers and Development*, Aldershot, Edward Elgar.

White, H. and Woestman, L. (1994) The quality of aid: measuring trends in donor performance, *Development and Change*, 25(3): 527–54.

Wittkopf, E. (1973) Foreign aid and the United Nations' votes: a comparative study, *American Political Science Review*, 67(3): 868–88.

Wolf, M. (1996) How the west failed Russia, *Financial Times*, 7 May.

Wood, R. (1980) Foreign aid and the capitalist state in underdeveloped society, *Politics and Society*, 10(1): 1–34.

World Bank (1981) *Accelerated Development in sub-Saharan Africa: an Agenda for Action*, Washington, DC, World Bank.

World Bank (1992) *Governance and Development*, Washington, DC, World Bank.

World Bank (various years) *World Development Report*, Washington, DC, World Bank.

World Commission on Environment and Development (1987) *Our Common Future*, Oxford, Oxford University Press.

Yasutomo, D. (1989) Why aid? Japan as an 'Aid Great Power', *Pacific Affairs*, 62(4): 490–503.

Yasutomo, D. (1995) *The New Multilateralism in Japan's Foreign Policy*, New York, St Martin's Press.

Yeoman, G. (1986) Aid to Africa: the great illusion, *Traveller*, 16(1): 25–6.

Yunling, Z. (1995) China in the post-cold war era, in H. Holm and G. Sørensen (eds) *Whose World Order?* Boulder, CO and Oxford, Westview.

Zhukov, S. (1995) Aid dialogue between Russia and the West: climbing the learning curve, in O. Stokke (ed.) *Aid and Political Conditionality*, London, Frank Cass.

Zimmerman, R. (1993) *Dollars, Diplomacy and Dependency*, Boulder, CO, Lynne Rienner.

Zinkin, M. (1978) Aid and morals: addressing the aspiration of poor countries, *Round Table*, 271: 222–8.

Zubok, V. (1995) Russia: between peace and conflict, in H. Holm and G. Sørensen (eds) *Whose World Order?* Boulder, CO and Oxford, Westview.

Index